LIFE HISTORIES
OF NORTH AMERICAN
GULLS AND TERNS

by Arthur Cleveland Bent

DOVER PUBLICATIONS, INC.
NEW YORK

Published in Canada by General Publishing Company, Ltd., 30 Lesmill Road, Don Mills, Toronto, Ontario.

Published in the United Kingdom by Constable and Company, Ltd.

This Dover edition, first published in 1986, is a republication of the 1963 Dover edition, an unabridged and unaltered republication of the work first published by the United States Government Printing Office in 1921 as Smithsonian Institution United States National Museum *Bulletin 113*.

Plates 78 through 93, which were reproduced in color in the 1921 edition, are reproduced in black and white in this edition.

Manufactured in the United States of America
Dover Publications, Inc., 31 East 2nd Street, Mineola, N.Y. 11501

Library of Congress Cataloging-in-Publication Data

Bent, Arthur Cleveland, 1866–1954.
    Life histories of North American gulls and terns.

    Originally published: Washington : U.S. G.P.O., 1921. (Smithsonian Institution United States National Museum bulletin ; 113)
    Bibliography: p.
    Includes index.
    1. Laridae. 2. Stercorariidae. 3. Black skimmer. 4. Birds—North America. I. Title.
QL696.C46B46 1986   598'.338   86-8840
ISBN 0-486-25262-0

ADVERTISEMENT.

The scientific publications of the United States National Museum consist of two series, the *Proceedings* and the *Bulletins*.

The *Proceedings*, the first volume of which was issued in 1878, are intended primarily as a medium for the publication of original, and usually brief, papers based on the collections of the National Museum, presenting newly-acquired facts in zoology, geology, and anthropology, including descriptions of new forms of animals, and revisions of limited groups. One or two volumes are issued annually and distributed to libraries and scientific organizations. A limited number of copies of each paper, in pamphlet form, is distributed to specialists and others interested in the different subjects as soon as printed. The date of publication is recorded in the tables of contents of the volumes.

The *Bulletins*, the first of which was issued in 1875, consist of a series of separate publications comprising chiefly monographs of large zoological groups and other general systematic treatises (occasionally in several volumes), faunal works, reports of expeditions, and catalogues of type-specimens, special collections, etc. The majority of the volumes are octavos, but a quarto size has been adopted in a few instances in which large plates were regarded as indispensable.

Since 1902 a series of octavo volumes containing papers relating to the botanical collections of the Museum, and known as the *Contributions from the National Herbarium*, has been published as bulletins.

The present work forms No. 113 of the *Bulletin series*.

WILLIAM deC. RAVENEL,
Administrative Assistant to the Secretary,
In charge of the United States National Museum.
WASHINGTON. D. C.

INTRODUCTION.

This Bulletin contains a continuation of the work on the life histories of North American birds, begun in Bulletin 107. The same general plan has been followed and the same sources of information have been utilized. Nearly all of those who contributed material for, or helped in preparing, the former volume have rendered similar service in this case. In addition to those whose contributions have been previously acknowledged, my thanks are due to the following contributors:

Photographs have been contributed, or their use authorized, by D. Appleton & Co., S. C. Arthur, A. M. Bailey, R. H. Beck, B. S. Bowdish, L. W. Brownell, G. G. Cantwell, F. M. Chapman, H. H. Cleaves, Colorado Museum of Natural History, E. H. Forbush, A. O. Gross, O. J. Heinemann, A. L. V. Manniche, W. M. Pierce, M. S. Ray, J. Richardson, R. B. Rockwell, R. W. Shufeldt, J. F. Street, University of Minnesota, C. H. Wells, J. Wilkinson, and F. M. Woodruff.

Notes and data have been contributed by S. C. Arthur, R. H. Beck, F. H. Carpenter, H. H. Cleaves, E. H. Forbush, F. C. Hennessey, R. Hoffmann, F. C. Lincoln, H. Massey, O. J. Murie, C. J. Pennock, J. H. Rice, Katie M. Roads, and G. H. Stuart. With the consent of Dr. L. C. Sanford and R. H. Beck, the American Museum of Natural History has placed at the author's disposal Mr. Beck's extensive notes made on the Brewster and Sanford expedition to South America.

The distributional part of this Bulletin has been done mainly by the author, with considerable volunteer help from Mr. F. Seymour Hersey, whose time is now otherwise occupied. Dr. Louis B. Bishop has devoted much time to revising the paragraphs on distribution and on plumages.

Our attention has been called to an error in Bulletin 107. On page 32 a quotation from Dr. T. S. Roberts was inserted as referring to the food of the eared grebe; this really refers to the food of Franklin's gull and not to that of the grebe.

Readers of Bulletin 107 have suggested some changes. Consequently, in this and subsequent Bulletins in this series, the exact details will be given, when available, in such casual records as are given; but it must be remembered that no attempt will be made to mention *all* casual records; only a few can be given, to suggest the limits of the wanderings of the species.   Another addition of value, suggested and furnished by Dr. T. S. Palmer, is information regarding reservations and the species which are protected in them.   As some readers have questioned the scale on which the eggs are illustrated, it seems desirable to say that in Bulletin 107, in this one, and in subsequent Bulletins, all eggs are, and will be, shown exactly life-size, the plates being produced by an exact photographic process.

THE AUTHOR.

TABLE OF CONTENTS.

LIFE HISTORIES
OF NORTH AMERICAN
GULLS AND TERNS

Family STERCORARIDAE, Skuas and Jaegers.

CATHARACTA SKUA Brünnich .

SKUA.

HABITS.

The following quotation from the graphic pen of Mr. F. St. Mars (1912) gives a better introduction to this bold and daring species than anything I could write, and his article, The Eagle Guard, from which I shall quote again, is well worth reading as a striking character study:

Then the scimitar wings shut with a crisp swish, and he became a statue in dull, unpolished bronze, impassively regarding the polecat, who lay with her back broken, feebly struggling to drag into cover. It is a shock to the human nerves to see the life blasted out of a beast almost 'twixt breath and breath; what one moment is 'a gliding, muscular form, instinct with life and energy, confident in power, and the next moment a crumpled heap of fur, twitching spasmodically. But it was a searchlight on the reputation of the eagle guard and the stories one had heard anent the superstitions of the natives.

The polecat, being hungry with the gnawing hunger of a mother and presuming on a swirl of mist. had tried to steal up the knoll to the two great eggs that lay in the hollow atop all unguarded. Had come then a thin, high, whirring shriek, exactly like the noise made by a sword cutting through the air, and a single thud that might have been the thud of a rifle bullet striking an animal. Then—well, then the scene described above.

Big, powerfully built, brown with the black brown of his own native peat bogs, armed to the teeth, long and slash-winged, whose flight feathers were like the cutting edge of a sword, insolent with the fine, swelling insolence of power, and greatly daring, no wonder men had chosen him as the eagle guard. this mighty bird, this great skua of the naturalists, this Bonxie, mascot, and superstitious godling of the fishermen. Wah! he was a bird.

We know so little about the skua, as an American bird, that I shall have to draw largely from European writers for its life history. It is rare on the American side of the Atlantic Ocean, and is not known to breed here regularly, although it probably does so occasionally or sparingly in Greenland or on the Arctic Islands.

Nesting.—Yarrell (1871) says:

The great skua arrives in the Shetlands about the end of April, and its nest, which consists of a neatly rounded cavity in the moss and heather of the highest moorlands, is prepared in the latter half of May. According to Maj. Feilden, the birds appear to prepare several nests before they decide on using one. There is no difficulty in finding the nests, as the parent birds at once attack any intruder upon their domain with fierce and repeated swoops. When handling the nestling the editor found their assaults were unremitting; first one bird and then the other wheeling short, and coming down at full speed, almost skimming the ground. At about 15 yards' distance the strong clawed feet are lowered and held stiffly out, producing for the moment a very ungainly appearance, and it seems as if the bird would strike the observer full in the center of the body, but on quickly raising the hand or stick the bird rises also, the whirr and vibration of its pinions being distinctly heard and felt. Its ordinary flight is soaring and stately. On leaving the territory of one pair, the attack is taken up by another, and so on; for the great skuas do not nest in close proximity.

Morris (1903) writes:

The nest of the skua is of large size,. as well as somewhat carefully constructed; the materials used being grasses, lichens, moss, and heath. The bird places it on the tops of the mountains or cliffs in the neighborhood of the sea, but not on the rocks themselves. They build separately in pairs.

Eggs.—The skua lays. ordinarily two eggs, rarely three, and sometimes only one. These vary in shape from ovate or slightly elongated ovate to short ovate. The shell is smooth, with a dull luster. The ground color is " Saccardo's olive," " Isabella color," or " deep olive buff." The markings are usually not profuse and consist of spots and blotches, scattered irregularly over the egg, of " sepia," " bister," " snuff brown," or " tawny olive." There are also usually a few faint spots or blotches of pale shades of drab or gray. Rev. F. C. R. Jourdain has collected for me the measurements of 68 eggs, which average 70.58 by 49.43 millimeters; the eggs showing the four extremes measure **76.3** by 50.4, 71.5 by **53.2,** and **62** by **44.5** millimeters.

Young.—Macgillivray (1852) quotes Captain Vetch as saying:

The young bird is a nimble, gallant little animal, and almost as soon as hatched leaves the nest. On the approach of danger he secretes himself in holes or behind stones with great art, and when captured at least makes a show of defense that is quite amusing.

Plumages.—I have never seen the downy young, but Coues (1903) describes it as "buffy-gray, ruddier above than below." Ridgway (1887) quotes Dresser as calling it "brownish or cinnamon-gray, rather darker in color on the upper parts than on the under surface of the body."

I have not been able to examine enough specimens to come to any definite conclusions as to the sequence of molts and plumages. Coues (1903) gives the following good description of the young of the year:

Size much less; bill weaker and slenderer; cere illy developed; striae not apparent and its ridges and angles all want sharpness of definition. Wings short and rounded, the quills having very different proportional length from those of adults; second longest, third but little shorter, first about equal to fourth. The inner or longest secondaries reach, when the wing is folded, to within an inch or so of tip of longest primary. Central rectrices a little shorter than the next. Colors generally as in adult, but duller and more blended, having few or no white spots; reddish spots dull, numerous, and large, especially along edge of forearm and on least and lesser coverts. On underparts the colors lighter, duller, and more blended than above; prevailing tint light dull rufous, most marked on abdomen, but there and elsewhere more or less obscured with ashy or plumbeous. Remiges and rectrices dull brownish-black; their shafts yellowish-white, darker terminally. At bases of primaries there exists the ordinary large white space, but it is more restricted than in adults, and so much hidden by the bastard quills that it is hardly apparent on outside of wing, though conspicuous underneath.

Young birds may become indistinguishable from adults at the first postnuptial molt, when a little over a year old, but perhaps not for a year or two later.

Adults seem to have but one complete molt—the postnuptial—in August. Adults can be distinguished by their larger size and by the elongated feathers of the neck with the whitish central streaks.

Food.—Yarrell (1871) writes of the food of the skua:

Their food is fish, but they devour also the smaller water birds and their eggs, the flesh of whales, as well as other carrion, and are observed to tear their prey to pieces while holding it under their crooked talons. They rarely take the trouble to fish for themselves, but, watching the smaller gulls and terns while thus employed, they no sooner observe one to have been successful than they immediately give chase, pursuing it with fury; and having obliged it from fright to disgorge the recently swallowed fish, they descend to catch it, being frequently so rapid and certain in their movements and aim as to seize their prize before it reaches the water. The stomachs of a pair which were shot were full of the flesh of the kittiwake, and the castings consisted of the bones and feathers of that small gull. Heysham has noticed an adult female on the coast of Cumberland, which allowed herself to be seized while she was in the act of killing a herring gull. It also feeds on fish offal, and the editor found by the side of a nestling some disgorged but otherwise uninjured herrings of large size.

Behavior.—In appearance as well as in habits the skua seems to share the attributes of the Raptores and the Laridae; its strong, hooked bill and its sharp, curved claws enable it to stand upon and rend asunder the victims of its rapacious habits. Its flight is also somewhat hawk like. Yet it stands horizontally and runs about nimbly like a gull. Morris (1903) says that it "soars at times at a great height, and flies both strongly and rapidly, in an impetuous, dashing manner." Mr. Walter H. Rich has sent me the following notes on the flight of this species:

When on the wing, which is the greater part of the time, the skua shows in the air hawk like, rather than like the gulls, with whom we rather expect to find its resemblances. Its appearance in the air is somewhat like the buteonine hawks, except that its wing action, in its seemingly restrained power and forceful stroke, suggests the unhurried flight of a falcon, or, perhaps, more accurately—since the wings are at all times fully opened, employing their full sweep in their action, their primaries slightly separated at the tips and slightly recurved—the majestic flight of an eagle. The wing spread is ample, the wing well balanced in its proportions of length and breadth, well combined to produce both power and speed. The figure is somewhat burly and chunky as compared with the lighter appearance of the gull and the more racy lines of the yager. The impression of muscularity is heightened by the short, square-cut tail, carried somewhat uptilted, giving the fowl an appearance unmistakable in the eyes of one having once recognized it. This peculiarity of tail, which to me seemed slightly forked instead of having the central feathers lengthened, as in others of this group, together with the broad white patch across the bases of the primaries, furnishes a good field mark for the identification of the species.

Macgillivray (1852) says:

Its voice resembles that of a young gull, being sharp and shrill, and it is from the resemblance of its cry to that of the word skua or skui that it obtains its popular name.

Mr. Rich's notes state:

Whatever the case elsewhere, on the fishing grounds this seemed a silent species. The writer heard no sound at all which he was able with certainty to trace to it during his acquaintance with it.

The most interesting phase of the skua's life history is its behavior toward other species. It is certainly a bold and dashing tyrant, more than a match for anything of its size and a terror to many birds and beasts of larger size. Mr. F. St. Mars (1912) describes its attack on the golden eagle, which dared to venture too near its nest, in the following graphic words:

Some minutes elapsed, in spite of the warnings, before the human eye could have made out a faint dot growing out of the mist round the tail of an inlet. It enlarged rapidly, however, that dot, and one saw that it was really a real, live eagle, a golden eagle of Scotland. Mind you, there was none of that sublime soaring in the infinite that the books tell of. He came, as any mere common bird might have come, beating up along the shore with heavy, flapping flight, which, by the way, looked much slower than it really was, and he said nothing as he came.

The picture, as it stood, of that somber, bronze-gold winged giant, beating slowly up against the wind in a setting of dim gray sky, jade sea, and dark-velvet land, was very fine. It seemed that nothing could have added to its bold, wild grandeur. Then something seemed to move across the heavens very quickly, and there was a hissing sound as if a mighty sword had cleaved the air. Followed then a second phenomenon just like the first, and almost in the same instant one realized two distinct facts: Firstly, that the two skuas were no longer near their nest; and, secondly, that the eagle had, with five stupendous flaps of those vast wings, shot upward into the clouds.

At the same instant it seemed as though a big brown projectile hurtled past exactly beneath him, and a fraction of a second later, as though another one had hit him. There was a burst of feathers and a whirl. The eagle appeared suddenly to grow much larger, miraculously to sprout an extra and smaller, thinner pair of wings, and to reel in his flight, recover, reel again, turn half over, as if grappling some invisible foe, drop like a thunderbolt some 200 feet, and then break into two pieces, the larger piece slanting upward on the one hand and the smaller executing the same wonderful aerial evolution on the other.

Then were the facts made plain. The smaller portion was the skua. He had darted like lightning upon the eagle's back and clung there for a second or two— only for a second or two, but it seemed minutes while the two fell—after the king had avoided his mate's first reckless, headlong, crazy rush.

I have no hope to describe to you what followed, because the laboring human eye was far too slow to see and the brain to grasp the electric-quick passage of events. I only know that one was dimly aware that some stupendous battle was going on up there in the dim northern heavens; that bodies, large bodies, bursting with life and a dozen uncurbed wild passions, were sweeping and swerving, and swooping, and swaying, and streaking, and stabbing, and slashing, and striving, and screaming in one wild welter of wildering speed. And all the while the land below, save for the huddled sheep, lay as deserted as if a hand had come down and swept it clean of life. Yet one knew that in reality hundreds and hundreds of sharp eyes were watching from cover that battle of the overlords of the air and calculating the chances of life upon its issue.

Slowly, second by furious second, inch by hard-fought inch it looked from the earth, but mile by mile it was really, up there in the unbounded airy spaces, the battle receded, receded upward and northward, till the straining eye was at last only conscious of a faraway blur, a dancing of specks, as it were gnats, on the vision, and then, with an almost audible sigh from the hidden spectators, of nothing.

Mr. Rich's impressions of the behavior of the skua are expressed in his notes as follows:

This is the overlord of the fishing grounds, fearing no bird here. Whether the skua would successfully contest with the black-backed gull the writer is unable to state, as the two did not come together under his observation, but he thinks that the skua need have little uneasiness as to the outcome of battle. The difference in size between the black back and the skua is mostly a matter of measurements, due in part, at least, to the skua's shortness of rudder. In bulk and weight there is less difference, probably, than is shown by these figures, and in physical powers, judging from appearances, there is little to choose between them. Of the two, the skua's armament seems the better fitted for damaging an enemy, and he seems to possess greater speed and skill in maneuvering—a flight of greater power and control than has his rival, who, gull-like, is a drifter rather than a flier. Certain it is that the hag, tern, kittiwake, and herring gull move respectfully aside when the "sea hen" comes sailing above them, for all these he harries and robs constantly, performing in the realms of the sea the same robber tactics which the raptorial birds carry on among the feathered people ashore. Are the hags or the gulls squabbling over a bit of waste or striving to tear a "poke-blown" fish which has drifted away from the steamer's side; over the struggling mass there comes the shadow of broad wings; a heavy body drops among them regardless of what may be beneath it; the weaker move respectfully aside and leave the newcomer in undisturbed possession of the spoil. Over his shoulder the skua gazes at the steamer, making only now and then a tentative pull at the body of his prey, until it has floated to a safe distance, when he begins to rip and tear it with his powerful beak. To lose all interest in that particular morsel, hag or gull that comes near the spoil needs to look but once at that lowered head with its bristling crest, and the powerful wing upraised to strike.

Winter.—The status of the skua as an American bird is based largely on its occurrence on the fishing banks off the coasts of Newfoundland and New England. Probably the birds which occur there in winter are of this species, but the following notes by Mr. Rich suggest the possibility that the birds seen there in summer may be of one of the Antarctic species:

In the main, the "sea hen" seems to have been considered a winter visitor to our coasts, somewhat unusual during the summer months, yet my records show its presence here from June 19 to November 5, with its period of greatest abundance from August 12 to September 10 (this in the "South part of the channel," 35 miles east; south from Sankaty Head, 68° —42′ W.; 41° —20′ N.), with numbers diminishing thereafter until the last appearance therein noted on November 5, 1913. The writer remained upon the fishing grounds 21 days later, but did not again note its presence there.

These facts have suggested to Mr. Norton that the "sea hen" of the summer months may have come from the Antarctic with the shearwaters, returning thither to breed among the penguin rookeries of that little-known continent on the underside of the world; while the skuas of the winter months may come from the northern breeding grounds of the species.

It is regrettable that I was unable to collect any specimens with which to make comparisons and to go deeper into this matter. There would have been very little difficulty in getting material, as the "sea hen," while more careful than the "gull-chasers," was not very shy, and shots at 30 yards or even less would have been frequent.

DISTRIBUTION.

Breeding range.—Islands of the North Atlantic Ocean, Greenland, Iceland, the Faroe and Shetland Islands. Said by Kumlien to breed at Lady Franklin Island north of Hudson Strait.

Winter range.—The North Atlantic Ocean, occasionally reaching land. From the Great Banks, off Newfoundland, and Georges Bank, off Massachusetts, to New York (Long Island). In Europe from the British Isles and Norway south to Gibraltar. Occasional in the Mediterranean Sea and on inland waters.

Spring migration.—Migration dates in North America are so few as to appear little more than straggling records. Labrador: Straits of Belle Isle, June 22.

Fall migration.—Birds reach Georges Bank in July. Massachusetts dates: Ipswich, September 17; Woods Hole, August 30 and September 19; Pollock Rip, September 10; and Nantucket Shoals, October 17. Recorded from New York (Long Island) as early as August 10.

Casual records.—Accidental inland in New York (Niagara River, spring, 1886).

Egg dates.—Iceland: Twenty-four records May 20 to June 23; twelve records June 3 to 15. Greenland: One record June 21.

CATHARACTA CHILENSIS (Bonaparte).
CHILEAN SKUA.

HABITS.

The preceding species, *Catharacta skua*, has been reported, as a straggler, on the coasts of California and Washington, where specimens have been taken, as recorded below.

These records have always seemed open to question as it seemed unlikely that a bird of the Atlantic Ocean would stray so far away from its normal habitat.

There are at least two other species of skua, which are fairly common in certain parts of the South Pacific and South Indian Oceans, which would be much more likely to wander to the coast of California. Thinking that these records might refer to *Catharacta chilensis* or *Catharacta lonnbergi*, I opened correspondence regarding them with Mr. Harry S. Swarth, which resulted in his sending me one of the birds. After consultation with Mr. Robert Cushman Murphy, who is familiar with these species in life, and after comparing it with series of specimens of *chilensis*, *lonnbergi*, and *antarctica* in various museums in Cambridge, New York, and Washington, I have decided to provisionally refer these birds to the above species, *Catharacta chilensis*, of which they probably represent an immature plumage or a dark phase.

DISTRIBUTION.

Breeding range.—Unknown.

Range.—Most abundant on the coasts of Chile and Peru, but found on both coasts of southern South America, from Rio Janeiro, on the Atlantic side, to Callao, Peru, on the Pacific side. Wanders northward, perhaps regularly, in the Pacific Ocean to Japan (Sagami Sea, August 23, 1903), California (Monterey Bay, August 7, 1907, and August 4 and September 21, 1910), Washington (off Gray's Harbor, June 28, 1917), and British Columbia (off Vancouver Island, June 20, 1917).

STERCORARIUS POMARINUS (Temminck).
POMARINE JAEGER.

HABITS.

To most of us this and the other jaegers are known only as summer and fall visitors on our coasts or on the fishing banks, where they are constantly harassing the smaller gulls, the terns, and the shearwaters, from whom they obtain by force a large part of their food supply. The pomarine is the largest of the three, but by no means the most aggressive. Few of us have ever seen it on its breeding grounds, which lie within the Arctic Circle, where it is widely scattered over the boundless plains of the marshy tundra.

Spring.—Dr. E. W. Nelson (1887) says of its arrival in northern Alaska:

The earliest arrival of this bird in spring was May 13 at the Yukon mouth where the writer found it searching for food along the ice-covered river channels. They became more common, until, by the last of the month, from a dozen to 20 might be seen every day,

Mr. Frank C. Hennessey, who accompanied the A. P. Low expedition to the regions north of Hudson Bay, says, in his notes, that " the first of this variety was seen to arrive in the spring at Winter Harbour on May 29th."

Nesting.—Very little has been published on the nesting habits of the pomarine jaeger. Mr. Hennessey, in the notes referred to above, which he kindly sent me, states that these birds are " abundant about Winter Harbour, where they breed on the low, flat, marshy land in the neighborhood, choosing the small mounds or slight elevations that abound in these places upon which to rear their brood. The nest is a slight depression in the soil of the elevation and just deep enough to admit the eggs and breast of the bird. No material is used in its construction, but the bottom is covered with much loose soil and rubbish apparently blown in accidentally." Mr. C. Boyce Hill (1900) published the following account of the nesting habits of this species in Siberia:

On our way down the Yenisei the steamer which was towing us fortunately ran ashore on one of the numerous sand banks which abound in this river. I say fortunately because it enabled us to discover this skua nesting. After having inquired the probable duration of our stoppage, Popan and I agreed to explore the small islands near at hand—a group named the Brekotsky. We took one each, and on mine, a large, flat marsh, I observed a Pomatorhine skua, which was presently joined by another. The birds did not appear at all demonstrative nor to resent intrusion, like the long-tailed skuas, so I thought they could not be nesting. But after much searching and watching I observed one settle right in the center of the marsh, so at once proceeded to the spot. The bird rose when I was within a few yards of it, and to my delight I saw the nest with two eggs. I waited a few moments for the skua to come within shot and killed it; after pursuing its mate, I captured that also. The nest was a mere depression in the ground, on a spot rather drier than the surrounding marsh, and to reach it I was at times up to my knees in swamp; so that had it not been for a foundation of ice at a depth of from 18 inches to 2 feet from the surface I do not think I should have been able to record this event. I also found nesting on this island some scaup ducks and red-necked phalaropes.

Mr. Ludwig Kumlien (1879) found this species breeding on the Greenland coast under very different conditions. He writes:

I have, however, nowhere found them so very common as on the southern shores of Disko Island; at Laxbught and Fortuna Bay there must have been many hundred pairs nesting. Their breeding place was an inaccessible cliff about half a mile from the seashore. The greater number of the birds nesting here were in the plumage described in Doctor Coues's monograph of the Laridae as the nearly adult plumage; but there were also a good many birds that were unicolored blackish brown all over, but with the long vertically twisted tail feathers. That these were breeding I think there can be no doubt, as I saw them carrying food up to the ledges on the cliff, for the young I suppose.

Eggs.—The Pomarine jaeger lays two or three eggs to a set, usually the former. They are said to be scarcely distinguishable from certain eggs of the parasitic jaeger or of the mew gull, but are more pointed. The shape is ovate or pointed ovate. The shell is smooth and slightly glossy. The ground color varies from "brownish olive" or "Brussels brown" to "olive lake" or "dark olive buff." They are rather sparingly spotted with "bone brown," "bister," "chestnut brown," or "snuff brown," and occasionally with underlying spots or blotches of various shades of drab or gray. The measurements of 49 eggs, in various collections, average 62 by 44 millimeters; the eggs showing the four extremes measure **72.6** by 44.9, 68 by **48, 57.2** by 43.6, and 58.5 by **40** millimeters.

Plumages.—The young when first hatched is covered with long soft down, of plain colors and unspotted; the upper parts are "clove brown" or "olive brown" and the under parts "drab" or "light drab." The plumage appears first on the scapulars, back, and wings, then on the breast, and the full juvenal plumage, which is not distinctly separated from the first winter, is acquired before the young bird is fully grown. The first winter plumage is the well-known brownish mottled plumage, in which the body feathers and particularly the scapulars are heavily barred transversely with dark browns or dusky tints and tipped with rufous or pinkish buff; the central tail feathers are only slightly elongated beyond the other rectrices. This plumage is worn with slight changes all through the first year, or until the first postnuptial molt, which begins in June and lasts until October. The rufous or buff edgings gradually fade out to white during the winter; during the molt into the second-year plumage August birds show old barred feathers with white edgings and new barred feathers with rufous edgings. The second winter plumage is still mottled or barred, but is much lighter colored; the browns are grayer and there is more white, the rufous edgings soon disappearing. There is less barring on the under parts and the belly is often wholly white centrally; the under tail-coverts are heavily barred with white and dusky. There are sometimes signs of the golden collar in this plumage. If there is any molt in the spring, it is only partial, and probably the young bird does not breed in this plumage the second spring.

At the second postnuptial molt the following summer, when the bird is about 2 years old, the third-year plumage is assumed. This plumage is practically the same as the adult in many individuals; the upper parts are uniformly dark, except that the white and golden collar encircles the neck; the two central tail feathers become much elongated; the under parts are mainly white, with more or less dusky mottling on the neck, upper breast, and sides; and the lower abdomen and under tail-coverts become dusky, but in some individuals these are veiled or mixed, more or less, with white. There is great individual variation in the amount and extent of the dusky mottling in the white areas, in the amount of white in the dark under tail-coverts, and in the extent of the white and golden collar at this age; but as there is not much further progress to be made toward maturity, the third-year birds may be considered practically adult. The fully adult plumage, without much mottling in either the light or the dark areas and with the fully developed golden collar, increases in perfection with subsequent molts; the clear dark crissum and under tail-coverts are assumed when the bird is about 3 years old, though vigorous birds may acquire them before that time. I have never seen a specimen in which the neck, breast, and shoulders were *entirely* free from dusky mottling.

Birds in the dark phase of plumage, apparently, undergo the same sequence of plumages to maturity, though I have not been able to trace the changes so satisfactorily. In the first-year plumage they are much darker than in the light phase, with the white barring much more restricted. During the second year they are almost wholly dark with some whitish and rufous edgings above and below. The third-year and adult plumages are hardly distinguishable, both being uniformly dark, but some specimens show an indication of the golden collar, more or less distinctly, which are probably the older birds. The molt of the contour feathers in both phases occurs in summer, from June to October, and the flight feathers are molted in October, beginning with the inner primaries and the central rectrices. The prenuptial molts of both young birds and adults are probably incomplete, but specimens of winter and early spring birds are too scarce to demonstrate it.

Food.—The predatory feeding habits of the jaegers are familiar to everyone who has studied the habits of our sea birds during the latter part of summer and fall. They are the notorious pirates and freebooters among sea birds, the highwaymen that persecute their neighbors on the fishing grounds and make them "stand and deliver." It is no uncommon sight on the New England coast to see one or two of these dusky robbers darting through a flock of hovering terns or small gulls, or giving chase to the lucky one that has caught a fish, following every twist and turn in its hurrying flight as it tries to dodge or escape, close at its heels as if attached by an invisible string. At last, in desperation, the harassed tern drops its fish and the relentless pursuer seizes it before it strikes the water. Occasionally the indignant tern voids its excrement instead, which the jaeger immediately seizes, as if it were a dainty morsel.

Off Chatham, Massachusetts, we often saw this and the next species, which are called "jiddie-hawks" by the fishermen, mingling with the shearwaters and browbeating them as they do the gulls and terns. As soon as the shearwaters began to gather about our boat to pick up the pieces of cod liver that we threw overboard, the jaegers would appear and take a hand in the general scramble for food. They are quick to sense the idea that a gathering flock of sea birds means a feast to be obtained by force. The "haglets" are greedy feeders, and soon gulp down what pieces of food they can find, but they have learned by many a painful squabble that they are no match for the active, fighting "jiddie-hawks," and they are soon forced to disgorge or to surrender the field.

Mr. Kumlien (1879) says that on the Greenland coast "they live to a great extent upon the labors of the kittiwake, though they do not hesitate to attack *Larus leucopterus*, and even *glaucus*. They are destructive to young birds and eggs. It is a common sight to see five or six after one gull, which is soon made to disgorge, and then the jaegers fight among themselves for the morsel, which often gets lost in the mêlée." In addition to the food stolen from other birds, the pomarine jaeger lives on what it can pick up in the way of offal, carrion, and scraps thrown from the galley. It devours young birds and eggs, and even small mammals, such as mice and lemmings.

Mr. Albert W. Tuttle (1911) publishes the following account, contained in a letter from Mr. Allen Moses, of Grand Manan, New Brunswick:

I saw a pomarine jaeger catch a phalarope. There was a pair of the jaegers. The female started after the phalaropes and chased them a long time. They were too smart for her, and after a long chase she separated out one, and then the male gave chase, and in a few minutes, with the two chasing the little fellow, one caught him within a hundred yards of the vessel; then they both lighted in the water and ate him.

Behavior.—Were it not endowed with splendid powers of flight the pomarine jaeger could never perform the feats indicated above. It is not only swift and powerful, but it has wonderful command of its powers on the wing. It can be easily recognized by its superior size and by the peculiar shape of its elongated, central tail feathers, which are broad and blunt and are held with their vanes in a vertical plane, like a rudder. Its ordinary flight is steady and direct, with rather slow, constant wing beats. Mr. Walter H. Rich has

contributed the following notes on one of its spectacular performances:

On several occasions I have seen the "gull chaser" turn a complete back
somersault in the air to make a dive upon some piece of food on the water which
the sweeping gale had caused it to overrun. Often, too, it thus makes its
piratical raids upon some luckless hag, which, almost too late, it finds in
possession of a morsel which it deems too dainty to be wasted on a mere
squealing shearwater. And so it rises against the breeze, turns itself upside
down and, with wings half closed, darts at its victim from above like a lance.
But the hag stands to his guns; a squealing, choking remonstrance, a mighty
gulp, and if the jaeger has luck he may capture a small fragment of the spoil.

Mr. Rich says that the usual "call is a sharp 'which-yew,' also
a squeaky whistle, and occasionally a squealing note like the 'week-
week' of the herring gull." Doctor Nelson (1887) says that it " has a
low, harsh, chattering cry when feeding with its companions."

Its behavior toward other species, which has been partially shown
above, is not above criticism; its motto seems to be that might makes
right; it therefore uses some discretion in the choice of victims for
persecution. The terns and the kittiwakes are the ones most regularly abused, the ring-billed and the herring gulls are less frequently
persecuted, and it seldom ventures to attack the glaucous or the
great black-backed gulls. Size and strength do not always bring
courage, and the pomarine jaeger seems to be lacking in the latter
quality. Doctor Nelson (1887) writes:

They are clumsy and cowardly as compared with their smaller relatives.
When one of this species chances to cross the path of the smaller species, the
latter almost invariably gives chase and beats its clumsy antagonist off the
field by repeatedly darting down from above. This attack embarrasses the
large bird, so that it flinches and dives and often alights and watches an
opportunity to escape from its nimble assailant. One that was driven to
alight in the river thrust its head under water at every swoop of its assailant
and exhibited the most ludicrous terror. When on the wing they usually ward
off an attack from one side by a half-closed wing, and if above, both wings are
raised, forming an arched shield above the back.

Fall.—The fall migration of the jaegers is governed largely by
the food supply, which depends on the movements of the fish on
which the gulls, terns, and shearwaters feed. On the New England
coast we usually look for the jaegers in August, especially where the
bluefish or mackerel are running in schools and driving the small
fry to the surface. During seasons when these fish are scarce the
jaegers and shearwaters are absent, perhaps following other schools
of fish far out at sea. And when the bluefish and mackerel move off
the coast in the fall the jaegers disappear with them. They are
seldom seen on our coasts in winter. We do not know very much
about their winter range and habits, but they probably spend this
season roaming at large over the open ocean wherever they can find
a chance to ply their trade as pelagic pirates.

DISTRIBUTION.

Breeding range.—Northern parts of the Northern Hemisphere. In North America east to central Greenland (latitude 64° to 73° N.). South to Cumberland (Exeter Sound) and Hall Peninsula (Grinnell Bay), Melville Peninsula (Winter Harbor), and the Arctic coast of North America. West to northwestern Alaska (Kotzebue Sound to Point Barrow. North to Melville Island, Banks Island, North Somerset, and probably others of the Arctic islands. In Europe from Iceland to Spitzbergen, and Nova Zembla, perhaps occasionally on the coast of northern Norway; also in northeastern Siberia and probably the entire Siberian coast. Siberian birds have been described as a distinct subspecies, but it is doubtful if on good grounds.

Winter range.—Poorly defined. Probably in Southern Hemisphere south to Peru (Callao Bay), northern Australia (Cape York), Burma, and South Africa (Walfisch Bay); also said to occur on inland waters of Europe south to the Mediterranean, and in small numbers from the coast of southern California to the Galapagos; occasional in winter in the Orkney Islands, off the south coast of England, and off Japan. It seems probable that these more northern records are not true wintering birds, but late migrants or stragglers.

Spring migration.—Northward off both coasts of North America. Early dates of arrival: North Carolina, Cape Hatteras, April 18; Massachusetts, May 23; Maine, May 29; New Brunswick, Grand Manan, May 26; Melville Peninsula, Winter Harbor, May 29; Greenland, June 10; California, San Francisco Bay, May 5; Alaska, St. Michael, May 23, and Point Barrow, May 23 to June 6; northeastern Siberia, Liakoff Islands, June 20.

Fall migration.—Southward by same routes. Early dates of arrival: Newfoundland, Bonne Bay, August 16; Nova Scotia, Sable Island, September 3; Rhode Island, September 13; New Jersey, October; Alaska, Kodiak Island, August 15; Washington, Puget Sound, September 7; California, Monterey Bay, August 2; Mexican coast, October 5; Peru, Callao Bay, November 17. Late dates of departure: Northeastern Greenland, latitude 75° 49′ N., August 6; western Greenland, Disco Island, September 6; Nova Scotia, Halifax, October 4; Maine, late October; Massachusetts, December 9; Rhode Island, October 11; New York, Long Island, October 30; New Jersey, December; Alaska, Point Barrow, August 15 to September 20; Washington, Puget Sound, October 22; California, Monterey Bay, October 27.

Casual records.—Spring records from Nebraska and Michigan and fall records from Pennsylvania, Ohio, Illinois, and Missouri are probably casual stragglers, but they may indicate a limited migration through the interior from Hudson Bay.

Egg dates.—Point Barrow, Alaska: Twenty-four records June 12 to 27; twelve records June 17 to 20. Iceland: Three records May 21, June 1 and 28.

STERCORARIUS PARASITICUS (Linnaeus).

PARASITIC JAEGER.

HABITS.

Contributed by Charles Wendell Townsend.

As one watches a flock of terns whirling like driven snow, now here, now there, and ever and anon plunging for fish, one may sometimes see a dark, hawk-like bird suddenly appear on the scene and spread devastation in the ranks. With relentless energy he singles out and pursues some hapless individual until it drops its prey. This is a jaeger, a gull-like bird, with hawk-like characteristics. A more appropriate name for him would be robber rather than jaeger or hunter, for he obtains his food by robbing other birds. He has, however, all the grace and agility of the true hunting birds—the hawks—but his actions rarely end in bloodshed. After all robbery is a less serious crime than murder, but the term robber is opprobrious, while that of hunter is not, so it is perhaps well that the name remains as it is.

The parasitic jaeger is circumpolar in its distribution and breeds throughout the barren arctic grounds in North America, Greenland, Europe, and Asia. In Europe it nests as far south as the Shetlands. It winters from the southern part of its summer range along the coast even as far as Brazil, Australia, and the Cape of Good Hope, but in the interior of the continents it is only of casual occurence.

Spring.—In the brief arctic spring, when the ice is breaking up and the snowdrifts are dwindling, the parasitic jaeger arrives on the breeding grounds on the tundra near the shores of the Arctic Ocean, or at a distance from the sea on the shores of ponds or lakes. It generally nests apart, not in communities. Of its courtship nothing is known. It is possible that the " wailing cries " described by Nelson and mentioned later may be in the nature of the love song. When surprised near the nest, Nelson (1887) says, " it creeps along the ground with flapping wings to decoy away the intruder."

Nesting.—The nest is a mere depression in the soil. Macfarlane (1908) says it is " scantily lined with a few withered leaves and grasses." Grinnell (1900) in the region of Kotzebue Sound, Alaska, says " the nest was a slight saucer-shaped depression on a low mossy hummock on the tundra. This depression was scatteringly lined with bits of white lichen, such as grow immediately around the nest." Thayer and Bangs (1914) report that Koren found it in northern Siberia nesting " in dry spots in swamps." Russell (1898) at the mouth of the Mackenzie, says that " the nest was simply a level bit of dry moss on the tundra a few yards from the water's edge."

Eggs.—Only two eggs are laid and one brood hatched. Nelson (1887) says the eggs are laid in northern Alaska by June 5. The egg is ovate in shape, of a dull olive varying to green, gray or brown ground color, with spots, blotches, and lines of a sepia, drab, dark chocolate, and umber-vinaceous color. These markings are sometimes distributed with great uniformity over the whole egg or gathered as a wreath about the larger end. The measurements of 50 eggs in various collections average 57 by 41 millimeters; the eggs showing the four extremes measure **61** by 41, 58 by **43, 51** by 40.5, and 56 by **38** millimeters.

Plumages.—[Author's note: I have never seen a small specimen of the downy young of the parasitic jaeger, but a half-grown young in my collection, which is still more than half downy, has the down of the upper parts uniform " natal brown," paler on the head and neck, and shading off to " drab-gray " on the under parts. There is no indication of any mottling anywhere. The juvenal plumage is well advanced on the wings and scapulars, where it evidently appears first; the feathers are appearing through the down all over the breast and belly and on the upper part of the back; the tail feathers are bursting their sheaths.

The sequence of plumages to maturity is practically the same, in both phases, as in the pomarine jaeger, except that the parasitic jaeger normally acquires its fully adult plumage when a little over 2 years old. The first-year plumage is heavily barred above and below with rufous edgings, which fade and wear away during the fall and winter. The second-year plumage is less heavily barred, with narrower and whitish edgings above, with much more white in the underparts, with heavily barred under tail-coverts, with somewhat elongated central rectrices and sometimes with a suggestion of the golden color. At the second postnuptial molt, when the bird is from 25 to 27 months old, the fully adult plumage is assumed with no mottling or barring anywhere, with the dusky under tail-coverts and crissum and with the elongated central rectrices.

During this molt the upper body plumage is completed first, and the last signs of immaturity to disappear are the barred feathers of the chest and flanks. The postnuptial molt of both adults and young is complete and occurs in August, September, and October, the wings being molted in October. There is probably an incomplete prenuptial molt also, but material is lacking to show it satisfactorily. Fall adults in fresh plumage have the chin, throat, and neck clouded with light drab and the dark crown less pronounced than in spring. This disappears partially by wear, but I have seen one adult, taken in California on April 29, in which this plumage was being replaced by a partial molt.

Adult parasitic jaegers can be distinguished in life at a long distance by the downward extension of the drab mantle on the sides of the neck which seems to form a partial collar; this is entirely absent in the long-tailed jaeger; the long central tail feathers are more pointed and are held differently in flight from those of the pomarine jaeger, as explained under that species; these feathers are, however, an unsafe guide by which to distinguish the parasitic and long-tailed jaegers, as there is much individual variation and overlapping. These last two species can hardly be distinguished in life in the immature plumages. For the best characters by which they can be distinguished in the hand I would refer the reader to Dr. Leonhard Stejneger's (1885) excellent remarks on the subject.

In the dark phase, which may prove to be a distinct species, the sequence of molts and plumages is practically the same as outlined above, though the birds are much darker in all stages. During the first year the brown edgings are conspicuous, but during the second they are replaced by narrower and whiter edgings, the under tail-coverts being heavily barred in both cases. The adult plumage is wholly sooty, with sometimes a trace of the golden collar.]

The proportions of the two phases vary considerably. At Ipswich in the migrations, which extend over most of the summer, the birds in light phase outnumber the dark birds in the proportion of 8 or 10 to 1. On the Labrador coast I found those in the dark phase more numerous in proportion than at Ipswich. Richardson (1825) says that on the banks of the Coppermine River in the beginning of July the greater part of them had dark abdomens. Grinnell (1900) in Alaska found a sooty bird mated with a light one and remarks that "one could scarcely believe them to be of the same species." He says that half of this species in June and July were in the dark plumage. Thayer and Bangs (1914) mention two pairs in northern Siberia, where all four birds were in the light phase, and one pair at Kodiak Island, Alaska, where the birds were in the dark phase. Nelson (1887) mentioned a similar dark couple. The difference between the two phases seems as great as that between the greater and the sooty shearwaters.

Food.—The feeding habits of the parasitic jaeger vary considerably with the locality. The host on which it preys is in some places, as on the New England coast, the common tern, although the arctic, roseate, and least terns, as well as the Bonaparte's gull, may in places be added. On the eastern Labrador coast I found the great flocks of kittiwakes to be the chief source of its supplies, as also is the case in Baffin's Land, for Kumlien (1879) says:

This species seems to depend on *Rissa tridactyla* for the greater part of its food.

Anderson (1913), under the heading "Parasitic jaeger," says:

The jaegers are the terror of the smaller birds, spending their time ceaselessly hawking back and forth over the tundra looking for eggs and young birds. Large numbers of eggs of eiders and gulls are destroyed in the rookeries by the jaegers. Whenever the Arctic terns are nesting their neighbors are comparatively safe, as the belligerent little terns speedily cause any marauding jaeger to beat a hasty retreat. I have also seen ruddy turnstones drive a jaeger away from the nests. I once observed a pair of jaegers chasing a flock of sandpipers. One sandpiper flew out of the flock, the jaegers in pursuit. They seemed to work together, one darting in while the other turned. The sandpiper finally escaped by flying upward until almost out of sight, and the jaegers finally gave up the chase. * * * Some other birds will also attack the jaegers, which are really cowardly birds when heartily opposed. I have on two or three occasions seen a rock ptarmigan fly fiercely at a jaeger which came too near his nesting place and put the jaeger to ignominious flight.

Its calling makes it one of the most interesting sea birds to watch. The advent of a jaeger among a flock of terns occasions loud cries of anger among the latter as they scatter to the right and left, while the hunter, singling out one individual, chases it with great energy. No matter how skillfully and rapidly the victim twists and turns, now up, now down, now to one side, now the other, sooner or later, with a few exceptions, it acknowledges defeat by dropping the fish from its beak or by disgorging the contents of its gullet. These, the jaeger, with great skill and agility, catches in mid-air and swallows at once, or on other occasions carries hanging from the beak for a short distance before satisfying its appetite. Sometimes it alights on the water, the better to enjoy its meal. Nelson (1887) says:

They are very greedy, and frequently swallow so much that they are unable to fly until a portion is disgorged.

The victimized tern meanwhile vents its wrath at the robbery in no uncertain language and must again set to work for its living. But the jaegers are not always successful. Thus, on one occasion, I saw a parasitic jaeger pursue a common tern in a straight line for nearly a mile, eventually to give up the chase. Not infrequently two hunters combine on one victim. Thus I have notes of two jaegers at Ipswich, one in the dark, the other in the light phase, that relentlessly followed a common tern. The bird that secured the prize was at once pursued by his companion and accessory in theft. On another occasion two jaegers at Ipswich were chasing a tern that twisted in sharp angles and small circles over the beach

Finally the tern dropped the fish, which one of the jaegers secured in mid-air. Later the two dashed into a flock of about a hundred terns and chased them right and left. The terns screamed and darted around in great confusion; some retaliated by chasing the jaegers.

Although this bird well justifies its name *parasitic*, it occasionally does some foraging for itself; thus King (1836) says that it also "subsists on putrid fish and other animal substances thrown up by the sea." Turner (1886), at St. Michael, Alaska, says it eats "fishes that had been cast on the beach, shell fish, and other animal food. They also eat the berries of *Empetrum nigrum.*" The latter is the crow berry or the curlew berry of the north, the berry on which the curlew formerly fatted in countless numbers. Turner also relates an instance where a parasitic jaeger picked up a freshly torn-off muskrat skin that was floating on the surface of the water.

It seized the skin in its beak and then passed it to its claws, by which it carried it off a little distance and began to strip the adhering muscle and fat from it.

Nelson (1887) reported that this species eats also shrews, mice, and lemmings. Eifrig (1905) found bones and feathers in the stomachs. Seton (1908) says that in the region of the lakes of the barren grounds "it lives much like a hawk or a raven, coming when a caribou is killed to share in the offal. Once saw one capture a Lapland longspur on the wing, and have often seen it pursuing ground squirrels." Preble (1908) gives the stomach contents of two taken near the Great Slave Lake; the first contained various insects and the bones of a small bird, evidently a young tern, and the other a dragon fly, various beetles, and a small fish. Anthony (1906) says:

These deep-sea individuals had their stomachs filled to overflowing with fish spawn about the size of No. 5 shot, evidently of some species spawning on the surface where the bird could pick it up without trouble. I have seen this jaeger in Bering Straits diving for surf smelt, together with Pacific kittiwakes; but, like all of their group, they found it difficult to get below the surface, even with the help of a drop of 6 or 8 feet above the water, and seldom neglected an opportunity to rob the Arctic tern or kittiwake.

Behavior.—The flight, swimming, and diving of this species have all been mentioned in the feeding habits. While the first is rapid, graceful, and falcon-like, the two last are seldom indulged in, and not very efficient. It is, indeed, a bird of the air and outside of the breeding grounds is rarely seen on shore. On one occasion, however, at Ipswich, I saw a flock of 10 of these birds on the smooth, hard beach.

In the chase of terns, it is the tern that uses its vocal powers, and the voice of the jaeger is rarely heard. Nelson (1887) says:

On cloudy days or in the dusky twilight, these birds have a habit of uttering loud wailing cries, interspersed with harsh shrieks, which are among the most peculiar notes heard in the northern breeding grounds.

Mr. W. Elmer Ekblaw says of the habits of this jaeger in Greenland:

The jaeger not only steals the food away from the other birds, but also preys upon their eggs and young. In 1914 I found in one day's tramp two eider nests and one nest of the ring-necked plover that had been despoiled by this ravager. The pierced egg shells were scattered about the nests, as if the jaeger had delighted in the destruction he had wrought. The knots and sandpipers of the land birds and the kittiwakes and terns of the sea birds cordially hate the jaeger. In protection of their nests and young these birds often valiantly attack and drive off the greedy jaeger, but usually he pursues them vindictively until they yield to him. He is the particular enemy of the kittiwakes, and whenever he dashes into a flock of them his vicious screams scatter them panic stricken. He then singles out one for his victim and pursues him relentlessly with buteonine tenacity of purpose.

Disliked, as parasitic jaegers must be by their victims, they are well able to take care of themselves and have few destructive enemies. Even man, although eagerly taking the eggs for food on the breeding grounds, disdains to eat the robber bird. It may, like the strongest of sea birds, at times succumb to the tempest. King (1836) records that one in a storm " sought refuge from the raging elements under the lee of our tent."

Fall.—The fall migration of the young of the year begins in Alaska, according to Nelson (1887), after the 20th of September and the birds keep out to sea on the New England coast. I have seen adults at Ipswich as early as July. Here they pursue their calling among the terns until these birds leave for the south, whither they follow them by September, and continue the same methods of making a living during the winter.

DISTRIBUTION.

Breeding range.—Arctic and subarctic regions of both hemispheres. In North America east to Greenland (Disco Bay and Baffins Bay and probably north to Thank God Harbor. South to northern Labrador (Killinek), and northern Hudson Bay (Southampton Island), central Keewatin (near York Factory), southern Mackenzie (Great Slave Lake), southwestern Alaska (Alaska Peninsula and Kodiak Island), and the Aleutian Islands. West to Bering Sea coast of Alaska. North to the Arctic coast of Alaska and Mackenzie, also Banks Land (Mercy Bay), Melville Island (Winter Harbor), and other Arctic Islands to about 80° north latitude. Has been recorded in summer in southeastern Alaska (Glacier Bay) and may occasionally breed. In the Old World breeds from Iceland, the Faroe Islands, northern British Isles (north coast Scotland, Orkney, and Shetland Islands, and many of the Hebrides), along the Arctic coast and islands of Europe and Asia to northeastern Siberia. South to the Commander Islands and probably the Kurile Islands.

Breeding grounds protected in the following national reservation in Alaska: Aleutian Islands (as Agattu, Amchitka, and Kiska).

Winter range.—From Florida (Gulf coast) and southern California (Point Concepcion) southward along both coasts of South America to Argentina (Mar del Plata) and Chile (Valparaiso) and occasionally as far as the Straits of Magellan. In the Eastern Hemisphere along the western coast of Europe and Africa to the Cape of Good Hope; also southwestern Asia from the Persian Gulf to the Mekran and Sind coasts, and occasionally New Zealand and Australia.

Spring migration.—Northward along both coasts. Early dates of arrival: Off Jacksonville, Florida, April 9; New Jersey, Stone Harbor, May 27; Massachusetts, May 24 and 31; Greenland, Thank God Harbor, June 14; Washington, Tacoma, May 17; Alaska, St. Michael, May 7; Point Barrow, May 29; Banks Land, May 31; Mackenzie River, June 8. Late dates of departure: Straits of Magellan, March 6; Chile, Valparaiso, March 28; Florida, Matanzas Inlet, May 18; Pennsylvania, Renova, June 18; Ontario, Toronto, June 20; southern Labrador, June 21.

Fall migration.—Southward along both coasts and irregularly in the interior. Early dates of arrival: Nova Scotia, Sable Island, September 9; New Hampshire, Seabrook, September 2; Massachusetts, August 30; Rhode Island, September 2; New York, Long Island, August 6; Brazil, October 26; Argentina, Mar del Plata, October 9; southern Alaska, Cook Inlet, August 22; Washington, Puget Sound, September 2; Chile, Valparaiso, November 6. Late dates of departure: Ontario, October 20; Massachusetts, October 22; Rhode Island, November 27; South Carolina, Charleston, November; Wellington Channel, September 2; Alaska, Point Barrow, September 9, and St. Michael, September 16; Pribilof Islands, October 18; Washington, Puget Sound, November 8; California, Monterey Bay, December 12.

Casual records.—Fall records from the interior are so numerous that they indicate a regular migration route in limited numbers.

Egg dates.—Iceland: Sixteen records, May 21 to June 24; eight records, May 26 to June 14. Northern Canada: Twelve records, June 10 to July 8; six records, June 29 to July 8. Northern Alaska: Four records, June 19 and 20 and July 10 and 18. Shetland Islands: five records, May 15 to June 26; three records, May 30 to June 15.

STERCORARIUS LONGICAUDUS Vieillot.

LONG-TAILED JAEGER.

HABITS.

On the rolling Arctic plains or tundra back of Nome, Alaska, we found these handsome birds very common and a conspicuous feature in the landscape, where they had probably reared their young and were spending the summer in congenial surroundings. Some of them were almost constantly in sight, and it was a pleasure to watch their graceful evolutions on the wing, as they coursed about the grassy borders of the little tundra ponds in search of food or perched on the little mossy hummocks to rest or to watch for passing birds that they might rob, or for some small mammal on which they might pounce. Certain of these little mounds seemed to be favorite lookout points for certain individuals or pairs, as there were signs of continued occupancy, and we frequently saw the same mound occupied at various times; perhaps each pair of birds has a sort of feudal domain of its own, from which intruders are driven away.

Spring.—The long-tailed jaeger retires to its Arctic summer home very early in the season and arrives on its breeding grounds in advance of its congeners. Dr. E. W. Nelson (1887) says that it arrives in the vicinity of St. Michael about May 12 or 15, but is not numerous until 10 days or more later. Mr. Lucien M. Turner (1886) writes:

On their first arrival they are somewhat gregarious, though this may be due to the limited portions of ground free from snow. At this time the little pools of the low ground are being rapidly thawed out; many cracks in the heaving sea ice expose the water to view. These places are then scanned for food. When the ice in the lakes and larger ponds is melted, these birds usually are hovering in the vicinity, or seated on some knoll watching a gull or tern dive for a fish.

Nesting.—Doctor Nelson (1887) says of the nesting habits of this species near St. Michael:

The mating occurs with a great amount of noisy demonstration on the part of several rivals, but once paired the birds keep by themselves, and early in June deposit their eggs in a depression on the mossy top of some knoll upon rising ground. In one instance, on June 16, while I was securing the eggs of a *Macrorhamphus*, a pair of these jaegers kept circling about, uttering harsh screams and darting down within a few feet. As I approached the spot where the snipe's eggs lay I had noticed these birds on a knoll just beyond, but had paid no attention; but as the birds kept leaving me to hover over the knoll and then return to the attack, I examined the spot, and there, in a cup-shaped depression in the moss, lay two dark greenish eggs marked with an abundance of spots. During the breeding season these birds and the preceding species have a cunning habit of tolling one away from their nest by dragging themselves along the ground and feigning the greatest suffering. They roll about among the tussocks, beat their wings, stagger from side to side, and seem to be unable to fly, but they manage to increase the distance from their starting point at a very respectable rate, and ere long suddenly launch forth on the wing.

Mr. Hersey found a nest of the long-tailed jaeger, with two eggs on the point of hatching, near St. Michael on June 19, 1915. The eggs were laid in a natural depression of irregular shape on the top of a dry mound slightly raised above the surrounding wet tundra; there were several higher mounds within a few yards. The female could be plainly seen sitting on her nest from a considerable distance. She allowed him to approach within 20 yards before she flew, when both she and the male swooped about his head. Within 50 feet of this nest a willow ptarmigan was sitting on her nest with six eggs.

Mr. Johan Koren, according to Messrs. Thayer and Bangs (1914), found a remarkable nest of this species, in northeastern Siberia, on June 22, 1912.

The eggs lay in a slight depression on the level, mossy ground in a dry, high, larch forest. Both parent birds were present, and both had acquired the habit of alighting and perching in the tree tops.

This was a decided exception to the rule, however, as the nest is usually placed on some slight elevation on the flat or rolling open tundra, where a few pieces of dry grass, bits of mosses or leaves are scraped together in a slight hollow. The birds are very courageous in the defense of the nest, swooping down at the intruder or flying straight at his face and turning or rising just in time to miss striking him. After the young are hatched, however, they become more cautious and seldom approach within gunshot, lest they betray the presence of the young, which are cleverly hidden in the grass.

Eggs.—The long-tailed jaeger lays almost invariably two eggs, occasionally only one, and very rarely three. The eggs are almost indistinguishable from those of the parasitic jaeger, but they average slightly smaller and are usually a little more blunt in shape. The shape varies from ovate to short ovate, usually nearer the latter. The shell is smooth and thin, but has very little luster. The ground color varies from " light brownish olive " or " Dresden brown," in the darkest eggs, to "tawny olive," " Isabella color," " light yellowish olive," or even " olive buff," in the lightest eggs. The eggs are irregularly spotted or blotched, chiefly about the larger end with " raw umber," " Prout's brown," or other lighter shades of brown. Often there are also numerous underlying spots and blotches of various shades of drab. The measurements of 48 eggs in the United States National Museum collection, average 55 by 39 millimeters; the eggs showing the four extremes measure **61.5** by 42.5, 56 by **50, 47** by 38.5, and 49.5 by **36** millimeters.

The period of incubation is 23 days. Both sexes incubate. Mr. A. L. V. Manniche (1910) writes:

As far as I could notice the sexes divided the breeding duties evenly between themselves. The posture of the bird while brooding is high, the neck and head erected. While the one bird broods, the other guards its mate and the hunting territory. As soon as a bird of the same species or another larger bird appears upon the scene, the watching bird utters a long penetrating cry and attacks the unwelcome guest; having chased him off, the skua again takes its seat near the brooding mate. If you retire some 50 meters the bird will quickly settle upon the nest again. The clamorousness and fearlessness of the bird make it easy to discover nearly every nest, even on a most extensive territory.

If the eggs be removed from the nest, the skua will nevertheless as a rule lie down upon the nest for some few minutes. In a certain case I saw a bird lying more than half an hour upon the empty nest.

Young.—The chicks, which soon after the hatching leave the nest, seem during the first days to be principally fed with insects. In the gullet of a newly hatched bird I found a crane-fly (*Tipula*), but they are even when quite young able to eat lemmings, which the parents hunt, eat, and afterwards disgorge before them. The young ones grow very quickly. It is a well-known fact that the young of this skua appear before the first molt in two-color varieties—a pale and a dark. The pale variety seems to occur somewhat more frequently than the dark.

Though this and the preceding species were both common in northwestern Greenland, the members of the Crocker Land Expedition failed to find the nest of either. To illustrate the peculiar behavior of this species near its nest, I quote from Mr. Ekblaw's notes of July 16, 1914, as follows:

Though I failed to find them I felt confident that I had been very near either the eggs or the young of *Stercorarius longicaudus* to-day. Among the rocks just above Moraine Lake a pair of these birds flew uneasily about me and alighted from time to time near me as I searched at length for the nest that I suspected was on the plateau. The male boldly perched within 40 feet of me, and though the female was shyer she did not leave me far either. An ingenious deceit that the female attempted is worthy of note. After flying nervously near and about me she flew to a large bowlder and settled down snugly beside it, to all appearance as if she were returning to her nest. I hastened to the place exultantly, only to find, when the bird flushed, that she had deceived me. After another nervous flight about me she repeated the performance, and again I was deceived, even though I waited until I thought she would tire of her strategy, if deceit it were. When she tried a third time to delude me I waited to let her tire, but her patience outwore mine and I finally flushed her. In an hour's search of the moraine afterwards I failed to find any nest.

Plumages.—The only downy young that I have seen is plainly colored without any dark markings. It varies from " bister " or " buffy brown " above to " wood brown " below, being darkest on the back. Yarrell (1871) describes "a nestling in half-down " as " pale smoke-brown on the downy head and under parts with very dark brown feathers tipped with rufous on the back and wings.

Although the adults of the long-tailed jaeger are not known to have light and dark phases, there seem to be two quite distinct types of coloration in the juvenal plumages. In the dark phase the upper parts are dark "brownish black," or "clove brown"); the head, neck, and chest are mainly dusky, the latter mottled with "wood brown"; the feathers of the back and wing-coverts are edged with "cinnamon" or "wood brown," and the rump is spotted with the latter color; the lower parts are mainly buff, mottled and barred, chiefly on the sides and under tail-coverts, with dusky. In the light phase the upper parts are much the same as in the dark phase, but much lighter colored, and the pale "wood brown" edgings are broader and more prevalent; the head and neck are mainly "pinkish buff" and the crown is but little darker; the head is uniformly covered with linear streaks of pale dusky; the under parts are largely whitish, tinged with pale "pinkish buff," nearly immaculate on the breast and belly, but heavily barred on the sides and under tail-coverts with dusky. These descriptions are taken from young birds, collected early in August, in full, fresh, juvenal plumage. Other specimens taken late in September show similar well-marked color phases, but birds a year older do not seem to show them. This plumage is worn, with slight modifications, during the first year; the brown edgings fade out to white and gradually wear away; probably a partial molt occurs during the winter and spring. At the first postnuptial molt, the following summer, a complete change produces the second-year plumage. In this plumage the upper parts are much as in the adult, except that there is only a trace of the yellow on the sides of the head, often none at all; the two central tail feathers now project decidedly beyond their fellows, which was hardly noticeable in the previous plumage; but the under parts are more or less barred with dusky, particularly on the flanks and chest, and heavily so on the under tail-coverts. This plumage is worn for about a year or so until the second postnuptial molt, which is complete, beginning in June and lasting through September. At this molt the long central tail feathers and the dusky under tail-coverts are assumed; the young birds then assume the adult plumage when a little over 2 years old.

Adults have a partial prenuptial molt in the early spring and a complete postnuptial molt in August, September, and October. The seasonal changes in adults are not conspicuous, though freshly molted birds in the fall have the chin, throat, and neck clouded with light drab and the dark crown less pronounced than in the spring. The characters by which this and the foregoing species can be recognized are somewhat involved and confusing; so, rather than discuss them here, I would refer the student to Dr. L. Stejneger's (1885) excellent remarks on the subject.

Food.—In their summer homes on the tundra these jaegers live on a varied bill of fare. They are said to feed largely on lemmings, field mice (*Microtus*), and other small mammals. They catch flies, butterflies, and other insects and eat their larvæ. In the summer they rob bird's nests to devour the eggs and young, and sometimes they pursue and kill wounded birds for food. Probably a few fish are caught and many are stolen from gulls and terns. They also pick up considerable offal of various kinds, as well as small crustaceans and worms. During the latter part of the season they feed largely on crow-berries (*Empetrum nigrum*) and other berries. While migrating or during the winter they associate with the smaller gulls and terns, depending largely for food on what they can steal from these industrious birds or what they can pick up, in company with these common scavengers, in the way of garbage.

Behavior.—To watch the long-tailed jaeger in flight is one of the delights of the Arctic summer, for it is one of the swiftest and most graceful of birds on the wing; its light and slender form is propelled by its long, pointed wings with the speed of an arrow, its broad tail serving as an effective rudder, as it twists and turns in pursuit of its fellows or some luckless gull or tern, with its long central tail feathers streaming in the wind. Doctor Nelson (1887) says:

They appear to be much more playful than the other jaegers, and parties of six or eight may be seen pursuing one another back and forth over the marsh. The long, slender tail feathers and extreme grace on the wing of these birds render them very much like the swallow-tailed kite.

Mr. Turner (1886) observes that it is "extremely swift on the wing, and when pursuing another bird thrashes the air with wing and tail, giving an undulatory motion to the body." It swims lightly and gracefully on the water, holding its long tail pointed upward; but I have never known it to dive below the surface.

Doctor Nelson (1887) describes the notes as follows:

They have a shrill phĕū-phĕū-phĕū-phĕŏ, uttered while they are flying, and when the birds are quarreling or pursuing one another the ordinary note is often followed by a harsh qua. At other times they have a rattling kr-r-r-r, kr-r-r-r, kr-r-r-r, krī, krī-krī-kri, the latter syllables shrill and querulous and sometimes followed by the long drawn pheū-pheū-pheū in the same tone.

All writers refer to the predaceous habits of the jaegers. Their behavior toward other species is certainly not above criticism. On their breeding grounds they have the reputation of being nest robbers, according to the reports of the natives, eating the eggs and small young of any of the birds which are smaller or weaker than themselves. Such pilfering is done on the sly, however, for the jaeger is far from courageous and is often attacked and driven away from the nests of gulls, terns, curlew, sandpipers, and other shore birds,

Doctor Nelson (1887) " saw a jaeger swoop down at a duck paddling quietly on the surface of a pond, and the latter went flapping away in mortal terror, while the jaeger passed on, probably highly pleased at giving the duck such a fright." Mr. Turner (1886) says:

Should one of their kind be shot and slightly wounded the others will gather around it, and if not frightened away will soon dispatch their comrade.

Mr. Hersey's notes on the long-tailed jaeger at St. Michael state:

I have found this jaeger to be more peaceable and less given to chasing the gulls than the parasitic. I have seen as many as five or six of this species and a dozen or more short-billed gulls feeding in company on the refuse from the hotel, which had been put on a scow to be carried out into the bay and dumped; each bird paid no heed to his companions and there was no quarreling. The small shore birds and longspurs seem to regard him as an enemy, however, and follow him about over the tundra whenever one appears. Both this and the parasitic jaeger show caution when among a flock of glaucous gulls, and I have never seen them attempt to molest one of these large birds. At times they bother the little Sabine's gulls.

Mr. Frank C. Hennessey, who has sent me his notes on the birds of Winter Harbor, says, on the other hand, that " they tyrannize all others of their tribe, including the snowy owl, and make known their presence by successions of sharp but not discordant cries. These birds, considering their size, are quite able to fight for and defend themselves, particularly when any intruder may happen to encroach on the locality in which their nest is situated; in such a case they have been known to even attack the Arctic fox."

Mr. A. L. V. Manniche (1910) writes:

Not rarely I observed falcons pursued by skuas (*Lestris longicauda*). At the end of August the young skuas will frequently be sitting around on stones, still cared for by their parents, which with extreme violence will guard their offspring against attack from falcons. The skuas exceed by far the gyrfalcons in ability of flight, and the falcons therefore always wish to escape the pursuit and retire to the rocks. Most frequently three or four skuas would join in an attack. The battle would usually be fought out immensely high up in the air.

Mr. Walter H. Rich has contributed the following notes on the behavior of jaegers on the fishing banks among the shearwaters:

Both yagers and skuas bully the " hags," dropping on their backs as often as these latter are found enjoying a dainty bit. The yagers fight and quarrel much among themselves also. On several occasions the writer saw them clinch in the air to fall 20 or 30 feet, striking and clawing all the while. Only rarely do they annoy the skuas, and then somewhat carefully, usually in breezy weather, when they may the more easily escape consequences through their superior abilities in maneuvering; less often still do they trouble the large gulls, as the " black backs." Of the latter species I saw one in the brown plumage, when weaving his dignified flight through a cloud of " kittiwakes," turn suddenly to shoot upward and seize a long-tailed yager by the flank, bringing away a mouthful of feathers with a wicked side wrench of his head, causing the victim to squeal in angry indignation and put on full power ahead.

It seemed to be sheer malevolence on the gull's part, for the yager was merely balancing before and above him in the gale, unmindful of his enemy's presence until the blow fell. Yet it may have been the payment of some ancient grudge.

The behavior of this and the foregoing species among the gulls and terns along on coasts is well known and has already been well described under the previous species. But the following passage from Audubon (1840) seems worth quoting:

It generally passes through the air at a height of 50 or 60 yards, flying in an easy manner, ranging over the broad bays, on which gulls of various kinds are engaged in procuring their food. No sooner has it observed that one of them has secured a fish than it immediately flies toward it and gives chase. It is almost impossible for the gull to escape, for the warrior, with repeated jerkings of his firm pinions, sweeps toward it with the rapidity of a peregrine falcon pouncing on a duck. Each cut and turn of the gull only irritates him the more and whets his keen appetite until, by two or three sudden dashes, he forces it to disgorge the food it had so lately swallowed. This done, the poor gull may go in search of more; the lestris is now for a while contented and alights on the water to feed at leisure. But soon, perceiving a distant flock of gulls, he rises on wing and speeds toward them. Renewing his attacks, he now obtains an abundant supply and at length, when quite gorged, searches for a place on which to alight unseen by any other of his tribe more powerful than himself.

Fall.—During the months of August and September the jaegers. old and young, leave their northern breeding grounds and start on their southward migration, and the first arrivals often appear on the coasts of New England and California during the former month, showing that some individuals must start very early or must migrate very rapidly. Doctor Nelson (1887) says that " the long-tailed species is less frequently found at sea than the last, and is rarely found about the ice pack north of Bering Straits." Numerous records from the interior of the United States and Canada would seem to indicate that the main migration route is overland rather than coastwise.

Winter.—Prof. Wells W. Cooke (1915) makes the remarkable statement that " it seems probable that the long-tailed jaeger does not regularly winter anywhere in the Western Hemisphere. The winter home is in the Eastern Hemisphere, south to Gibraltar on the Atlantic side and to Japan on the Pacific." He evidently regards all the numerous fall records on both coasts and in the interior as accidental occurrences and either overlooks or disregards Audubon's (1840) statement that this species " often ranges " to the coasts of Florida and the Gulf of Mexico in winter; as well as Wayne's (1910) more recent records for South Carolina in December and Florida in February, where it was " observed in numbers."

DISTRIBUTION.

Breeding range.—Arctic coasts of both hemispheres. In North America from northwestern Alaska (Yukon Delta) along the coast at least as far east as Franklin Bay; on Ellesmere Land, Grinnell Land, and northern Greenland (on the west coast from Disco Bay north to 82° and on the east coast from Scoresby Sound north to 80°); probably on other islands in the Arctic Archipelago. South to northern Labrador (Cape Chidley), Southampton Island, and the west coast of Hudson Bay (probably as far south as York Factory). In the Eastern Hemisphere Iceland, Spitzbergen, Nova Zembla, the coast of northern Scandinavia, the Kola Peninsula, the Lower Petchora River, and the Arctic coast of Siberia south at least to the Gulf of Anadyr and St. Lawrence Island.

Winter range.—American winter records are very scarce. Has been seen at Caper's Island, South Carolina, on December 21, and off the St. Johns River, Florida, in February; has been taken once in California (Hyperion), January 26; taken and reported common in Argentina (Mar del Plata) in October; and taken in Chile (Valparaiso) in March and November. In the Eastern Hemisphere it winters south to Gibraltar and the Mediterranean, and on the Asiatic side to the northern Kurile Islands.

Spring migration.—Early dates of arrival: Florida, east coast, April 8; New Jersey, 80 miles off Barnegat, May 6; Ellesmere Land, Cape Sabine, May 23; northeastern Greenland, latitude 80°, May 28 to June 6. Dates of arrival in Alaska: St. Michael, May 12 to 15; Nulato, May 15; Kowak River, May 22; Point Barrow, May 30; Demarcation Point, May 24. Taken at Vancouver Island, May 11.

Fall migration.—Southward along both coasts and through the interior. Early dates of arrival: Massachusetts, Woods Hole, August 12; Connecticut, Wallingford, August 30; Alaska, Forrester Island, August 24; British Columbia, Chilliwack, August 23; California, Monterey Bay, August 2. Late dates of departure: Ellesmere Land. Fort Conger, August 30; Massachusetts, Monomoy Island, September 29, and Woods Hole, October 13; Alaska, Point Barrow, August 21, and St. Michael, September 12; British Columbia, Okanagan Landing, September 18; California, September 19. Interior dates: Southampton Island, August 17; Manitoba, Lake Winnipeg, September and October 8; Missouri, Lake Como, October; Indiana, August 20, September 11 and 12, and November 30; Illinois, Cairo, November.

Egg dates.—Northern Alaska: Ten records, June 6 to July 12; five records, June 8 to 19. Northern Canada: Sixteen records, June 16 to July 12; eight records, June 27 to 30. Lapland: Nine records, June 2 to 20; four records, June 14 to 18.

Family LARIDAE, Gulls and Terns.

PAGOPHILA ALBA (Gunnerus).

IVORY GULL.

HABITS.

This beautiful, snow-white gull of the Arctic regions is decidedly boreal in summer and seldom wanders far south even in winter. It is circumpolar in its distribution and has been noted by nearly all Arctic explorers in both hemispheres. The names " ice-partridge " and " snow-bird," which are applied to this species, are both very appropriate, for the bird lives almost constantly in the vicinity of ice and snow, where its spotless plumage matches its surroundings. It is largely a bird of the open polar seas, frequenting the edges of the ice floes in company with the fulmars and other Arctic sea birds, and seldom resorting to the land except during the breeding season.

Nesting.—Prof. Robert Collett (1888) has given us a very good account of the nesting habits of the ivory gull, based on information furnished by Capt. Johannesen, who visited a breeding colony on the small island of Storöen, near Spitzbergen, in 1887. I quote from his excellent paper, as follows:

On the 8th of August, when he visited the island, he found young birds in all stages, from newly hatched to fully fledged, together with a small number of eggs, which, however, were on the point of hatching, and in all probability not one would have been left a week later. Storöen is about 9 English miles in length and 6 in breadth; the greater part of its surface is covered by a glacier, which rises to a height of about 400 feet; the remaining portions consist of sand and gravel, with here and there small stones, likewise oases covered with moss; while in a few places the ground consisted only of rock.

L. eburneus was breeding on the northeast side of the island, close to, or only a short way above, high-water mark, on low-lying ground like *L. canus*, *L. fuscus*, etc., and not in the cliffs. Capt. Johannesen estimated the number of nests at from 100 to 150; they were somewhat apart, at distances varying from 2 to 4 yards. There were one or two eggs or young, but never more in a nest. On being examined at Tromsö it was found that all the 19 eggs contained almost fully developed young chicks. Many of the nests contained young of various ages, whilst others were already empty. Several black-spotted young, capable of flight, were seen, likewise several young birds of the previous year's brood remained on the breeding ground. The nest is composed chiefly of green moss, which forms about nine-tenths of its mass. The rest consists of small splinters of driftwood, a few feathers, single stalks, and leaves of algae, with one or two particles of lichen. No trace of straw is to be found; a couple of pebbles may possibly have appertained to the underlayer of the nest. The mosses occur in pieces the size of a walnut, or less, and have evidently been plucked in a fresh state from a dry subsoil, either on rocks or gravelly places. The mosses are all sterile. Several of the splinters of driftwood were found of a length of about 100 millim. Under the microscope they all proved to be of conifers, probably larch, drifted from the Siberian rivers. Some were very old;

others, however, being still hard and possessing a fresh appearance. The feathers, of which only a few were found, are snowy white and have probably fallen from the brooding bird. Some portions of the algae were dry, crumpled leaves and stalks of seaweed. Only a few bits of a lichen were found, which appear to have got in accidentally.

A most interesting account of the home life of this species in Franz Josef Land is published by Mr. W. Eagle Clarke (1898); in which he quotes from the journal of Mr. William S. Bruce, of the Jackson-Harmsworth Expedition, as follows:

August 7. To-day we landed at Cape Mary Harmsworth, and the first thing we noted was an immense number of ivory gulls, and from their demonstrations and shriekings it soon became evident that they were nesting. As we traveled across the low-lying spit we found this was so. Here there are 5 or 6 square miles or more of fairly level ground, more or less terraced, being evidently a series of raised beaches. This, if not the largest, is one of the largest areas of bare ground in Franz Josef Land. Beyond a few lichens and occasional patches of moss there is very little vegetation, only two flowering plants being found—a saxifrage and a grass, and these very sparingly, indeed. There is very little actual soil, and the surface is rough and rugged with large stones. Scattered all over it are numerous fresh-water ponds, the largest of them perhaps 200 yards across. The first signs of the ivory gulls' nests were patches of old moss every here and there, which at first we could not make out. As we advanced we saw more of these patches, and these seemed more compact. On approaching closer to these the birds made still more vehement demonstrations, swooping down upon us and giving vent to their feelings by uttering a perfectly deafening shriek close to our heads.

Once in the midst of their nests—for these patches of moss were their nests—we had many hundreds of birds around us, first one swooping down to within a foot of our heads, and immediately after another. In some cases they actually touched us, and in one instance knocked the hat off a man's head. Most of the nests were empty, owing to the late date; but here and there was a single egg, and in two nests I found two eggs. Going on through this gullery we found that near certain nests, which were apparently empty, the birds made even more violent demonstrations than before, and in looking carefully about we descried a young ivory gull in its greyish-white downy plumage, and hardly visible against the stones, which were of a very similar color. Even the older ones, which were more whitish, were difficult to see among the stones. These young birds would sit crouched in between two or three large stones, and one might at first sight take them for stones also. On picking up a young bird the parents became quite distracted and threatened us more vehemently than ever. By-and-by we passed out of this gullery, but further along we could see others, each with many hundreds of these birds, and we advanced toward them. The gullery we left gradually became quiet; but the birds in the one which we were approaching were beginning to demonstrate in the same way as those at the last. The cries became louder and louder, and in a few minutes we were again in the midst of the deafening shrieks of a host of terrified yet defiant birds. Again they swooped down upon us, and it seemed quite likely that at any moment they might dash into our faces. So we passed on from gullery to gullery among many thousand of these birds. It was a magnificent sight; the sun was shining brightly in a blue sky, the air was clear, and these handsome birds in their pure white plumage added brilliancy to the scene. Each nest is, as I have said, composed of a pile of moss, in shape a truncated cone, and may be from 6 to 9 inches in height and from 18 inches to 2 feet in diameter. There is no hollow on the top of this more or less level pile, upon which the egg is deposited or the young bird sits. I noticed many dead young birds, some quite recently deceased, for they were still warm, while others had been dead for some time. In nearly every case their crania had been indented.

Doctor Malmgren, of the Swedish expedition to Spitzbergen in 1861, found a colony of ivory gulls breeding in entirely different situations. Baird, Brewer, and Ridgway (1884) quote from his notes, as follows:

On the 7th of July, 1861, I found on the north shore of Murchison Bay, latitude 80° N., a number of ivory gulls established on the side of a steep limestone precipice some hundred feet high in company with the *Rissa tridactyla* and *Larus glaucus.* The last named occupied the higher zones of the precipice. The *Larus eburneus,* on the other hand, occupied the niches and clefts lower down, at a height of from 50 to 100 feet. I could plainly see that the hen birds were sitting on their nests, but these were inaccessible. Circumstances did not permit before the 30th of July my making the attempt, with the help of a long rope and some necessary assistance, to get at the eggs. With the assistance of three men I succeeded in reaching two of the lowest in situation, and each contained one egg. The nest was artless and without connection and consisted of a shallow depression 8 or 9 inches broad in a loose clay or mold on a sublayer of limestone. Inside the nest was carefully lined with dry plants, moss, grasses, and the like, and a few feathers. The eggs were much incubated and already contained down-clad young. Both of the hen birds were shot upon their nests and are now in the National Museum. The male birds were at first observable, but disappeared when we began the work of reaching their nests.

Eggs.—The ivory gull lays a set of one or two eggs. Two of the eggs taken by Captain Johannesen are in our National Museum, and Major Bendire (1888) has described them as follows:

Their ground color is buffish olive; in one egg, somewhat paler, perhaps more of an olive-drab tint. The surface markings, more or less irregularly distributed over the entire egg, vary from clove-brown to bistre. The underlying or shell markings vary from slate to lilac-gray in tint and predominate in the larger specimen. In the smaller and darker one, both styles of markings are about equally distributed. The two kinds of spots vary considerably in size and shape.

Professor Collett (1888) describes nine of the eggs, as follows:

The ground color of five specimens is almost entirely alike—viz, a light grayish-brown tint, with faint admixture of yellowish green, such as often appears on the eggs of *L. canus;* which, however, have often a deeper brown or green hue. In structure and gloss all nine eggs greatly resemble those of *L. canus;* but the granulations under the microscope are a little coarser, more uneven, and in larger numbers; on the other hand, the granulations are perceptibly finer than in *L. fuscus.* The eggs are easily distinguished from those of *Rissa tridactyla* by their greater gloss, and the small excrescences do not lie quite so crowded, and are a little more flattened than they usually are in the last-mentioned species.

The measurements of 32 eggs in various collections average 60.5 by 43.6 millimeters; the eggs showing the four extremes measure **69.3** by 41.5, 62.6 by **44.6, 57** by 43. and 60.5 by **40** millimeters.

Plumages.—Prof. Collett (1888) describes the downy young as " white all over; the down white to the root "; and says that " even in this first stage the young in down may be distinguished from the young of other species by the strong and hooked claws, especially on the hind toe, the somewhat marginated web on the toes, and the forward nostrils. The downy covering is particularly close; *L. eburneus* in this respect is more closely related to the other species of *Larus* than to *Rissa*, the hairlike tips being shorter." A downy young bird in Doctor Bishop's collection, collected on King Charles Island on August 3, 1901, is covered with long, soft down, evenly colored above and below, " pallid mouse gray " shading into " pearl gray " at the base of the down. This is an older bird, however, as the first feathers are appearing on the scapulars.

Mr. Howard Saunders, in his edition of Yarrell (1871) says:

The nearly fledged young are described by Richardson [1] as having ash-gray backs; but with regard to the subsequent stages of plumage there is an absence of satisfactory details, and the editor can only place the following facts before his readers: In the autumn of 1880 Mr. Leigh Smith brought back from Franz-Josef Land a bird which was supposed to be the survivor of several young taken from the nest, and which was presented to the zoological gardens. Its prevailing tone was gray, owing, perhaps, to the saturation of the plumage with grease and dirt acquired on board the steam yacht, where the bird is said to have frequented the stokehole; but after constant washing since its arrival at the gardens the bird still remained of a smoke gray, nearly as dark as a fulmar petrel on the upper parts, and especially so on the tail coverts, the feathers of the back and wing coverts having slightly darker shafts, and the head bearing not merely a mask but a short hood of a darker gray than the neck and the underparts. The tail was reduced by abrasion to a mere stump. Such was the description given by the editor when the bird was supposed to be from three to four months old,[2] and its correctness can be corroborated by other observers. It was naturally expected that at the next moult the bird would pass into the well-known spotted plumage, but no spots made their appearance, and this example at once assumed the pure white plumage which it now (April, 1884) displays. This omission of the spotted stage may, perhaps, be owing to captivity in a comparatively warm climate; the editor is unable to account for it.

The ordinary immature or first-winter plumage is white, heavily mottled with dusky or dark grayish spots on the sides of the head and throat, concentrating into almost solid color in the loral region; scattering spots of the same slate-gray are on the hind neck and upper back. The scapulars have subterminal dusky spots, as do also many of the lesser and nearly all of the greater wing coverts and tertials. The primaries, secondaries, and rectrices are broadly

---

[1] Journal of a boat-voyage, p. 281.   [2] Zoologist, 1880, p. 484.

tipped with dusky, narrowly edged with white. As to how long this plumage is worn or at what age the adult, pure white plumage is acquired, I am in doubt. Selby (1833) says:

As the bird advances in age the brown spots and bars gradually decrease at each molt, and it is supposed to be perfectly matured in two years and a half.

I very much doubt if it requires any such time as two years to reach maturity, and I have never seen a bird with any spots on it at all, except a few on the edge of the wing, which I thought was over a year old. Probably the dusky tips wear away somewhat during the winter or are partially replaced by white feathers at an incomplete prenuptial molt, and at the first postnuptial molt the pure white adult plumage is assumed; but, unfortunately, I have not been able to study sufficient material to determine this with certainty or to understand fully the seasonal molts of adults. Adults apparently have but one complete annual molt in July and August. I have seen an adult which had not begun to molt its much-worn plumage on July 3, and another, in fresh plumage, which had completed the molt on August 30. These are in the Dwight collection, which also contains two specimens, taken July 6 and 13, molting both wings and tails, and another, taken on May 30, in which the wings are molting, beginning with the inner primaries.

Food.—The feeding habits of the ivory gull are hardly becoming a bird of such pure and spotless plumage. It is a greedy and voracious feeder and is none too particular about the quality of its food or how it obtains it. When some of these birds have been feeding on the carcass of a whale they present a sorry spectacle, for in their eagerness to satisfy their gluttonous appetite they crowd themselves into the entrails of the animal and their beautiful white plumage becomes smeared with blood. They are particularly fond of the blubber and flesh of whales, walruses, and seals, even when somewhat putrid, and, when busily engaged in such a feast they are tame and unsuspicious. Nothing in the way of animal food comes amiss to them and they even frequent the holes in the ice used by seals for the purpose of feeding on the excrement of these animals. Pieces of meat, blood, or offal from slain animals scattered on the ice or snow will always attract them. Any refuse thrown from the galley of a ship is readily picked up. Mr. Kumlien (1879) says that he once saw one try to swallow the wing of an eider, which the cook threw overboard. They also feed to a large extent on lemmings and other small rodents. On their breeding grounds, in the Polynia Islands, Captain McClintock (1856) found the bleached bones of lemmings scattered about their nests, " also fresh pellets, consisting of their bones and hair."

Behavior.—The flight of the ivory gull is said to be light and graceful. Yarrell (1871) says "that its note is shrill and not unlike that of the Arctic tern, and its flight is more like that of a tern than of an ordinary gull." Nuttall (1834) writes: "Its only note consists of a loud and disagreeable scream." Selby (1833) says: "Its voice is strong and harsh." Mr. A. L. V. Manniche (1910) says: "This pretty bird, with its short but sonorous note, would make a wonderfully animating impression in these silent and desolate surroundings."

Winter.—The migration amounts merely to a withdrawal from its breeding grounds and such northern portions of its summer range as are rendered uninhabitable by the closing in of ice and snow. The species is merely forced southward by the advance of winter conditions and frequents the more or less open edge of the ice pack all winter. Mr. Clarke (1898) makes this statement:

Dr. Neale records that in the autumn of 1881 the ivory gulls departed from Cape Flora (Franz Josef Land) at the end of October, and arrived there the following spring on the 20th of April. Dr. Nansen observed them for the first time in 1896 as early as the 12th of March, at his winter quarters on Frederick Jackson Island.

On the Labrador coast it seems to occur in the late fall only. Mr. Kumlien (1879) noted it as "very common" in Cumberland Sound "just before it froze up, for a few days only." Doctor Townsend (1907) writes:

Dr. Mumford, Mr. Frank Lewis, and others at Battle Harbor told us of shooting "ice patridges," which came with the ice and seals in November or December. They stay for about two weeks or a month and then depart, not to be seen again for a year. At times they are very abundant and even fly about the houses. These birds are shot for food, and are often obtained in the following manner: About a gallon of seals' blood is poured on the ice near the rocks, and as the birds hover about they are easily shot. Some of the birds in their eagerness to obtain the blood dash themselves with such force against the ice as to kill themselves.

A recent occurrence of the ivory gull in Portland Harbor, Maine, is recorded by Mr. Arthur H. Norton (1918); he and Mr. Walter H. Rich observed it at short range on January 5, 1918. He says:

The snowy whiteness of its plumage was always noticeably different from any other gull in the harbor, which contained at the time an abundance of *Larus argentatus* in all plumages, *Larus kumlieni*, and *Larus leucopterus*. Its habits and flight also differed distinctly; it was much more restless, now alighting on the ice, either to remain at rest for a few minutes, or to feed at the water's edge, and then away to search the edge of the ice field or to feed near some of the docks. It seemed to pay little or no attention to the other gulls or their feeding. On the ice it ran rapidly, suggesting the action of a large plover.

Its restlessness and independent action suggested to me the action of *Larus atricilla*, as it appears in the company of *Larus argentatus*. Its dashing flight seemed more like that of a jaeger than that of a gull. The wing was used at full extent with very little flexure at humero-radial and carpal joints, and was broad and wedge shaped in comparison with the narrower wing of *Larus argentatus*. It was seen for the last time January 7 by Mr. Rich, though daily watch has been kept to the present time (Feb. 22, 1918). During the period that the bird was seen the mercury was hardly rising above 0° F., and the harbor and bay was a solid field of ice except as broken by the ever busy tugs laboring to keep an open channel.

DISTRIBUTION.

Breeding range.—High northern latitudes, probably circumpolar. Known breeding places: Prince Patrick Island, Melville Island (Winter Harbor), northern Baffin Land (Port Bowen), and northern Greenland (Kane Basin and Kennedy Channel, and on the northeastern coast from latitude 74° to 81°); also said to have bred at Darnley Bay, east of Franklin Bay, on the Arctic coast. In the Eastern Hemisphere, at Storöen near Spitzbergen and Franz Josef Land.

Winter range.—Probably the open circumpolar seas as far north as unfrozen water occurs. Said to occur in some numbers in winter in southern Greenland and along the Labrador coast. In Europe it occasionally winters about the coasts of Great Britain and Ireland and northern France. Many winter records are of single birds, probably stragglers.

Spring migration.—Early dates of arrival: Melville Island, Winter Harbor, May 24; Ellesmere Land, Peterman Fiord, May 28; Greenland, Etah, June 1; Prince Patrick Island, June 12. Late dates of departure: Quebec, Godbout, March 7; Labrador, Sandwich Bay, June 12; Alaska, Point Barrow, May 22 to June 2.

Fall migration.—Fall and winter wanderings are erratic. Dates of arrival: Cumberland Gulf, October 24 and November 5; Anticosti Island, October; Quebec, Godbout, December 9; New Brunswick, St. John, November; Maine, Portland, January 4 and 5; Massachusetts, Monomoy Island, December 1; Long Island, Sayville, January 5; Bering Strait, November 9; Commander Islands, December 2. Dates of departure: Ellesmere Land, Lincoln Bay, September 1; Wellington Channel, September 15; Boothia Felix, September 21; Alaska, Point Barrow, September 25 to October 10.

Casual records.—Has occurred twice in British Columbia (Dease Lake, Cassiar, September, 1899, and Penticton, Okanagan Lake, October, 1897).

Rare or accidental in Ontario (Toronto, December 25, 1887).

KITTIWAKE.

HABITS.

The hardy kittiwake has been well named, on the New England coast, the " frost gull " or the " winter gull," for its arrival seems to indicate the coming of hard frosts and the beginning of real winter. It seems to bring with it the first cold breath of ice and snow from the rugged Arctic coasts where it makes its summer home. This species is always associated in my mind with icebergs and the great Greenland ice packs, which drift southward with the Arctic current, and in its summer home, with the dark, frowning cliffs of the frozen north, which tower for hundreds of feet above the stormy ice-bound seas until lost to sight in shrouds of mist and fog, where the " frost gulls " find a safe retreat in which to rear their hardy offspring.

Spring.—According to Hagerup (1891) the kittiwakes arrive in Greenland early in April:

From their arrival till the middle of May they keep together in one or more large flocks, and are then very timid and noisy. This is, perhaps, because the fjord is to a great extent covered with ice, so that their nesting ground lies 8 to 10 miles from open water. On clear days in April a flock of some 2,000 may be seen rising to a great height, say 3,000 and to 4,000 feet, sometimes going out of sight, so that one can only hear their screeching as they rapidly wheel about. They are then wont to make an excursion inland, above the ice, toward their breeding place. On returning they descend somewhat more scattered; but at once, on reaching the water, they gather close together. These exercises they often go through many times a day. In May they assemble in smaller flocks and are less shy. About 2,000 lay their eggs on the front of a perpendicular cliff situated at the head of the fjord. The lowest nests may easily be reached from a boat; the highest are about 150 feet above the sea. The eggs are laid chiefly during the first 10 days of June, and the young fly from their nests about the middle of August. (The earliest date on which I have seen a young bird is the 7th of August.) After that they generally go about in small flocks or singly and keep comparatively silent. On a few occasions only, on August afternoons, I have seen large flocks of 500 to 1,000 individuals rise to a great height and fly toward the ocean.

Courtship.—Mr. Edmund Selous (1905) says, in referring to the courtship of the kittiwake, that the inside of the mouth is of " a fine rich red, or orange red color," and that " both sexes open their bills widely and crane about, with their heads turned toward each other, whilst at the same time uttering their shrieking, clamorous cry. The motion, however, is often continued after the cry has ceased, and this we might expect if the birds took any pleasure in the brilliant gleam of color which each presents to and, as it were, flashes about in front of the other."

Mr. W. Elmer Ekblaw, in his Greenland notes, says:

About June 10 the kittiwake begins mating. The rivalry for mates and nests is keen, and the struggles over the nests are bitter and prolonged. I watched two birds fight for a nest for over an hour. When one alighted upon the nest he turned at once with open bill and angry scream to meet the rival which he expected to attack him at once. Usually the other claimant for the nest was quick in his attempt to eject the first. With bills locked like the jaws of fighting bull terriers, they wrestled with each other, shaking and tugging and pulling fiercely until they fell off the ledge and fluttered to the ice still in death grip. Once on the ice they soon ceased their combat, and separated, both angrily screaming. The contest was many times repeated.

Nesting.—The kittiwake is decidedly an oceanic gull, being seldom seen inland, except as a wanderer on migrations, and breeding on the rocky cliffs and crags of our Arctic coasts exposed to all the fury of ocean storms in which it seems to delight. On the Greenland coast most of the large breeding colonies are on the high cliffs near the heads of deep fjords, but farther south the preference seems to be for lofty rocky islands.

My first intimate study of the nesting habits of the Atlantic kittiwake was made on the famous Bird Rocks, in the Gulf of St. Lawrence, in 1904, one of the southernmost outposts of its breeding range. We landed here in a small boat, late in the evening of June 23, under rather exciting circumstances. As the great cliffs towered above us in the moonlight we saw a lantern coming down the ladder to show us where to land and we ran in among the breakers. There was a crash which brought us to our feet as we struck an unseen rock; but the next wave carried us over it and landed us among the rocks and flying spray. We were overboard in an instant, struggling in the surf up to our waists, for the boat was rapidly filling, as wave after wave broke over us. A few moments of rapid work served to unload our baggage and attach a stout line to the boat, the signal was passed aloft and the powerful steam winch above landed her high and dry. After exchanging hearty greetings with our genial host, Captain Bourque, we enjoyed the novel experience of being hoisted up in a crate to the top of the cliff, over 100 feet high. It was certainly a new and interesting sensation to feel ourselves slowly rising in the darkness up the face of these somber cliffs, with the surf thundering on the rocks below us and with a cloud of screaming seabirds hovering about us, barely discernible in the moonlight, like a swarm of ghostly bats whose slumber had been disturbed and who were protesting at our rude intrusion.

On the following day the wind was blowing a gale and clouds of sea birds were drifting about the rock in a bewildering maze, 10,000 of them in all. There were great white gannets sailing on long powerful wings, tipped with black; clouds of snowy kittiwakes hovering in the air; hundreds of swift-winged murres and razor-billed auks darting out from the cliffs; and quaint little parties of curious puffins perched on the rocks. There was a constant babel of voices, the mingled cries of the varied throngs; deep, guttural croaks and hoarse grunts from the gannets; a variety of soft purring notes from the murres; and sharp, piercing cries from the active kittiwakes distinctly pronouncing the three syllables for which they are named, as if beseeching us to "keep away" from their precious nests.

For a more intimate study of their nesting habits we were lowered down the face of the cliff in a crate, dangling at the end of a long rope and whirling helplessly about in space, but within a few feet of the confiding, gentle birds on their nests. They were so accustomed to the intimacy of man that it was an easy matter to study and photograph the dainty creatures at short range. Their nests were scattered all over the perpendicular face of the cliff, on every available little shelf. I was surprised to see how small and narrow a ledge could support a nest in safety. The nests were firmly and well built of seaweeds, grasses, and mosses, and were securely plastered on to the rock; apparently they were made of wet seaweed which adhered firmly to the rock as it dried; evidently the nests had been used for successive seasons, fresh material being added each year. They were deeply cupped and well built up on the outer sides, so as to form safe cradles for the young. Incubation was far advanced at this date (June 24), and many of the eggs had hatched. The nests must, indeed, be well built to hold the weight of two lusty young and the brooding parent in such precarious situations. Mr. Ora W. Knight (1908) gives the dimensions of a nest found on Baccalieu Island, Newfoundland. "Its diameter at base was 1 foot, and at top 8 inches; interior diameter, 6 inches; and depth, 2 inches."

Eggs.—The kittiwake is said to lay as many as four or five eggs, but I believe that two is the usual number; that three eggs are rarely laid; and that larger numbers are very unusual. I am quite sure that more than 90 per cent of the nests that I have seen have held only two eggs. Often only a single egg is hatched. The eggs vary in shape from somewhat pointed ovate to short ovate, rarely elongate ovate; the shell is thin and smooth, but without much lustre. The ground color varies from "pinkish buff" or "olive buff" to "cartridge buff," "pale olive buff," or bluish white. The spots are irregular in arrangement, size, and shape; most eggs have underlying spots or blotches of "light Quaker drab" or "light mouse gray"; these are either overlaid or mixed with darker spots, blotches, or scrawls of "clay color," "snuff brown," "tawny olive," "Vandyke brown," or "sepia" of various shades. The measurements of 41 eggs in various collections average 56.1 by 40.8 millimeters; the eggs showing the four extremes measure **62.5** by 42.5, 58 by **43.5, 53** by 39 and 55 by **37.5** millimeters.

Young.—The period of incubation is said to be 26 days. Probably both sexes incubate, as both parents are usually together at the nest and both are devoted to the young. The young remain in the nest, where they are fed by their parents, until they are fully fledged. The narrow confines of the usual nest, on its small shelf of rock, permit no wandering habits, as common among other gulls. Any attempt to stray from the nest would usually result in a disastrous fall from a dizzy height to dangerous rocks or surf below; so the young birds must of necessity stay in the nest until able to fly. Many such fatal accidents probably occur, which serve to keep in check the increase of the species, which is otherwise secure from molestation on its nesting grounds.

On North Bird Rock, where many of the nests are on the lower ledges, I noticed on July 24, 1915, that many of the nearly fledged young had been able to crawl or jump out of the nests and were wandering about over the flat rocks below the cliffs, though they were not able to fly. Many of the older young were already on the wing at this date and a few were still in the nests.

Plumages.—The newly hatched young is covered with long, soft, glossy down, which is white and spotless, but tinged basally with yellowish gray and buffy on the back and thighs, and tipped with dusky, giving it a grizzly appearance, quite unlike other young gulls. The young bird grows rapidly and soon begins to assume the first winter plumage, which appears first on the scapulars, then on the wings, back, and neck. There is no strictly juvenal plumage in this species. In the first winter plumage the bill is black; there is a blackish patch on the hind neck; the lesser wing-coverts and sometimes the greater wing-coverts and scapulars are largely black; the tail has a broad black band at the tip; the dusky spots on the head, before and behind the eye, are darker than in adults. A partial molt occurs early in the spring, usually in February and March, but sometimes as early as December, in which most of the dusky feathers in the head are replaced by white or lighter colored feathers and the black lesser wing-coverts disappear. At the first postnuptial molt in August young birds become indistinguishable from adults when one year old, a complete molt producing the adult winter plumage. A partial prenuptial molt, involving the head, neck, and body feathers, produces the adult nuptial plumage with the pure white head and yellow bill. Adults have a complete molt in the summer, producing the well-known winter plumage.

Food.—A flock of feeding kittiwakes is an animated and a pretty sight. During the latter part of the summer they assemble in enormous numbers in the numerous bays and " tickles " of the Labrador coast, and congregate about the fishing vessels to pick up the scraps that are thrown overboard. A school of small fry, swimming near the surface, soon attracts an interested throng of these little gulls which hover over them and scream excitedly as they gently swoop down with elevated wings to pick the small fish from the surface without wetting a feather. Although small fishes procured in this way constitute the principal food of the kittiwake, it also eats crustaceans, aquatic larvæ, and other marine animals which it gleans from the water. It feeds to some extent along the beaches and on the bare sand flats at low tide, where it finds various small mollusks, crustaceans, and other marine invertebrates. Often large flocks are seen feeding in the flats. It is less of a scavenger than the larger gulls and less given to frequenting the inner harbors. It is said to drink salt water exclusively, being seldom seen inland. Mr. Brewster (1883) reports a captive kittiwake that refused fresh water and drank salt water eagerly.

Behavior.—The flight of the kittiwake is buoyant, graceful, and easy. Audubon (1840) describes its movements, in his usual graphic style, as follows:

Bearing up against the heaviest gale, it passes from one trough of the sea to another as if anxious to rest for an instant under the lee of the billows; yet as these are seen to rear their curling crests, the gull is already several feet above them and preparing to plunge into the next hollow. While in our harbor, and during fine weather, they seemed to play with their companions of other species. Now with a spiral curve they descend toward the water, support themselves by beats of their wings, decline their heads, and pick up a young herring or some bit of garbage, when away they fly, chased perhaps by several others anxious to rob them of the prize. Noon has arrived. High above the masthead of our largest man-of-war the kittiwakes float gracefully in wide circles until all, as if fatigued, sail downward again with common accord toward the transparent deep, and, alighting close to each other, seem to ride safely at anchor. There they now occupy themselves in cleaning and arranging their beautiful plumage.

It flies more swiftly than the larger gulls and with more rapid wing beats. It can be readily recognized by the flight, even at a long distance, by one who is familiar with it. Dr. Charles W. Townsend writes to me:

Although the flight of the kittiwake is characteristically graceful, rapid, and swallow like, with quick wing strokes, I have seen them get up from the surface of the water just in time to clear the bow of the advancing steamer and fly off with slow and heavy wing beats, as if loath to leave a good fishing ground. In the adult the black wing tips are short and cut squarely across, as if the wings were dipped in black. In the immature plumage it most closely resembles the young Bonaparte's gull, but the black nuchal crescent and the black wing coverts are conspicuous, and there is more black on the primaries, in which the color pattern is also different.

The ordinary cry of the kittiwake suggests its name, which it seems to pronounce quite distinctly. This is the soft and mellow note most often heard about its breeding grounds, but when much excited or alarmed, it indulges in loud, shrill, piercing screams, as it darts down upon the intruder. When hovering in large flocks over a school of fish or other tempting feast it becomes very noisy, uttering loud, harsh cries, somewhat resembling the notes of the gull-billed tern. Doctor Townsend adds the following notes:

Besides the cry, which recalls its name *Kit-ti-wake*, I have noted down the syllables *Ka-ake;* sharp and piercing *Ki, Ki, Ki;* rapidly repeated and harsh rattling *Kaa, Kaa, Kae, Kae,* and *Kaak Kaak.*

The gentle kittiwake is a highly gregarious and sociable species. Among the various sea birds, with which it is intimately associated on its breeding grounds, it is a harmless and a friendly neighbor. It does not seem to molest the eggs or young of the other species at all and it has no enemies among them. At other seasons it is often persecuted by the jaegers, the relentless pursuers of all the smaller gulls and terns, the highway robbers of the northern seas. The worst enemy of the kittiwake is man. In winter, when these gulls are abundant on the New England coast, they are shot in large numbers. They are tame and unsuspicious, gathering, like terns, in large flocks over a fallen companion, making it easy for the gunner to kill as many as he chooses. They may easily be attracted about the fisherman's boat by throwing overboard cod livers or other refuse, where they are easily shot and may often be caught on a baited hook. Their bodies are used for food or for bait and their plumage is, or was, sold for millinery purposes; but often they are killed in purely wanton sport. Macgillivray (1852) says of the way these birds have been killed on the British coast:

Parties are formed on our eastern coast for the sole purpose of shooting them; and I have seen a person station himself on the top of the kittiwake cliff of the Isle of May, and shoot incessantly for several hours, without so much as afterwards picking up a single individual of the many killed and maimed birds with which the smooth water was strewn beneath.

Fall.—The fall migration starts early; that is, the birds move away from their breeding grounds early and begin to work down the coast in August and September. Dr. Charles W. Townsend (1907) saw about 5,000 kittiwakes at the mouth of Hamilton Inlet, Labrador, on July 18, 1906. He describes their behavior as follows:

At Hamilton Inlet thousands of kittiwakes covered the water, and as we steamed on they rose in bodies of 500 or more and whirled about like gusts of snow driven by the wind, their pure white plumage lit up by the rays of the setting sun. Silent for the most part, they occasionally emitted cries of *kae kae,* or *ka-ake,* and at times one could imagine the syllables of *kittiwake.* On our return trip we ran into a flock of nearly the same size near Cape Harrison. The appearance of a snowstorm here was more perfect, for there was a thick fog bank, on the edge of which the kittiwakes played. The sun shining on the birds before the fog shut them out was very striking. They were occasionally plunging for capelins, at times disappearing entirely under water with a splash. One could often be seen flying with a fish hanging by one end from its bill. A jaeger suddenly appeared on the scene, and the twisting and turning of pursuer and pursued was interesting to see. The kittiwake finally dropped his prey, and the jaeger settled on the water to pick it up.

On my way south along the Labrador coast on August 21, 1912, I saw large numbers of old and young kittiwakes near Makkovik and Ragged Islands, far south of their breeding grounds. Mr. Lucien M. Turner says of their habits on the Labrador coast:

Scores and hundreds of the kittiwake gull were observed on the Labrador coast in the early part of July, 1882. They were most numerous in the Arctic current bearing icebergs, on which these birds at times assembled in thousands as the mass of ice towered at times over 200 feet high and presented an area of over half a mile square on the top of it. Here the birds sat compactly, slowly moving to the southward; they probably congregated during these times after having gorged themselves with capelins and lance fishes to allow the process of digestion to be completed. A single rifle shot reverberating against the wall of ice or a ball projected in the midst of these birds was sufficient to startle the entire community into flight, and upon which they would lazily circle round and round the vessel or sway back and forth across her wake, always at a provoking distance, until one would be dropped while on wing with a rifle ball. The living birds wheeled over their dead companion in angry curiosity as they clamored their rattling cry.

Winter.—The kittiwake does not become common on the Massachusetts coast until about the middle of October, after which it is common off our coasts all winter, where it is known as the " winter gull," " frost gull," or " pinny owl." Dr. Charles W. Townsend (1905) says of its winter habits:

The kittiwake is an offshore gull, one that is to be found especially about fishing vessels in winter, gleaning the waves for the refuse which is always to be found in the neighborhood of these boats. In my notes of a trip to Nova Scotia from Boston, in December, 1883, I have entered that they were very abundant everywhere off the coast. Off Rockport in winter, kittiwakes begin to be common 2 or 3 miles from land, and are generally abundant on the fishing grounds, 8 or 10 miles out. They may, however, be frequently seen from the shore, especially if the day be stormy and the shore an open one. They often visit the little harbor of Rockport with its wealth of fish gurry. They also fly occasionally over the beaches, and under these circumstances I have had no difficulty in shooting them for specimens, as, unlike the herring gull, they do not hesitate to fly within gunshot. I have never seen them in the tidal estuaries.

Mr. Walter H. Rich has sent me the following notes on the behavior of the kittiwake or " winter bird," as it is called, on Georges Banks:

As might be guessed from the name, it is during the coldest weather that this bird is most abundant, and at this season, so the writer was informed, not infrequently they became so tame as to perch in rows upon the main booms of the vessels on frosty mornings, awaiting their breakfasts.

The first arrivals (five birds) appeared on the morning of October 12, 1913. Every day following their arrival showed increasing numbers until in a fortnight there were always "hundreds," and at times "thousands" would make but a moderate estimate of their flocks. My records for November 16 says, "winter birds in millions"—perhaps an exaggeration, yet so it seemed. Scarcely a daylight hour after their arrival but was filled with their chattering squeal; scarcely a moment but saw them wheeling about the steamers, appearing just before sun up and standing by to give any needed assistance as long as the sun held above the western rim of the ocean.

The signal for hauling the net brought great activity among the flocks banked up on either side of the steamer's path in 2½-mile-long lines of white birds roosting upon the water. There were literally thousands of gulls that rose and drifted along over the swells, just keeping pace with the steamer's slow progress. Other gulls there were, both brown plumaged and full plumaged—ring-bill, herring gull, black-backed, and a few of the large white or pearly gulls, of species undetermined where they wheeled in a safe offing. But all these were at a disadvantage, both numerically and otherwise, with the kittiwakes, who stole from them and beat them to every piece of liver and waste thrown overside. If the prize sinks the big gull has lost it; not so the little "winter bird," who dives swiftly and gracefully from the wing and brings it up. This is the only gull which the writer has ever seen to dive. Naturally their success makes them unpopular with the losers, who pursue and harry the kittiwake, but to little effect, since the small gull is too active to suffer much in these attempts at reprisal.

In fair weather during midday the gulls of all species soar far aloft to wheel in wide circles and drift in the sunshine of the upper air. The "winter bird" indulges in this also, but to a somewhat lesser extent than do the gulls of other species. The greater part of the kittiwake flocks prefer to bank up along the steamer's course, so as to be at hand at the haul, utilizing the interval to preen their feathers and bathe and dip like sparows in a puddle. In fact, it was a considerable time before I could be sure that the kittiwake joined in these lofty aerial maneuvers; yet they surely did, sweeping on motionless wings in great spirals at a height where the eye could hardly follow them or distinguish them, but never failing to drop with all swiftness when warned by the whistle that the feast was about to be spread for them. What an enormous amount of food must be needed to support all this great sea-bird population—the hags and petrels in the summer months, the gulls in the colder weather, the full round of the year.

DISTRIBUTION.

Breeding range.—Northern parts of the Northern Hemisphere; in North America east to Greenland and the Labrador coast. South to the Gulf of St. Lawrence (Newfoundland, Bird Rock, Bonaventure Island, and Anticosti) and probably parts of Hudson Bay. The western limit of its range, where the subspecies *pollicaris* takes its place, is unknown, but it has been stated to occur west to Franklin Bay. North to Prince Albert Land (near Princess Royal Islands); the south shore of North Somerset; north of Wellington Channel (latitude 77°), and northern Greenland (Thank God Harbor on the northwestern coast, and between latitude 80° and 81° on the northeastern coast). In the Old World breeds from Iceland, Great Britain (Shetland and Orkney Islands, Hebrides, coast of Ireland and England, except southern parts) ; Spitzbergen, probably Franz Josef Land, Nova Zembla and coast of western Siberia (said by Koren to range east to Chaun Bay, northern Siberia. South to northwestern France.

Breeding grounds protected in the Canadian reservations on Bird Rock, Bonaventure Island, and Percé Rock.

Winter range.—Offshore from Gulf of St. Lawrence (Prince Edward Island), Nova Scotia (Halifax), New Brunswick (Grand Manan), and coast of Maine; occasionally on the Great Lakes; south to New Jersey and the Bermudas, and even farther south (latitude 25° 57′ N., east of Miami). In Europe winters from the coasts of Great Britain south to the Mediterranean and Caspian Seas, the Canary Islands, and Azores.

Spring migration.—Return from ocean wandering to its breeding grounds. Early dates of arrival: Prince Edward Island, March 15 (average March 26) ; Quebec, Godbout, March 25 (average April 6) ; Greenland, Ivigtuk, March 26; Dover Strait, May 20; and Cape York, June 10. Late dates of departure: Bermuda, April 4; New York, Orleans County, April 10; Connecticut, New Haven, April 13.

Fall migration.—Offshore and southward. Early dates of arrival: Massachusetts, October 2 (average November 6) ; Long Island, October 13; Pennsylvania, Erie, October 17. Late dates of departure: Northeastern Greenland, latitude 75° 20′, August 1; Ellesmere Land, Lincoln Bay, September 1; Wellington Channel, September 2; Frobischer Bay, September 2; Cumberland Gulf. September 19; Newfoundland, October 17.

Casual records.—Wanders occasionally to various points in the interior; to the Great Lakes frequently, as far west as Michigan (Neebish Island, fall 1893–94) and Wisconsin (Racine, March 17, 1884) ; up the Mackenzie Valley (Fort Resolution, May 23, 1860) : west in the interior to Wyoming (Douglas, November 18, 1898).

Egg dates.—Great Britain: Thirty-one records, April 6 to June 27; sixteen records, June 4 to 12. Newfoundland: Ten records, May 30 to July 1; five records, June 14 to 20. Gulf of St. Lawrence: Ten records, June 10 to 26; five records, June 13 to 25.

RISSA TRIDACTYLA POLLICARIS Ridgway.

PACIFIC KITTIWAKE.

HABITS.

The Pacific form of the well-known kittiwake differs from its eastern relative in having a larger hind toe and more extensive black tips on the primaries, but its habits are practically the same and its life history is similar. The two subspecies together occupy a wide range throughout the northern part of the northern hemisphere, giving the species a circumpolar distribution.

Spring.—The spring migration is early, reaching Bering Island, in the Commander group, according to Stejneger (1885), about the 1st of April. In Bering Sea the migration is delayed until the breaking up of the ice. Nelson (1887) says:

At St. Michaels each year they arrive from the 10th to the 18th of May, and were first seen searching for food in the narrow water channels in the tide cracks along shore. As the open spaces appeared they congregated there until in early June, when the ice broke up and moved offshore. At this time the kittiwakes sought the rugged cliffs along the shore of the mainland or the precipitous islands dotting Bering Sea and the adjoining Arctic.

Courtship.—Very little seems to be known about the courtship or mating performances of this bird, but Mr. H. W. Elliott (1875) says that "the male treads the female on the nest, and nowhere else, making a loud shrill, screaming sound during the ceremony."

Nesting.—We saw plenty of kittiwakes near the eastern end of the Aleutian Islands, where they were probably breeding in the vicinity of Akutan Island. West of Unalaska we saw very few birds and no signs of breeding colonies. Doctor Stejneger (1885) found them breeding in "astonishing numbers" at certain places in the Commander Islands, at the western end of the chain, where they choose "steep walls, rising perpendicularly out of the deep sea, and especially high pinnacles standing lonely amidst the foaming breakers, provided they are fitted out with shelves and projections upon which to place the nests." Dr. W. H. Dall (1873) gives us the following good account of a breeding colony in the Shumagin Islands, south of the Alaska Peninsula:

On entering Coal Harbor, Unga, we were at once struck with the peculiar white line which wound around the precipitous cliffs of Round Island, and was seen to be caused by the presence of birds; and as soon as an opportunity was afforded I took a boat and went to the locality to examine it. The nests, in their position, were unlike anything I had ever seen before. At first it appeared as if they were fastened to the perpendicular face of the rock, but on a close examination it appeared that two parallel strata of the metamorphic sandstone of the cliffs, being harder than the rest, had weathered out, standing out from the face of the cliff from 1 to 4 inches, more or less irregularly. The nests were built where these broken ledges afforded a partial support, though extending over more than half their width. The lines of nests exactly followed the winding projections of these ledges, everywhere giving a very singular appearance to the cliff, especially when the white birds were sitting on them. The nests were built with dry grass, agglutinated together and to the rock in some unexplained manner; perhaps by a mucus secreted by the bird for the purpose. The nests had a very shallow depression at the top in which lay two eggs. The whole establishment had an intolerable odor of guano, and the nests were very filthy. The birds hardly moved at our approach; only those within a few yards leaving their posts. I reached up and took down two nests, one containing two young birds, and the other empty. Wind coming up, we were obliged to pull away, and the bird, which came back, lighted on the rock where her nest and young had been with evident astonishment at the mysterious disappearance. After flying about a little she again settled on the spot, and, suddenly making up her mind that foul play on the part of some other bird had taken place, she commenced a furious assault on her nearest neighbor. As we pulled away the little fellows began to be effected by the motion of the boat, and with the most ludicrous expression of nausea, imitating as closely as a bird could do the motions and expression of a seasick person, they very soon deposited their dinner on the edge of the nest. It was composed of small fishes or minnows, too much disorganized to be identified. Eggs, in a moderately fresh condition, were obtained about the same time, but most of them were far advanced toward hatching.

In Bering Sea we found this to be one of the commonest gulls and found it breeding on all of the islands where it could find high, rocky cliffs. On Walrus Island, where there are no high cliffs, we had an unusually good opportunity to examine the nests. Among the hosts of sea birds which made their summer home on this wonderful island a few little parties, of from four to six pairs each, of Pacific kittiwakes found a scanty foothold on the vertical faces of the low, rocky cliffs. Here their nests were skillfully placed on the narrow ledges or on little protuberances which seemed hardly wide enough to hold them, and often they were within a few feet of nesting California murres or red-faced cormorants, with which the island was overcrowded. The nests were well made of soft green grass and bits of sod securely plastered onto the rocks and probably were repaired and used again year after year. They were well rounded, deeply cupped on top, and lined with fine dry grass. Most of the nests, on July 7, contained two eggs, some only one, but none of them held young. The incubating birds and their mates standing near their nests were very gentle and tame. We had no difficulty in getting near enough to photograph them.

Eggs.—The eggs of the Pacific kittiwakes are practically indistinguishable from those of the Atlantic kittiwake, though they will average a trifle larger and a trifle more pointed. The ground color seems to run more to the lighter shades, from " tilleul buff " or " olive buff " to " cartridge buff " or " pale olive buff." Many sets show very pale shades of " glaucous green " or even greenish or bluish white. The markings are about the same as in the Atlantic bird, but average lighter with a larger proportion of the drab or gray spots. The measurements of 40 eggs in the United States National Museum and the writer's collections average 58.4 by 41.3 millimeters, the eggs showing the four extreme measure **63 by 43.5, 55.5** by 41.5 and 58.5 by **37.5** millimeters.

Young.—The young remain in the nests and are fed by their parents until they are able to fly. Both old and young birds spend much of their time on their breeding grounds and frequent their old nests until ready to migrate in September. The description of the downy young and the sequences of molts and plumages, already given for the Atlantic kittiwake, will do equally well for the Pacific subspecies. I can find no essential points of difference.

Food.—Nelson (1887) says of their feeding habits:

From the end of August they frequent the inner bays and mouths of small streams, and are often seen in large parties feeding upon the myriads of stickle backs which are found along the coast at this season. They pursue their prey in the same graceful manner as the terns, by hovering over the water and plunging down head foremost. In the bay at St. Michaels they were frequently seen following a school of white whales, evidently to secure such fragments of fish or other food as the whales dropped in the water. It was curious to note how well the birds timed the whale and anticipated their appearance as the latter came up to blow.

Along the beach at Nome we saw kittiwakes almost constantly where they seemed to be picking up bits of garbage. Mr. A. W. Anthony (1906) saw them in winter at Puget Sound, associated with other gulls about the garbage heaps.

Behavior.—Dr. E. W. Nelson (1883) pays the following tribute to the flight powers of this kittiwake:

During our cruising in the summer of 1881 I had repeated occasions to notice the graceful motions and powers of flight possessed by this handsome gull. Its buoyancy during the worst gales we met was fully equal to that possessed by the Rodger's fulmar, with which it frequently associated at these times. These birds were continually gliding back and forth in graceful curves, now passing directly into the face of the gale, then darting off to one side on a long circuit, always moving steadily, with only an occasional stroke of the wings for long periods if there was a strong wind.

Mr. William Palmer (1890) also shows his admiration of it in the following words:

Viewed from the cliffs the flight of these birds is remarkably graceful, and especially so when they have been disturbed from a midday siesta. I thus disturbed several dozen one day and carefully watched them as they passed and repassed the spot where I sat on the edge of the cliff. They were all within 20 yards and continually paraded parallel with the cliff, all the while intently watching me. They would pass by for some 30 to 40 yards, then turn and fly an equal distance on the other side before again making a turn. Usually the whole distance was accomplished by sailing, and often the turns and several lengths were traveled in the same way. Thus, selecting an individual and keeping my eyes on him I often counted from two to three trips without a flap of the wing. One individual thus noted made the trip seven times without once changing his wings from their rigid outstretched position. The length of his parade was fully 50 yards and he sailed in an almost straight line, and rarely varied his level, being about as high above the sea as I was on the cliff. Not a movement of the air was perceptible to my senses. He was often so close that as he passed I could distinctly see the movement of his eye as he slightly turned his head to view me. Several times the fly lines of two birds would cross at about the same level, but rarely would one flap to gain impetus enough to get rapidly out of the way. It was more often accomplished by a quiver of the wings on the part of one of the two, a slight rise as the other passed beneath, and then a similar descent, and the continuation of the journey without any distinct flapping whatever. They thus sailed in plain view as long as I remained on the rocks, probably 30 minutes.

Winter.—These hardy birds of Arctic seas seem quite at home among the drifting ice and snowstorms, and it is not until their summer feeding grounds become permanently closed with winter ice, in October, that they are forced southward to spend the winter months in the Aleutian Islands, along the Alaska coast, and south to Puget Sound, or even California. Here they associate freely with the other common gulls on the coast or spend their time offshore. They are so much more pelagic in their habits than other gulls that they seem much less abundant than they really are.

DISTRIBUTION.

Breeding range.—Coasts and islands of the North Pacific, Bering Sea, and the adjacent Arctic Ocean. East to Cape Lisburne and other suitable parts of the western Alaskan coast. South to Seldovia, Alaska, the Shumagin, Aleutian, Commander, and Kurile Islands. West along the coast of Kamchatka and northeastern Siberia to the Koliutschin Islands. Occurs in summer, but has not been found breeding on the coast of southern Alaska (Yakutat and Sitka) at Point Barrow and on the Siberian coast from Koliutschin Islands to Chaun Bay.

Breeding grounds protected in the following national reservations in Alaska: Aleutian Islands (as Kiska, Near Islands, Unga, Unimak Pass), Pribilofs, St. George Island.

Winter range.—From southeastern Alaska (Sitka) and perhaps from the Aleutians, south along the coast of British Columbia, Washington, Oregon, and California to northern Lower California (San Geronimo Island). On the Asiatic side south to the Kurile Islands and Japan (Yezo and Tokyo).

Spring migration.—A return from ocean wandering to its breeding grounds. Early dates of arrival: Commander Islands, Bering Island, April 1; Pribilof Islands, St. Paul, April 20; Alaska, St. Michael, May 6, and Point Barrow, June 2. Late dates of departure: Lower California, San Geronimo Island, March 17; California, Point Pinos, April 25; Washington, Port Townsend, May 19; British Columbia, May 24.

Fall migration.—Mainly eastward and southward off the coasts, beginning in July and reaching British Columbia in September. Average date of arrival at Point Pinos is November 14, earliest November 5. Late dates of departure: Alaska, Point Barrow, August 31, and St. Michael about October 15; Pribilof Islands, St. Paul, October 12; Siberia, Koliutschin Island, September 22.

Egg dates.—Pribilof Islands: Thirteen records, June 10 to July 7; seven records, June 25 to July 3. Northern Bering Sea: Nine records, June 10 to July 20; five records, June 20 to July 6.

RISSA BREVIROSTRIS (Bruch).

RED-LEGGED KITTIWAKE.

HABITS.

This is one of the species which I expected to find breeding abundantly among the Aleutian Islands, but I was disappointed to find that it was far from common about any of the islands that were visited. As we passed Akutan Island on the way to Unalaska I saw a large number of kittiwakes hovering about the rocky cliffs at a distance. I supposed that they were of this species, which is recorded as breeding on this island, but I was unable to stop and did not go near enough to identify them. I saw several about the Pribilof Islands, but only one specimen was taken. I did not find it on Walrus Island, where it is said to breed.

Nesting.—Mr. Henry W. Elliott (1880), to whom we are indebted for practically all that we know about the habits of the red-legged kittiwake, says that it arrives on the fur-seal islands, for the purpose of breeding, about the 9th of May and of its nesting habits he writes:

It is much more prudent and cautious than the auks and the murres, for its nests are always placed on nearly inaccessible shelves and points of mural walls, so that seldom can one be reached unless a person is lowered down to it by a rope passed over the cliff. Nest building is commenced early in May, and completed, generally, not much before the 1st of July. It uses dry grass and moss cemented with mud, which it gathers at the fresh-water pools and ponds scattered over the islands. The nest is solidly and neatly put up; the parents work together in its construction most diligently and amiably. Two eggs are the usual number, although occasionally three will be found in the nest. If these eggs are removed, the female will renew them like the " arrie " in the course of another week or 10 days.

Dr. L. Stejneger (1885) found the red-legged kittiwake breeding abundantly in the Commander Islands, and says:

Like its black-legged cousin, it only selects steep and inaccessible rocks, and in none of its habits at the breeding place could I detect any marked difference. They also arrive at the islands about the same time, hatching their young simultaneously with the other species. The two species usually keep apart from each other. In the great rookery at Kikij Mys only one solitary red-legged bird was seen among the thousands and thousands of black feet, while a still greater colony at Gavaruschkaja Buchta consisted of red legs exclusively. On Copper Island, however, I found the two species breeding together on the same rocky wall—the black feet always higher up than the present species. The two kinds were easily distinguished when sitting on the nests, *brevirostris* having the gray of the mantle of a perceptibly darker shade than *pollicaris*.

Eggs.—The set usually consists of two eggs, rarely three, and often only one. The eggs are usually about ovate in shape, and in a general way resemble those of the common kittiwake, though they average lighter in color and are somewhat less heavily spotted. The ground color is bluish white, buffy white, creamy white, or even pure white. The markings consist of spots, blotches, or scrawls scattered irregularly over the egg or occasionally concentrated in a mass at the larger end or in a ring around it.

These markings are in various shades of drab, lavender, or lilac, overlaid with various shades of brown, mostly the lighter shades, but sometimes as dark as "bister" or "sepia." The measurements of 43 eggs, in various collections, average 55.8 by 40.9 millimeters; the eggs showing the four extremes measure **66.5** by **45** and **50** by **37** millimeters.

Young.—Mr. Elliott (1880) says:

Both parents assist in the labor of incubation, which lasts a trifle longer than the usual time—from 24 to 26 days. The chick comes out with a pure white downy coat, a pale whitish-gray bill and feet, and rests helplessly in the nest until its feathers grow. During this period it is a comical-looking object. The natives capture them now and then to make pets of, always having a number every year scattered through the village, usually tied by one leg to a stake at the doors of their houses, where they become very tame; and it is not until fall, when cold weather sets in, that they become restless and willingly leave their captivity for the freedom of the air.

Plumages.—The downy young are not distinguishable from those of the Pacific kittiwake, being covered with white down without spots. So far as I have been able to learn from the available material the molts and plumages are similar to those of the common species. There is no juvenal plumage, the young bird going directly from the downy stage into the first winter plumage; in this plumage the young bird has a well-marked, dark, cervical collar, considerable dusky about the eyes, and a mantle variegated with grayish-white tips; but it has no black on the wing coverts, secondaries, or tail, as in the common kittiwake. These dark markings are usually wholly or partially lost during the first spring, but they are sometimes retained through the summer by failure to molt in the spring or by a partial renewal of feathers in sympathy with the first winter plumage. At the first postnuptial molt (in August) the adult winter plumage is assumed.

Adults have a complete postnuptial molt in August and apparently a partial prenuptial molt early in the spring. Winter adults have the cervix and the auriculars washed with plumbeous. In the adult nuptial plumage this is one of the most beautiful birds in Bering Sea, where we learned to recognize it by the short, yellow bill, bright red feet, dark mantle, and wings.

Behavior.—I can not find any data on the food of the red-legged kittiwake, but probably it does not vary materially from that of closely related species. Mr. William Palmer (1899) writes, concerning his impression of this species on the Pribilof Islands:

To my mind this is the most beautiful species on the islands. Always graceful, whether on the cliffs or flying, its beautiful form and delicate snow-white plumage, with its vermilion feet, adds much to the avifaunal wonders of these islands. Unlike its cousin, which carries its feet extended when flying, this species nearly always buries them in the feathers of its under body, as if fearful of showing their beauty except when absolutely necessary. When fog envelops these islands, both the land and sea, the sea birds away from home find their way by flying along the edges of the bluffs, where the stored heat in the rocks dissipates the rapidly drifting fog. The wily aleut, knowing these characteristics, ensconces himself behind a rock in a suitable location and with a large dip net intercepts the birds on their way along the bluffs. Thus many a meal is obtained, and, unfortunately, our pretty red-legged kittiwake too often falls a victim.

Winter.—When the young birds are fully fledged and able to fly, both old and young birds desert their breeding places on the rocky cliffs, but do not migrate far away. They are resident throughout the year in the vicinity of the Pribilof and Aleutian Islands, and probably spend most of their time at sea during the winter months.

DISTRIBUTION.

Breeding range.—Islands of Bering Sea (the Pribilof, Near, and Commander Islands) are the only places where this species has been found breeding. It is supposed also to nest at various places in the Aleutians from Akutan Island westward.

Breeding grounds protected in the following national reservations in Alaska: Aleutian Islands, as Near Islands, Round Island, Unimak Pass, and Pribilof Islands.

Winter range.—Unknown. Probably the open sea not far from its breeding grounds. It has been stated not to winter on the Near and Commander Islands. Elliott says it occurs about the Pribilofs at all seasons.

Spring migration.—Apparently comes to the breeding grounds about May 9.

Fall migration.—Birds leave the Pribilofs as soon as the young can fly, usually early in October, latest November 11. Has been seen near Unalaska Island, October 5.

Casual records.—Taken at Forty Mile, Yukon Territory, October 15, 1889; St. Michael, Alaska, September 18, 1876; Kamchatka (specimen, but no date); and Wrangel Island (specimen, but no date).

Egg dates.—Pribilof Islands: Three records, July 1, 3, and 10. Kamchatka: Two records, June 12 and 22.

LARUS HYPERBOREUS Gunnerus.

GLAUCOUS GULL.

HABITS.

The name burgomaster is a fitting name for this chief magistrate of the feathered tribes of the Arctic seas, where it reigns supreme over all the lesser water fowl, levying its toll of food from their eggs and defenseless young. Well they know its strength and dread its power, as it sails majestically aloft over the somber, rocky cliffs of the Greenland coast, where, with myriads of sea fowl, it makes its summer home; and useless is it for them to resist the onslaught of its heavy beak when it swoops down to rob them of their callow young. Only the great skua, the fighting airship of the north, dares to give it battle and to drive the tyrant burgomaster from its chosen crag. Its only rival in size and power among the gulls is the great black-backed gull, and where these two meet on the Labrador coast they treat each other with dignified respect.

Spring.—The glaucous gull is more oceanic in its habits than other large gulls. Though it resorts somewhat to inland lakes and rivers during migrations and in winter, it seems to prefer the cold, bleak, and rugged coasts of northern Labrador, Greenland, and the Arctic islands, whither it resorts in the spring as early as the rigors of the Arctic winter will allow. What few birds winter in southern Hudson Bay and the region of the Great Lakes, migrate across Ungava and through Hudson Straits to the Atlantic coast; but the main migration route is northward along the seacoast following the open leads in the ice with the first migration of the eiders. Kumlien (1879) says:

This gull is the first bird to arrive (at Cumberland Sound) in the spring. In 1878 they made their appearance in the Kingwah Fjord by the 20th of April. It was still about 70 miles to the floe edge and open water; still, they seemed to fare well on the young seals.

At Ivigtut, Greenland, according to Hagerup (1891), "some, chiefly young birds, remain over winter. An old bird, in complete summer dress, was shot on the 20th of March." In Alaska, also, this species is the earliest migrant to arrive. Turner (1886) observes that they arrive at St. Michael by the middle of April, " sailing high in the air, almost out of sight. Their note, being the first intimation of their presence, is always gladly welcomed as a sign that the ice, farther south, is breaking up." Nelson (1887) says:

They wander restlessly along the coast until the ponds open on the marshes near the sea, and then, about the last half of May, they are found straying singly or in pairs about the marshy ponds, where they seek their summer homes. Here they are among the noisiest of the wild fowl.

Grinnell (1900) noted their arrival in Kotzebue Sound May 11, 1899, when he " discovered 10 sitting close together out in the middle of the river ice." Winter was still unbroken at this date, and there was no open water in the vicinity " so far as he knew."

Nesting.—The southernmost breeding grounds of this species are in Newfoundland. Here in the summer of 1912 I saw them at several places, where they were probably nesting on the high and inaccessible rocky cliffs of the west coast. Other observers have also reported them from this region. Mr. J. R. Whitaker, of Grand Lake, told me that he had taken the eggs of this species on an island in Sandy Lake. While investigating a breeding colony of great black-backed gulls on an island in Sandy Lake, on June 23, 1912, I saw a pair of glaucous gulls flying overhead. The young of all the gulls had hatched at that date and were hidden among the rocks and underbrush, so I did not succeed in identifying any young of the glaucous gull, but I have no reason to doubt that the pair had nested there, perhaps on one of the small rocky islets by themselves. Mr. Edward Arnold (1912) reports that " several pairs had their nests built out on large bowlders in the center of ponds, but as the water was very cold and over our heads in depth we could not examine them."

On the Labrador coast in 1912 I found the glaucous gull common all along the coast from the Straits of Belle Isle northward. I saw a large breeding colony on the lofty cliffs of the Kigla-pait range between Nain and Okak. The nests were quite inaccessible on the narrow ledges of precipitous cliffs facing the sea. On August 2 we visited a breeding colony of 30 or 40 pairs of glaucous gulls on a rocky islet near Nain. It was a precipitous crag, rising abruptly from the sea to a height of 100 or 150 feet, unapproachable in rough weather, and an invulnerable castle except at one point, where we could land on a rock and climb up a steep grassy slope. Numerous black guillemots flew out from the lower crevices, and my companion, Mr. Donald B. MacMillan, succeeded in finding a few of their eggs still fairly fresh. Rev. Walter W. Perrett, of Nain, had taken a set of duck hawk's eggs from the cliffs earlier in the season. The upper part of the rock was occupied by the gulls, where their nests were mostly on inaccessible ledges. Near the top of the rock, which was flat and covered with grass, we found quite a number of nests that we could reach, but all of these were empty. Below us we could see nests containing young of various ages and one nest still held two eggs. Some of the young were nearly ready to fly and probably some had already flown. The nests were made of soft grasses and mosses, and were not very elaborate or very bulky for such large gulls; probably they had been somewhat trampled down by the young.

Kumlien (1879) found the glaucous gull breeding abundantly in the Cumberland Sound region. He describes one nesting site as " an enormous cliff about 1½ miles in length and over 2,000 feet in height, and nearly perpendicular. This cliff is about 4 miles from the sea-shore to the east-northeast of America Harbor. Many hundreds of nests are scattered about on the little projecting shelves of rock, and the birds sitting on them look like little bunches of snow still unmelted on the cliff. The ascent to this locality is very laborious; but the marvelous beauty of the place will well repay any future explorer to visit it, for the plants that grow in such rich profusion at the base of the cliff, if nothing more." He also says:

I have examined some nests that were built on the duck islands, always on the highest eminence. The structure seemed to have been used and added to for many years in succession, probably by the same pair. In shape they were pyramid-formed mounds, over 4 feet at the base and about 1 foot at the top, and nearly 2½ feet in height. They were composed of every conceivable object found in the vicinity, grass, seaweed, moss, lichens, feathers, bones, skin, egg shells, etc.

Regarding the breeding habits of this species in Greenland, Mr. J. D. Figgins writes me that on Saunders Island:

The nest is composed of moss and grass, often of considerable height because of the yearly repair, always near the top of the cliffs and never approachable from below. The nests are rarely placed other than near rookeries of murres and other gulls, where the glaucous gulls prey upon the eggs and young. When the gulls make forays upon the murre and kittiwake rookeries, the latter birds make no defense whatever and, besides uttering their usual querulous complaints, offer no resistance, seemingly knowing that it is quite useless. The glaucous gulls prefer small young, which their advanced young gulp whole. Young in various stages of growth, from newly hatched to those ready to leave the nests, were found abundantly on August 15. No eggs were seen at that time. Both adults were invariably nearby, screaming protest when the nest was approached and following the intruder for considerable distance when leaving.

On the Arctic coast of Mackenzie, Macfarlane (1908) found some 20 nests of this species on sandy islets in the bays and rivers:

The nest was usually a shallow depression in the beach, while in one of them we discovered an egg of the black brant which was being incubated by a bird of this species.

Nelson (1887) describes two nests found by him on the Yukon delta, as follows:

On June 4 their first nest was found. It was placed on a small islet, a few feet across, in the center of a broad shallow pond. The structure was formed of a mass of moss and grass piled up a foot or more high, with a base 3 feet across and with a deep central depression lined with dry grass. There was a single egg. The female, as she sat on the nest, was visible a mile away, and not the slightest opportunity was afforded for concealment on the broad surrounding flat.

On June 15, near St. Michaels, another nest was found, an equally conspicuous structure. Like the majority of their nests found by me, it also was located on a small islet in a pond. It was 2 feet high, with a base from 3 to 4 feet long by 2 wide and measured about 18 inches across the top. In the apex was a depression about 5 inches deep and 9 inches in diameter. This bulky structure was made up of tufts of moss and grass rooted up by the birds' beaks. The ground looked as though it had been rooted up by pigs in places near the nest and on the outer edge of the pond; and while I was examining the nest, which contained three eggs, one of the old birds came flying up from a considerable distance, carrying a large tuft of muddy grass in its beak and dropped it close by on seeing me. One of the eggs taken was white, without a trace of the usual color marks. While I was securing the eggs the parents swooped down close to my head, uttering harsh cries.

On July 7, 1911, I visited Walrus Island, in the Pribilof group in Bering Sea, where among all the hordes of water fowl that breed in this wonderful islet was a nesting colony of glaucous-winged and glaucous gulls. Their nests were scattered among the tufts of short, coarse grass, which covered the highest and central part of the island, where soil had been formed by the accumulation of guano. The nests were rather bulky and well made of seaweed and soft grasses; a few of them still contained eggs, but nearly all of the young had hatched and were hiding in the grass and among the rocks. We were not allowed to shoot any birds here and the gulls were too shy to enable us to identify any nests, but I am positive that both species were breeding here. The glaucous-winged gull seems to have been overlooked by some of the others who have visited this island, though it may not have been breeding there then.

Eggs.—As with most gulls, only one brood is raised in a season and the set usually consists of three eggs, though two eggs frequently complete the set. The eggs are similar to those of other large gulls, varying in shape from ovate to elongate ovate. The shell is rather coarsely granulated and without luster. The ground color shows the usual variations from " buffy brown " to " deep olive buff " or " pale olive buff." The eggs are usually not very thickly and more or less irregularly spotted with small spots or blotches of various shades of the darker browns, such as " bone brown," " bister," or " Saccardo's umber "; also sometimes with lighter browns and often with underlying spots of various shades of the lighter drabs and lavender grays. The measurements of 56 eggs in the United States National Museum average 75.8 by 52.4 millimeters; the eggs showing the four extremes measure **85.5** by 50.5, 78 by **57, 70** by 52.5 and 76.5 by **48** millimeters.

Young.—Both Turner (1886) and Elliott (1875) give the period of incubation as about three weeks, but probably four weeks would be more nearly correct; Evans (1891) gives it as 28 days. Probably both sexes incubate, for the pairs keep together at this time, and the male usually stands guard near the nest while the female is incubating. The young leave the nest after a few days and become quite lively; they are expert at hiding under whatever shelter they can find, often lying flat in some slight hollow with the eyes tightly closed. Kumlien (1879) says that he " had an opportunity of seeing how these young hopefuls are instructed in egg sucking. The parent carried a duck's egg to the nest and broke a hole in it, and the young one just helped himself at his leisure. After the young are full-fledged these birds are eminently gregarious, and are often seen feeding in considerable flocks." The young are voracious feeders and become very fat, when they are much esteemed by the natives for food.

Plumages.—The young chick is covered with long, soft, thick down, grayish white above and almost pure white below, tinged with buff on the throat and breast. The back is clouded or blotched with " smoke gray," and the head and throat are distinctly marked with numerous large and small spots of " fuscous black," the number and extent of the markings varying in different specimens. Before the young bird is half grown the juvenal plumage begins to appear, about the last of July, showing first on the wings, scapulars, flanks, and back.

Doctor Dwight (1906) has given us a full and accurate account of the molts and plumages of this species. Of the juvenal plumage he says:

August or early September finds birds wholly in the brown barred or mottled plumage, of which the flight feathers and the tail are retained for a full year, the body plumage and some of the lesser wing coverts being partially renewed at two periods of moult, the post juvenal in November or later and the prenuptial beginning often as early as the end of February.

The first winter plumage only partially supplants the juvenal, " chiefly on the back. The overlapping of the post-juvenal and pre-nuptial moults obscures the question of whether all young birds pass through one or two moults during their first winter, but the evidence is in favor of two. Before the time of the prenuptial arrives birds have faded out a good deal and are often quite white in appearance, with the brown mottling very obscure. The paler of the drab primaries apparently fade to white in some cases." At the first post-nuptial molt in August and early September, when the bird is 14 or 15 months old, a complete change takes place, producing the lighter but still mottled plumage of the second year. There is, however, great individual variation in the purity of this plumage, some birds still retaining mottled feathers like those of the first year and others acquiring advanced signs of maturity. Doctor Dwight (1906) says further:

In a very few birds brown mottled feathers still predominate, although birds with fairly developed gray mantles, white tails sprinkled with brown, and having pale ecru-drab or white primaries are perhaps the most usual type of plumage. The white heads and bodies are much obscured with smoky gray. An extreme is represented by birds absolutely pure white, the "*hutchinsii*" type. The dark bill of the young bird is replaced by a bill which is partially yellow. A partial prenuptial moult occurs in April, producing the second nuptial plumage, in which some birds, except for wings and tail, are now like adults.

The adult winter plumage is acquired by a complete postnuptial molt, in August and September, when the bird is 26 or 27 months old. This plumage is characterized by the pure white head and body plumage, pale pearl-gray mantle and wings of the same shade, fading to white at the tips of the remiges. A few birds still retain traces of immaturity, such as an occasional mottled feather or some signs of dusky clouding on the head, which disappear at the third partial prenuptial molt. In the complete postnuptial molt the remiges are shed in pairs, in regular rotation, beginning with the inner secondary and ending with the outer primary.

Food.—The glaucous gull is noted for its ravenous appetite, for it is a voracious feeder and is not at all particular about its diet, which includes almost any kind of animal food whether fresh or carrion. Its fresh food consists of fish or mollusks, which are usually stolen from other sea birds, starfish, sea-urchins, surface-swimming amphipods and crustaceans, and the eggs and young of other sea birds. Yarrell (1871) says that "it feeds also on *Cancer pulex* and *araneus;* extracts the soft animals from the shells of *Venus islandica, Pecten islandicus,* and searches closely for the lump-sucking fish, *Cyclopterus lumpus.*" That it is not content with devouring the eggs and young of dovekies, murres, and other small sea birds is shown by the much quoted statement by Swainson and Richardson (1831) that "one specimen killed on Captain Ross's expedition, disgorged an auk when it was struck, and proved by dissection to have another in its stomach." As a consumer of carrion it is undoubtedly useful; it feeds freely on dead fish or other animal refuse, which it finds along the shore, the entrails of fish, which are thrown overboard, the carcases of seals and the remains of animals or birds killed by hunters. Murdoch (1885) says:

If a duck be shot so that he fall in the water or any not easily accessible place, an hour is generally time enough for him to be reduced to a skeleton by the gulls.

Nuttall (1834) states that they "are said to attend on the walrus to feed on its excrement"; also that when "pressed by hunger," they sometimes even condescend to share the crow berry with the ptarmigan. Hagerup (1891) observes that "after the young leave their nests in August they gather on the flat tracts along the shore and feed on the berries of *Empetrum nigrum*, of which they consume a vast quantity."

Behavior.—The flight of this gull is not especially different from that of other large gulls, though it is particularly strong and at times quite swift, as when chasing the smaller sea birds to rob them of their food. The white-tipped wings serve to distinguish it from all other gulls except the Iceland gull, from which it differs only in size—a very unsatisfactory field mark. Even in young birds the primaries are much whiter than in other species, so that on the Pacific coast the glaucous gull can usually be recognized at short range.

Its voice is usually loud and harsh, often shrill and penetrating, but on its breeding grounds I have heard it utter a variety of soft conversational notes after the first excitement was over. Nelson (1887) gives us a good description of its notes as follows:

They have a series of hoarse cries like the syllables ku-ku-ku, ku-lee-oo, ku-lee-oo, ku-lee-oo, ku-ku-ku, ku-ku-ku. The syllables ku-ku are uttered in a hoarse nasal tone; the rest, in a shrill, screaming cry, reaching the ear at a great distance. These notes are used when quarreling or communicating with each other, and when disturbed on their breeding ground. At Unalaska, during May, 1877, I found them about the cliffs on the outer face of the island, and they protested vigorously against our presence as they glided back and forth overhead or perched on craggy shelves.

Elliott (1880) says:

It has a loud, shrill, eaglelike scream, becoming more monotonous by its repetition; and it also utters a low, chattering croak while coasting.

Turner (1886) observes:

The note of this bird is variable; in spring a harsh *Kaou*, which changes to a deep *honk*, in a few weeks. When flying along the shore a prolonged, grunting croak is uttered.

Chamberlain (1891) gives it as " something like the syllables *Kuk-lak;* I have seen it written *cut-leek*."

I quote from Mr. Hersey's notes his observations on the behavior of this species near St. Michael:

The glaucous gull is a bird of marked individuality. Though often solitary, when a number do assemble together they are usually rather noisy. A large flock has kept close to the ship for several days while we have been anchored in the bay and this gave me a good opportunity to study them. Often while all were resting quietly on the water one would extend his neck, open his mouth to its widest extent, and swim rapidly along, voicing his wild harsh notes. Sometimes he would swim in circles while calling, or two birds would swim side by side, either in a straight course or circling. At other times they would face one another on the water, or when on the wing one would rise above the other, the lower bird stretching his neck up and the other reaching downward, and both with dangling legs and motionless wings cry lustily. At one time while two birds were struggling with a piece of food two others sat on the water near by and added their cries to the general commotion. Both adult and immature birds do this.

They are strong swift fliers, and probably pugnacious toward smaller or weaker species, but I did not see them molest any other birds, although

I often noticed that the Sabine's and short-billed gulls, Pacific kittiwakes and jaegers kept at a respectful distance and never attempted to pick up food from the water if these gulls were near but left it for them. When no food was in sight all the above species rested on the water together in one flock. When food was thrown out the glaucous gull was slower in taking wing than the others and often lost his share on this account.

The glaucous gull is decidedly predatory in its habits. Nuttall (1834) says:

They wrest prey from weaker birds, and are often seen hovering in the air or seated on some lofty pinnacle of ice, whence, having fixed their eye upon some favorite morsel, they dart down on the possessor, which, whether fulmar, guillemot, or kittiwake, must instantly resign the prize. The auk, as well as the young penguin, they not only rob but often wholly devour.

Kumlien (1879) gives the following account of how it robs the eiders:

June 4, I saw a few *L. glaucus* among a large flock of *Som. mollissima* that were diving for food outside the harbor in a small lead in the ice. As soon as the duck came to the surface the gull attacked it till it disgorged something, which was immediately gobbled up by the gull. The gull picked several times at what was disgorged, which leads me to the belief that the food was small crustaceans. This piratical mode of living is very characteristic of *Larus glaucus*.

A similar performance has been noted by Hagerup (1891) in Greenland.

The Eskimos find the breasts of this and other gulls desirable as food, the young birds being considered a delicacy, and the eggs are very good to eat when fresh. Many an Arctic explorer also has found these birds a welcome addition to the food supply. Kumlien (1879) thus describes the primitive methods of the Eskimos in capturing these birds:

One of the most popular is to build a small snow hut on the ice in a locality frequented by the gulls. Some blubber or scraps of meat are exposed to view on the top and seldom fails to induce the bird to alight on the roof of the structure. This is so thin that the Eskimo on the inside can readily see the bird through the snow and, with a quick grab, will break through the snow and catch the bird by the legs. Some use a spear, thrusting it violently through the roof of the hut. Many are killed by exposing pieces of blubber among the hummocky ice and lying concealed within proper distance for bow and arrow practice.

Murdock (1885) tells us of another method practiced at Point Barrow:

They are a favorite bird with the natives, and many are shot in the autumn as they fly up and down the shore. They are also occasionally caught with a baited line in the autumn when there is a light snow on the beach. A little stick of hardwood, about 4 inches long and sharpened at both ends, has attached to its middle a strong line of deer sinew. The stick is carefully wrapped in

blubber or meat and exposed on the beach, while the short line is securely
fastened to a stake driven into the sand and carefully concealed in the snow.
The gull picks up the tempting morsel and swallows it and, of course, is caught
by the stick, which turns sidewise across his gullet, and his struggles to
escape fix it more firmly.

Winter.—Although some individuals, principally young birds, remain as far north as Greenland in winter, the great majority of
these gulls migrate southward when the sea ice freezes, and their
feeding grounds are covered with ice and snow, but winter must
be well upon us before we need look for them on the New England
coast. They are always rare here and find the southern limit of
their normal winter range about Long Island. When on our coasts
they may be seen among the flocks of herring gulls which frequent
our harbors and beaches, acting as scavengers, intent only on finding
a good food supply. McIlwraith (1894) says:

During the winter months the "burgomaster," as this species is usually
named, may be seen roaming around the shores of Lake Ontario, seeking what
it may devour, and it is not very scrupulous either as regards quantity or
quality.

On the Pacific coast it winters as far south as Monterey, associating with the common winter gulls of that region.

Many years ago Mr. Ridgway (1886) described the glaucous gulls
of the coasts of Alaska and adjacent waters as a new species under
the name *Larus barrovianus*, the size and the shape of the bill being
the chief distinguishing character. Twenty years later Doctor
Dwight (1906) argued that this species was untenable, and it was
removed from the check list. Recently, however, Dr. H. C. Oberholser (1918) has resurrected *barrovianus*, as a subspecies of *hyperboreus*, on the claim that the Alaska bird is smaller and has a
darker mantle than the birds from Greenland or from Europe.
Whether this claim is well founded or not, it is apparently a fact
that the characters he ascribes to the Alaska bird hold true in a
large majority of the specimens, though there are some exceptions
to the rule. Doctor Dwight, however, still maintains that the pro-
posed race is unworthy of recognition in nomenclature.

DISTRIBUTION.

Breeding range.—Circumpolar, including practically all the Arctic
coasts and islands of both hemispheres. In North America south to
eastern Labrador (Cape Harrison), Newfoundland (west coast and
in the interior), James Bay (east side), northern Hudson Bay (Cape
Fullerton), Arctic coast of Canada and Alaska, Bering Sea coast of
Alaska (south to the Kuskoquim River) and Pribilof Islands (Wal-

rus Island). North on all the Arctic islands and northern Greenland to at least latitude 82° 34' North. In the eastern hemisphere from Spitzbergen and Nova Zembla eastward to northeastern Siberia and Wrangel Island. South to Iceland, Arctic coasts of Europe and Asia and to Kamchatka.

Breeding grounds protected in the following national reservations in Alaska: Bering Sea, St. Matthew Island; Pribilofs, Walrus Island.

Winter Range.—In North America south along the coast fairly regularly to Massachusetts and Long Island and casually farther south. In the interior rarely to the Great Lakes (Lakes Ontario and Michigan). And on the Pacific coasts south to central California (Monterey) and Japan, rarely to the Hawaiian Islands. In Europe south to the Azores and the Mediterranean, Black, and Caspian Seas. North to limits of open water.

Spring migration.—Early dates of arrival: Southern Greenland, March 20; northeastern Greenland, latitude 80° 20' North, June 9; Baffin Land, Kingwah Fiord, April 20; Fort Conger, May 14; King Oscar Land, May 27; Prince Albert Land, May 31; Winter Harbor, June 3; Wellington Channel, May 16; Alaska, Yukon Delta, May 13; Kowak River, May 11; Point Barrow, May 11; and Demarcation Point, May 14. Late dates of departure: Long Island, Rockaway, May 1; Massachusetts, Rockport, April 24; Maine, Portland, April 27; Quebec, Godbout, April 29; California, Monterey, May 4; Washington, Tacoma, May 2.

Fall migration.—Early dates of arrival: Massachusetts, Cambridge, November 29; Long Island, Orient, November 30; California, Monterey, November 6. Late dates of departure: Ellesmere Land, Cape Union, September 1; Greenland, Thank God Harbor, September 3, and Bowdoin Bay, October 17; Mackenzie River, October 9; Alaska, Point Barrow, November 1; Kotzebue Sound, October 13; Unalaska, November 12; Diomede Islands, December 7; Pribilof Islands, December 13.

Casual records.—Wanders in winter along Atlantic coast to North Carolina (Cape Lookout, Carteret County, March 30 or 31, 1895), and to Bermuda (April 28, 1901). Accidental at many places in the interior, westward to Wisconsin (Milwaukee, January 8, 12, and 14, 1895), and southward to Texas (Clay County, December 17, 1880).

Egg dates.—Canadian Arctic coast: Twenty records, June 10 to July 8; ten records, June 25 to July 5. Northern Alaska: Eleven records, May 26 to June 28; six records, May 30 to June 12. Greenland: Nine records, May 26 to July 2; five records, June 7 to 14. Iceland: Ten records, May 12 to June 21; five records, June 1 to 10. Newfoundland: Three records, June 3, 5, and 8.

LARUS LEUCOPTERUS Faber.

ICELAND GULL.

HABITS.

Contributed by Charles Wendell Townsend.

The Iceland gull is a smaller edition of the glaucous gull, which it resembles closely in appearance and habits. Like its larger relative it breeds in the Arctic regions in Victoria Land, Boothia Peninsula, Greenland, Iceland, and east to Nova Zembla. It winters wherever there is open water in its range and south to Long Island and the British Isles. In the interior it is rare. Rather more arctic in its distribution than the glaucous gull, it seldom comes as far south in winter.

Nesting.—The Iceland gull nests in communities by itself and with other species of gulls both on high rocky cliffs and on low, sandy shores. Ross (1835) found it breeding on the faces of precipices on the shores of Prince Regent's Inlet with the glaucous gull, "but at a much less height and in greater numbers." Hagerup (1891) at Ivigtut in Greenland says:

About a thousand pair nest on the "bird cliff," above the kittiwakes. The lowest nests are built at a height of about 200 feet; the highest at about 500 feet above sea level. In 1888 a single pair hatched their young away from the rest on the face of the cliff, close by the edge of the ice, and at the height of 40 feet. Two pair raised their young during the three summers I was in Greenland on a cliff which was formerly the home of numerous kittiwakes. One of these nests was at the height of 15 feet, the other 100 feet above sea level.

He writes that the birds arrive in March and often lay their eggs while the fiord below is still covered with ice. The earliest young leave their nests at the close of July.

The nest is rather a bulky affair, made up of mosses and grasses. One set of eggs is laid, either two or three in number.

Eggs.—The eggs are of a clay color with numerous chocolate-colored markings. They are exactly like those of *hyperboreus*, but smaller. The measurements of 54 eggs, in various collections, average 68 by 48 millimeters; the eggs showing the four extremes measure **75.5** by 49.5, 72.5 by **51, 62.5** and 49.6, and 65.7 by **44.7** millimeters.

Plumages.—The downy young are dingy white, with brownish-gray spots above, especially about the head. In July and August they are feathered out in the juvenal plumage, which is white, more or less barred and mottled above with black and brown. Below they are gray with indistinct cloudings. Dwight (1906) says of this stage that "the primaries more frequently have white or brownish shafts, untinged with the yellow, so prominent in *glaucus*." Kumlein (1879) says that the first plumage of the young is darker than that of the yearling bird, while the opposite is the case in *glaucus*. According to Dwight (1906), "the sequence of molts and plumage is precisely the same as in the larger *glaucus*, of which it is a small edition. There is, however, no overlapping of dimensions, for even the largest male fails to reach the size of the smallest female *glaucus*." The first winter plumage resembles the juvenal, and is acquired by a partial postjuvenal molt. In this plumage the bird looks white, but rather soiled and buffy or coffee-stained in places. There is considerable variation, and in some individuals the mottling is quite dark. After the first postnuptial molt the bird loses much of its mottling and becomes nearly white, the *candidus* and *glacialis* of early writers corresponding to the *hutchinsii* of the glaucous gull. Dwight says that "second-year birds more often have adult mantles than do second-year *glaucus*, but the creamy or pinkish drab, or white primaries and brown mottled feathers in wings of tail, betray their age." The full adult plumage is assumed in the third winter, and is characterized by a pearl-gray mantle and pure white color of head, breast, tail, and the tips of all of the wing feathers. The bill is yellow. According to Dwight the color of the mantle is somewhat darker than that of *glaucus*. This stage is rarely seen on the New England coast, although full adults of the glaucous gull are not uncommon.

The recognition of a white-winged gull in the field is not difficult. The general whiteness of the birds as compared with herring gulls, for example, makes them conspicuous. In all cases where the diagnosis is suspected it is necessary to examine carefully the wing tips with the glasses before one can speak with certainty. The entire absence of dark markings on the wing tips at once settles the general diagnosis, but it is often extremely difficult to differentiate between the glaucous gull and the present species. Particularly is this the case if a white-winged gull is seen alone or with others of the same species. Size in absence of other objects for comparison is very deceptive. In company with the glaucous or the herring gull, the Iceland gull is seen to be a little smaller. The glaucous gull is not only larger than the Iceland gull, but is also larger than the herring gull; but here again appearances without careful comparison are apt to be deceptive. In fact, size alone is of little value, for a large male Iceland gull may nearly equal in size a small female glaucous gull. The size of the head, neck, and bill are, however, important field marks, for these are noticeably smaller in proportion to the size of the bird in the Iceland gull than in the glaucous gull.

Food.—The feeding habits of the Iceland gull are similar to those of the glaucous and herring gulls. They are ever on the alert to pick up dead fish, crustacea, or other edible substance from the surface of the water and from the beaches. About Eskimo encampments seal and fish refuse are eagerly sought. Hagerup (1891) states that in Greenland the young feed on the berries of *Empetrum nigrum.* He also says:

> For a while after leaving the nests they are accompanied by one of the parents, or by both, and these give warning in a wise and unmistakable manner: "Don't go near those treacherous boats," they seem to cry. Later on the young mingle with the young of the glaucous gull, but not with young kittiwakes. In voice and habits the young birds quite resemble young glaucous gulls.

Behavior.—Like other gulls and terns the Iceland gull is sometimes of value to man in indicating the presence of fish. Baird, Brewer, and Ridgway (1884) quote from Faber a statement that in 1821 " on the 1st of March the shore was full of sea gulls; but early on the 2d the air was filled with numbers of this species which had arrived during the night. The Icelanders concluded from the sudden appearance of the birds that shoals of codfish must have arrived on the coast, and it was soon found that this conjecture was correct." He adds that these gulls " would indicate to the seal shooters in the fiord where the seals were to be looked for, by following their track to the sea and hovering over them in flocks with incessant cries." In both cases it is probable that the larger creatures stirred up the water so that the smaller food of the gulls could be obtained. In the same way flocks of terns follow whales, not with any expectations of feeding on the whale, but on the smaller marine life stirred up by the whale and on which both feed.

Winter.—Iceland gulls, as well as glaucous and Kumlien gulls, visit the New England seacoast more in some than in other winters, dependent, no doubt, on the amount of open water and on the sufficient or insufficient food supply in the north. In the winter of 1907 and 1908 we were favored with an unusually large number of these northern birds in the vicinity of Boston. F. H. Allen (1908) reported one or two Iceland gulls in immature plumage in Charles River Basin and in Boston Harbor, at least three at Swampscott, and one at Lynn and Marblehead.

DISTRIBUTION.

Breeding range.—Portions of the Arctic regions; from Victoria Land (Cambridge Bay), Boothia Peninsula, and west-central Greenland east probably to Nova Zembla; southern limits not well defined. Said to breed in Hudson Bay. Mackenzie Bay and other western records are not well established and should be discredited.

Winter range.—From the northern limits of open water in southern Greenland south along the Labrador coast to the Bay of Fundy and Maine, more rarely Massachusetts and Long Island. Occasionally on the Great Lakes as far west as Michigan (Sault Sainte Marie). Recorded off North Carolina (Cape Hatteras). In Europe from Iceland, the northern British Isles, and Scandinavia south; rarely to northern France and the Baltic Sea.

Spring migration.—Early dates of arrival: Ellesmere Land, Fort Conger, May 19 to June 5; northeastern Greenland, June 20. Late dates of departure: New York, Rochester, April 14; Maine, Portland, April 27, and Richmonds Island, May 20; Ontario, Port Sidney, April 6; Quebec, Godbout, May 1.

Fall migration.—Early dates of arrival: Massachusetts, Boston, November 4; New York, Lansingburg, November 21. Late dates of departure: Northeastern Greenland, September 25 to 30; Gulf of Cumberland, September 6.

Casual records.—Accidental in Maryland (Baltimore, November 23, 1893) and at various places in the interior, as far west as Nebraska (Dorchester, January 15, 1907). Two specimens taken at Point Barrow, Alaska, August 4 and September 19, 1882.

Egg dates.—Iceland: Eleven records, May to July 2; six records, June 6 to 28. Greenland: Nine records, May 29 to July 1; five records, June 10 to 20.

LARUS GLAUCESCENS Naumann.

GLAUCOUS-WINGED GULL.

HABITS.

This, the most abundant, the most widely distributed, and the characteristic gull of the north Pacific coast, is an omnipresent and familiar sight to the travelers along the picturesque coast and through the numerous inside passages leading to Alaska. From the coast of Oregon southward it is replaced by the dark-mantled western gull during the breeding season, and in Bering Sea it mingles with the large white Arctic species, the glaucous gull, by which it is replaced northward. During the latter part of April, in 1911, we first became familiar with the glaucous-winged gull in Puget Sound, where it was very abundant, feeding with the herring gull in large numbers about the harbors. As we steamed northward in May through various channels and sounds to Ketchikan, Alaska, the grand and picturesque scenery of those inside passages was enlivened and made more attractive by the constant presence of these gulls following the ship, drifting northward to their breeding grounds, or merely wandering in search of food. At Ketchikan they were particularly abundant in a great variety of plumages of different ages. But when we passed through Dixon Entrance and out into the Pacific Ocean we left the gulls behind, as the land faded away from sight, and when 50 or 100 miles from land they had been replaced by the more pelagic fulmars and albatrosses. We did not see them again until we came within sight of the Aleutian Islands, and from that time on they were always with us throughout the whole length of the Aleutian chain.

Spring.—As this gull is practically resident, or, at least, always briefly a few typical breeding colonies in different localities. present throughout all but the extreme northern portions of its breeding range, it is difficult to tell just when it arrived on its breeding grounds; but it usually begins to frequent or to resent intrusion upon its nesting grounds at least a fortnight before egg laying begins, the dates varying greatly in the different latitudes. To illustrate the wide variations in its nesting habits I propose to describe

Nesting.—The largest and most interesting colonies of the glaucous-winged gull, in the southern part of its range, are among the spectacular sea-bird colonies on the rocky islands set apart as reservations off the coast of Washington, and divided into three groups, known as the Copalis Rock Reservation, the Quillayute Needle Reservation, and the Flattery Rocks Reservation. Mr. W. Leon Dawson (1908a) and Prof. Lynds Jones visited the various islands in these groups in 1905 and 1907, and made careful estimates of the numbers and kinds of birds found breeding there. The full report is well worth reading to gain a fair impression of what these wonderful reservations contain, but I shall confine my quotations to a few striking facts taken from it. Only two pairs of glaucous-winged gulls were found nesting on Destruction Island, which seems to be the southern limit of its breeding range. Thence northward, colonies of this species became more frequent and increased in size. The largest colony was found on Wishalooth Island, from 2,000 to 3,000 glaucous-winged gulls, 100 to 500 western gulls, 1,000 tufted puffins, 5,000 to 15,000 Kaeding's petrels, and 100 Baird's cormorants. This is an island of about 20 acres, three-quarters of a mile offshore in the Quillayute Needles Reservation. It is "a lofty jagged ridge of metamorphic conglomerate with sharply sloping sides covered with guano ledges and resulting areas of shallow earth, which are clothed with grass and other vegetation—yarrow, painted cup, and the like; 175 feet high; 200 yards long along the crest." Carroll Islet, "the gem of the Olympiades," as Mr. Dawson calls it, contained the following wonderful colonies of breeding water birds: Five thousand tufted puffins, 1,000 Cassin's auklets, 20 pigeon guillemots, 700 California murres, 1,000 glaucous-winged gulls, 50 western gulls, 500

Kaeding petrels, 100 white-crested cormorants, and 500 Baird's cormorants. Professor Jones (1908) has well described it, as follows:

Seaward Carroll Islet presents a rock precipice some 200 feet in height. A stone dropped from the top, within 2 rods of our camp, would fall clear into the ocean below. Landward the islet slopes at first gently, but finally at an angle of nearly 70° to within 30 feet of the water, ending in another precipice there. It was only along the landward side that ascent was possible, and even there one must clamber up vertically for 10 or more feet, finding foothold in the weathered rock. Two sharp rock ridges jut out, one at the northeast corner, the other landward easterly. The gentler slope of the top is covered with Sitka spruce trees, two of them old monarchs, with a few deciduous trees, growths of elder bushes, a sort of red raspberry bush, and the ever-present salal bushes. Bordering on the steeper slopes there is a growth of grass clinging to masses of soil which has lodged in the interstices between rock chips. In some places this grass is seen clinging to shelves on the face of precipices. Exposed rock faces are pitted and hollowed by the elements into nesting places for cormorants and gulls. Other rock masses, a good deal worn down, project from the other angles of the island. The waves have worn a hole completely through the island parallel to the landward side and about a hundred feet from it. Practically the entire island was covered by the nests of this species, except the area covered by the taller trees, and also a relatively small area on the steep slope of the northeastward side.

By covered is meant that there were nests in all sorts of situations and within reasonable distance of each other, but never within striking distance of the birds occupying adjoining nests. A number of nests were found beneath the dense fringe of salal bushes, and many of the larger grottoes of the perpendicular rock faces contained a nest. Ledges, which were broad enough to afford us secure footing, were also occupied by nests. Often nests could be seen on small niches in the rocks. There was one nest on the murre ledge fully exposed on the bare rock. Many of the more exposed nests showed unmistakable signs of having been pilfered by crows.

Professor Jones noticed that all of the gulls which were nesting under the bushes were old birds with pure white heads, while many of those nesting in the open showed signs of immaturity. The nests were also better made than those in the open.

We found this species nesting under somewhat different conditions in the Aleutian and Pribilof Islands, where it was decidedly the commonest large gull and universally distributed. On Bogoslof Island on July 4, 1911, we found a colony of between 100 and 200 pairs of glaucous-winged gulls nesting on the flat sandy portions of the famous old volcano. The steep, rocky pinnacles in the center of the island were densely populated by countless thousands of Pallas's murres. Recent eruptions had thrown up so much volcanic dust, ashes, and sand that extensive sand dunes and flat sandy plains had been formed all around the island, which was entirely bare of shelter and devoid of vegetation. The nests of the glaucous-winged gulls were widely scattered over this area, no two being anywhere near together. They were well made of seaweed, rockweed, kelp, and straws, and were sometimes decorated with feathers or fish bones; some of the nesting material must have been carried a long distance, for the nearest land on which any grass was growing was many miles away. Many of the eggs were pipped and there were quite a number of downy young running about, but a few of the eggs were only slightly incubated. The nesting grounds of the gulls were closely adjacent to a large breeding rookery of Steller's sea lions (*Eumetopias stelleri*), with which they seemed to be on friendly terms.

A few days later we landed on Walrus Island, the most wonderful bird island in North America. Here we found a breeding colony of this species mixed with glaucous gulls on the highest part of the island, where the accumulations of guano had formed a rich soil, supporting a luxuriant growth of grass. Other portions of the little island, which I have described more fully in the history of the red-faced cormorant, contained, in close proximity to the gulls, the most densely populated colonies I have ever seen of California and Pallas's murres, tufted puffin, paroquet, crested and least auklets, Pacific kittiwakes, and red-faced cormorants. At the time of our visit (July 7, 1911) most of the gulls' eggs had hatched, but a few eggs were still to be seen in the nests among the tufts of grass. Mr. William Palmer (1899) says of the nests on these islands:

On Walrus Island the nests are quite numerous. On June 13 many contained three eggs well incubated; some had two fresh eggs, while a few had one or two young and an egg or two. Larger young were picked up on the rocks near the nests. The nests are well made, clean, and are generally composed of dead grass stems, which the birds bring from St. Paul. While most were placed on the flat rock, a few were in depressions of the sand which filled some of the larger crevices of the rocks.

Dr. E. W. Nelson (1887) says:

The usual nesting places of this species are the faces of rugged cliffs, at whose base the waves are continually breaking and the coast exposes its wildest and most broken outline.

He seems to think that instances of these gulls nesting in other situations are exceptional. They nest on the steep, rocky cliffs of St. George Island and in similar situations elsewhere, but they also nest frequently on the flat, grassy tops of many small islands, and are found on the sandy plains of Bogoslof Island. We never found them nesting on the larger islands in the Aleutian chain, where they might be disturbed by foxes. On June 19, 1911, I saw a large number of glaucous-winged gulls frequenting a high grassy plain on Kiska Island and acting as if they were breeding in the vicinity, but I could not find any nests.

Eggs.—The glaucous-winged gull normally lays three eggs, though frequently two constitute a full set; four eggs are very rarely, if ever, laid by one bird. Only one brood is raised in a season. The eggs are not distinguishable from those of other species of gulls of similar size. The prevailing shape is ovate, with variations toward short ovate on one hand and elliptical ovate on the other. The shell is thin and finely granulated, with only a dull luster. The ground color shows various shades of buff, " olive buff," and pale olive. The eggs are spotted, generally uniformly over the entire surface, with small spots or occasional larger blotches of " wood brown," " raw umber," " burnt umber," or " seal brown," and with underlying spots of " lilac gray." The measurements of 47 eggs in the United States National Museum average 72.8 by 50.8 millimeters; the eggs showing the four extremes measure **82** by 51.5, 73.5 by **55, 66** by 47.5 and 70.5 by **46.5** millimeters.

Young.—Mr. George Willett (1912) noted the following incident in the education of the young:

I was considerably interested in observing the swimming lessons given the nearly grown young by the adult birds. In some cases, where the young seemed afraid to take to the water, they were shoved from the rocks by the old birds. The old bird would then swim beside the young one, occasionally poking it with her bill. I was unable to satisfy myself whether this was meant as a caress or as punishment for poor swimming.

Plumages.—The period of incubation does not seem to be definitely known. The downy young is " drab gray " above, variegated with " avellaneous," and a paler shade of the same color below, fading to " tilleul buff " on the center of the breast. It is heavily spotted on the back with " fuscous black " and on the head and throat with pure black. The young birds somewhat resemble those of the western gull, but the latter has more of the buffy shades and less of the gray; and the markings on the back are not quite so heavy. Perhaps in large series they might intergrade.

Dr. Jonathan Dwight (1906) has fully described the sequence of plumages in this species as follows:

The juvenal plumage is deep plumbeous gray with broad dark barring or mottling and obscure whitish edgings. The tail is nearly solidly gray, sprinkled basally with white, and the flight feathers, including the quills, are also dark gray. Birds in this plumage are never so pale (especially the primaries) as the darkest *leucopterus*, nor are they ever so dark as the palest of the black-primaried species. They fade to a decidedly brown shade, almost mouse gray, but their color (especially that of the primaries) and the size of their bills, even when young birds, are cardinal points by which to recognize them. The first winter plumage is like the juvenal, but at the prenuptial molt white about the head and body and gray on the back begins to appear in some specimens, thus marking the first nuptial plumage. In the second winter plumage unpatterned drab or mouse-gray primaries are most frequent, together with the gray mantle of the adult. The white head and neck, as in the other species, are much clouded with dusky markings, which are lost at the next prenuptial molt. I do not think that primaries with the apical white spots of the adult bird are ever developed until a year later, but in some birds there is a fore-shadowing of the white spots on the first primary. The third winter plumage, that of the adult, is the result of the second post-nuptial molt, after which very few birds can be found showing traces of immaturity. The new primaries are slaty, and white tipped, the first and sometimes the second with subapical or sometimes terminal white "mirrors," quite unlike the unpatterned feathers of *glaucus* or the smaller *leucopterus*. The mantle varies from cinereous to plumbeous gray, the color running over into the primaries, which become de-cidedly slaty toward their apices. The white of the head and neck is still clouded, the dusky markings being characteristic of winter plumages until the birds are quite advanced in age. At prenuptial molts, as in the other species, these feathers are replaced by white ones.

Food.—These, like other large gulls, are useful scavengers all along the coast and are practically omnivorous. They were constantly fol-lowing our ship in search of small scraps that might be picked up, and, while we were at anchor at Ketchikan and Unalaska, they were especially numerous and always in sight, eagerly waiting for the garbage to be thrown overboard. They are abundant, in winter, in the harbors of nearly all the large cities on the Pacific coast as far south as southern California, where they feed largely on refuse and seem to fill the place occupied by the herring gull on the Atlantic coast. They are particularly numerous about the garbage heaps which are dumped on the shore to be washed away by the advancing tides. In such places they appear to realize that they are protected and are very tame. In their eagerness to secure the choice morsels of food they seem to forget all about the presence of human beings, even within a few feet. At other times it is difficult for a man to walk up within gunshot distance of them. They become much excited and clamorous in their scramble for food, competing at close quar-ters with other species of gulls, with dogs, and with the lazy Indians. They are none too particular in their choice of food and will eat almost anything that is edible.

During the summer they frequent the vicinity of the salmon can-neries, where they gorge themselves on the refuse from the factories or fishing vessels and on the bodies of dead salmon along the shores. As a result they become very fat. On the Pribilof Islands they regularly visit the killing grounds to feast on the entrails and other waste portions of the slaughtered seals, which furnish an abundant food supply. Among the Aleutian Islands, where sea urchins are abundant, we found numerous broken shells of these creatures on the rocky heights frequented by the gulls. Evidently they had been dropped on the rocks to break the shells. In the colonies, where they were nesting with other species, we saw no evidence to prove that they feed on the eggs or young of their neighbors, though they may, perhaps, do so occasionally. On Walrus Island we kept some of the murres and cormorants off their nests for several hours without any apparent damage from the gulls.

Behavior.—The flight of the glaucous-winged gull is buoyant, graceful, and pleasing, and its plumage is always spotlessly clean and neat. A gull in flight is one of nature's most beautiful creatures and one of its triumphs in the mastery of the air. It was a never-ending source of delight to watch these graceful birds following the ship at full speed without the slightest effort, dropping astern to pick up some fallen morsel or forging ahead at will, as if merely playing with their powers of flight. Sometimes the same individual could be recognized day after day by some peculiarity of marking. They seem thoroughly at ease on the wing. Several times I saw one scratch its head with its foot, as it sailed along on set wings, without slackening its pace at all. When traveling against a strong head wind I have seen one sail along for miles without moving its wings, except to adjust slightly the angle at which they were held, keeping alongside the ship, forging ahead, or dropping astern, as it wished, and rising or falling to suit its fancy. When left far astern to pick up food off the water it would give a few flaps when rising, set its wings, and soon catch up with the ship. This power to sail almost directly into the teeth of a strong wind has caused much discussion, as it has been noted in the herring gull and other species. Various theories have been advanced to account for it, all of which are more or less unsatisfactory. To my mind it is simple enough to understand if we can realize that a gull is a highly specialized, almost perfect sailing vessel, endowed with instinctive skill in navigating the air to use the forces at its command to advantage. With a clear knowledge of the forces at work when a ship sails, close hauled, to within a few points of the wind, we can imagine the gull sailing along a vertical plane, in which the force of gravity replaces the resistance of the water against the keel and the wind acts against the gull's wings as it does on the sails of the ship; the resultant of these two forces is a forward movement, which the gull controls by adjusting its center of gravity and the angle of its wings.

It is evident from the foregoing accounts that the glaucous-winged gull is decidedly a sociable species on its breeding grounds where it seems to nest in perfect harmony with its neighbors in close quarters. It also associates on migrations and during the winter with various other species of gulls, with all of which it seems to be on good terms. The adults can readily be distinguished from the white-winged species or from those having black-tipped wings by the peculiar color pattern of the primaries. Birds in immature plumage are not so easily recognized, but a careful study of the descriptions given in the manuals will help to identify them. They are not likely to be confused with the dark-mantled western gull, but Mr. Dawson's (1908) reference to the large number of "mulattoes" on Carroll Islet suggests the possibility that these two species may hybridize.

Mr. Dawson (1909), who spent a week studying the vocal performances of this species and their significance, has thus classified its various notes:

1. *The beak-quaking notes*—Harsh, unmusical, and of moderate pitch, used to express distrust and continued disapproval. During the delivery the mandibles are brought together three or four times in moderate succession. This is the ordinary scolding or distress cry of characteristic and uniform pitch, save that it is raised to a higher key when the speaker becomes vehement. The phrase varies from three to five notes, and is uttered in the following cadences: *kak-ako; ka ka, ka ka; ka ka kaka; kaka; kaka, ka kakak; kak-a-ka.*

2. *Kawk.*—A note of inquiry or mere communication; has many modifications and varies from a short trumpet note to the succeeding.

3. *Klook.*—A sepulchral note of uniform interest but uncertain meaning.

4. The trumpet notes, long or short, single or in prolonged succession, high-pitched, musical, and far-sounding. During delivery the head is thrust forward, the neck arched, and the throat and mandibles opened to their fullest capacity. These are pleasure notes and are used especially on social occasions, when many birds are about, *keer, keer, keer, keer.*

5. *A(n)k, a(n)k, a(n)k, a(n)k, a(n)k, a(n)k.*—Minor trumpet notes of regular length and succession, used in expostulation or social excitement; frequent and varied.

6. *Klook, klook, klook.*—In quality a combination of *kawk* and the trumpet tones, uttered deliberately and without much show of energy. Used chiefly in domestic conversation of uncertain import.

7. *Oree-eh, oree-eh, oree-eh, an an an.*—An expression of greeting as when uttered by a sitting bird welcoming one about to alight. The notes of the first series are trumpet tones, in which the second syllable of each member is raised to a higher pitch, while the voice is dropped again on the third. The second series is lower and more trivial, but still enthusiastic, as though congratulatory to the guest arrived.

8. *Ko.*—Shouted once, or thrice repeated, in quelling a clamor. "Hist! Hist! You're making too much noise; he's watching us."

9. *Arahh.*—A slow and mournful trumpeting, usually uttered awing, to express anxiety or grief, as at the loss of a chick.

10. *Oo anh, oo anh.*—Repeated indefinitely. Notes of coaxing and endearment usually addressed to children, but occasionally to wedded mates. The cooing of doves does not express so much adulation or idolatrous devotion as the gull throws into these most domestic tones.

Winter.—When winter, with its snow and ice, drives the glaucous-winged gull from the northern portion of its breeding range, there is a general movement southward; but the migration is more in evidence along the California coast, where this species spends the winter in large numbers, frequenting the harbors in company with glaucous, herring, California, western, and short-billed gulls. It winters commonly as far north as the Aleutian Islands, where it can always find open water.

DISTRIBUTION.

Breeding range.—Coasts and islands of the North Pacific Ocean and Bering Sea, from St. Lawrence Island and the Pribilof Islands southward to southern Alaska, British Columbia, and Washington to Destruction Island; westward throughout the Aleutian and Commander Islands; northward to Kamchatka and northeastern Siberia (Providence Bay). Occurs rarely in summer in northern Bering Sea (St. Michael and Port Clarence), but probably does not breed there.

Breeding grounds protected in the following national reservations: In Alaska, Aleutian Islands, as Adak, Atka, Attu, Kiska, Tanaga, and Unalaska; Bogoslof; St. Lazaria; Forrester Island; in Washington, Flattery Rocks and Quillayute Needles, as Alexander Island, Carroll Islet, and Destruction Island.

Winter range.—From the Aleutian Islands, Kodiak, and southern Alaskan coast southward to lower California (San Geronimo and Guadalupe Islands), and from the Commander Islands to Japan (Hakodadi). Birds remains late at the Pribilof Islands, but probably rarely, if ever, stay throughout the entire winter.

Spring migration.—Northward along the coast. Late dates of departure: Lower California, San Geronimo Island, March 10 to 15, and Guadalupe Island, March 22; California, Santa Cruz Island, May 2, and Monterey, May 10.

Fall migration.—Southward along the coast. First arrivals reach California, Monterey, October 25 to 30.

Casual records.—Rare visitor to Hawaii (taken December 9, 1902). Rare straggler north of Bering Strait; taken in Kotzebue Sound May 11, 1899, on Wrangel Island April 3, 1916, and at Point Barrow September 19, 1882.

Egg dates.—Alaska, south of peninsula: Fifty records, June 3 to July 16; twenty-five records, June 20 to July 3. Washington: Nineteen records, May 29 to July 23; ten records, June 14 to 19. British Columbia: Sixteen records, June 14 to July 16; eight records, June 16 to 24.

LARUS KUMLIENI Brewster.

KUMLIEN'S GULL.

HABITS.

Very little is known about the distribution, much less about the habits, of this and the following species—the two gray-winged gulls—as both are very rare. Kumlien's gull was described by Brewster (1883*a*) from a specimen secured by Ludwig Kumlien in Cumberland Sound on June 14, 1878.

Nesting.—When Kumlien (1879) found this species breeding in Cumberland Sound in 1878 he supposed that it was identical with the glaucous-winged gull of the Pacific coast and so reported it. He then gave us the following brief account of its habits:

They are quite common in the upper Cumberland waters, where they breed. Arrived with the opening of the water and soon began nesting. The nest was placed on the shelving rocks on high cliffs. Two pairs nested very near our harbor, but the ravens tore the nest down and destroyed the eggs. Only a single well-identified egg was secured. This gull is unknown to Governor Fencker on the Greenland coast. They remained about the harbor a great deal and were often observed making away with such scraps as the cook had thrown overboard; were shy and difficult to shoot. Full-grown young of this species were shot in the first days of September. These were even darker than the young of *L. argentatus*, the primaries and tail being very nearly black.

Since that time nothing further has been learned of its breeding habits, eggs, or young.

Eggs.—Several sets of eggs were collected by Mr. J. S. Warmbath on one of the Peary expeditions, which have since found their way into collections as eggs of Kumlien's gull. These eggs were taken in Ellesmere Land on June 15, 1900, and are probably eggs of a new species of gull, to be known as *Larus thayeri*. Probably the only authentic egg of *Larus kumlieni* in existence is the one referred to above as taken by Kumlien. This egg is now in the United States National Museum; it is a miserable specimen, too badly broken to measure accurately, and is tied together with thread. In shape it is practically elongate ovate. The ground color is " olive buff "; it is sparingly spotted over the entire surface with small spots of " bister," " sepia," several lighter shades of brown, and various shades of brownish drab. If a series of eggs were available for study they would probably show the usual variations which are found in nearly all gulls' eggs.

Plumages.—Dr. Jonathan Dwight (1906) has made a careful study of the plumages of this rare species and, based on the examination of 22 specimens, has given us the following conclusions:

The natal down is unknown, as no chicks have as yet found their way into collections. The juvenal plumage may be described as follows:

Above, drab-gray mottled with dull white and obscurely barred and mottled with darker gray; below, more solidly gray, paler about the head and throat. Flight feathers a brownish gray, darker than the body, the outer webs of the primaries darkest. Tail almost solidly drab-gray, the basal portion and the outer pair of rectrices sprinkled with dull white; the upper and under tail coverts similar in color, but with a good deal of blotching or barring. They might easily pass for specimens of *glaucescens* if it were not for the small bills and rather smaller dimensions. They are considerably darker (especially the primaries) than the darkest *leucopterus* I have seen, and the nearly solid gray of the tail is a feature not seen in *leucopterus*. Besides this, the barring and mottling is much coarser and darker. In one of the birds there is a faintly indicated whitish subapical spot on the first primary, but similar spots may be found in other species of gulls, and it seems to be a variable character of little importance. These specimens are perhaps not in full juvenal plumage, for they are probably partly in first winter dress; and two of them, just beginning the prenuptial molt, having acquired a few gray nuptial feathers of the mantle; but it must be remembered that the differences between juvenal and first-winter plumages of the gulls are inappreciable. It is probable that the brown shade is due to fading and that earlier in the season these birds were grayer.

First winter plumage.—From what has just been said it has been made evident that this plumage differs in practically no respect from the juvenal. The post-juvenal molt is variable in the time of its occurrence, just as it is in all the gulls, and overlaps the prenuptial so as to be in many cases confused with it.

First nuptial plumage.—This plumage doubtless closely resembles the juvenal or the first winter, but birds may be expected to become whiter about the head and with a few gray feathers on the back.

Second winter plumage.—Like *leucopterus*, this species attains a considerable amount of adult plumage at this moult. The gray mantle, clouded white head and body, and white tail indicate a close approximation to the adult plumage; but the primaries and other feathers of the wings are usually drab and not very much paler than in first winter birds. Dark gray or mottled feathers may also be found on the wings or tail or on the body posteriorly. The bills are yellow, but often clouded and with the red spot lacking. The variation is considerable, just as in *glaucus* or *leucopterus* or *glaucescens*, but the darkness of flight feathers or tail, or both combined, is a character useful in separating *kumlieni* from the two species last mentioned. The tail feathers, like those of *glaucescens*, while largely white, may show gray patches, chiefly on the inner webs.

Second nuptial plumage.—The body plumage is renewed more or less at the second prenuptial moult, and I find evidence of this in several specimens.

Third winter plumage.—Just as in the other gulls, this species after the second post-nuptial moult assumes (except perhaps in a very few cases) the adult plumage.

Behavior.—It is fair to assume that the habits of Kumlien's gull probably do not differ materially from those of the other large gulls, for they are all very much alike in general behavior with the possible exception of the tyrannous great black-backed gull.

Winter.—Kumlien's gull wanders southward late in the fall and winter, probably regularly, though sparingly, as far south as southern New England and New York, where it is associated with herring gulls and other species, acting as savengers about our harbors.

DISTRIBUTION.

Breeding range.—Known to breed only in Cumberland Sound. Specimens taken in Ellesmere Land prove to be *thayeri*.

Winter range.—So far as known, the Gulf of St. Lawrence (Prince Edward Island) and Bay of Fundy (Grand Manan); southward rarely to Massachusetts (Plymouth and Boston), and New York (Long Island and Mohawk River).

Spring migration.—Long Island, Rockaway Beach, March 8; Maine, Portland, April 27.

Fall migration.—Gulf of Cumberland, September 27; Prince Edward Island, October 7; Bay of Fundy, November 1.

LARUS NELSONI Henshaw.

NELSON'S GULL.

HABITS.

This large gray-winged gull of the Pacific coast and Bering Sea is so rare that its status, as a species, is none too well established, though the four specimens which had been studied by Doctor Dwight (1906) led him to the conclusion that "*nelsoni* seems to have as good a claim for specific distinctness as does *kumlieni*, of which it appears to be a large edition." Nothing seems to be known about its breeding habits or its breeding range.

Plumages.—Doctor Dwight (1906) after examining the scanty material available, suggests the following, regarding the probable plumage changes of this rare species:

The young bird has never been described, but inasmuch as *kumlieni* in juvenal plumage is scarcely to be distinguished from *glaucescens*, there is every reason for expecting the corresponding plumage of *nelsoni* to be practically the same. The birds, though, ought to be larger than *glaucescens*, and I have no doubt that very large specimens now labeled "*glaucescens*" in various collections will eventually prove to be *nelsoni*. Such a bird has been recorded in the British Museum Catalogue, but somehow I overlooked it when examining the collection. In the American Museum, however, I find two specimens (Nos. 26234 and 61536) so much larger than *glaucescens* usually is that I believe them to be *nelsoni*. The tarsi and feet are unusually large and massive and the bills very heavy. The bird in the Philadelphia Academy is completing an adult post-nuptial moult, but the other specimens throw very little light on the subject of moult in this species.

I have never recognized the bird in life and can not find anything in print regarding its habits, in which it probably closely resembles Kumlien's and the glaucous-winged gulls. Some day, when its breeding grounds are discovered, we may know more about it. I am inclined to think that it may prove to be identical with *Larus kumlieni*, or at best only subspecifically distinct from it. The fact that a young gull, possibly referable to *kumlieni*, has been taken on the coast of California adds weight to this theory, which may be established when more material has been collected.

DISTRIBUTION.

Range.—Three specimens taken in Alaska—St. Michael, June 20; near Bering Strait; and Point Barrow, September 5. One taken in Lower California, San Geronimo Island, March 18. One taken in

Hawaiian Islands, Hilo, March 13. One taken on Vancouver Island, December 20. Its ranges and migration are otherwise unknown.

LARUS MARINUS Linnæus.

GREAT BLACK-BACKED GULL.

HABITS.

While cruising along the bleak and barren coasts of southern Labrador I learned to know and admire this magnificent gull, as we saw it sailing on its powerful wings high above the desolate crags and rocky islets of that forbidding shore, its chosen summer home. Its resemblance to the bald eagle was striking, as it soared aloft and wheeled in great circles, showing its broad black back and wings in sharp contrast with its snow-white head and tail, glistening in the sunlight. It surely seemed to be a king among the gulls, a merciless tyrant over its fellows, the largest and strongest of its tribe. No weaker gull dared to intrude upon its feudal domain; the islet it had chosen for its home was deserted and shunned by other less aggressive waterfowl, for no other nest was safe about the castle of this robber baron, only the eider duck being strong enough to defend its young.

Spring.—Early in May, when winter is breaking up on the south coast of Labrador, the loud defiant cries of the great black-backed gulls are heard as the birds return from their winter resorts to take possession of their summer homes. Mating and nest building begin soon after their arrival. They are not so gregarious here as other gulls. We found no large breeding colonies on this coast, seldom more than four or five pairs on an island, and often only one pair. They seem to prefer solitude and isolation, where each pair can hold undisputed sway over its own territory. We never found them breeding on the mainland, but always on the bare tops of islands, from which they could have a good outlook. They were never taken by surprise and always left the island long before we reached it, soaring high above us, screaming in protest. They were exceedingly shy and would never come within gunshot unless outwitted by strategy, which was no easy task. While walking along the shore at the base of a cliff a black-backed gull flew out over the cliff unexpectedly, and I dropped him with a charge of heavy shot, but this was the only specimen I was able to obtain.

Nesting.—The first nest we found was on a little low islet with sandy and rocky shores, over which a single pair of great black-backed gulls were soaring, as if interested. The nest was conspicuous enough when we landed, for it had been built over the base and about the roots of a dead tree which had been washed up on the beach—a large pile of coarse grasses, seaweeds, sods, and mosses neatly lined with fine grasses. It measured 52 inches across the pile, and the inner cavity, which was deeply hollowed, was 10 inches in diameter. It contained three fresh eggs on May 25, 1909. Another nest was found the next day, which also contained three fresh eggs, on the moss-covered rocks on the highest portion of a small island. It was a shallow nest of mosses, grasses, twigs, and rubbish, with a few feathers and a little seaweed. It measured 20 inches in outside and 10 inches in inside diameter, hollowed to a depth of about $2\frac{1}{2}$ inches. There was only one pair of gulls on this island, but a pair of eiders were nesting in a hollow among some fallen dead trees. On some of the islands the nests were mere depressions in the turf 9 or 10 inches across, and the eggs were laid on the ground. The fresh green grass made a handsome border to these nests, but there was no lining of any sort, and not even a twig or bit of straw was used in the construction. Some of them had evidently been used for several seasons.

On the northeast coast of Labrador, in 1912, I found the great black-backed gull common and evenly distributed all along the coast, breeding in single pairs on low rocky islands, well inland in the deep bays and among the outer islands. They are locally known as " saddlers " or " saddle backs." They are intimately associated with the eider ducks, affording them some protection as sentinels to warn them of approaching dangers. There is almost always a pair of great black-backed gulls nesting on every island where the American eiders or northern eiders are breeding. The fishermen rob the ducks' nests persistently all through the summer, but do not disturb the gull's nests, for they believe that if the gulls are driven away the ducks will not return to breed again. Apparently the adult gulls do not rob the eider's nests, for they are too shy to do so while egg collectors are on the island, and at other times the eiders are able to defend their eggs; but I saw some evidence to indicate that the young gulls, when unable to fly but large enough to run about, do sometimes eat the eider eggs. While exploring a low rocky island in one of the bays, where several pairs of northern eiders and one pair of great black-backed gulls were breeding, on August 2, 1912, I noticed an eider's nest in which the eggs had been broken and eaten. One young gull was seen swimming away from the island and one long-legged youngster, about half grown, was running about over the smooth rocks so fast that we could hardly catch him. I suspected that he was responsible for the broken eggs. Probably the damage done in this way is more than offset by the benefits derived from such wary sentinels and such powerful defenders against the depredations of other gulls and ravens. Young gulls are considered to be very good eating and are often kept in confinement by the residents of Labrador and fattened for the table.

In Newfoundland the great black-backed gull breeds on the islands in fresh-water lakes. On June 23, 1912, I visited a small breeding colony of this species on an island in Sandy Lake, Newfoundland, where about seven pairs of gulls had already hatched their broods and where they had been known to breed regularly for many years. It was a small island, heavily wooded in the central higher portion with birches, poplars, alders, and thick underbrush, but with broad, stony beaches around its shores. The gulls' nests were scattered along the higher portions of the beaches among the loose rocks. All of the nests were empty and most of the young birds were so well hidden among the stones, under piles of driftwood, or in the woods that we found only two. I saw several downy young, only a few days old, swim away from the beach and out onto the rough waters of the lake, where their parents watched them anxiously and finally drove them back to the island after we had left. A pair of glaucous gulls and one or two pairs of herring gulls were flying about the island, but their nests were probably on some of the neighboring islands.

The southern limit of its breeding range seems to be in Nova Scotia, where there are several breeding colonies in the lakes of Kings County. Mr. Watson L. Bishop (1888) reported several sets taken on May 22 and May 25:

These were collected on rocks and small islands in the Gaspereaux Lake, where quite a number of these birds breed every year. It is about 18 miles from salt water.

There is also said to be a colony of 50 or 100 black-backed gulls nesting on rocky islets in Methol Lake in this county. The largest colony seems to be the well-known colony in Lake George, on which Mr. Howard H. Cleaves has sent me the following interesting notes:

In 1912 there were from 600 to 800 adult great black-backed gulls in the breeding colony at Lake George, Yarmouth County, Nova Scotia. At that time the birds were confined to two islands near the northern end of the lake, but Mr. Harrison F. Lewis observed that the colony had increased in 1913 and 1914 so that in the latter year the birds were occupying four or five islands. The writer and Mr. G. K. Noble spent the period from July 21 to 28, 1912, encamped on an island within a quarter of a mile of the gull islands, visiting the latter daily, when weather conditions permitted, for the purpose of photographing and otherwise studying the birds. The islands selected by the gulls were not large, each comprising probably between two and three acres. They were bordered with glacial bowlders of varying sizes, upon which the young and old habitually stood or squatted. The highest portions of the islands were not more than 8 or 10 feet above the level of the lake. The topsoil, evidently not deep, supported thick growths of weeds and bushes, chief among the latter being alders and raspberry. There were a few spruces, but these were small and scattering, and there were also several open areas of coarse turf. The lateness of the season at the time of our visit accounted for the finding of only one nest with eggs (three in number), but there were enough empty nests to justify the belief that all the adult birds present had bred, which would mean an aggregate of 300 or 400 nests.

The birds had used a diversity of sites, some being on rocky peninsulas, others on the turf back from the shore, and many among bowlders or beside stumps a short way from the water line. All seemed to have been situated with a view to affording the owners a clear outlook, it being noted that apparently no birds had selected locations beneath the canopy of the thicket or under the low, spreading branches of spruces.

Eggs.—The great black-backed gull lays usually three eggs, but sometimes only two. The ground color varies from " pale olive buff " to " wood brown," " buffy brown," or " Isabella color," with a tendency in some specimens toward " tawny olive " or " cinnamon." They are more or less heavily spotted or blotched with various shades of brown, varying from " Brussels brown " to " clove brown," and are often more or less spotted or clouded with pale lilac, drab, or lavender gray. The measurements of 59 eggs, in various collections, average 77.9 by 54.2 millimeters; the eggs showing the four extreme measure **86.5** by 54.5, 79 by **57.5, 73** by 53, and 73.5 by **51** millimeters.

Young.—The period of incubation is said to be 26 days. Both sexes incubate and assist in the care of the young. The young remain in the nest for a day or two, but are soon able to crawl out and run about. They spend much of their time hiding in the grass, in crevices between stones, among the underbrush, or anywhere that they can find a little shelter, where they probably sleep most of the time; but when disturbed they can run with surprising swiftness. I have had to exert myself to the utmost to catch one of the larger young, whose long legs could carry it about as fast as I could run. They are fed by their parents on soft, semidigested food at first, but gradually they are trained to accept more solid food. Mr. Cleaves has sent me the following notes on the feeding process:

Young of all ages spent much energy in beseeching their parents for food, and the old birds often displayed a discouraging apathy toward their young at such times, even taking to flight or swimming away from the shore to escape the entreaties of their progeny. The older youngsters would sometimes swim after their parents in their eagerness for rations. In begging for a meal it was usual for a young gull to utter a whining cry and to run his bill along the neck or body of his parent. Not infrequently two or three young were thus besieging one old bird simultaneously.

In delivering food to her young the old gull first threw her head forward and downward (with a deliberation of movement which must have been painful to the waiting babies), then opened her spacious mouth and began a series of contortions with her neck muscles. The youngsters, being well aware by now of the imminent, centered attention on the flat stones in front of their mother, where the disgorged dainties presently appeared. Both parents were observed to feed the young. Immediately after delivering a meal the old birds sometimes stood by until the young were well underway with it—this so far as we could see, being for the purpose of keeping off neighbors, either young or old, who might be inclined to piracy. On one occasion an old bird chased into the water a half-grown youngster belonging to another pair, and, with her blows at the back of his head with her beak, might have murdered him had he not been able, by the use of both his wings and feet, to make the beach and scramble into the brush. A violent encounter lasting many seconds also took place between two adult birds, the striking of their beaks and the thrashing of their giant wings against the alders creating a commotion such as might do credit to a bull moose. It could not be determined whether the origin of these differences was a matter of food or trespass.

Plumages.—The downy young is mainly " pale olive gray," paler on the head and flanks and white on the central breast portion. The head is distinctly marked with well-defined spots, of various sizes and shapes, of " fuscous black "; the back is indistinctly spotted or variegated with " fuscous " and the wings are more heavily marked with an intermediate shade of " fuscous." The lower parts are unmarked. By the time that the young bird is half grown it is nearly fledged in its juvenal plumage, which appears first on the scapulars, wings, breast, and back, in about the order named. The dorsal feathers of this plumage are dusky, broadly tipped or margined with " avellaneous " or " vinaceous buff." This color pattern, which varies considerably in different feathers, is more pronounced in the scapulars and wing coverts than elsewhere. The color patterns in the different feathers vary from a solid dusky center, with broad buffy edges, to a herring-bone pattern, showing a dusky central streak with lateral processes, or to heavy transverse barring. The underparts are also variegated with dusky and " vinaceous buff " or " tilleul buff." The change from the juvenal to the first winter plumage is not well marked, as it is very gradual and is accomplished with a limited amount of molt. The buffy edgings on the dorsal surface fade and wear away during the winter until they become practically white before spring, when the back appears to be transversely barred with dusky and white. The head, which was heavily streaked with dusky in the fall, and the underparts also become much whiter before spring. In this first-year plumage the primaries are wholly black, with only the narrowest suggestion of white tips on the innermost; the secondaries and tertials are dusky and more or less broadly edged with buffy white; the greater coverts are somewhat variegated; and the lesser coverts are like the back. The tail is basally white, much mottled or variegated with " fuscous " or " fuscous black," with a broad subterminal band of " fuscous black." This band is broadest and the mottling is thickest on the central rectices, decreasing outwardly, so that the outer feather has only a large subterminal spot and a few dusky markings. The bill is wholly dark.

The second-year plumage shows only a slight advance toward maturity, and is mainly characterized by the mixture of several different types of feathers in the back, scapulars, and wing coverts. Some of these are wholly " slate color " or " blackish slate," as in the adult; others are basally so colored and terminally barred, spotted, or variegated; still other new feathers are reproductions of those seen in the first year plumage. There is great individual variation in the amount of "slate color" assumed during this year, but probably it increases as the season advances. The wings are not strikingly different from those of the first year. There are more conspicuous white tips on the tertials, secondaries, and inner primaries, and the coverts contain more "slate color." The underparts are largely or wholly white, increasingly so toward spring. The bill is lighter near the base and has a light tip.

The third-year plumage shows about the same stage of advance toward maturity as the second year in the herring gull. The mantle is now more than half "blackish slate"; the wing-coverts, both greater and lesser, are still mottled with dusky and white, but there are many adult feathers among the mottled ones; the secondaries and tertials are as in the adult; the primaries are black, tipped with white, and the outer primary now has a broad subterminal white space an inch and a half long. The tail is white, more or less variegated with dusky near the tip. The underparts are pure white, and so is the head, except for a few dusky streaks on the hind neck, which disappear before spring. The bill still shows traces of dusky.

At the next postnuptial molt, when a little over 3 years old, some birds probably assume the adult plumage, with the pure white tail, the complete dark mantle and the broad white tips of the primaries, which in the first primary measures $2\frac{1}{2}$ inches. But probably a large majority of the birds still retain traces of immaturity in the primaries and the tail, which do not reach their full perfection until a year later; and apparently the white in the primaries increases a little at each succeeding molt until the maximum is reached.

Both adults and young have a complete postnuptial molt in August and September, and an incomplete prenuptial molt during the winter and early spring. The adult winter plumage differs from the nuptial only in having a few faint, narrow streaks of dusky on the hind neck, which are more conspicuous in the younger birds and less so in the older ones.

Food.—The great black-backed gull is a voracious feeder, omnivorous, and not at all fastidious. On or about its breeding grounds it feeds largely on the eggs of other birds, particularly sea birds, when it can find them unprotected, or upon the small young of such birds as are unable to defend them. Mr. M. A. Frazar (1887) describes its method of capturing young eiders as follows:

Two or three gulls will hover over a brood in the water, which, of course, confuses the mother duck and scatters the brood in all directions. Then, by following the ducklings after each dive, they would soon tire them out, and a skillfully directed blow at the base of the skull, which seldom missed its aim, would in an instant finish the business, and, before the unhappy duck would know which way to turn, its brood would be one less. On several occasions I have seen the mother duck drawn several feet in the air by clinging to the gull as it dove for its prey, and several times I have seen a venturesome "black-back" get knocked over with a charge of shot when he happened to get too interested in his pursuit and allow of my too close approach.

He writes in the same paper that some of these gulls partially devoured some cormorants which he had shot and allowed to drift on the water for a short time. It feeds largely on fish, but probably seldom succeeds in catching them itself. It does not object to carrion, and will gorge itself on the carcass of a dead whale or pick up anything that it can find in the way of animal food along the shore. While wintering on our coasts it does its part as a scavenger, feeding on floating garbage with other gulls.

Mr. Cleaves contributes the following notes on its feeding habits:

From remains discovered on the ground it was evident that the food of the birds consisted exclusively of fish and allied sea food. The greater portion of a large squid was once found where it had been abandoned, evidently by a fleeing youngster; and on another occasion we discovered a 10-inch mackerel that had been very little affected by the digestive juices of the old gull that had delivered it to her young. Lesser remains of fish were frequently found, and occasionally we came to bones where it would seem they had been disgorged in the shape of pellets. None of the food was secured in the fresh-water lake, but was obtained from the ocean, which lay more than 5 miles distant to the west. From early morning until late in the evening the old gulls were seen flying either toward the ocean or returning from it, their course being always the same. The birds traveled in companies of twos or threes, and while passing over the land barrier always sought an altitude which insured safety from any possible gunshot.

Behavior.—The soaring flight of the great black-backed gull is majestic and grand in the extreme. It has been well likened to the flight of an eagle, for the resemblance to the king of birds is certainly striking, as it floats in great circles high above its rocky home, the monarch of its tribe. When traveling its flight is slow and heavy, as might be expected in the largest of the gulls, but it is always strong, dignified, and protracted. Macgillivray (1852) writes:

Its flight is strong, ordinarily sedate, less wavering and buoyant than that of smaller species, but graceful, effective, and even majestic. There, running a few steps and flapping its long wings, it springs into the air, wheels to either side, ascends, and on outspread and beautifully curved pinions hies away to some distant place. In advancing against a strong breeze it sometimes proceeds straight forward, then shoots away in an oblique direction, now descends in a long curve so as almost to touch the water, then mounts on high. When it wheels about and sweeps down the wind its progress is extremly rapid. It walks with ease, using short steps, runs with considerable speed, and, like the other gulls, pats the sands or mud on the edge of the water with its feet. It generally rests standing on one foot, with its head drawn in; but in a dry place it often reposes by laying itself down.

Although usually silent elsewhere, it is a very noisy bird on its breeding grounds, indulging in a variety of loud, harsh cries or raven-like croaks. It has a long drawn-out scream—*keeaaw*—on a lower key than that of the herring gull. It also has a short, more quickly uttered note—*kow*, *kow*, *kow*—very much like the other gulls; also a high pitched *ki ki* and a hoarse laughing *ha*, *ha*, *ha*. Its courtship note is softer and more prolonged, sounding at times like *kowaat*, but varied and modulated in a most human manner. Mr. Cleaves describes some of the vocal performances as follows:

There were few moments of the day or night when absolute silence prevailed in the colony. The sounds produced by the birds were varied, both in form and in volume, and ranging from the baby whine of the downy young to the great bellow or trumpet of a giant adult black-back standing above the lake on a 6-foot bowlder. The calls intermediate between these two extremes were mostly variations of groans or kindred sounds, some of which were soft and to be heard only at short range. There were two cries, given perhaps with greater frequency than all others, which the writer can now recall with most distinctness. One was the mellow " kuk-kuk-kuk," uttered when the birds were disturbed and far aloft over the islands; the other, the inspiring trumpeting bellow, emitted when the gulls were unmolested, and usually when standing on some prominence or on the open shore. Each syllable of the latter cry sounded like " oo " in " loon," given slowly and with comparative softness at first, but repeated slightly more rapidly as the call proceeded and the syllables gaining volume until, at the end, when the sound had been uttered 8 to 14 times, the noise was tremendous at a range of only a few feet. The uproar caused by a chorus of 50 trumpeting gulls could no doubt be distinctly heard over the lake on an otherwise still morning at a range of a mile or more. In producing this bellowing call a bird usually began on the introductory notes with his head lowered, raising it as the call advanced, until, at the finish, his open bill pointed toward the zenith and his neck was inflated from the force of his " challenge."

Mr. Cleaves relates in his notes the following interesting incident:

One pair of old birds, who apparently had but a single chick of probably two weeks, engaged in a curious performance only 3 feet from the wall of the blind. Amid rumbling sounds and groanings from the parents and whining from the baby one of the old birds picked from the beach a dried fern leaf and waded slowly and with apparent gravity into the lake with it until he was belly deep in the water. He then stopped and thrust his bill and its contents beneath the surface, moving his head rather vigorously from side to side as he did so. The female (?) followed a few paces behind with empty beak, and when she was a little way from the shore she submerged her entire head, holding it below for two or three seconds. After withdrawing it she took a step or two forward (following the first bird) and then immersed her head again. Throughout the entire ceremony the youngster whined, apparently for food, and waded as far in the wake of his elders as he could, with comfort, in the choppy waves. The bird carrying the fern then came slowly back to shore where his burden was dropped without further formality. Some minutes later, however, the same bird picked up a cast primary from the beach and reenacted almost the exact ceremony through which he had gone with the dead fern, and the other members of the family repeated their parts of the act also. Whether all of this was mere play or whether it possessed a greater significance it would no doubt be difficult to determine.

Winter.—About the middle of August, or as soon as the young are able to fly and care for themselves, these gulls leave their breeding grounds and wander about or start to migrate southward. They sometimes appear on the Massachusetts coast in August, though not regularly until September, where they are more or less common all winter until the second or third week in April. Dr. Charles W. Townsend (1905) records them as common on the coast of Essex County, Massachusetts, from July 17 to May 1, and says, " as early as July 17, 1904, I found seven adults in a flock of herring gulls on Ipswich Beach," though these may have been summer stragglers and not migrants from their breeding grounds farther north. Their normal winter range extends from southern Greenland to Delaware, with straggling records farther south. While wintering on our coasts they associate freely with the herring gulls, with which they seem to be on good terms, feeding with them on what refuse they can pick up in our harbors or along the shores. They are practically silent and not nearly so tyrannical as on their breeding grounds, though they may occasionally be seen chasing the other gulls and robbing them of their food. Adult birds can, of course, be easily recognized and the superior size of the immature birds is distinctive. While roosting on a sand bar or on floating ice a black-backed gull always looms up large in a flock of herring gulls. They are exceedingly shy at this season, and it is useless to attempt to approach them in an open situation.

DISTRIBUTION.

Breeding range.—Coasts and islands of northeastern North America and northern Europe. In the Western Hemisphere, from North Devon Island and central western Greenland (Disco) southward, along both coasts of Labrador to eastern Quebec (Godbout), Anticosti Island, Newfoundland (Sandy Lake), Nova Scotia (Pictou, Halifax, and Kentville) and Bay of Fundy (Isle au Haute). In the Eastern Hemisphere, Iceland, Shetland, and Faroe Islands, Scotland, and northern Europe east to eastern Russia (Petchora River), and south to about 50° N.

Winter range.—Regularly on the coast of the United States from Maine to New Jersey. More rarely north to southern Greenland and south to northern Florida (St. Augustine) and Bermuda. Occasionally south to Ohio (Columbus) and west to Michigan (Detroit) on the Great Lakes. In Europe from Great Britain south to the Azores and Canary Islands, the Mediterranean, and the Black Sea.

Spring migration.—Early dates of arrival: Newfoundland, St. Johns, March 1; Labrador, Romaine, March 26, and Rigolet, April 9. Late dates of departure: New York, Long Island, May 13; Massachusetts, Boston, May 25, and Woods Hole, June 10. Nonbreeding birds linger on the coasts of New England late into or all through the summer.

Fall migration.—Early dates of arrival, excluding summer stragglers: Massachusetts, Woods Hole, September 24 (average October 8); Long Island, Orient, September 12 (average October 5). Late dates of departures: Greenland, Gothaab, September 3; eastern Labrador, November 2; Prince Edward Island, November 12; Nova Scotia, Pictou, December 13.

Casual records.—Accidental in Nebraska (Missouri River, May, 1871), Kerguelen Island (June 5, 1840), and Japan (Hakodadi).

Egg dates.—Quebec, Labrador: Twenty records, May 25 to June 28; ten records, June 5 to 15. Nova Scotia: Fifteen records, May 15 to June 13; eight records, May 22 to 27. Great Britain: Eleven records, April 28 to July 20; six records, May 20 to June 1. Iceland: Three records, May 18 and 28, and June 6.

LARUS SCHISTISAGUS Stejneger.

SLATY-BACKED GULL.

HABITS.

Dr. Leonhard Stejneger (1885) has demonstrated, by an exhaustive treatise on the subject, that this is a well-marked species, although one can not read his remarks without realizing how much confusion has arisen over the nomenclature and relationships of the Laridae. In both size and color it is intermediate between the great blackbacked gull and the western gull; but its best and most constant character is the color pattern of the primaries, which Doctor Stejneger has well described and illustrated. It is an Asiatic species, with its center of abundance in northeastern Siberia, which has established a slight foothold on some of the islands of Bering Sea and in northern Alaska, chiefly as a straggler. It may eventually become better established in Alaska, as several other Asiatic species have done.

Spring.—Doctor Stejneger (1885) first saw it on Bering Island, in the Commander Islands, but afterwards found it common near Petropaulski, Kamchatka. Mr. N. G. Buxton's notes, published by Dr.

J. A. Allen (1905), give the best life history of the species in that region. He writes:

This is the most conspicuous and one of the most abundant birds along the Okhotsk Sea. From the time of its arrival until it departs there is scarcely a time when one can not either hear or see one or more of these birds. The first arrivals are usually reported about the 20th of April, and from that time on they increase in numbers daily until May 1, when they have nearly all arrived. From the time of their arrival until the nesting season begins they make daily excursions up the rivers in the morning and return to their roosting places along the seacoast in the evening. They go up the Gichiga River at this time as far as Christova, 30 miles above its mouth. Also at this time many may be seen soaring in large circles high over the tundra and marsh above the mouth of the river, when they utter a cry very similar to that of the red-tailed hawk during the breeding season. None of the dark phase are seen among the earlier arrivals, but by the 15th of May they begin to appear, and increase in numbers until they have all arrived, although at no time during the spring and early summer do they form any considerable per cent of the thousands that one sees. Before the ice goes out of the head of the bay and river, their food supply is limited to the few dead salmon which the melting snow exposes on the gravel bars along the river beds and the mussels they pick from the rocks along the seacoast at low tide.

Nesting.—By the first of June all of the breeders have repaired to the rugged seacoast and rocky islets lying off it, below the mouth of the river, to breed. Only the roughest and most inaccessible places are chosen for nesting sites, generally at the headlands, where sections of the solid rocks have been partly or wholly separated from the mainland. The nests, which are loose, bulky structures, composed of grass and with but a slight depression in the center, are placed on ledges and the tops of rocks. Three eggs constitute a set, and they show the usual large variation in color and size found in the eggs of other species of *Larus*. The height of the nesting season is reached about June 10, when the koraks visit their rookeries and obtain large numbers of their eggs by being lowered down the cliffs with sealskin lines. Many more breeders spend the summer on the bars and along the marsh near the mouth of the river, and on the gravel bars along its bed.

Rev. W. F. Henninger (1910) refers to three sets of eggs of the slaty-backed gull, containing three, two, and one eggs, respectively, that were " taken on the coast of Siberia, near the Bering Strait, on June 4, 1905. The nest was a mere depression or hollow in some moss." There are two sets, of three eggs each, in Col. John E. Thayer's collection, taken by Capt. H. H. Bodfish in Harrowby Bay, on the Arctic coast of northwestern Canada, June 11, 1901. The nests are described as made of grass, roots, and mud and lined with dry grass; they were placed on a point making into the bay. The parent birds were collected and the skins were identified by Mr. Robert Ridgway and Dr. A. K. Fisher. These are probably authentic sets, though they were taken outside of the previously known breeding range of the species.

Eggs.—These two sets might easily be matched with eggs of some of the commoner species of *Larus*. The shape is practically ovate and the ground color is " Isabella color." They are more or less evenly covered with small spots of " clove brown," " blackish brown," " sepia," and " bister," as well as several shades of " brownish drab."

Two eggs in the writer's collection, from the Asiatic coast, show other extremes of coloration. The darker one has a ground color of " Saccardo's umber " and is spotted with " blackish brown " and " brownish drab;" the lighter one has a " deep olive-buff " ground color and is spotted with " snuff brown," " bister," and several shades of " brownish drab," some very light and some very dark shades. The measurements of 34 eggs, in various collections, average 74 by 51.5 millimeters; the eggs showing the four extremes measure 81 by 52, 77 by 54, 67.1 by 50 and 72 by 48 millimeters.

Plumages.—I have never seen the downy young of this species, nor can I find any description of it in print. The sequence of molts and plumages, so far as can be learned from the limited amount of material available for study, is practically the same as in the great black-backed gull. Young birds during the first fall and winter are darker than those of the commoner species, particularly on the underparts, which are nearly uniform dusky.

Behavior.—For the remainder of the life history of this little-known species I must again quote from Mr. Buxton's notes, as follows:

After the nesting season is over, about the 1st of August, the breeders and young of the year join the nonbreeders and they all spend the rest of the season in flying up and down the river, collecting in large flocks along the water front, and gorging themselves on the worn-out salmon that they find there. At this time they begin to fly up the river at 2 or 3 o'clock in the morning, continuing to fly until the middle of the forenoon, and then begin the return flight at 5 p. m., and continue to fly until long after dark, which does not occur at that time until 10 or 11 p. m. They are so abundant that on these flights there is one continuous long, loose flock of them without any considerable break or intermission. The height of the return flight is from 6 to 8 p. m. When the wind is strong they fly high, but when it is calm they fly low and are easily attracted. When one is killed on the wing, or a decoy is thrown into the air, all the gulls in the vicinity will immediately " land about " and circle once or twice over the dead bird or decoy, changing their usual guttural cackle to hoarse " squeals " of alarm before proceeding on their way. I have often seen them attempt to take a fish from the mouth of a seal when it arose to the surface and which the gull had been watching catch the fish. By the last of August one dark or young one is seen to every four or five adult or white ones, and later the proportion of the dark ones is much higher, as the adults begin to leave first. By the 1st of October the migration is well advanced, and decreases daily until by the 15th of October few remain, although the last of them do not leave until the last week of the month. They are the last of the migrants to leave in the fall.

Breeding range.—Asiatic coasts of North Pacific and Bering Sea; from northern Japan (Yezzo), Kurile Islands, Kamchatka, and shores of Sea of Okhotsk north to Gulf of Anadyr and vicinity of Bering Straits. The breeding record from Harrowby Bay, Arctic coast of Canada, appears to be authentic, although far outside of the known breeding range.

Winter range.—So far as known, only from Japan to the Kurile Islands.

Spring migration.—Migrants recorded at Commander Islands, Bering Island, April 20 to May 5; Copper Island, June 13; Sakhalin Island, May 11. They arrive on their breeding grounds in the Anadyr district by April 20.

Fall migration.—During migration birds occur along the Alaskan coast, Diomede Islands, September; off Nome, August 31 to September 8; St. Michael, September 9; Port Clarence, Sakhalin Island, late September. The last birds leave the Anadyr district late in October.

Casual records.—Stragglers have been recorded at Herald Island (Ridgway), Unalaska (Chernofsky Bay, October 1, 1880), and taken in Mackenzie (Franklin Bay, June 9, 1901).

Egg dates.—Japan: Eight records, May 23 to June 18; four records, May 29 to June 15.

LARUS OCCIDENTALIS Audubon.

WESTERN GULL.

HABITS.

Along the numerous beaches of the California coast the dark-mantled western gull is the most conspicuous and the most universally abundant sea bird throughout the whole year, everywhere much in evidence and everywhere tame and familiar—a welcome visitor as a useful scavenger and a pretty feature in the seashore scenery. The immaculate purity of its snow-white plumage is kept spotlessly clean, in spite of its untidy feeding habits. As we see these beautiful black and white birds sailing along the ocean cliffs they seem to reflect the clear freshness of the beach and sea and sky; and as we see them walking daintily on their long legs over the clean sand it seems incongruous to associate them with the struggling screaming mob of hungry birds that we have just seen fighting for and gorging themselves on the refuse from the sewers or the garbage dumps.

During my stay at Redondo Beach, in June, I spent considerable time watching these interesting and familiar birds. There were always plenty of them to be seen flying along the beach or resting in groups on the flat, smooth sand, adults and young in several different stages of plumage, and generally a few Heermann's gulls were mingled with them. It was in the height of the breeding season and I wondered whether the adults had nests on the islands off the coast or were birds that were not breeding that season. Some of them were standing on one leg, with bills tucked under their scapulars, sound asleep; but more of them were resting on their breasts. One old male seemed to be the boss of the beach and acted as a disturber of the peace by walking around, driving off the Heermann's gulls and waking up all the gulls that were asleep, making them move on, as a policeman does with loafers on a sidewalk. One was seen playing with a feather, picking it up, letting it blow away and running after it again, as if he enjoyed the fun. Occasionally one would walk down to the surf line to pick up a morsel of food, to drink or to bathe, and return to dry land to preen its feathers. They were tamer than any large gulls I had ever seen. I had no difficulty in shooting them, picking out the exact plumage that I wanted to complete my series. As soon as one was shot a flock gathered about me, hovering over my head with intimate curiosity; and while walking along the beach with dead gulls in my hand there were always several following me, close at hand. Even about the much-frequented wharves they were very unsuspicious, standing on the posts and railings within 10 or 15 feet of numerous human beings, in whom they justly had perfect confidence, for they are never molested. About the fish houses, where men were cleaning fish, they were particularly familiar, standing in rows along the roofs, or on the stringers waiting for the offal to be thrown into the water. No one seemed to notice them at all, but to me it was a novel and interesting sight.

There was a time when persistent egging on the Farallones was reducing the population of western gulls, but since that has been stopped they are increasing again. They are probably not much disturbed on their breeding grounds and are generally protected. Hence they have become familiar and useful birds on the coast, but they are more of a nuisance than ever on the islands where they do so much damage to other species.

Spring.—As this gull is practically a resident throughout its range, it has no well-marked migration. The spring migration merely amounts to a concentration on its breeding grounds or a withdrawal, and only a partial one at that, from its somewhat wider winter range. In the southern portion of its breeding range in Lower California this occurs early in March, in southern California in April, and correspondingly later farther north. It retreats in the spring from the Puget Sound region to the northern limit of its breeding range in the bird reservations on the coast of Washington, where it mingles with the glaucous-winged gull at the southern limit of the latter's breeding range.

Nesting.—Dawson (1909) says that the northernmost colony of unmixed *occidentalis* on the Washington coast is on Willoughby Rock, off Cape Elizabeth; "but scattered pairs occur, along with glaucous wings, as far up as Carroll Islet." He says of its nesting habits:

Nesting is undertaken in May, and by the 20th of that month, or by June 10 at the latest, the complement of three eggs is laid. Nests are composed almost exclusively of dried grasses plucked by the birds, roots and all; and these become quite substantial structures if the grass is convenient. Ledges, crannies, grassy hill sides, and the exposed summits of the rocks are alike utilized for nesting sites; while occasionally a bird ventures down so close to the tide line as to lose her eggs in time of storm. Chicks are brought off by the third week in June or by the 1st of July, according to season, if unmolested. If the first set is removed, however, the birds will prepare a second, consisting almost invariably of two eggs, and these are deposited as likely as not in the same nest as the former set. Deposition occurs at intervals of two or three days.

On the Three Arch Rocks, Oregon, Mr. W. L. Finley (1905) describes the nesting of this species as follows:

The gull picks out a comfortable spot and builds a respectable nest, and that is about the only creditable thing he does on the rock. The grass-covered roof of the island is his favorite nesting place, although many select the niches in the bare rock on the face of the cliff. The gull's eggs lie right out in the open and never seem to be bothered by other birds; they themselves do not ravage the homes of their own kindred. The eggs are of dull earthy and chocolate-brown tints, with darker blotches, matching their surroundings so perfectly that we had to be constantly on the lookout to keep from stepping on them. When the eggs were hatched we found the nestlings were protected by equally deceptive clothes of a mottled gray color.

The best known breeding grounds of the species are on the Farallon Islands, which have been well described by several writers. According to Mr. W. Otto Emerson, who sent some original notes on the subject to Major Bendire, the gulls begin building or repairing their old nests about May 1, and the nesting season is prolonged through May and June. The nests are built wholly of dry Farallon weed, *Baeria maritima*, the old nests being used year after year. After being robbed the birds soon begin laying again, and he noted, by watching a certain nest, that an egg was laid every other day.

Mr. Milton S. Ray (1904) has given us the following good account of the Farallon colonies:

While this bird builds in colonies, so to speak, they are not like those of the cormorant or murre. There is always fighting room between the nests, and only the aggregations near Shell Beach, Indian Head, and at Guano Slope on West End, and about Tower Point on East End, could well deserve this term.

Besides these places we found them breeding in scattered congregations all along the rocky terrace west of the Jordan, from the shore to the highest points. On the east, in addition to the rookery at Tower Point, we observed a dozen isolated nests at Bull Head Point, near Arch Rock, and about half that number right at the Weather Bureau observatory, where, rewarded for their confidence in man, they brooded unmolested. The great mass of driftwood, thrown up by winter storms, was a favorite spot in the Shell Beach rookery. We did not, however, observe any of these birds nesting off the main island.

While they are somewhat wary, many allowed us to come quite close before rising from their nests. The latter are placed in natural basinlike hollows among the rocks, by which they are partially sheltered, although some were in the most open and windy situations. The nest is a bulky structure, composed of various dry island weeds and grasses, and has about as much claim to ingenuity as those of most sea birds. They vary little in size, averaging 13 inches across, the cavity being 8 inches by 4 deep. About many of them I noticed small heaps of ejected fishbones.

Mr. Brewster (1902) says of the nesting habits of this species in the Cape Region of Lower California:

Mr. Frazar found a breeding colony of about 25 pairs on a small rocky island a little to the westward of Carmen Island. Most of the nests were only just begun, and but two contained eggs, one set, however, comprising the full complement of three. This was on March 13—a date about two months earlier than that at which the first eggs are usually taken on the Farallon Islands near San Francisco. The next day another breeding ground was discovered on the northern end of the island of Montserrat. Here some 50 pairs had congregated. Few of their nests were finished and only eight contained eggs, the number in each set varying from one to three. At both of the places just mentioned the nests, which were made of seaweed, were built at the foot of the cliffs, just above high-water mark, and often in nooks or crevices.

Although the nest may be frequently robbed and several sets of eggs may be laid, only one brood of young is raised in a season. The normal set consists of three eggs, though two eggs often constitute a full set in the later layings, and sometimes a single egg is incubated. Sets of four eggs are rare.

Eggs.—The eggs of the western gull can not be distinguished with certainty from those of other gulls of similar size, and they are subject to the usual variations. The ground color is " buffy brown," " tawny olive," " cinnamon buff," " deep olive buff," or " pale olive buff." They are usually heavily spotted, blotched, or scrawled, more or less evenly, with " clove brown," " bister," " burnt umber," and various lighter shades of brown, as well as various shades of " Quaker drab " and " mouse gray." The measurements of 70 eggs, in various collections, average 72.4 by 50.4 millimeters; the eggs showing the four extremes measure **78** by 47, 73 by **53, 67.5** by 48 and 78 by **47** millimeters.

Young.—Mr. Emerson gives the period of incubation as 24 days. He says that both sexes take turns at the duties of incubation, but there are no set times for relieving each other. The bird which is off duty usually stands near the nest, on guard, slipping onto the nest when the sitting bird leaves. The young remain in the nest for a few days and are brooded by their parents, who are very bold and devoted in their defense. The young gulls soon learn to run about, becoming very lively, and are taught by their parents to become experts in the art of hiding. Mr. Finley (1905) says:

They teach their young to keep hidden and to lie close. I have seen more than one gull impress this upon her children. One day I was walking along a ledge and came abruptly to a place where I could look down the top slope. Below me a few yards I saw two half-grown gulls; one crouched beside a rock, but the other started to run down the ridge He hadn't gone 2 yards before the mother dove at him with a blow that knocked him rolling. He got up dazed and struck off in a new direction, but she swooped again and rapped him on the head till he seemed glad enough to crawl in under the nearest weed.

Occasionally we found the gulls very pugnacious. There was one mother that had a nest of three young birds on a narrow ledge, and every time the photographer approached her nest she would dart at him. She swooped at his head with a loud bark, something like a watchdog; at 6 or 8 feet distant she dropped her legs and took a sharp clip with her feet. Twice she knocked the hat from the intruder's head.

Mr. Dawson (1909) visited a colony of this species in July and found that:

Young birds, from infants to those half grown, were in hiding everywhere. The danger sign had, of course, been passed around, and not a youngster on the island but froze in his tracks, no matter where he happened to be. It was pathetic to find, as I did now and then, babes soaking heroically in the filthy green pools left in hollows of the rocks by ancient rains rather than attract attention by scrambling out. One youngster had evidently been nibbling playfully at a bit of driftwood cast high up, for I found him with the stick between his mandibles as motionless as a Pompeian mummy.

So bold and solicitous were the anxious mothers in the defense of their young that he was struck three times upon the head, always from behind, by vicious beaks while engaged in gathering up babies for a picture.

The young gulls are fed at first on semidigested foods, but their parents soon begin to feed them on small fish and other animal food. They become more omnivorous in their diet as they grow older, and are very voracious feeders. Their parents keep watchful guard over them until they are able to fly and will not let them attempt this hazardous feat until the proper time comes. Mr. A. B. Howell has noted that "if when full grown but still timid on their wings, they are thrown into the air, they will essay unsteady flight and are sure to be pounced upon by their elders, who, for some reason or other, knock the youngsters heels over head as long as they remain in the air "—a decided hint that the time for flight has not arrived.

Plumages.—The downy young is "drab gray" above variegated with "avellaneous" or other shades of buff. Some individuals are grayer and others are brighter buff in color. The lower parts are lighter colored, paling to "tilleul buff" on the center of the breast; sometimes the breast is bright, clear, "avellaneous" buff in newly hatched young, the colors fading as the youngster grows. The back is heavily spotted with "fuscous black," and the head and throat with pure black.

By the time that it is fully grown, at an age of about 2 months, the young bird has assumed its juvenal or first real plumage, in which it is heavily mottled above with "hair brown" and pale "avellaneous"; the feathers of the lower back and the scapulars are "clove brown" centrally, broadly edged with "avellaneous" or "wood brown"; the cheeks are plain "hair brown"; and the crown is "hair brown" streaked with "light buff." This plumage is worn but a short time and is replaced in the fall by the first winter plumage, which is acquired by a partial molt, involving part, or perhaps all, of the contour feathers, but not the wings and tail. I am inclined to think that part of this change is effected by wear and fading of the brown edgings.

The first winter plumage, deep blackish brown, mottled with grayish white, with the uniform dark primaries and rectrices, and with the bill wholly dusky, is worn throughout the first year or until the first postnuptial molt, when the bird is about 13 or 14 months old. A complete molt then occurs, at which time the slaty blue mantle is, at least partially, acquired, and the bill becomes yellow on the basal half. The new primaries are still wholly black and the tail wholly black or mottled with white near the base. The contour feathers or head and underparts are still mottled with dusky, but become lighter during the year by wear and fading. There is much brown still remaining in the wing-coverts. During the second spring there is a steady advance toward maturity, with great individual variation, the molt beginning as early as April in some cases. At this second postnuptial molt, which is complete, the wings of the adult, with black primaries tipped with white, are acquired, but there is sometimes more or less brown in the wing coverts; the tail becomes white with a subterminal black bar; the white body plumage appears, though it is much clouded with dusky in the fall; and the bill still remains dark at the tip. The fully adult plumage seems to be acquired perhaps a year later, when the bird is 3 years of age; this, of course, is characterized by the pure white tail and the yellow bill. Some birds, otherwise adult, during the fourth winter, have more or less dusky mottling in the tail, and some lack the subapical white spot, or have only a small one, on the outer primary. As these birds and those with the black-banded tail and brown wing coverts are comparatively rare, it may be that these are merely backward or less vigorous birds, and that normally vigorous birds acquire their fully adult plumage when 3 years old. I am inclined to think that this is so, but, as I am not sure of it, I have given what seem to be the facts in the case. The seasonal molts of the adult consist of a complete postnuptial molt in the summer and a partial molt about the head and neck in the spring. In spite of statements in some of the books to the contrary, adults have the heads streaked with dusky in the fall, which markings disappear by wear or fading, or perhaps by molt, before spring.

Food.—Before the encroachments of civilization gave the western gull an easy way of earning its living as a scavenger, its principal food supply was gleaned from the sea; it followed the schools of small fish in flocks, hovering, screaming, and struggling for its prey in strenuous competition. When its appetite was satisfied a game of tag sometimes ensued, such as Mr. J. H. Bowles (1909) described as follows:

One catches a herring, and instead of eating it flies with the fish hanging from its bill, past three or four comrades. These accept the challenge and rush madly after, while the pursued goes through all sorts of evolutions in seeking to elude them. If overtaken, the order of chase is reversed, and the game goes merrily on until all are tired. The fish, or tag trophy, is not eaten but is dropped upon the playground in a condition decidedly the worse for wear.

Although fish still form a large part of its food, especially about its breeding grounds, it is primarily a scavenger, like the other large gulls, and has learned to frequent harbors and populated shores, where it can easily gorge itself on the garbage dumping grounds, pick up unsavory morsels at the outlets of sewers, and feed on whatever refuse it can find scattered along the beaches. It also follows vessels to pick up whatever scraps of food are thrown overboard. It feeds at low tide on the sand flats, mud banks, river shores, and mussel beds, where it finds dead fish, clams, seaworms, dead rats, or any kind of fresh animal food or carrion. It understands how to break the shells of a clam or a sea urchin by flying up into the air with it and dropping it on hard ground or on a rock, sometimes making several attempts before succeeding.

Mr. Walter E. Bryant (1888) says of its feeding habits:

The gulls are indiscriminate feeders; in addition to their usual articles of diet, they subsist largely upon eggs during the summer. They do not eat the eggs of their own species, nor do they trouble the cormorants after the murres have commenced laying. Sea-urchins, crabs, young murres, and rabbits, and fish stolen from the cormorants' nests are eaten. Not being quick enough to swoop upon the rabbits they catch them by patient watching at their burrows, and will patiently try for 15 minutes to swallow a squealing young rabbit, and finally fly away with the hind feet protruding. The dead bodies of murres are also eaten; they detach pieces of flesh by backing away and dragging the body, meanwhile shaking their heads, till a piece breaks off.

Perhaps the most important food supply of the western gull on its breeding grounds consists of the eggs of other birds, near which it almost always nests. The sagacity displayed by the gulls in taking advantage of the human egg hunters is well described by Dr. A. L. Heermann (1859) as follows:

At 1 o'clock every day, during the egg season, Sundays and Thursdays excepted (this is to give the birds some little respite), the egg hunters meet on the south side of the island. The roll is called to see that all are present, that each one may have an equal chance in gathering the spoil. The signal is given, every man starting off at a full run for the most productive egging grounds. The gulls understanding, apparently, what is about to occur, are on the alert, hovering overhead and awaiting only the advance of the party. The men rush eagerly into the rookeries; the affrighted murres have scarcely risen from their nests before the gull, with remarkable instinct, not to say almost reason, flying but a few paces ahead of the hunter, alights on the ground, tapping such eggs as the short time will allow before the egger comes up with him. The broken eggs are passed by the men, who remove only those which are sound. The gull then returning to the field of its exploits, procures a plentiful supply of its favorite food.

I have repeatedly seen this gull drink salt water, and I believe that all ocean gulls do so, though I have heard it stated that they prefer fresh water. They do not, however, like their food too salt, as the following instance, related by Mr. A. W. Anthony (1906) will illustrate:

I was one day watching some western gulls, a few yards from me on a wharf, when a large piece of salted fish was thrown out from an adjacent boathouse. It fairly glistened with a thick incrustation of salt, and I was somewhat curious to see if the gulls would eat food so highly seasoned. No sooner had it fallen than it was seized upon by a gull and as quickly swallowed; but from the surprised actions of the bird it was evidently not to his liking; no sooner had it reached the stomach than it was ordered out again. Dropping the fish on the wharf the bird eyed it for a moment, turning its head from side to side, and, to judge from its soliloquy, made a number of uncomplimentary remarks on the depraved tastes of mankind that would spoil good fish in that manner. Then picking up the fish it flew down to the water, and holding it under the surface shook its head from side to side violently "sozzeling" the meat about for several seconds. It was then taken back to the wharf, laid down and inspected, and carefully sampled; this time, however, it was not bolted as at first, but held for a moment in the mouth and again rejected, and carried back to the water, where it was even more roughly laundered. This operation was repeated several times; and the piece of fish, which must have weighted 4 ounces at the outset, was reduced to half that size before it reached a state of freshness that suited the palate of the gull.

Behavior.—The flight of the western gull is not unlike that of other closely related species; it has the same power of sailing directly into the wind, or within a few points of it, on motionless wings. I have seen it travel for long distances in this manner without any apparent effort. It also has the same soaring habits as other large gulls, rising to great heights and circling about on outstretched pinions, as if enjoying the exercise. While soaring it occasionally preens the feathers of its breast with its bill or raises one foot to scratch its head, without losing its poise. Once, while sailing before a strong wind, almost a gale, a lot of these gulls were following us to pick scraps of food which we were throwing overboard; it was necessary for them to face the wind and drift along tail foremost, so as to keep pace with our boat; they were not sailing or drifting, but were maintaining their positions by constant flapping and were apparently flying backwards. While flying the feet are extended backwards and buried in the plumage, but when about to alight they are dropped and spread. A sudden descent from a considerable height is quickly accomplished by a spiral or a zigzag glide, on half extended wings, with frequent quick tipping from side to side.

The cries and call notes of this gull are much like those of other species. Mr. Charles A. Keeler (1892) has given a good description of them, as follows:

Their most common note may be expressed by the syllables *quock kuck kuck kuck*, uttered very rapidly in a low, guttural tone. Sometimes it was varied thus *kuck kuck kuck ka*, the quality of tone being the same as in the first instance. Frequently a higher cry would be heard, which may be indicated by the letters *ki aa*, with a strong accent on the first syllable. Again, one would utter a rattling, guttural cry, which sounded like a man being throttled.

The behavior of western gulls toward their neighbors is truly scandalous. They must be cordially hated and seriously dreaded by the various species among which they nest, for they are arrant thieves, ever on the alert to improve every opportunity to steal and devour any unprotected eggs or young which they can find. They usually select a breeding place among nesting colonies of cormorants, murres, or pelicans, chiefly because they can there find an abundant food supply in the nests of their peaceful neighbors. Cormorants, being rather shy, are easily driven from their nests by human intruders and do not readily return, so that the gulls often succeed in cleaning out a whole colony. Eternal vigilance is the price of success in rearing a brood with such rogues roaming about and looking for the slightest chance. The cormorants and pelicans have to sit on their eggs constantly from the day they are laid, or the gulls will get them. This will account for the fact that the young in the nests of these species are often of widely differently ages. Even the young have to be constantly brooded, for the gulls will swallow the smallest young whole and mutilate or beat to death the larger ones. Mr. A. W. Anthony (1906) has graphically described this perforance as follows:

The advent of man in the region of a cormorant rookery is hailed with delight by every gull on the island, but to the poor cormorant it is a calamity of the darkest hue. As the frightened birds leave the nests, which have so far never been for a moment left without the protection of at least one of the parents, the screaming gulls descend in swarms to break and eat the eggs or kill the young, as the case may be. Small cormorants are bolted entire, despite their somewhat half-hearted protest; larger birds are dismembered by two gulls assisting in the operation, after the well-known manner of barnyard chicks with a worm; and before the adult cormorants have recovered from their fright and returned to protect their homes a colony of several hundred nests will be almost destroyed. I have found young western gulls feasting on cormorant squabs half a mile or more from the nests from which they had been abducted.

Mr. A. B. Howell writes:

These robbers are surely the pest of their range during the spring months. When the pelicans and cormorants are flushed from their nests, down comes a devastating army of the marauders, spearing the eggs with their bills and neatly devouring them on the wing, pecking holes in the skulls of the young pelicans for the fun of it, and bolting the shiny cormorant chicks with a great gulping and show of satisfaction. A favorite pastime of theirs is to pester a half grown pelican until the latter relinquishes his last meal as a peace offering, and this the gulls greedily fight over. The gulls themselves have few enemies, except man, and now that egging has been practically stopped they are free to increase and flourish.

Winter.—After the breeding season is over and the young gulls have become strong on the wing, they begin to scatter and spread out all along the coast, extending the winter range of the species northward to Puget Sound, where it is one of the common winter gulls. They are given to wandering at this season, following the vessels up and down the coast, chasing schools of fish, feasting on the garbage dumps, roosting on the islands at night, and associating freely with other species of gulls, cormorants, pelicans, and other sea birds.

DISTRIBUTION.

Breeding range.—Pacific coast of North America, from British Columbia and Washington (various islands off the coast) southward along the coasts of Oregon, California, and Lower California, on nearly all suitable islands, at least as far as Cerros and Guadalupe Islands; also in the Gulf of California (San Pedro Martir, Ildefonso and Carmen Islands).

Breeding grounds protected in the following national reservations: In California, Farallon Islands; in Oregon, Three Arch Rocks; in Washington, Copalis Rock and Quillayute Needles, as Carroll Islet.

Winter range.—Practically resident throughout its breeding range. North in winter to British Columbia and south to southwestern Mexico (Isabella and Tres Marias Islands, Tepic).

Egg dates.—Farallon Islands: Fifty-five records, May 12 to July 10; twenty-eight records, June 3 to 24. Coronados Islands: Ten records, May 6 to June 30; five records, May 11 to June 4. Washington: Seven records, June 3 to July 12; four records, June 3 to 14. Gulf of California: Three records, April 5, 6, and 7.

LARUS FUSCUS AFFINIS Reinhardt.

LARUS FUSCUS AFFINIS Reinhardt.

BRITISH LESSER BLACK-BACKED GULL.

HABITS.

The Siberian gull is no longer entitled to a place on our list, which it has held ever since the type specimen of *Larus affinis* was taken in Greenland and described by Reinhardt. The lesser black-backed gull of Europe and Asia has been subdivided into three subspecies— *Larus fuscus fuscus* Linnaeus of northern Europe, Scandinavia, etc.; *Larus fuscus affinis* Reinhardt of the British Isles, Faroes, and Greenland; and *Larus fuscus antelius* Iredale of Siberia. Reinhardt's bird, the type of *Larus affinis* and the bird which occurs as a straggler in Greenland was, until recently, supposed to be of the Siberian form. But Iredale has recently examined Reinhardt's type specimen and found it to be referable to the British form, the well-known lesser black-backed gull. He therefore gave a new name to the Siberian form, which necessitated the above rearrangement of the group, and makes it necessary for us to eliminate the Siberian gull from our list and enter in place of it the British lesser black-backed gull (*Larus fuscus affinis* Reinhardt).

Nesting.—This well-known gull occurs in Great Britain, both as migrant and as a resident, throughout the year. Much has been written about its habits. Dr. Henry O. Forbes (1898) writes of its breeding habits:

In May the lesser black-backed gulls select their nesting place, betaking themselves, as Macgillivray states, " to unfrequented islands, headlands, and sometimes inland lakes (and mosses), often in considerable numbers, and there remain until their young are able to fly, although they make extensive excursions around in search of food." On the Teifi Bog, in mid-Wales, about 12 miles from the sea, the nests are placed " on slight hillocks, generally in deep heather, the vicinity, with trampled grass and scattered feathers, being suggestive of a goose green " (Salter). " In Hoy (in the Orkneys) anyone," writes Mr. Moodie-Heddle to Harvie-Brown, " can create a breeding place of the lesser black-backed gull by burning a large tract late in the season; the gulls then come on the bare ground (through the following summer and autumn) to catch moths and winged insects, which have no heather left to go down into. They then usually begin to breed on the tufts of white moss left unburnt the following season. The breeding places by the water of Hoy and down to Pegal Burn were thus formed by accidental fires. No gulls bred there for many years before, and we could kill 60 to 70 brace more grouse.

In Iona, Mr. Graham notes that this gull made its nest on the flat, marshy summits of all the lesser islands. The nest is sometimes on the bare rock, but more often on a grassy slope, if such exist near. The most remarkable situation for a nest, perhaps, is that cited by Doctor Sharpe, which was placed in the middle of a sheep track, and the sheep, in passing to and fro, had to jump over the back of the sitting bird. This nest (with its four eggs) is now in the British Museum.

This species breeds in colonies, which in some places are very large, when their nests are placed so close to each other, that it is by no means easy to traverse their nursery without treading upon either the eggs or young. The nest, if on the ground, is little more than a scraped out hollow in the ground, lined with grass, seaweed, or herbage of any kind within reach; if on a rock, a larger pile of the same substances is built up in the selected niche or ledge. It is not at all uncommon to find the herring gull nesting in close proximity to it, only, however, in the more inaccessible ledges or summits. Three eggs are laid as a rule—four occasionally, sometimes only two—which vary very greatly in size, shape, and color. Many of them are hardly, if ever certainly, to be distinguished from those of the herring gull. They vary in size from 2⅝ to 3 inches in length, by 1⅗ to 2 in diameter. Ground color, from very pale gray, through olive-brown to greenish-blue or chocolate-brown, spotted and blotched, often more abundantly at the greater end, with black or dark brown. From the end of May, through June and into July, eggs and chicks of all stages and ages may be found.

Eggs.—Rev. F. C. R. Jourdain has sent me the following measurements of eggs of this gull from the British Isles: Eighty eggs average 68.04 by 47.39 millimeters; the eggs showing the four extremes measure **77.1** by 49, 72.5 by **52.1, 58.6** by 45 and 61.3 by **43** millimeters.

Young.—Doctor Forbes (1898) says of the young:

After about three weeks' incubation the chicks break through their prison, as lively and nimble balls of down, grayish-buff above, with the head, neck, and back spotted with brown; the under side paler and unspotted. On the least intrusion on their cubicle they are ready to be off—running, as Mr. Battye remarks, head down and shoulders up like a falcon—to the nearest herbage or water for security; but if left undisturbed they may be found for a fortnight or more in the nest, most assiduously tended by the parents. The approach of any intruder when the helpless young are in the nests is the signal to set the whole of the colony on wing, wheeling round his head, swooping down upon and screaming at him.

Plumages.—When fledged, the bill, legs, and feet are livid corneous. The feathers, which are white in the adult, have a center streak, or a bar of ashy-brown, and pale edges; and where black they are reddish-brown, with yellowish-white edges. The wing feathers are sooty or black, and the tail is mottled with brown, which, near the end, becomes almost a continuous bar, the tips of the feathers being grayish-white; the bill is horn color, and the legs and feet brownish-white.

During its first autumn the bird undergoes no true molt, but the brown becomes less marked in some parts by loss of pigment, and more uniform through the wearing off of the pale tips. In the next spring there is a more general but slow molt, in which the brown comes in of a less deep shade, and during the second autumn its color becomes a little paler still. During the next year, in spring and autumn by feather-changes, and loss of pigment in them, the brown is still further lost; bill yellow at its base, but without the red spot on the angle of the mandible.

In the fourth autumn this gull has assumed almost the complete winter dress of the adult—the white spot near the end of the primaries perhaps alone not being well marked. The following spring, when the bird is in its fifth year, sees it in its first nuptial plumage. As soon as that interesting period is over the gull begins to assume its first mature winter garb, which differs only from that of the summer in showing brown streaks on the head and neck.

Behavior.—Macgillivray (1852) writes:

The flight of this bird is peculiarly elegant, resembling, however, that of the greater black-backed gull, but more easy and buoyant, with the wings considerably curved. Its ordinary cry is loud, mellow, and somewhat plaintive, and when a number join in emitting it, which they sometimes do, when assembled for repose on an unfrequented beach or island, may be heard at a great distance and is then far from being unpleasant. It also emits occasionally a cackling or laughing cry, more mellow than that of the species above named. It searches for food on the open sea, in estuaries, on the beaches, and frequently on the land, sometimes flying to a great distance from the coast. Small fishes, crustacea, echini, shellfish, land mollusca, and earthworms are its habitual food, but it also eats of stranded fishes and devours young birds. When shoals of young herrings are in the bays, creeks, or estuaries it may often be seen in great numbers, intermingled with other gulls; but when reposing, whether on the sea or on land, it generally keeps separate in small flocks.

Doctor Forbes (1898) adds the following:

Mr. Thompson notes that this gull is very fond of ascending rivers, as well as visiting inland lakes. Several of these birds may be seen, in winter and spring, in the river Lagan as far as the first fall above the sea, where the canal commences, the snowy whiteness and pure black of their plumage contrasting finely with the background of dark foliage of the river banks. On one occasion [continues the same naturalist] I observed an adult bird fishing * * * high up the Lagan, * * * while soon afterwards two immature birds flew up the course of the river until they joined him. They were no doubt the bearers of some particular intelligence, as immediately on their reaching the old bird he wheeled about and the three proceeded with their utmost speed down the river. In like manner I once observed several of the black-headed gulls feeding in a ploughed field, half a mile from the shore of the bay, whence a single bird flew direct to them; the moment it arrived they all wheeled about, and, with their best speed, made for the bay, where it was low water at the time. They were not in any way alarmed in the field; the courier seemed to convey some special news.

DISTRIBUTION.

Breeding range.—The British Isles from the Faroes to the Channel Islands, on the coasts of France and probably Spain; south to Alboran Island off Morocco. From the Scandinavian Peninsula eastward it is represented by another subspecies.

Winter range.—From the British Isles south to the western Mediterranean, the Canary and Madeira Islands, and the west coast of Africa.

Casual records.—The type specimen was taken in Greenland, which is the only North American record.

LARUS ARGENTATUS Pontoppidan.

HERRING GULL.

HABITS.

Contributed by Charles Wendell Townsend.

The most widely distributed sea gull of the Northern Hemisphere and the one that is best known because it frequents the haunts of man, visiting his most populous harbors,, is the herring gull. But slightly inferior in size to the great black-backed and burgomaster gulls, it is distinguished from the former by its pearly gray back and from the latter by the black tips to its wings. Not only is it a bird familiar to those dwelling along the seacoast and to the voyagers on the ocean, but it is found about lakes and rivers. Owing to better protection given to breeding colonies, which were formerly systematically robbed of their eggs, and to the fact that the birds are not molested in the neighborhood of large cities, the herring gull has not only held its own, but is undoubtedly on the increase.

Circumpolar in distribution the herring gull breeds from Ellesmere Land to Manitoba and Maine, and in Europe to northern France and the White Sea. It winters wherever there is open water throughout its range, and as far south as Cuba and the Mediterranean Sea. In northern regions the return of open water in the spring often determines the arrival of these gulls as well as of other water birds. An interesting example of this is shown in the case of Cobalt Lake, Ontario, where a constant stream of hot water flows into the lake from the silver mines. As a consequence the ice leaves sometimes as much as two weeks earlier than it does in any of the surrounding lakes. Arthur A. Cole (1910) reports that in 1910 "the lake opened on March 31, and within 24 hours two herring gulls were seen floating in the lake."

On the eastern coast of the United States the herring gull spends not only the winter but also the summer to a considerable distance to the south of its breeding range, the most southern point of which is No-Man's-Land in Penobscot Bay, Maine.[1] In southern Maine and on the New Hampshire and Massachusetts coasts it is difficult to state the dates of migration, for the birds is always to be found there.

Courtship.—In the spring one may often see on a sand bar some of the herring gulls walking proudly about raising and lowering their heads and emitting from time to time loud sonorous notes, a bugle call which I believe to be their love song, while others stand quietly by. As this song is given the head, with wide-open bill, is raised until it points vertically upwards and then lowered to the horizontal

---

[1] A few herring gulls have recently bred near Marthas Vineyard.

position. As the sex can not be distinguished one may only guess that it is the males that are thus parading themselves. At this time of year, more than at other times, they are frequently to be seen chasing each other in the air, and that too without the object of stealing coveted food morsels. Mr. Ralph Hoffman reports seeing a pair of these birds bowing to each other at Ipswich beach just prior to the act of mating. On the ground they sometimes seize each other by the bills and strike with the wings and feet. H. L. Ward (1906) describes an action on the part of the gulls which suggested to him the dance of the albatross at Laysan. He says:

> Two adults may be standing near together, when one will stop, hold its neck nearly horizontal, its bill pointed down, wave its head in and out from its body, and slightly up and down, in a rapid, jerky way, reminding one somewhat of the motions of a duck feeding in shallow water, at the same time emitting a peculiar chickenlike chatter. The other one immediately joins in, apparently directing its attention to the same place in the ground, and the performance is kept up for a minute or two, when the birds straighten up, perhaps to repeat the operation two or three times with short intermissions.

Nesting.—The herring gull breeds in small or large colonies, but always in the neighborhood of some body of water—a river, lake, or the sea. Single nests are rare, and usually point to the breaking up and scattering of a colony, for the herring gull is a very social creature and prefers to nest, feed, rest, and sleep in companies. Mr. Brewster in 1881 found many of the herring gulls on the southern coast of Labrador nesting in widely scattered regions, and says (1883) "the policy of scattering over wide areas, however, probably preserves the majority of nests from discovery."

At the Duck Islands off the coast of Maine is a large breeding colony which has been protected for some years. Previously the colony was despoiled of eggs every year by fishermen, and many of the birds had acquired the habit of nesting in trees, where they were less likely to be robbed. Herring gulls have resorted to trees as nesting sites when disturbed by man in places other than these Duck Islands. Audubon (1840) in 1833 found the gulls nesting in fir trees on Grand Manan Island. He was informed that the habit had been acquired within the recollection of those living there, and that previously they had nested on the ground. Dr. Henry Bryant visited the same locality in 1856 and found that fewer were building in trees than in Audubon's time—a fact he attributes to greater freedom from persecution. Barrows (1912) says that he has never known herring gulls to nest in trees in the Great Lakes region. When I visited the Duck Island in 1904 the birds under protection had returned with few exceptions to the normal habit of nesting on the ground.

Maj. G. Ralph Mayer, United States Army, contributes the following description of the nesting colony at Great Duck Island, Maine, which he visited on June 20, 1913:

Great Duck Island is about 2 miles long and from three-fourths to 1 mile wide at its greatest width. The gulls' nesting ground extends clear across the island in the open rocky ground and even back into the edge of the woods among the second or third growth. The nests are placed almost anywhere, though usually against a tree trunk or stump. Some are placed among the rocks along the shore. There are three nesting trees on the island. The greater part of the nesting ground has a peculiar soil of rotten vegetable matter and is thickly scattered over with dead trees, standing and fallen. There are probably 4,000 pairs of birds nesting on Great Duck. Little Duck Island, which is about 1 mile north of Great Duck, is the home of about 6,000 pairs of the birds.

The nests, as a general rule, are very rough looking structures, though there are some exceptions. The shape and size varies considerably with the location. The materials used were varied. In one part of the island where chickweed was plentiful this was used to the exclusion of all other materials excepting a few sticks for the base of the nest. On the higher ground the predominating materials were chips and pieces of the dead and rotten trees in the vicinity. Some nests were lined with grasses or feathers; others had no lining whatever, but were more like mere beds of chips and decayed vegetable matter. In the walls of one nest I found a bristle brush of the kind used in washing bottles. The tree nests were composed of branches and were lined with grasses. Several nests found in the woods on Little Duck were composed of sticks and were lined with mosses, principally *Usnea longissima*, which was very plentiful in the vicinity. These were the best constructed nests I found. In all cases they were larger than those in the open. Mr. Gray, the head light keeper, told me that this was the first year he had seen them nesting in the heavy timber.

The birds are quite bold in the defense of their breeding grounds. I have repeatedly seen them drive sheep and lambs from the vicinity of the nest, and only once did I see the sheep offer any resistance whatever, and in that case she very quickly decided that it was better to leave the vicinity. On two occasions I was charged by the birds. They did not touch me, but would swoop down straight at me until from 15 to 25 feet from me and directly overhead, when they would go up almost vertically and circling back, repeat the performance. When passing overhead they would utter their piercing " kee-ew." It was really exciting at times to see the bird heading directly at me and coming so fast. Mr. Gray told me that they made little attempt, however, to defend their nests against the crows, and that in some years a great deal of damage was done in this way. I watched the birds for some time from a tent. My notes show that six minutes after I entered the tent the birds had quieted down. I noticed one bird picking up nesting material several times, but it appeared to be a nervous action rather than a desire to collect nest material. Several times the birds had fights, in which each got hold of the other's bill and pulled.

The following, taken from my notebook, was written about 5 p. m. on a clear, bright day:

This is one of the most wonderful sights I have ever witnessed. The air is literally full of gulls. In sight there must be at least 4,000 gulls and all screaming. It is a weird sound. The air is so full of them that it looks like a snowstorm. They are perched on the trees and standing on the ground, where they resemble nothing so much as a national cemetery with its thousands of white stones. When I first arrived at Great Duck the birds did not appear to mind my walking around among the nests so much as they did later on. When I entered the nesting ground the birds within 50 to 100 feet of me would rise and fly around, calling. Later on during my stay the birds within 200 to 250 feet would rise. This may have been due to the fact that young were hatching out every day.

On the ground the nests are placed in hollows or in plain sight on sand or gravel or rocks, or in grassy fields. Sometimes they are placed at the foot of stumps or close to an overhanging rock or pile of driftwood; sometimes on the ground in thick spruce woods. They also nest on ledges on the face of cliffs, as at the Gaspe Peninsula. A. H. Jordan (1888) found a few nests on an island in Lake Champlain, where the birds were much persecuted, " quite well concealed in the edge of the woods under low-hanging trees." An unusual nesting site of the herring gull is mentioned by F. S. Daggett (1890), who found on Isle Royale in Lake Superior four nests of this bird built on the ice accumulated on the rocks by the dashing of the waves in winter. A few warm days had already so melted the ice that the nests with their contents were in danger of falling into the lake. He also speaks of nests made in hollows in the accumulated droppings of the bird.

Dutcher and Bailey (1903) say:

During incubation the weight of the sitting bird breaks down or packs the nest, so they are continually being repaired and built up around the edges with new material, which is always green grass or weeds, the effect being very pretty indeed. On several occasions gulls were seen gathering this material in their bills. The grass is bitten off or pulled up by the roots until the bird has a ball in its bill larger than a man's fist. This material is gathered where it is most plentiful and is usually carried by flight to the nest site.

Baird, Brewer, and Ridgway (1884) describe a nest built in the top of a spruce, 60 feet from the ground, at Grand Manan, which was firmly built and " composed entirely of long, fine, flexible grasses, evidently gathered, when green, from the salt marshes, and carefully woven into a circular fabric. The nest measured about 18 inches in diameter, its sides being 3 or 4 inches thick, and its cavity at the center at least 4 inches deep." Ward (1906) observed incipient nest building at Gravel Island in Lake Michigan, and says that " there seemed to be no attempt to arrange the material with the bill," but that the bird molded the nest with her breast.

Dutcher and Bailey found at Duck Island, Maine, the average depth of the bowl to be 3 inches and its diameter 10 inches. The diameter of the nests at the base varied from 13 to 24 inches; they are sometimes built up to a height of 10 inches. Maj. G. Ralph

Meyer found that the size of the nests at the Duck Islands varied greatly. He writes:

The average of seven nests was: Outer diameter, 15 inches; inner diameter, 8 inches; depth outside, 4¾ inches; depth inside, 3¼ inches. One nest in the heavy timber measured 22 by 8 by 6 by 5. One of the tree nests was 28 inches in diameter.

Eggs.—Only one brood is raised, but when the nests are frequently robbed the birds are kept laying all summer. Three eggs constitute a set, although the number is sometimes only two, and in very rare cases one or four. The color of the eggs varies within wide limits. Dutcher and Bailey, from an examination of many hundreds at Duck Island, Maine, found that:

The ground colors were light sky blue, dead blue, light blue-gray, light gray-blue, dark lilac-gray, light gray, light pea-green, green drab, warm drab, ocher drab, pink drab, light brown, and cinnamon. The colors of the markings were chocolate brown, rich brown, light brown, snuff brown, asphalt, black, lilac, mauve. The shape of markings was almost infinite—large and small spots, indistinct specks, blotches, lines, and irregular streaks, somewhat like the markings on the eggs of blackbirds. One egg was found with a light sky-blue ground color with tiny indistinct specks of lilac and light brown. Some of the markings were so confluent that they resulted in a distinct line around the egg.

Major G. Ralph Meyer writes:

The eggs varied greatly in shape, size, and color. Eggs were found varying from short ovate to cylindrical ovate. The most common shape was the elongate ovate.

The measurements of 45 eggs, in the United States National Museum and by Major Meyer, average 72.3 by 50.5 millimeters; the eggs showing the four extremes measure **82** by **52**, 74.5 by **53** and **58** by **45** millimeters.

Young.—The period of incubation varies from 24 to 28 days, the average being 26 days. Dutcher and Bailey found an interval of about 12 hours between the hatching of each egg. Dutcher and Bailey (1903) show conclusively that in some cases at least both sexes incubate. They say:

It was also observed that as the period of incubation neared its end the anxiety of the parents increased in a marked degree, so that it was easy to determine the stage of incubation by the action of the parents. During the last few hours, before the pipping and cracking of the egg, the parent birds were so fearless that they would leave the nest only on a near approach.

Several observers have found that the eggs were turned slightly by the bird's bill, feet, and breast. The mate of the sitting bird is often stationed near at hand.

The young are soon on their feet after leaving the egg, and, according to Dutcher and Bailey, "the instinct to hide seems to be developed within an hour or two after hatching." They conceal themselves or sometimes only push their heads under pieces of wood or projecting rocks or in the grass. The object of this habit may be also a desire for coolness and shade. Audubon (1840), speaking of the herring gulls breeding in trees at Grand Manan, says:

> The most remarkable effect produced by these changes of locality is that the young which are hatched in the trees or high rocks do not leave the nests until they are able to fly.

This is conspicuously the case at Percé Rock in the Gaspé Peninsula and on the lofty cliffs of Bonaventure Island and Bon Ami.

One of the parents guards the young during the first week or two of life, repelling intruders, and the young are brooded and shielded from the sun.

R. M. Strong (1914) describes the feeding of young only a few hours old as follows:

> The adult bird did not insert its bill in the mouth of its offspring, but the latter took food from the ground just below the bill of the parent. * * * A quantity of food in a fine and soft condition was disgorged in more or less of a heap.

Meyer writes that " in feeding the very young bird the parent holds the food in the bill and the young bird picks it out. The older birds take their food from the ground, where it is placed by the parents." Ward (1906) thus describes the feeding of young nearly able to fly:

> The young comes in front of an adult and with a bowing and courtesying movement puts up its bill to that of the old one, continuing the bowing for several minutes, resting between times. Sometimes it took hold of the adult's bill with its own; at other times merely touched bills. When the adult opened its mouth the young put its bill within. Failing to get indications of food it went to another adult, and repeated the operation, passing in succession to several, until at length it seemed to get some favorable signs, for it remained by this one, alternately begging and resting. After some time, it was apparent to me that the adult was striving to regurgitate. It would open its mouth, stretch its neck nearly horizontally, then bring its head down to the ground. * * * Perhaps half an hour after these efforts began I saw a portion of a fish appear in its mouth, and a moment later it was deposited on the ground, where the young promptly seized it. The fish appeared to be a herring about 7 or 8 inches long and so mascerated that it readily fell apart.

I have observed adults at Percé Rock very promptly regurgitate for their young on alighting near them.

This feeding is done by both parents; and even after the young are able to gain a fair livelihood by their own exertions, and have gathered in companies by themselves, they are ever on the alert to beg food not only from their own parents, but from any adult that may come in their way. It is thought by some that the adults in their turn feed any that come along, but it is probable that the adults recognize their own offspring and as a rule refuse to feed any other, except when they are so set upon by the mob of clamorous young that they must perforce submit. The young are fed for at least five weeks, or until they are able to fly, and even for some time after this whenever the adult can be induced to part with some of its food. Young gulls swim readily, and when frightened will sometimes take to the water and swim rapidly away.

An astonishing habit of herring gulls that has been observed and described by various writers is that of infanticide, and the murder is committed not only on the very young, but also on those nearly grown. Ward (1906a) says:

The main point of attack was the back of the head. To this region a number of severe blows were given with the point of the bill, after which it was grasped between the mandibles of the adult and the bird was pulled about until the skin and flesh were cut through to the skull.

He was unable to find that these victims were abnormal or had given offense. The habit may perhaps be due to the ferocity of the guarding and fighting instincts in the old birds, and a lack of attunement in the instincts of the young, in consequence of which a chick will occasionally stray from its own preserve and trespass on the domain of a neighbor. Meyer quotes Mr. Gray, the lighthouse keeper of Great Duck Island, as saying " that some of the old birds would kill young gulls and even young chickens. They would take the young bird by the neck and choke it. He put a stop to that by killing the bird found in the act."

Examination of stomach contents of young herring gulls reported by Dutcher and Bailey (1903) showed that, besides fish and squid, various insects (moths, flies, and beetles) had been eaten. As a rule the young are given the same food that is consumed by the adults and this will be described later. In two stomachs of birds 1 and 2 days old examined by me I found wasps and large June beetles.

Plumages.—The downy young are of a buffy yellow color, nearly white below and dusky on the back. They are thickly marked with black spots above. The bill is horn color, with a pink tip after the white pipping knob has disappeared; the feet, dusky pink. The growth of the young gull is rapid, and at the age of 5 or 6 weeks it has donned the juvenal dress, of which the prevailing color is dark gray tinged with brown. The upper parts are mottled and barred with grayish buff and white; the head and neck are streaked with white; the breast and belly nearly uniform ashy-fuscous. The primaries and tail are brownish black. The eyes are brown; the bill dark, pale at the base; the tarsi and feet grayish flesh color. There is a partial molt in the fall of the first year into the first winter plumage and a partial one in the spring into the first nuptial plumage; but no essential change in the general color of the feathers. In the spring and summer the large flocks of herring gulls that are to be found south of the breeding range are largely made up of these dark plumaged year-old birds. In the fall of the year following the one in which the birds are hatched—that is, in the second winter—the "gray gull" molts into its second winter plumage, a dress which approaches that of the adult in its pearl-gray back and white belly, but the former is mottled with brownish and the latter clouded with dusky. The head, neck, and rump are heavily streaked with gray, the primaries are black, and the tail appears to be tipped with black, owing to the dusky brown mottling of the white feathers. A partial molt in the spring into the second nuptial plumage still further improves the dress. A few individuals of this age (2 years) with black tips to the tails and streaked breasts are to be found in the breeding colonies, but none of those in the gray of the first nuptial plumage. Not until the third year or later is the full dress assumed with perfect blue gray mantle, snowy heads, breasts, rumps, and tails, and with primaries tipped with white. Astley (1901) states that the bright yellow bill is not attained until the fourth year. There is then a carmine spot on the lower mandible; the irides are yellow.

There is also a seasonal molt, by which a slight streaking of the neck is assumed in winter, but it is probable that this diminishes and may vanish with age. According to Dwight (1901) the limited prenuptial molts occur on the Atlantic coast in March and April, and the complete postnuptial molts in August and September.

Food.—The food habits of the herring gull are of considerable importance, for the bird is a scavenger and renders great service in keeping the harbors and beaches free from decaying fish and refuse of all sorts. All is game that comes in their way, but their greatest prizes are thrown from fishing vessels when the men are cleaning fish. At these times they crowd around the sterns of the vessels and dash eagerly for the choice pieces, the air being filled with their screams. The method of picking up food from the water is characteristic and graceful. Down they swoop on outstretched wings and spread tails with feet dropped to the water, where they often seize the morsel without wetting a feather save perhaps only the tips of their tails, which are curved downward. Often the birds must needs check their course by back paddling with their wings or even by flying up almost backwards. If the morsel is large thy sit on the water for a moment or two to swallow it, and thus drop behind the fishing vessel which, however, is easily overtaken. There is many a slip twixt the cup and the lip, however, for the birds are often made to share the booty with other gulls who have had their eyes on the same dainties, or even to lose it altogether when pursued by a more powerful rival. The great black-backed gull plays this rôle with great effect.

The scows which carry off the city garbage to be dumped in deep water are also eagerly followed by the gulls and much booty is gleaned when the vessel is discharged. In the harbors of populous cities there is always food to be found floating on the water, particularly in the neighborhood of fish wharves and at the mouths of sewers. The service to sanitation in these places is of great value. At Boston large quantities of sewage are poured out into the harbor at Moon Island just after the tide begins to ebb. Gulls collect from all sides in anticipation of this event and rest on the water offshore or fly to and fro until the sewer gates are opened. Then, heedless of the onlookers, they fly in crowded ranks close to the unsavory fountain head and dip gracefully for the titbits to be found there. It is an interesting fact and an indication of considerable intelligence that gulls, although very wary in regions where shooting is carried on, become entirely tame and confiding where this is forbidden, as is the case in harbors and bird reservations.

At times, however, but not often, the herring gull resorts to the tactics of the tern, and captures small live fish by plunging headlong into the water. Occasionally this plunge is made from a height of 15 or 20 feet, and the bird disappears below the surface, soon to emerge with its prey. Sometimes a whole flock can be seen engaged in this occupation as they follow a school of fish. At other times, the plunge with partly open wings is made from only a few feet above the surface, and the bird is only partially immersed. I have seen the members of a flock of herring gulls riding in shallow water fly up a few feet into the air in order to obtain impetus for a short dive below the surface for some prey. Knight (1908) describes the plunging of these gulls from the air and says:

They flew about the open water in circles * * * and as their keen eyes detected some fish at this upper portion of their range they plunged with force into the water, quickly rising to the surface as a usual thing, though on at least one occasion a bird was out of sight so long that I had grave fears that it would be carried under the ice by the swift current, but it finally emerged at the edge of the ice and took wing with an unusually large tomcod. Nearly every plunge seemed to be successful, the birds swallowing the smaller fish before taking wing, but when a large fish was captured they would fly to the ice near by and after batting the fish from side to side on the ice would finally swallow it.

When herring are caught in pounds and traps there are some dead or dying fish that are captured by the gulls, which have, therefore, been accused of damaging the fishery. It is probable that their work here is more properly that of scavengers in keeping the traps free from dead fish, and, therefore, beneficial.

The sand beaches are at times covered with stranded fish, small and large; sand launces, herring, cod, hake, haddock, pollock, dogfish, and skates are often thrown up or cast themselves ashore, pursued and pursuers alike. Their dead bodies would soon become intolerable were it not for the greediness of the gulls who come from all sides to the feast. The small fry are eaten whole, while the larger bony fishes are gradually hacked to pieces until nothing but the skeleton is left. The tough spiny skin of the dogfishes and skates protect them until decay has allowed an entrance, and these are then partly consumed. Squid are also thrown up on the beaches and are relished by the gulls.

The herring gull has a curious habit of dragging dry fish from the upper beach to the water. I found on Ipswich Beach a fish, 18 inches long, that had been dragged by a gull 134 yards in an irregular course from the upper beach to the edge of the water. During the whole transit the gull walked backward, as was plainly shown by the tracks. In this connection the following by Strong (1914) concerning his captive gulls is of interest: He found that these gulls often rinsed a piece of food that " has been lying in a chemical solution, or when it has accumulated considerable dirt as a consequence of having been dragged on the ground. Such rinsing of the food does not occur at every feeding, but is usual." In the case of the gulls at Ipswich it would seem as if they wished to soften the food by maceration in the water.

From the beach and among the rocks of the seashore the herring gull obtains a variety of food other than dead refuse—crabs and other crustaceans, mollusks of all sorts, such as clams, mussels, sea snails, etc., and echinoderms and worms. Many crabs and mollusks are broken with the bill, but if this can not be accomplished the gull seizes the difficult morsel and flies up with it into the air, nearly vertically or in circles, drops it onto the hard sand or rocks, follows closely the descent, and alights to regale itself on the exposed contents. If unsuccessful the first time the gull tries a second and sometimes a third or fourth time. This habit, which is also a common one with crows, explains the fact that mollusk shells, crabs, and sea urchins are scattered so universally along our coast, sometimes half a mile from the sea. On the rocky coast of Maine, where the sea urchin (*Strongylocentrotus dröbachiensis*) is abundant, the gulls sometimes turn them over and pick out the flesh from the circular hole about the mouth without breaking the shell. Isely (1912) speaks of seeing a herring gull in Kansas " following a corn lister, picking up grubs like the blackbirds." In England, where the birds are more familiar with man, herring gulls not infrequently follow the plow to pick up worms and grubs.

From time to time complaint is made of the damage done by herring gulls in eating fish or fish refuse spread on land as a fertilizer, and one can hardly blame the gull for his failure to discriminate between harmful and useful refuse. It is probable that these reports are exaggerated, and it has been found that the birds are easily kept away by scarecrows.

Seton (1908) says of the herring gull in the region of the Great Slave Lake that it "will pursue wounded game and often follows the hunter to share in the kill." Mackay (1892) says that herring gulls will eat dead ducks with avidity, cleaning off the flesh and rejecting the skin and feathers as if it had been done with a sharp knife. He has known them to carry a dead red-breasted merganser "for nearly a quarter of a mile by stages of about 25 yards, holding it by the neck, in order to eat it in security." He also states that they watch mergansers and rush at them when they appear with a fish in the mouth, and he believes that they often secure the fish.

As has been stated above, insects of all kinds have been found in the stomachs of young birds. Coues (1877) speaks of finding the remains of a hare in a gull's stomach, and Eifrig (1905) seeds and berries.

The herring gull under some circumstances robs nests of the eggs and young, but not to such an extent as some other gulls. Mr. Manly Hardy reports finding a herring gull nesting within 8 or 10 feet of three red-breasted mergansers' nests and close by the nests of spotted sandpipers and common terns, none of which was in the least disturbed.

Herring gulls eject from their mouths the harder particles of food, such as fishbones and crab's claws, in the form of loosely compacted pellets; some 2 inches in length. These may be seen about their resting places. I have sometimes found a few feathers in these pellets, probably plucked from the bird's own breasts.

The fresh-water ponds and reservoirs along the coast are frequently visited by this splendid gull, and it is the common idea that they resort to these to drink fresh water; but it is to be remembered that in some places and times they stay continuously near salt water, and that Mr. Brewster's captive kittiwake refused fresh water, but drank salt water. In the interior on the fresh-water lakes and ponds where the herring gull breeds, and in similar regions where it spends the winter, it is evident that the bird must drink fresh water. Anthony (1906) says:

That gulls drink sea water, and can thrive on it, is a fact not to be questioned; but I am of the opinion that when fresh water can be obtained without too much trouble they will drink it in preference.

Strong (1914) found that his captive gulls showed an aversion for salted food, and washed their bills and drank fresh water afterwards.

Behavior.—The flight of the herring gull varies greatly under different circumstances. At times, especially in calm weather, the birds flap along slowly with broad, slow wing beats like those of herons or cormorants. In this manner they may fly close to the water or high in the air, and they are usually massed in loose flocks.

Occasionally, however, their flight is in a long line, one behind the other, or in broad lines abreast, and rarely they may be seen in the typical V formation of ducks. In rising, a flock often ascends nearly vertically in a great circle all together, or in many intersecting circles. The play of light and shade, of sun and shadow, alternately make the birds appear dark and light. Many hours are spent by the gulls in this graceful and beautiful sport of soaring in circles— a sport which apparently requires but little effort, as, under favorable conditions, few wing beats are necessary. The descent may be made in the same manner as the ascent by circling, but at times the birds drop swiftly down by tipping or rocking from side to side.

In windy weather the flight of the herring gull is far from slow and heron-like. Then it is extremely graceful, as the bird alternately sails with great rapidity before the wind or beats up into it.

At times these gulls are able to sail directly into the teeth of the wind without a single stroke of the wing. Mr. William Brewster (1912) has described the manner in which herring gulls keep pace with a vessel, gliding along on almost motionless wings into the teeth of the gale, sometimes within a few yards of the deck, but always on the windward side. He says:

As the gale increased they flapped their wings less and less often, until most, if not all of them, were gliding ceaselessly, minute after minute, over distances certainly exceeding a mile, without a single wing beat, but not without changes or readjustments in the bend or the inclination of the wings, which took place not infrequently and often were very obvious.

Several explanations of this mysterious means of propulsion have been offered, but the following by F. W. Headley (1912) seems to me the most satisfactory. He says:

There is a feat perhaps more striking than any of the others already described—a feat which, nevertheless, gulls often achieve. A steamer is advancing against a fairly strong wind, which, if not absolutely a head wind, strikes the vessel at an acute angle. There results a steady up current over the stern of the vessel, or slightly to one side or the other of the stern. Poised on this up current the gulls hang in mid-air, their wings held rigidly expanded. Only very slight wing movements, evidently for purposes of balance, can be detected. Standing on the deck and watching these gulls one is irresistibly reminded of the poising of the kestrel high in air, with wings held motionless, when he finds a wind that is all that he could wish. It is sometimes easy to forget that, unlike the kestrel, they do not remain in one spot, but that all the while they are moving forward and, in fact, keeping pace with the steamer. The gulls, like the kestrel, are poising on an up current of air; but they give their bodies a rather different incline, with the result that they keep traveling forward. * * * The general incline of their body and wing surfaces is slightly downward. Hence the upward-streaming wind not only maintains them in the air or lifts them higher, but, acting at right angle, also drives them forward.

A similar explanation is given in detail by A. Forbes (1913).

It is probable that gulls take advantage of ascending currents of air when they soar in circles without perceptible wing beat. In descending from a height they often glide, or *vol-plane* in the modern language of the aviator, with amazing speed at a steep angle. At other times, as remarked above, they descend almost vertically by tipping first to one side and then to the other, with a suddenness that suggests falling. The last 20 or 30 feet is often accomplished slowly with upstretched wings and downstretched legs. There are very few birds whose flight is more beautiful or which will so well repay study as that of the herring gull.

In flight the feet are stretched behind under the tail, where they can be seen; but it is not very rare to discover a gull flying with one or both feet imbedded in the feathers of the breast, entirely covered or showing only a bit of the darker surface of the feet. I can hardly believe that this is for the sake of warmth, for it may occur on comparatively warm days; while even in the coldest weather the great majority of gulls fly with their feet exposed behind. In quick turns the feet are sometimes dropped, as if to aid in holding the air like a centerboard. They are also dropped as they approach the water, and at times dangle for several seconds as the birds rise into the air. Rising from the water or beach is easily accomplished against a strong wind, but in calm weather the bird is obliged to run along the sand or water for a variable distance before it can rise above the surface.

Although gulls are able to swim rapidly when winged and unable to fly, they rarely swim any distance under natural conditions. Their buoyant position on the water, with elevated tails, is well expressed by Oliver Wendell Holmes when he says:

> The gull, high floating like a sloop unladen.

The young just out of the egg are rapid swimmers and instinctively take to the water.

It is said by some writers that the herring gull never dives. This statement is, however, incorrect, as has already been shown in describing the feeding habits. In fact, under exceptional circumstances the herring gull dives as well as a tern.

The vocal powers of the herring gull have a wide range. This is particularly the case during the breeding season, when they indulge in all sorts of sounds, uttered it may be in conversational manner, in moods of love and passion, or anger and fear. Writers have described these sounds by syllables or by comparisions with other sounds in nature. Thus Ward (1906) says:

> Sometimes one hears sounds like the lowing of cattle, except that the pitch is higher, like the bleating of sheep, the mewing or snarling of cats, the clucking of hens, the crowing of cocks, hoarse human chuckles, and sounds for which I could find no comparisons.

Olive Thorne Miller says that the young herring gull has "a querulous cry like a puppy in distress."

I have often been struck with the resemblance of some of their notes to the rattling of blocks in the rigging of a vessel.

The usual alarm cry may be represented by the syllables, *kak-kak-kak*, or by a series of *ha ha has*. Herrick writes it as "*waw-wak-wak! wak-wak! wak-wak!*" Strong decided on the syllables "*kek-kek-kek*," with the accent on the first syllable. Ward also distinguishes a "challenge cry where the bird stretches its neck up at an angle of 45° and holds its whole body rigidly while the cry is emitted with great vehemence. This I have previously described under courtship. Bent's notes refer to this cry as the "trumpeting call" and state that this is

the most striking and spectacular vocal performance of all the varied notes heard on the breeding grounds. It is usually given from a tree, stump, or other perch, but often from the ground. The neck is outstretched to its full extent, pointing upwards at an angle, and the mouth is opened wide. The call begins with a loud, shrill, prolonged scream, which is followed by a long series of shorter notes, rapidly uttered, sometimes as many as 10 or 12 in the latter. It sounds like *queeeee-ah, quak, quak, quak, quak, quak, quak, quak, quak, quak, quak*. As one bird starts on this call it seems to challenge others to join in the chorus, until perhaps a dozen birds are all giving it at once like a loud ringing chorus of college cheers.

Strong represents the call as *keee, kee ek, kee ek, kee ek, kee ek*, etc. I have noted it as *ko-ah, ko-ah*, etc., as well as *ku-ku*, or *kee ke, kee*, the last named high pitched and rapidly repeated. At times the notes are clear and bugle like; again squeaking or rattling; again the birds emit hissing whistles, which are very different from the other notes and very characteristic. There is evidently great individual variation in the notes as well as variations due to many moods and circumstances.

The herring gull associates with a number of other sea birds in the same haunts. With the great black-backed gull it has not infrequent encounters on the score of food, but it is fair to say that the larger bird is more often the aggressor.

Arthur Saunders writes:

I have seen the common crow rob the gull of mussels which they have dropped on the rocks to break. The crows sit on the rocks until a gull drops a mussel near it, then walk up and seize the mussel before the gull has time to get it again. The gulls do not seem to resent this at all. They generally act as though they did not know where the mussel had gone to and fly off to hunt for another.

I have several times seen a herring gull fly at a whistler who was swimming near-by. The whistler always dove at the approach of the gull, who would settle on the water where the duck went down. In a few seconds he would start off for another duck, and the process

would be repeated again and again. The gull never picked up any
food from the water and never molested any ducks swimming near;
and none of them showed any fear, except the one directly flown at,
who would always dive before the gull reached it. It seemed to be
a matter of play on the part of the gull that was understood as such
by the duck, although it is possible that the gull hoped to obtain
food. On one occasion I saw a herring gull fly directly at a female
American merganser which with another was being courted by a
male. The merganser flew vigorously away just as the gull alighted.
Then began an active chase by short flights on the part of the gull,
who was eluded by rapid turns and occasional dives on the part of
the merganser. Finally the merganser came up close to the two
other mergansers, who had remained passive during the pursuit, but
as the gull pounced at the group they all took flight, closely followed
by the tyrant. The mergansers easily distanced the gull, who in his
eagerness spit out a small fish, but soon after gave up the pursuit
and alighted on the ice.

Well endowed by nature to resist the destructive agencies of storm
and cold, with practically no enemies among birds and mammals,
the herring gull would indeed be a prosperous species were it not for
the arch enemy, man. Fortunately, at the present date, the idea of
bird preservation from an esthetic as well as from a utilitarian point
of view is gaining ground, and since the beginning of the present century the herring gull has been more and more protected from gunners and eggers.

With many the benefit derived from this gull in sanitation (the
removal from harbors of floating organic matter) is a strong argument in favor of protection. In the past, and to a large extent in
such out-of-the way regions as Labrador at the present day, these
gulls were and are incessantly persecuted during the breeding season. Their eggs are highly valued as a food supply, and the young
are cooped up and fattened for eating. Adult birds are shot for food
or for mere sport. It is fortunate that such practices are now
frowned upon in all well-regulated communities.

A destructive agency of the young at breeding colonies is the surf
on the shore. In stormy weather when the waves are high many
young gulls, still unable to fly, are killed by being dashed on the
rocks.

Like many other birds, it is probable that herring gulls enjoy considerable longevity, barring accidents. American ornithologists are
familiar with the case of " Gull Dick," often reported by Mackay in
" The Auk." For 24 years this bird—easily recognized by markings,
voice, and disposition—visited the neighborhood of the Brenton's
Reef Lightship in Narragansett Bay. Here it stayed from about

October 12 to April 7. The bird was fed regularly with boiled pork and fish. It would fly close to the vessel and would respond to calls or waving of the hand at mealtimes, and it jealously drove off all other gulls. Morris (1903) records another individual that was observed for at least 30 years.

Fall.—The fall migration from the breeding grounds at the Duck Islands, Maine, has been observed by the lightkeepers to begin about August 8, and by the 20th three-quarters of the birds have left. At Ipswich I have noted a decided diminution in the summer birds and a migration past the beach of adults by the 20th of August. As the herring gull is found in summer as well as in winter to the south of the breeding range, it is difficult to set exact limits in time for the migrations.

The usual explanation given for the occurrence of the herring gull in summer south of its breeding grounds is that these birds are immature or, if adults, barren individuals. On the coast of Essex County, Massachusetts, especially at Ipswich, is a place where nonbreeding summer birds can be studied to good advantage. Here, on the sandy beaches, they collect in numbers, which have noticeably increased of late years, since adequate protection has been extended to the breeding colonies farther north. As a large proportion of the summer birds at Ipswich are in immature plumage, it is probable that immaturity is the cause for nonbreeding to a considerable extent. A certain proportion, however, sometimes as many as 5 or even 10 per cent of the flocks, are in adult plumage. This fact and the fact that the number of gulls varies greatly from day to day, and that their numbers are greatest at the times when the beaches are covered with stranded fish, suggests that a certain proportion, perhaps only a small one, may be daily excursionists from their breeding places, the nearest of which, No Mans Land, is 111 miles northeast of Ipswich Light. Confirming this supposition are some observations made by me in June, 1904, on the Maine coast, where I found flocks of gulls flying southwest in the morning and northeast at night. The following from Dutcher and Bailey (1903) in the study of the gulls at No Mans Land and Great Duck Island, also bears this out:

At daylight large numbers of gulls leave the island and go to sea for food; and the length of time they remain away is governed probably by the distance they have to go to find fish. Some days they return quite early and on others much later. The manner of flight when returning from one of these food trips is entirely different from that of the ordinary excursions made from the breeding grounds; it is made close to the surface of the water, very direct, one bird following another, and is quite rapid. Sometimes the birds show marked evidences of fatigue.

The numbers of these summer birds at Ipswich I have estimated at various times with considerable care and by various methods. Sometimes, I have measured the sand bar which they covered, or the strip of beach or the length of the line in the water abreast of the beach, and, by allowing a certain number to the square or linear yard, have arrived at a fairly accurate estimate, which I believe in most cases has been below rather than above the mark. The following are some of the dates and the numbers: June 21, 1903, 2,000; July 27, 1903, 2,500; November 20, 1904, 8,000; July 16, 1905, 28,800; July 20, 1907, 5,000; July 12, 1908, 5,000. The large number given for July 16, 1905, was obtained from the measurement of the area occupied by a flock. This was an area of 28,800 square yards, where the birds had stood nearly shoulder to shoulder. Even if there was only one bird in every square yard, the numbers would almost exceed belief.

After the middle of September the ponds about Boston where shooting is forbidden are frequented daily by this bird. The numbers are sometimes so great that the authorities have at times been alarmed lest the waters of the reservoirs be polluted by the droppings of the birds, or by typhoid baccilli, which they fear may be carried on the feet or plumage from sewage on which the gulls feed. I have made especial note of the gulls visiting the Back Bay Basin of Boston, bounded by Boston and Cambridge, and the center of a great area of brick and mortar. For some years past the tides have been excluded and the water is fresh. The gulls do not spend the night here, but come in from the sea, flying high over the houses at sunrise or from time to time during the day. At times companies of many hundreds ride the water. Later in the winter the gulls collect in great flocks on the ice. I have seen several acres of ice here, as well as on Fresh Pond, Cambridge, covered thickly with gulls.

The duration of the visits of the gulls to the fresh-water ponds varies. Sometimes they fly back to the harbor or sea within half an hour, sometimes they tarry much longer; but, as often happens, some are coming and going all day, so it is difficult to say how long the majority remain. However that may be, the ponds are deserted by them at sunset. On one occasion a large flock of gulls remained in Charles River Basin as late as 9 o'clock on a mild December night. It is possible that some food may be obtained on the surface of these bodies of fresh water, but the gulls appear to spend most of their time there gossiping in groups as they float in closely crowded ranks on the surface of the water or stand shoulder to shoulder on the ice.

The subject of the drinking of fresh water has already been discussed above. As the gulls do not spend the night in the small fresh-water ponds on the coast, and as they fly toward the sea at sunset, it is evident that they must spend the night on or near salt water.

One such night chamber—it can not be called a roost—I have found off the beach at Revere, close to Boston. Here in November and December I have seen great companies of these splendid white birds gathering about sunset from a quarter to a third of a mile offshore. Sometimes there are two groups of many hundreds each. Once I saw one that looked like a coral atoll, for it was annular with a calm, open area in the middle. I have seen these birds in a strong offshore wind keep in exactly the same place; so it was evident that each bird, headed up into the wind, must have been paddling hard. This, to our way of thinking, would seem to be a poor manner in which to spend the night—sleep walking with a vengeance. It is possible and indeed probable that later in the evening and during the night, when the beach is free from human intrusion, the birds seek rest on the beach. In fact at sunrise one December day I saw a large flock of herring gulls at Revere, partly on the beach and partly in the water. In the summer at Ipswich the gulls often spend the night on the beach, although they sometimes resort to the marshes and doubtless also sleep on the water. Many of them fly to the small rocky islands, the Salvages, off the end of Cape Ann, and there, secure from human intrusion, spend the night. In some regions herring gulls roost in trees during the night.

It is stated that sometimes herring gulls follow a vessel for food for many miles and even across the Atlantic Ocean. Anthony (1906) states that herring gulls turn back some 25 miles at sea on the Pacific coast.

DISTRIBUTION.

Breeding range.—In North America east to the Atlantic coast. South to central Maine (Penobscot Bay), central New York (Lake Champlain, Hamilton, Herkimer, and Oneida Counties), southern Ontario (Great Lakes), northern Wisconsin (Green Bay), northern Michigan (Sanilac County), central Minnesota (Mille Lacs), southern Manitoba (Shoal Lake), and central British Columbia (Sabine Lake). The western and northern limits are uncertain. Saskatchewan and North Dakota records are confused with *californicus;* breeding records from Forrester and Kodiak Islands, the Alaska Peninsula, Mount McKinley region, and Yukon River are not substantiated by specimens and may refer to *thayeri.* A breeding female has been taken at Lake Tagish, Yukon. For the same reason the northern limits which extend up to southern Ellesmere Land are equally uncertain. The species breeds in Iceland, the British Isles, and in Europe east to the White and Baltic Seas and south to northern France.

Breeding grounds protected in the following national reservations: In Alaska, Forrester Island; in Michigan, Huron Island, and Siskiwit Islands; in Wisconsin, Gravel Island and Green Bay; in Canada, protected on Percé Rock.

Winter range.—From the Great Lakes irregularly and the Gulf of St. Lawrence rarely, southward to Bermuda, the West Indies (Cuba and Jamaica), and the Gulf of Mexico (Florida, Texas, and Yucatan); on the Pacific coast from British Columbia (Puget Sound), south to Mexico (Tres Marias Islands); in Europe from the British Isles south to the Canary Islands and the Mediterranean; and east to the Black and Caspian Seas.

Spring migration.—Dates of early arrival: Prince Edward Island, April 1; Quebec, April 10; Montreal, April 13; Ottawa, March 13; Wisconsin, Madison, March 2; Minnesota, Heron Lake, March 20; Manitoba, Aweme, April 2; Alberta, Edmonton, May 1; Mackenzie, Fort Simpson, May 14; Franklin, Bay of Mercy, May 31, and Prince of Wales Strait, June 7. Dates of late departure: Florida, Clearwater Harbor, May 21; North Carolina, Pea Island, May 3; Maryland, Baltimore, May 28; Rhode Island, Providence, June 12; Massachusetts, Woods Hole, July 4 (average June 11); Louisiana, New Orleans, March 25; Missouri, St. Louis, May 28 (average April 15); Illinois, Chicago, June 15 (average April 23).

Fall migration.—Average dates of arrival: Massachusetts, Woods Hole, August 21; New Jersey, Jersey City, September 21; Georgia, Savannah, November 3; Iowa, Keokuk, October 8. Average dates of departure; Ungava, Fort Chimo, September 18; Labrador, Nakvak, October; Montreal, November 5; Ontario, Ottawa, November 7; Mackenzie, Fort Resolution, September 22; Manitoka, Killarney, October 18.

Egg dates.—Maine: Forty-eight records, May 4 to August 8; twenty-four records, June 12 to 30. Michigan: Twenty-five records, May 21 to June 24; thirteen records, May 27 to June 10. Gulf of St. Lawrence: Nine records, June 7 to 23. Great Britain: Nine records, April 28 to May 26; five records, May 12 to 20.

LARUS THAYERI Brooks.

THAYER'S GULL.

HABITS.

A new species has recently been described by Mr. W. Sprague Brooks (1915), based on the discovery that certain gulls collected by Mr. J. S. Warmbath, in Ellesmere Land in June, 1901, supposed to be Kumlien's gulls, were in reality a distinct and undescribed species. The discovery was made in attempting to identify a gull collected by Mr. Joseph Dixon at Demarcation Point, Alaska, on August 28, 1913. Practically nothing is known about the distribution or life history of this decidedly boreal species.

There are two sets of two eggs each, in Col. John E. Thayer's collection, taken by Mr. Warmbath in Ellesmere Land on June 15, 1910. These, and I believe a few others, were sold as eggs of Kumlien's gull, which they were honestly supposed to be at that time. These eggs are not strikingly different from many other gulls' eggs, though they are rather more pointed than the average; the shape varies from ovate to elongate ovate. The ground color is "dark olive-buff," "buffy brown," or "buffy olive." The markings are similar to those of other large gulls. The four eggs measure 80 by 51.5, 83 by 52, 73 by 49, and 75 to 52 millimeters. There is a set of three eggs in the author's collection, taken by Captain Bernard on Victoria Island, Arctic America, on June 27, 1914. The nest is described as the "usual nest of vegetation on rocks close to the sea." In these three eggs the ground color is, respectively, "deep olive buff," "yellowish glaucous," and "sea foam yellow." All three are quite uniformly and rather thickly covered with small spots of "vinaceous drab" and various shades of dark brown, from "bister" to almost black. In one egg the darkest markings are in scrawls. They measure 67 by 46, 67 by 48.5, and 70.4 by 46.5.

Very little is known about the distribution and habits of Thayer's gull, but, as it is now supposed to be a subspecies of the herring gull, its habits and plumage changes are probably similar to those of the common species.

Mr. Brooks (1915) says of its distribution:

Though there is no data to determine the range of this species it must be a very boreal form, and perhaps comparatively small in numbers. The Alaskan specimens may have wandered from Ellesmere Land, but it seems reasonable to believe that the bird may inhabit Prince Patrick, Melville, or Bathurst Islands, nearly all this territory being north of 75°.

Dr. Jonathan Dwight (1917) has studied practically all of the specimens of this gull now available, some 25 in all, which he says:

demonstrate that the supposed new species is nothing more than a geographical race of the herring gull, and should stand as *Larus argentatus thayeri*—Thayer's herring gull. Complete intergradation between the two forms occurs, *argentatus* prevailing south of Hudson Strait and of the northern shores of Hudson Bay, while northward probably throughout the Arctic Archipelago of Canada, *thayeri* seems to be the common form.

Breeding birds of Fort Chimo, Ungava, are *argentatus*, and those of Cape Fullerton, north of Chesterfield Inlet, not quite typical *thayeri*, but farther north and west all the birds are *thayeri*. The localities from which I have seen breeding specimens are Buchanan Bay, Ellesmere Land, Browne Island (south of Cornwallis Island), Kater Point, Coronation Gulf, Bernard Harbor, Dolphin and Union Strait, and Cape Kellett, Banks Island.

Thayer's herring gull probably winters chiefly on the Pacific coast, for I have examined a number of specimens from Barkley Sound, Departure Bay, and Comox, Vancouver Island, British Columbia. I also have an adult female in my own collection taken on the north shore of the St. Lawrence at Tadousac, Quebec, July 26; but this specimen is doubtless a wanderer from the north, for dissection showed it to be a bird past the breeding stage.

DISTRIBUTION.

Breeding range.—Breeding range imperfectly known. Presumably breeding herring gulls from the Artic coast of North America are this form, but it is not possible to verify all records; neither do we know the area where intergradation takes place. Breeding specimens have been examined by Dwight from Buchanan Bay, Ellesmere Land, Browne Island (south of Cornwallis Island), Cape Fullerton, Kater Point, Coronation Gulf, Bernard Harbor, Dolphin and Union Strait, and Cape Kellett, Banks Island. Eggs have been taken at Ellesmere Land (type locality) and Victoria Island.

Winter range.—Probably largely on Pacific coast. Specimens examined by Dwight from Barkley Sound, Departure Bay, and Comox, Vancouver Island, British Columbia.

Migration.—Practically nothing is known regarding the migrations of this gull. It apparently passes north along the Pacific coast at least to southeastern Alaska (Ketchikan, specimen taken); and, lacking negative evidence, we may infer the return is made by the same route.

Casual records.—One was taken at Tadousac, Quebec, July 26.

Egg dates.—Ellesmere Land: Two records, June 15 and July 1. Victoria Island: One record, June 27.

LARUS VEGAE Palmén.

VEGA GULL.

HABITS.

This (so-called) species seems to be nothing more nor less than a dark-backed herring gull, and I doubt very much if it will prove to be more than subspecifically distinct from *Larus argentatus*, if even that. Mr. William H. Kobbé (1902) has presented a very thorough and convincing argument to prove that the two forms intergrade, and suggests that but one species be recognized. The characters on which *Larus vegae* is supposed to stand have been apparently confused with those of *Larus cachinnans*, or are variable and unsatisfactory. For a full discussion of the merits of the case I would refer the readers to Mr. Kobbé's excellent paper.

The distribution of the Vega gull has not been very thoroughly worked out, for our knowledge of the bird life of the region it inhabits is very meager. Until the limits of its breeding range are well known, and until a large series of specimens have been collected in that region, the correct status of the species can not be determined.

If not identical with the herring gull it is certainly closely related to it, and its habits, so far as we know, are similar. It is therefore fair to assume that its life history closely resembles that of the commoner species, due allowance being made for any differences in environment.

Nesting.—There are three sets of eggs of this species in the author's collection, all of which were taken by Mr. Johan Koren at the mouth of the River Kolyma in northeastern Siberia, where he found it an abundant species along the Arctic coast. Two of these nests were photographed for illustration in this work. The first nest was located on a shelf on a steep bluff 200 feet high, on the bank of the river, where glaucous gulls were also nesting. It contained three eggs, which were nearly ready to hatch on July 10. Another set of three eggs, incubated about 15 days, was taken on July 2. A large nest of moss and straws had been built over the root of a stranded tree trunk, which drifted onto a low, grass-grown islet of the delta. The third set was taken on July 6 and consisted of two eggs, incubated seven days. The nest was made of moss and straws in a bog on a low island of the delta; a colony of six pairs of Vega gulls were breeding on the island.

Eggs.—The above three sets of eggs are so different in coloring that they are worth describing, as representing the usual variations in eggs of this species. In the first set the ground color is " deep olive buff"; the eggs are sparingly spotted over the entire surface with rather small spots of " fuscous," " Vandyke brown," " Dresden brown," and " chestnut brown," over underlying spots and blotches varying from " pale drab gray " to " hair brown." The second set is paler, " olive buff," one egg having a decidedly greenish tinge; this latter egg is heavily and fantastically blotched with dark shades of " chestnut brown " and "Vandyke brown." The third set represents the brownish type; the ground color carries from dull " snuff brown " to dull " tawny olive"; the three eggs are all heavily spotted, chiefly about the larger ends, with confluent spots of " hair brown," " drab," " warm sepia," and dark " Vandyke brown." All of these eggs could be closely matched with similar types of herring gull's eggs, which they resemble in general appearance. The measurements of 30 eggs, in various collections, average 70.4 by 49.5 millimeters; the eggs showing the four extremes measure **77.5** by 50.5, 75.5 by **53.1** and **65** by **47.5** millimeters.

Plumages.—The downy is similar to that of the herring gull, but what specimens I have seen average darker gray in color, less buffy, and are somewhat more heavily spotted with black. Although specimens of this bird are scarce in collections, I have seen enough to convince me that the molts and plumages are similar to those of the herring gull.

Winter.—Our check list states that this species migrates south in winter to Japan, and does not mention any southward migration down the Pacific coast of North America; but Mr. Kobbé (1902) collected a series of herring gulls in San Francisco Bay during December, 1900, and January, March, and April, 1901, some of which might easily be referred to this form. His series, and that of the California Academy of Sciences, show every gradation of color, from the darkest vega to the lightest herring gull. The more one studies such material the less faith one has in *Larus vegae* as a species.

DISTRIBUTION.

Breeding range.—Northeastern Siberia, known to breed on the Kolyma River and its delta; Cape Bolshaja Baranof; Cape Kibera Island; and coast of Tchonkatch (Idligass Island). Taken in summer, and probably breeds on the Siberian coast from the Taimir Peninsula and the Liakoff Islands to Plover Bay and Kamchatka. Alaska breeding records are doubtful.

Winter range.—South along the coasts of Japan and China to Formosa and the Bonin Islands. Records from the Pacific coast of the United States are usually not accepted.

Spring migration.—Northward along the Asiatic coast. China, Formosa Channel, March 9; Japan, Kanagana, March 29; Saghalin Island, June 2 (may breed there).

Fall migration.—Eastward to Norton Sound, Alaska, and then southward along the Asiatic coast. Alaska, Nome, August 31; St. Michael, October 16.

Casual records.—Taken at Laysan Island and Marcus Island in the Pacific Ocean.

Egg dates.—Northeastern Siberia: Eight records, June 4 to July 12; four records, June 24 to July 6.

LARUS CALIFORNICUS Lawrence.

CALIFORNIA GULL.

HABITS.

It has always seemed to me that the above name should have been applied to the western gull, *Larus occidentalis*, the characteristic gull of the California coast, for the subject of this sketch, *Larus californicus*, is essentially a bird of the inland plains. It is common enough on the California coast in winter, together with several other species, but it is not known to breed within that State except in the elevated regions east of the Sierras in the northern part of the State. Although we are accustomed to associate gulls with the seashore this species seems to be confined, during the breeding season, to the interior, where it is widely distributed and in many places abundant, particularly in the vicinity of the larger lakes, from northern Utah to the barren grounds on the Arctic coast. The exact limits of its distribution are none too well known, for the casual observer might easily mistake it for the herring gull, which it closely resembles. The ranges of the two species come together at the eastern edge of the Great Plains, and undoubtedly many mistaken identifications have been made where specimens have not been collected. Such was the case at Crane Lake, Saskatchewan, where the herring gull had been reported as breeding abundantly, but where all of the large gulls that we collected during two seasons' work proved to be California gulls, which were very common.

Nesting.—The finest breeding colony of this species that I have ever seen was at Big Stick Lake in that same region, 30 miles north of Maple Creek. On June 14, 1906, our guide drove us out through shallow water to a small island, about 300 yards from the shore. It was a low, flat island, surrounded by gravelly or muddy beaches, largely bare on the higher portions, except for a scattered growth of coarse, dead weeds, but supporting quite a thick growth of long grass on the lower or flatter portion. It may have contained more than 1 acre of land, but certainly not over 2 acres at the most. As we landed a flock of American white pelicans flew off from the farther end and a great cloud of California and ring-billed gulls arose from the center of the island, but we devoted our attention at first to the American avocets, which had flown out to greet us with their yelping notes of protest. Their nests were placed in the short grass near the beach or on the windrows of driftweed which lined the shores. There were not over a dozen pairs in the colony. A small colony of common terns were nesting in the short grass, two nests of spotted sandpipers were found, Wilson's phalaropes were flying about, and specimens of northern phalaropes and semipalmated sandpipers were collected. In the long grass we found a pintail's nest with nine eggs in the process of hatching and five ducks' nests, with apparently fresh eggs, which we took to be baldpates, though we could not identify them with certainty, as the birds were not incubating. On the higher portion of the island, among the tall dead weeds, we found three ducks' nests, referred to hereafter under the American merganser, which we were unable to satisfactorily identify. The California and ring-billed gull colony occupied the whole of the main portion of the island, which was thickly covered with their nests. We could form no accurate idea of their number, as we did not have time to count the nests; but to say that there were at least 1,000 pairs of each species would be a conservative statement. The nests of the ring-billed gulls were chiefly on the higher portion of the island, while those of the California gulls were mostly around the shores and on a bare, flat point, though both species were somewhat intermingled where the two colonies came together. I should say that about half of the eggs had hatched, for we found hundreds of the downy young hiding among the scanty vegetation and saw them swimming out from the shores in large numbers. This island was visited again by the other members of our party July 18–21, 1906, when they found the bird population of the little island increased by a nesting colony of 14 pairs of American white pelicans and 4 pairs of double-crested cormorants.

The California gulls' nests in this colony were well made of dead weeds, rubbish, straw, and feathers. Most of them were on the bare dry ground on the open shores, but many of them were actually in the water; probably these latter were originally built on the dry beach, but recent heavy rains had raised the level of the lake and surrounded them with water; fortunately they had been built high enough to keep the eggs and young dry. The nests varied greatly in size; average nests measured from 14 to 18 inches in diameter. The inner cavity was usually 7 inches wide by 2 inches deep; the outer edges of the nests were built up from 2 to 5 inches above the ground. One extra large nest measured 26 inches in diameter and 7 inches high.

Mr. W. L. Finley (1907) found an interesting colony of California and ring-billed gulls on a tule island in Lower Klamath Lake, Oregon, in May, 1905; I quote from his account of it as follows:

We were led to the place by watching the course of the small flocks that spread out over the lake in the morning and returned homeward about dusk each evening. From a full mile away, with our field glass, we could see the gulls rising and circling over the low-lying islands. As we rowed nearer the birds came out to meet us, cackling excitedly at the dubious-looking craft approaching so near their homes. They swam about on all sides, curiously following in the wake of our boat. Cormorants flapped along over the surface, pelicans rose heavily from the water, and gulls and terns got thicker and thicker, until when the nose of the boat pushed in at the edge of the island, the air seemed completely filled with a crying, chaotic swarm. We stepped out among the reeds, but had to tread cautiously to keep from breaking eggs or killing young birds. Many youngsters crouched low in their tracks and others scudded off in all directions.

Although there were at least 500 pairs of gulls nesting so close together, yet housekeeping was in no sense a communal matter. The nests were within 2 or 3 feet of each other, but each pair of gulls had its own home spot, and the invasion of that place by any other gull was the challenge for a fight.

Several times we were the excited spectators of fights that were going on just outside our tent. I watched one old hen, who was very angry because she could not find her chicks. As one of her neighbors lit near she grabbed the tail of the intruder and gave it a sharp jerk. At that both birds grasped each other by the bill and a lively set-to followed. They pulled and tugged till suddenly the old hen let go and grabbed her opponent by the neck and began shaking and hanging on with all the tenacity of a bull pup, till the intruder got enough and departed, leaving the victor with a mouthful of feathers.

Mr. Oliver Davie (1889) says of the nests of the California gull:

The nests of this species are made on the ground or built on rocks, and sometimes where the birds are breeding in vast colonies the nests are placed on stunted sage or greasewood bushes. They are built of sticks, grass, and a few feathers.

Eggs.—As with most water birds, only one brood is raised in a season. The usual set consists of three eggs, but two are often considered sufficient; four eggs are laid occasionally, and five have been reported. The eggs are similar to other gulls' eggs, but they are usually handsomer and often more boldly marked with striking colors. The shell is thin and lusterless. The shape varies from short ovate to elongate ovate. It is usually more pointed than in other gulls' eggs, and is sometimes nearly ovate pyriform.

The ground color shows a variety of shades from " Saccardo's umber " or " buffy brown," in the darker specimens, to " light drab," " smoke gray," or " olive buff," in the lighter specimens, which are much commoner. The commonest types of eggs are spotted more or less evenly with rather small spots of irregular sizes and shapes, but many of them are boldly marked with large spots and blotches; often lighter and brighter shades of brown seem to be overlaid on spots of darker brown or gray, producing handsome effects. Some eggs are oddly decorated with fantastic scrawls and irregular lines, such as are seen on murres' eggs. These markings are generally in the darker and richer shades of brown, such as " bone brown," " olive brown," " warm sepia," and " Vandyke brown." Nearly all eggs show underlying spots of " light violet gray," or similar colors. The measurements of 50 eggs in the United States National Museum average 67.5 by 45.5 millimeters; the eggs showing the four extremes measure **71.5** by 47.5, 69 by **50.5,** **57.5** by 41, and 65.5 by **40.5** millimeters.

Young.—I have no data on the period of incubation, which is probably about the same as with other large gulls. Probably both sexes incubate. The young are quite precocial; after a few days in the nest, they learn to run about and hide among the stones or under the vegetation near their nests. They are good swimmers and, even when very small, will take to the water readily and swim away until driven back by their parents, who keep a careful watch over them. Mr. Finley (1907) says of their behaviors at this time:

I soon discovered that their greatest anxiety seemed to be to keep their children crouching low in the nest so they would not run away and get lost in the crowd. I saw one young gull start to run off through the reeds, but he hadn't gone a yard before the mother dived at him with a blow that sent him rolling. He got up dazed and started off in a new direction, but she rapped him again on the head till he was glad to crouch down in the dry reeds.

The parents seemed to recognize their own chicks largely by location. Several times I saw old birds pounce upon youngsters that were running about and beat them unmercifully. It seemed to be as much the duty of a gull mother to beat her neighbor's children if they didn't stay home as to whip her own if they moved out of the nest, but often this would lead to a rough and tumble fight among the old birds. Sometimes a young gull would start to swim off in the water, but it never went far before it was pounced upon and driven back shoreward.

Plumages.—The young bird, when first hatched, is covered with thick, soft down of plain, light colors to match its surroundings, "light buff" to "cartridge buff," brightest on the head and breast; the upper parts and throat are clouded or variegated with light grayish, and the head is sparingly spotted with dull black. These colors fade out to a dirty grayish white as the bird grows older. The juvenal plumage is much like that of the herring gull; the head and underparts are dark and mottled, the dusky markings prevailing; the upper parts are boldly mottled, each feather being broadly edged with buffy white and centrally dusky. The first winter plumage, which is acquired early in the fall by a partial molt of the body feathers, is everywhere mottled with dusky, the underparts, especially the neck and breast, being tinged with cinnamon; the tail, which in the young ring-billed gull is basally gray, and the primaries are uniform brownish black and the bill is dark. This plumage is worn for nearly a year or until the first postnuptial molt, when the bird is a year old. This molt is complete, producing the second winter plumage, which is more or less mottled with dusky, except on the mantle, which now becomes more or less clear "gull gray." The new primaries are nearly black, but with little or no white tips; the tail is white at the base, becoming dusky near the tip. The bill becomes yellow at the base, but the outer half remains dusky. A partial prenuptial molt occurs during the latter part of the winter or early spring in both old and young birds, producing whiter heads and necks.

A nearly adult winter plumage is acquired at the second postnuptial molt, when the bird is a little over 2 years old. At this molt, which is complete, the black primaries with limited white tips and the pure white tail, often subterminally marked with dusky, are acquired; the bill becomes wholly yellow. Winter adults have elongated dusky markings on the crown and a necklace of dusky spots on the hind neck, which are lost at the partial prenuptial molt before the next breeding season. The bright chrome yellow of the upper mandible and the vermilion of the lower mandible are characteristic of the breeding season. Subsequent seasonal molts of the adult are merely repetitions of the complete postnuptial in the summer and the partial prenuptial molt in early spring, involving only the head and neck.

Food.—The feeding habits of the California gull make it one of the most useful of birds to the agriculturist of the western plains, where it makes its summer home. Rev. S. H. Goodwin (1904) says of its habits in Utah:

I have watched them for hours as they circled about the newly plowed field, or followed close behind the plowman, as blackbirds do in some localities, or sunned themselves on the ridges of the furrows after a hearty meal of worms. I have studied them as they fared up and down the river in search of dead fish and other garbage, or assembled in countless numbers in some retired, quiet slough where they rent the air with their harsh, discordant cries and demoniac laughter, or sailed on graceful wing in rising circles till lost in the deep blue of heaven.

Mr. Dutcher (1905) publishes the following interesting letter from Mr. John E. Cox, of the Utah Board of Agriculture:

Gulls go all over the State for insects, the greatest number visiting the beet fields, where they keep down the crickets, grasshoppers, cutworms, etc. They took a new diet this summer. Some alfalfa fields were so badly honeycombed with mice holes and runs that it was impossible to irrigate them, and they were plowed up, mostly for beet culture. When the water was turned into the irrigation ditches the mice were forced out of their holes, and the gulls then caught them. They became so perfect in their work that they kept abreast of the head of the water and picked up every mouse that appeared. When gorged with victims they would vomit them up in piles on the ditch bank and recommence their feeding. Gulls are sacred in Utah, and are so tame that oftentimes they may be caught by hand as they follow the plow so closely.

Dr. A. K. Fisher (1893) reports that a specimen of this species, shot at Owens Lake, California, " on December 28, had its craw full of duck meat and feathers, and from the actions of its associates when a duck was shot it was evident that they prey upon such game, since the lake affords little other food." During the two seasons that I spent in Saskatchewan we saw the California and ring-billed gulls almost daily visiting the garbage heaps on the outskirts of Maple Creek, where they found a good supply of food to vary their natural diet of insects and other animal food picked up on the prairies and about the lakes. During their winter sojourn on the Pacific coast they follow the example of others of their kind and become largely scavengers about the harbors. They also, probably, feed on fish to some extent.

Behavior.—Mr. Finley (1907) refers to their powers of flight as follows:

These gulls are masters in the air. I have watched by the hour birds similar to these following along in the wake of a steamer, but had never before had such chances with a camera. Often they poise, resting apparently motionless on outstretched wings. It is a difficult feat. A small bird can not do it. A sparrow hawk can only poise by the rapid beating of his wings. The gull seems to hang perfectly still; yet there is never an instant when the wings and tail are not constantly adjusted to meet the different air currents; just as in shooting the rapids in a canoe the paddle must be adjusted every moment to meet the different eddies, currents, and whirlpools, and it is never the same in two different instants. A gull by the perfect adjustment of its body, without a single flap of the wings, makes headway straight in the teeth of the wind. I saw one retain a perfect equilibrium in a stiff breeze and at the same time reach forward and scratch his ear.

Mr. Dawson (1909) pays the following tribute to their prowess on the wing:

Graceful, effortless, untiring, but above all mysterious, is that power of propulsion by which the bird moves forward into the teeth of the gale; indeed, is advanced all the more certainly and freely when the wind is strong. From the deck of a steamer making 15 miles an hour against a 15-knot breeze, I once stretched my hand toward a soaring gull. He lay suspended in mid-air without the flutter of a feather, while the air rushed past him at the rate of 30 miles an hour; and he maintained the same relative position to my hand, at 5 or 6 feet, for about a minute. When he tired of the game, he shot forward. And again, there was not in the motion the slightest perceptible effort of propulsion, but only a slightly sharper inclination of the body and wings downward. We see clearly how it must be, yet we can not understand it. The gull is a kite and gravity the string. The bird is a continually falling body, and the wind is continually preventing the catastrophe. Yes, we see it—but then, gravity isn't a string, you know; and so why doesn't the wind take the kite along with it? Well, there you are; and not even Hamilton, who discovered quaternions, could have given the mathematics of it.

My knowledge of the vocal powers of the California gull is confined to what I heard and noted on its breeding grounds, where its vocabulary was limited. The ordinary cry was a soft, low " kow, kow, kow," or " kuk, kuk, kuk," much like the notes of other gulls. When the birds became much excited or alarmed they indulged in shrill, sharp, piercing cries. Gulls are usually silent birds, but while feeding, quarreling, or showing active emotions, they have a variety of notes to express their feelings or to communicate their ideas to their fellows, all of which seem to be understood.

California gulls seems to be quiet, gentle, harmless birds, and I have no evidence to show that they do any appreciable damage to the various species with which they are associated on their breeding grounds, though they do occasionally steal a few eggs from unprotected nests. They have been found nesting in colonies with ring-billed gulls, Caspian terns, white pelicans, double-crested cormorants, and great blue herons. So far as I know they have no formidable enemies among birds and are not much molested by man. They select for their breeding grounds islands in remote lakes far from the haunts of man, where they are probably safe until the encroachments of civilization drive them out. They are not suspicious or wild; in fact, they are much tamer than most gulls, but they do not seem to be fond of human society.

Winter.—The fall migration is westward to the Pacific coast or southwestward to the large inland lakes of the Southwestern States and Mexico, where they spend the winter, associating on the coast with various other species of gulls.

DISTRIBUTION.

Breeding range.—Western North America. East to Great Slave Lake and northeastern North Dakota (Stump and Devils Lake). South to northwestern Wyoming (Yellowstone Lake), northern Utah (Great Salt Lake), western Nevada (Pyramid Lake), and northeastern California (Eagle Lake). West to central southern Oregon (Klamath Lakes) and central British Columbia. North to northern Mackenzie (Anderson River region). Occurs in summer from Washington (Bellingham Bay) to southeastern Alaska (Ketchikan), but not known to breed there.

Breeding grounds protected in the following national reservations: In California, Clear Lake; in Nevada, Anaho Island (Pyramid Lake); in Oregon, Klamath and Malheur Lakes; in Wyoming, Yellowstone National Park.

Winter range.—Pacific coast, from southern British Columbia southward to southwestern Mexico (San Mateo), and from northern Utah (Great Salt Lake) southward to the Gulf of California; rarely east to the coast of Texas.

Spring migration.—Northeastward to the interior. Early dates of arrival: North Dakota, Devils Lake, April 24; British Columbia, Okanagan Lake, April 11. Late dates of departure: Lower California, San José del Cabo, May 17; California, Monterey, May 19.

Fall migration.—Southwestward toward the coast. Early dates of arrival: British Columbia, Chilliwack, August 26; Washington, Seattle, August 31; Oregon, Netarts Bay, September 8; California, Monterey, August 21 to October 9; Lower California, Magdalena Bay, November 24. Late dates of departure: Mackenzie, Hay River, November 5; Kansas, Reno County, October 20.

Casual records.—Has been recorded in the Hawaiian Islands (Bryan) and in Japan (Seebohm)

Egg dates.—Utah and Nevada: Fifty-six records, May 8 to June 26; twenty-eight records, May 13 to 20. North Dakota and Saskatchewan: Twelve records, June 4 to 22. California: Six records, May 18 to 25.

LARUS DELAWARENSIS Ord.

RING-BILLED GULL.

HABITS.

Audubon (1840) referred to this species as " The Common American Gull," a title which would hardly be warranted to-day, although, with the possible exception of the herring gull, it is the most widely distributed and most universally common of any of the large gulls. In Audubon's time it was probably more widely distributed and certainly more abundant in some localities than it is now; he refers to its breeding on " several islands between Boston and Eastport, another close to Grand Manan at the entrance of the Bay of Fundy, the great Gannet Rock of the Gulf of St. Lawrence, and certain rocky isles in the deep bays on the coast of Labrador." I have visited all of these localities without finding or hearing of any breeding colonies of ring-billed gulls, and I can not find anything in the published records to indicate that they have bred at any of these places in recent years, except a few shifting colonies near Cape Whittle in southern Labrador, found by Mr. M. Abbott Frazar (1887) in 1884, and one found by Dr. Charles W. Townsend, referred to below. The ring-billed gull yields readily to persecution, is easily driven away from its breeding grounds, and seems to prefer to breed in remote unsettled regions, far from the haunts of man. It could never survive the egging depredations which the herring gull has withstood successfully; hence its breeding range has been gradually curtailed as the country has become settled. Although its former breeding range was nearly as extensive as that of the herring gull, it is now mainly restricted to the interior, in the lakes of the prairies and plains of the Northern States and Canada, where it far outnumbers the herring gull and is still *the common gull.* Here it is probably holding its own except where civilization is driving it out. In North Dakota in 1901, in Saskatchewan in 1905 and 1906, and in Manitoba in 1913 we saw it almost daily about nearly all the lakes we visited and we found numerous breeding colonies. Dr. P. L. Hatch (1892) stated that they had become much more numerous in Minnesota through a gradual increase since 1857, being " extensively distributed over the lacustrine regions of the Commonwealth, breeding in all places adapted to their habits."

Courtship.—According to Audubon (1840) mating takes place before the birds reach their breeding grounds. He says:

When spring has fairly commenced, our common gulls assemble in parties of hundreds, and alight on mud flats or sandy beaches, in out eastern estuaries and bays. For awhile they regularly resort to these places, which to the gulls are what the scratching or tooting grounds are to the pinnated grouse. The male gulls, however, although somewhat pugnacious, and not very inveterate in their quarrels, making up by clamor for the deficiency of prowess in their tournaments. The males bow to the females with swollen throats, and walk round them with many odd gesticulations. As soon as the birds are paired they give up their animosities, and for the rest of the season live together on the best terms. After a few weeks spent in these preparatory pleasures, the flocks take to wing, and betake themselves to their breeding places.

Nesting.—My first experience with the nesting habits of the ring-billed gull was on "the enchanted isles" of Stump Lake, North Dakota, three small islands in a western arm of the lake, now included in the Stump Lake Reservation. On May 31, 1901, and again on June 15, 1901, I visited these interesting islands, with Mr. Herbert K. Job (1898) who had previously described and named them. Two of the islands contained breeding colonies of ring-billed gulls, consisting of about 100 pairs each; one held a colony of about 75 pairs of double-crested cormorants; and one a large colony of common terns. All of them offered suitable nesting sites for various species of ducks, of which we found no less than 40 nests on June 15. Certainly the bird population of these little islands warranted Mr. Job's title. The gulls' nests were placed upon the ground along the upper edges of the beaches and among the rocks and bowlders which were scattered all over the islands. They were made of dried grasses and weeds, sometimes of small sticks; were lined with finer grasses and were often decorated with feathers. On May 31 all the nests contained eggs, many of which had been incubated a week or 10 days; on June 15 not over one quarter of the eggs had hatched and many of them still held incomplete sets.

One of the most interesting gull colonies I have ever found was on a small island in Big Stick Lake, Saskatchewan, on June 14, 1906, where large numbers of this and the preceding species were breeding, together with a number of other water birds. I have already described this colony more fully in my account of the nesting habits of the California gull. The nests of the ring-billed gulls were on the higher portions of the island, somewhat apart from those of the larger species, but mingled with them to some extent. The nests were made of dead weeds, straws, rubbish, and feathers; they measured from 10 to 12 inches in diameter, and the inner cavity was about 9 inches across and 2 inches deep. Most of the nests were in open situations, but some were partially hidden among the rocks and low bushes. About half of the eggs had hatched, and the downy young were running about or hiding.

Ring-billed gulls were common at Lake Winnipegosis, Manitoba, in 1913. We saw them almost daily and examined several breeding colonies. They were on small rocky islets or reefs, where bowlders had been piled up a few feet above high water and a little soil had accumulated about them. On one very small reef, not over 25 yards long, I counted 10 nests of ring-billed gulls and 45 nests of double-crested cormorants. The islet was thickly covered with nests of the common tern, of which I estimated that there were about a thousand pairs. Another thickly populated island, but slightly larger, was visited on June 19. It was similar to the other reefs—an accumulation of bowlders, with sandy or stony shores and some soil in the center, sparsely overgrown with nettles. A cloud of gulls and terns were hovering over it, which I estimated to contain about 100 pairs of ring-billed gulls and 500 pairs of common terns. There was also a small colony of double-crested cormorants nesting on the rocks at one end. The nests of the gulls and terns were closely intermingled, sometimes three or four nests within one square yard, showing that the two species were living in apparent harmony. The gulls' nests were very poorly built affairs, the poorest I had ever seen, consisting in many cases of mere hollows lined with a few sticks and straws. Some of them were more elaborate and some were prettily decorated with feathers or lined with green weeds or leaves. Most of the nests contained three eggs, but many of them only two. No young were seen.

Audubon (1840) found them breeding on the Gannet Rock, early in June, " on the shelves toward the summit, along with the guillemots, while the kittiwakes had secured their nests far below." This undoubtedly refers to Bird Rock in the Gulf of St. Lawrence, where none of this species have been found breeding in recent years.

Dr. Charles W. Townsend writes me:

On July 16, 1915, I found a breeding colony of ring-billed gulls on Gull Island near Sealnet Point or Point au Maurier, on the Canadian Labrador coast. The island is close to the shore, is composed of granitic rock with sparse vegetation of grass and low herbs, and is some 10 acres in extent. On the highest ground about 200 pairs of ring-billed gulls had their nests. These nests were composed of moss, sprigs of curlew-berry vine, dried grass, and dried-weed stalks. The nests were 12 inches in outside diameter, 6 or 7 inside diameter, generally very thin, but sometimes built up to a height of 3 or 4 inches. They were placed on the bare rock or among the grass. A few herring gulls, eiders, razor-billed auks, and black guillemots were also nesting on the island.

Mr. William L. Finley (1907) describes a large colony of California and ring-billed gulls which he found breeding on a marshy island of floating tules in Klamath Lake, Oregon, which is a decided departure from their usual habit of nesting on solid ground.

Mr. George G. Cantwell has sent me a photograph of a remarkable nest of a ring-billed gull which he found at Prince William Sound, Alaska, in June, 1912. His notes state that the nest was " made of usual material, but unique in the matter of situation, placed in the crown of a dwarf spruce, that grew to the height of about 4 feet above the surface of a small rock, upon which it had taken root. The rock set in an open bay of the salt water, about one-half a mile from shore. On other near-by islands a colony of Arctic terns were nesting, and on the bars of a stream on the near-by mainland other ring-billed gulls had nests. This was the only nest noted in the trees there, or on any other occasion."

Eggs.—The ring-billed gull normally raises but one brood, and the full set usually consists of three eggs; often only two eggs are laid, and sets of four are very rare. The eggs are subject to the usual variations in gulls' eggs. In shape they are usually ovate or short ovate; the shell is smooth, thin, and almost lusterless. The ground color varies from " Brussel's brown " or " snuff brown " to " pinkish buff " or " cartridge buff " in the commoner types of eggs; in the greener types of eggs, which are rarer, the ground color varies from " deep olive buff " to " pale olive buff," or in some cases to " yellowish glaucous," which makes the egg look much greener than it really is. The prevailing types of eggs show the usual markings of gulls' eggs— spots and blotches of various sizes and shapes irregularly distributed; some eggs are finely speckled all over; in some the markings are confluent into a ring; and some are handsomely decorated with irregular scrawls, splashes, or blotches. Nearly all eggs show underlying spots or blotches of various shades of " quaker drab," lavender or " mouse gray." These markings are very faint in the lighter types. The heavier and darker markings are made up of various shades of brown, often several shades on the same egg overlapping each other as if superimposed; these vary from " blackish brown " or " fuscous black " to " burnt umber," " russet," or " Dresden brown." Often the darkest markings are on the lightest colored eggs, making strong contrasts. The measurements of 40 eggs in the United States National Museum and the author's collections average 59.3 by 42.3 millimeters; the eggs showing the four extremes measure **64.5** by 42.5, 59.5 by **44.5, 54** by 40.5, and 60.5 by **40** millimeters.

Young.—The period of incubation is about 21 days. The young remain in the nest for a few days, but soon learn to run about and hide among the rocks or under the vegetation near their nests. They learn to swim at an early age, and may often be seen swimming out from the shores of their island home when disturbed. They are carefully guarded by their anxious parents and driven back to dry land as soon as the dangerous intruder has departed. They seem to appreciate the value of their protective coloring, and will remain hidden until forced to run, when they become very lively. They are fed by their parents until able to fly and forage for themselves.

Plumages.—The downy young have at least two distinct color phases, both of which are often found in the same nest. In the gray phase the upper parts are "smoke gray" or "pale smoke gray"; in the buffy phase the upper parts are "pinkish buff" or "vinaceous buff." They are lighter below and almost white on the breast; they are distinctly spotted with "hair brown" or "sepia" on the head and neck, and more faintly mottled with the same color on the back.

The juvenal plumage is not fully acquired until the young bird is about fully grown, the down disappearing last on the chest and thighs. The upper parts are heavily and boldly mottled; each feather of the back, scapulars, lesser wing coverts, and tertials is centrally dusky, broadly tipped, and margined with "pinkish buff," most conspicuously on the scapulars. The greater wing coverts are largely "gull gray," becoming dusky near the tips, and some are tipped or edged with buffy. The primaries are mostly black, with narrow white tips; the tail is largely "gull gray," somewhat mottled, and with a broad subterminal band of dusky, tipped with white or buffy white. The tail is never wholly dusky, as in the young California gull, a good diagnostic character. The under parts are largely white; the crown and breast are heavily mottled with dusky, and the sides are barred with the same. The bill is dusky, with the inner half of the lower mandible light yellowish.

Except for a molt of some of the body plumage, the first winter plumage is a continuation of the juvenal; the buffy edgings fade out to white and wear away; many new feathers, partially "gull gray" with dusky markings, come in on the back; and the dusky markings fade and wear away or are replaced by white on the breast and head during the winter. A partial prenuptial molt increases the amount of white on the head and under parts.

A complete postnuptial molt produces the second winter plumage, in which the back is mainly or wholly "gull gray," the feathers narrowly edged with whitish, and the greater wing-coverts are largely the same; the lesser wing-coverts are still mottled with dusky; there is much dusky in the tertials and secondaries, and the primaries are plain brownish black. The tail is whiter basally, but has a broad subterminal dusky band. The head and neck are heavily streaked and spotted with dusky, but the under parts are mainly white. The inner half of the bill is yellowish and the outer half black. The partial prenuptial molt produces pure white under parts and nearly a pure white head, with a clear "gull gray" back.

At the next complete molt, the second postnuptial, when the bird is 2 years old, the fully adult plumage is perhaps assumed by some birds; but many, probably a decided majority, still retain signs of immaturity during the third year. The new primaries in such birds are black, but they have only a faint suggestion of the subterminal white spot on the outer primary or none at all; undoubtedly these spots increase in size with the successive molts. There is more or less dusky in the tertials, and the tail has the black subterminal band more or less clearly indicated. The remainder of the plumage and the bill is now like the adult. Such birds would become fully adult at the age of 3 years. I have one bird in my series which is quite heavily mottled with dusky on the breast, but is otherwise fully adult.

The complete postnuptial molt of both adults and young occurs mainly in August and September, but I have seen the molt beginning as early as June. The partial prenuptial molt, involving the contour feathers only, occurs mainly in March. The winter adult is similar to the spring adult, except for a few narrow streaks of dusky on the crown and hind neck; these are less in evidence in older birds.

Food.—The feeding habits of this species make it as fully beneficial as any of the gulls. Throughout the agricultural regions of the western plains, where it is more abundant, it is often seen in the spring following the plow, picking up worms, grubs, grasshoppers, and other insects. It also does effective work by feeding on field mice and other small rodents. Dr. J. A. Allen, according to Baird, Brewer, and Ridgway (1884), states in regard to their feeding habits in Salt Lake Valley:

At the period of his visit these birds spent much of their time on the sand bars of Weber River, and at certain hours of the day rose in the air to feast on the grasshoppers, on which they seemed at this time almost wholly to subsist. The stomachs of those gulls that were killed were not only filled with grasshoppers, but some birds had stuffed themselves so full that these could be seen when the birds opened their mouths. And it was a curious fact that the gulls captured the grasshoppers in the air and not by walking over the ground, as they have been said to do. Sailing around in broad circles, as though soaring merely for pleasure, the birds seized the flying grasshoppers as easily, if not as gracefully, as a swallow while in rapid flight secures its prey of smaller insects.

I have seen ring-billed gulls hovering over a flock of feeding redbreasted mergansers and darting down at them as they rose to the surface. They were apparently trying to rob them of or make them drop some of the fish they had caught.

We found this and the foregoing species frequenting regularly the garbage dumps on the outskirts of the prairie towns and acting as scavengers along the shores of the lakes in Saskatchewan. On the seacoasts it does its part with other species in cleaning up the floating refuse in our harbors, and gathers in large numbers where garbage is regularly dumped, feasting on the miscellaneous diet it finds. It does considerable damage on its breeding grounds by destroying the eggs of other species associated with it.   I have seen a party of ring-billed gulls break and suck nearly every egg in a colony of double-crested cormorants when the latter had been kept off their nests for an hour or two; but I doubt if they would have dared to molest them if the cormorants had not been driven away by our presence.   It occasionally robs the nests of the avocet, but it does not seem to molest the nests of the common tern, with which it is intimately associated; and I have never known of its disturbing any of the ducks which nest on its breeding grounds.   Probably the terns are able to defend their eggs and the duck's nests are too well hidden.

Behavior.—The flight of the ring-billed gull is not markedly different from that of the other larger gulls; it is light and graceful as well as strong and long sustained.   It can poise stationary in the air when facing a good breeze without moving its wings except to adjust them to the changing air currents, and can even sail along against the wind in the same manner.   It is often so poised while looking for food on the water, but if the wind conditions are not favorable it is obliged to hover.   When food is discovered it either plunges straight downward or floats down more slowly in a spiral curve, and picks up its food without wetting its plumage.   When alighting on the water its wings are held high above it as it drops lightly down with dangling feet.   It swims gracefully and buoyantly, sitting lightly on the surface.   It rises neatly from the water.   It has no very distinctive field marks and closely resembles several other species. but it is somewhat smaller than the California gull and very much smaller than the herring gull; it also has a lighter gray mantle and less white in its black wing tips.   The black ring in its bill is not always in evidence and can not be seen at any distance.

Its notes are similar to those of other closely related gulls, but they are on a higher key than those of the two larger species referred to above.   When alarmed or when its breeding grounds are invaded it utters a shrill, piercing note of protest—*kree, kreeee*—like the cry of a hawk, but when its excitement has somewhat subsided this note is softened and modified and the subdued *kow, kow kow* notes are often heard from a flock of gulls floating overhead.   It is often noisy while feeding, while a cloud of hovering gulls show their excitement by a chorus of loud squealing notes and shrill screams. While pursuing its ordinary vocations it is usually silent, except for an occasional soft, mellow *kowk.*

The ring-billed gull is a highly gregarious species, both on its breeding grounds and in its winter resorts, congregating in large flocks of its own species and associating with a variety of other species, with all of whom it seems to live in perfect harmony.   Except for its cowardly, egg-robbing habits, it is a gentle and harmless creature. It seems to have no enemies from which it has much to fear except man. Its universal habit of nesting on islands saves it from the attacks of predatory animals.

Winter.—During the winter months much of its time is spent at sea following the coastwise vessels in company with other gulls in search of such morsels as it may pick up, hovering in clouds about our harbors where garbage is dumped, or resting in large flocks on sand bars or mud flats at low tide—a season of rest and recreation, with freedom to roam where it will.

DISTRIBUTION.

Breeding range.—Mainly in southern Canada. East to Hamilton Inlet and southern Labrador (Point au Maurier). South to northern New York (Adirondacks, casually), central Ontario (Muskoka Lake, Georgian Bay, etc.), Lakes Huron and Michigan (formerly), Wisconsin (Green Bay, formerly), northern North Dakota (Devil's Lake region), and northern Utah (Great Salt Lake). West to central southern Oregon (Klamath Lakes) British Columbia (Shuswap Lake), and southern Alaska (Prince William Sound). North to central Mackenzie (Great Slave Lake), eastern Keewatin (north of Fort Churchill), and James Bay (Fort George).

Breeding grounds protected in the following national reservations: In Oregon, Malheur Lake; in North Dakota, Stump Lake.

Winter range.—From Massachusetts (irregularly) southward along the Atlantic coast to Florida and Cuba; and along the Gulf Coast to Mexico (Tehuantepec); west to the Pacific coasts of Mexico and the United States, southward to Oaxaca, and northward to British Columbia; in the interior north to Colorado (Barr Lakes), more rarely Idaho (Fort Sherman), Montana (Lewiston), and the Great Lakes (Chicago and Detroit).

Spring migration.—Northward along Atlantic coast and in the interior; northeastward from the Pacific coast. Early dates of arrival: Connecticut, Saybrook, March 8; Newfoundland, April 19; Missouri, St. Louis, March 7; Iowa, Keokuk, March 8, and Storm Lake, March 15; South Dakota, Sioux Falls, March 19, and Vermilion, March 31; North Dakota, Devils Lake, average April 16, earliest April 11; southern Manitoba, average April 25, earliest April 21; Mackenzie, Pelican River, May 9. Late dates of departure: Florida, Big Gasparilla Pass, May 22; North Carolina, Pea Island, May 10; New Jersey, Atlantic City, June 20; Texas, Corpus Christi, April 12; Louisiana, New Orleans, April 28; Missouri, Kansas City, May 3; Wisconsin, Madison, May 17.

Fall migration.—Eastward, southward, and westward to the coasts. Early dates of arrival: Massachusetts, Chatham, September 7; South Carolina, Charleston, September 26; Florida, Fernandina, September 16; Mississippi, Bay St. Louis, October 10; California, Los Angeles County, September 17. Late dates of departure: Gulf of St. Lawrence, Anticosti Island, September 18; Massachusetts, Woods Hole, November 17; North Dakota, Harrisburg, October 17; Colorado, Denver, November 12; Utah, Provo, November 30.

Casual records.—Accidental in Hawaiian Islands (one taken in winter 1901) and in Bermuda (January 1, 1849).

Egg dates.—North Dakota: Forty-eight records, May 9 to June 22; twenty-four records, May 31 to June 15. Saskatchewan and Manitoba: Seventeen records, June 4 to 23. Quebec Labrador: Ten records, June 20 to 30.

LARUS BRACHYRHYNCHUS Richardson.

SHORT-BILLED GULL.

HABITS.

The North American counterpart of the common mew gull of Europe is so closely related to it that many ornithologists question the specific distinction of the two species. The characters on which they are separated are very slight and not very constant; there is so much individual variation in both forms that they seem to intergrade and may yet be proven to be no more than subspecies. The short-billed gull is a widely distributed and common species throughout the whole of the interior of Alaska and the northern portions of the northwest territories. It is a marsh-loving species and frequents all the flat marshy country of the coast and interior, as well as much of the wooded region in the vicinity of lakes, ponds, and streams.

Spring.—Mr. Lucien M. Turner (1886) says:

The short-billed gull arrives at St. Michael according to the openness of the season. It comes in few numbers as soon as large cracks are made in the ice. This may be early as the 1st of May or as late as the 25th. The season of 1874 was unusually open. Upon our arrival at St. Michael, on May 25, hundreds of these gulls were flying over the bay. In the course of a few days they became less, so that by the middle of June only few pairs were seen. In later years they were not abundant at any time, though the breaking up of the ice was accompanied with visits of numbers of them.

Turner's failure to note them after the middle of June was doubtless due to their being busy with family duties. Early in June they forsake the outer bays and scatter over the tundra where they construct their nests. Often their breeding places are several miles back from the coast, which they visit less frequently until after the young are on the wing.

Nesting.—Mr. Hersey found a nest of this gull near St. Michael, Alaska, on June 19, 1915, containing an egg on the point of hatching and a young bird only a few hours' old. The nest was on a small islet in a tundra pond; the islet was only a few yards long and about 2 feet above the level of the water. The nest was merely a hollow in the ground, about 8 inches in diameter and 3½ inches deep, scantily lined with dry grass; it was located in the center and on the highest part of the islet. His notes say:

When about one-eighth of a mile away one of the parents flew about above me screaming loudly. As I drew nearer the bird came lower down and when within 75 yards of the nest she flew directly over it and hovered. While photographing it both birds darted repeatedly at my head, and when I finally left they followed me for half a mile.

Dr. Joseph Grinnell (1900) made some interesting observations on the nesting habits of this species on the Kowak delta, Alaska. He writes:

The lakes which the short-billed gulls mostly frequented were usually surrounded by spruce trees, which in the delta are more low and scrubby than farther in the interior. I had in vain searched for the gulls' nests on small bare islets in the lakes and on grassy points, such as the gulls with which I was previously familiar would be likely to select for nesting sites. Although I failed to find any sign of nests, still the birds, by their uneasy actions, intimated that there must be eggs or young somewhere. Finally on the 16th of June I determined to discover the secret, and, armed with patience, selected a secluded hiding place among some scrub spruces near a lake, yet where I had a good view of it. Two pairs of short-billed gulls kept flying about above me for a long time, occasionally alighting on the tops of the spruces surrounding the lake. I kept track of each of the four gulls as best I could, and finally saw one settle close down on the bushy top of a tree on the other side of the lake. Then it dawned on me that the nests might be in trees. I took my bearings on the tree, and started around the lake. Before I had nearly reached the vicinity I was met by the gulls, one of which began to dive at me again and again. It would fly high above me and then swoop down past my head with a shrill, startling scream. Just as the bird passed me it would void a limy mass of faeces, and with such disagreeable precision that I was soon streaked with white. On climbing the spruce, which was about 12 feet tall, I discovered the nest. It was almost completely hidden from below by the flat, bushy top of the spruce on which it was placed. The nest was a shapeless mass of slender twigs and hay, 9 inches across on top. There was scarcely any depression and I found the shells of two of the eggs broken on the ground beneath, probably pitched out by a severe wind of the day before. The single egg secured was considerably incubated. After I left the nest the gulls followed me a long ways, dashing down at me at intervals as before described. I found several more nests by carefully examining the bushy topped spruces around lakes, but none contained eggs. Probably the jaegers which I saw in the vicinity were responsible for this. One of the nests was only about 7 feet above the water on a leaning spruce at the edge of a pond. The rest of the nests were from 10 to 20 feet above the ground in spruces growing nearest the water's edge.

Mr. Roderick McFarlane (1891), who collected many sets of eggs in the Anderson River region, says:

Its nest is usually a small cavity in the sand by the side of a stream or a sheet of water; but it also frequently builds on a stump or tree, and in such cases dry twigs, hay, and mosses, are used in its construction. The parents do their utmost to drive away intruders.

Eggs.—The short-billed gull ordinarily lays three eggs, but often only two. They are ovate or short ovate in shape; usually the former. The ground color varies from " Saccardo's umber " or " Isabella color " to "olive buff." The eggs are spotted and blotched evenly or irregularly or in a wreath near the larger end, with the darker shades of brown, such as " bone brown," " bister," " sepia," or " snuff brown "; also with various shades of " brownish drab." Sometimes the eggs are finely scrawled. The measurements of 40 eggs, in the United States National Museum average 57 by 41 millimeters; the eggs showing the four extremes measure **63** by 41.5, 58.5 by **43, 50.5** by 40.5, and 51.5 by **37** millimeters.

Plumages.—The young, when first hatched, is well covered with a warm coat of soft, thick down, " pale drab-gray " to " pale smoke-gray " on the upper parts, sides, and throat; " pale pinkish buff " on the breast and belly; and tinged with the latter color on the sides of the head and neck. The frontal and loral region is clear black. The sides of the head and neck are boldly and clearly spotted with black in a very distinct pattern, the spots coalescing into an indistinct Y on the crown; an irregular W on the occiput; a large, distinct crescent on the cervix; and a small crescent on the throat. The remainder of the upper parts are heavily but less distinctly mottled with duller black, becoming grayer posteriorly. The under parts are unspotted.

I have not seen any specimens showing the development of the first plumage from the downy stage, but I have a good series of young birds collected in August. This plumage shows considerable individual variation, but is always more or less heavily mottled both above and below. Often the throat, and sometimes the belly, is nearly or quite immaculate white; sometimes the entire under parts, below the throat, as well as the neck and head, are uniform " drab-gray," or " vinaceous gray," and always these parts are heavily clouded with these colors. The feathers of the back, scapulars, and wing-coverts are centrally dusky and broadly edged with pale-grayish buff; the primaries are uniformly dusky; the rectrices are basally gray, somewhat mottled, with nearly the terminal half dusky, and white-tipped. From this plumage the progress toward maturity begins early and continues all through the first year, by fading, wear, and molt. The " gull gray " of the mantle sometimes begins to appear in November, and by April or May this color predominates on the back. The white increases on the head and underparts, so that in the spring some individuals are largely white below; but in most cases the bellies are more or less clouded with dusky. The wings and tail also fade out to nearly white in the lighter areas.

A complete postnuptial molt produces the second winter plumage, which is worn for one year. This much resembles the adult plumage. The head and neck are heavily mottled with dusky in the fall, but become pure white by wear and molt during the winter and spring. The back is wholly " gull gray," and the wings are largely so, but there is some dusky mottling on the bend of the wing. The tail is largely white, but there is a subterminal black band, varying in extent in different individuals. The primaries are brownish black, not deep black as in adults, with a large white spot near the tip of the outer and sometimes a smaller one on the second.

At the second postnuptial molt, which is complete, the adult winter plumage is usually assumed at the age of about 2 years. This is the same as the adult nuptial plumage, except that the head is streaked, the throat is spotted, and the neck is clouded with dusky, all of which disappears at the partial prenuptial molt. The white spaces and gray wedges in the primaries are not always fully developed in third-year birds, but become more pronounced at succeeding molts. Other traces of immaturity are often retained during the third winter.

Food.—Mr. Turner (1886) gives the following account of the feeding habits of the short-billed gull:

At Atkha Island, in the early part of August, 1879, a small species of fish (*Mallotus villosus*) was thrown up by the waves onto the beach. These fish cast their spawn in the sand and is covered by the next wave. The gulls of this species follow the wake of these fishes, and during the spawning season devour many thousands of them. At Amchitka Island I observed this species frequenting the beach at low tide and securing the sea urchins, which occur plentifully. The birds seize the prey, carry it several yards into the air and then drop it on the rocks, or, as it frequently happens, into the little pools left by the receding tide. These pools are of variable depth, but when of not more than a few inches deep, the bird again took the object to drop it, perhaps into the same place; evidently not with the intention of washing any objectionable matter from its surface, but simply from the fact that the bird had not yet learned to calculate the law of falling bodies, yet when the shellfish was dropped on the rocks and broken open the bird greedily devoured the well-filled ovaries. These gulls and the ravens frequently carry the shells far to the inland and there break them open with their beaks. The old shells may be frequently found on a knoll of ground or tuft of grass.

Doctor Nelson (1887) says that " along the coast of Bering Sea they feed upon sticklebacks and other small fry which abound in the sluggish streams and lakes." Mr. E. A. Preble (1908) found that " three specimens collected May 12 had been feeding on water beetles (*Dytiscus dauricus*)." Mr. Hersey frequently saw them feeding on the garbage dumps near St. Michael. During the fall and winter they forage regularly with the larger gulls about the harbors and shores where garbage and other offal is to be found.

Behavior.—In its flight and swimming habits the short-billed gull does not differ materially from the larger species. Mr. Hersey observed that the adults show considerable curiosity, following the intruder about over the tundra, and that the young are even tamer, circling about within 15 or 20 feet for several minutes at a time, turning the head from side to side and watching intently, but making no sound.

Doctor Grinnell (1900) remarks:

Their usual notes are louder and sharper than those of the glaucous gulls and remind one of the bark of a terrier.

Doctor Nelson (1887) says:

They show considerable curiosity upon the appearance of an intruder, and very frequently follow one for some distance, uttering a sharp, querulous "kwew," kwew." When one or more are shot the others circle about a few times, but show very little solicitude over the fate of their companions. From the 18th to 25th of July most of the young are able to fly, and early in August old and young gather along the courses of streams or near the larger lakes. From this time on many of the birds are found also about low spits and mud flats along the coast. The young frequently follow boats for long distances on a stream or near shore, and they are so unsuspicious that they may almost be knocked down with a paddle. The old birds pass through the fall moult the latter half of August, and by the middle of September they are in the new dress and gradually disappear from the north, until by the end of this month they become rare. In September they fraternize more commonly with the kittiwake than at any other season in the bays and along the coast.

Mr. Hersey's notes, however, state:

When the young are well grown and able to fly they join the flocks of glaucous gulls feeding about the bays and tide creeks. They appear to prefer the society of this species to that of their own kind, as I have repeatedly observed. Flocks of adult short-billed gulls have been met with continually without seeing any young, but practically every flock of glaucous will contain at least two young short bills. Generally two are found together, probably a family.

Winter.—The fall migration carries the short-billed gulls down the Pacific coast to their winter range from Puget Sound to southern California, where they are fairly common all winter, associated with Pacific kittiwakes, glaucous-winged, western, herring, and Bonaparte's gulls—a mixed party of seacoast scavengers. Mr. W. L. Dawson (1909) gives the following account of this species on the coast of Washington in winter:

A certain childish innocence and simplicity appear to distinguish these birds from the more sophisticated herrings and glaucous-wings. They are the small fry of the great gull companies which throng our borders in winter, allowed to share, indeed, when Petro dumps a rich load of restaurant waste, but expected to take a grumbling back seat when the supply of food is more limited. One may see at a glance that they are not fitted for competition. Their bills are not only shorter, but much more delicately proportioned than those of the other gulls; while their gabbling, duck-like notes oppose a mild alto to the screams and high trumpetings of their larger congeners.

Gulls of this and allied species are quick to appreciate the advantages of protected areas. Along the water front or near steamers, where shooting would not be allowed, they become very bold. Short-bills, however, do not stand about on palings, piles, and roofs, as do the glaucous-wings, but rest, instead, almost exclusively on the water. Thus, if one attempts to bait the gulls with an offering of bread laid on the wharf rail, the larger gulls will begin to line the neighboring rails and posts, craning their necks hungrily or snatching exposed fragments; but the short-bills will settle upon the water and draw near to the piling below, content to catch such crumbs as fall from the high-set table.

DISTRIBUTION.

Breeding range.—Northwestern North America. East to Mackenzie Valley. South to northern Saskatchewan and Alberta (Athabasca Lake), northern British Columbia (Atlin Lake) and southern Alaska (Glacier Bay and Prince William Sound). West to the Bering Sea coast of Alaska (Nushagak and Norton Sound) and St. Lawrence Island. North to northern Alaska (Kowak River and Cape Lisburne), Herschel and Baillie Islands, and northern Mackenzie (Fort Anderson).

Winter range.—Pacific coast of the United States from the southern end of Vancouver Island and the Puget Sound region southward to southern California (San Diego).

Spring migration.—Northward along the coast and eastward to the interior. Early dates of arrival: British Columbia, Queen Charlotte Sound, April 6; Alaska, Admiralty Island, April 24, Mount McKinley, May 10, St. Michael, May 11, and Kowak River, May 15; Mackenzie, Fort Simpson, May 8, and Great Bear Lake, May 23.

Fall migration.—The reverse of the spring. Early dates of arrival: British Columbia, Chillawack, August 26; Oregon, Scio, September 21; California, Berkeley, October 9, Monterey, October 29, Ventura, November 26 and San Diego, December 11. Late dates of departure: Alaska, Icy Cape, July 30, Cape Nome, August 28, Camden Bay, September 8, St. Michael, September 23, Unalaska, October 1, and Sitka region, October 7; Mackenzie, Lake Hardisty, August 25.

Casual records.—Has been taken in Quebec City (Dionne), in Wyoming (Wind River Mountains, August 28, 1893), and in Kurile Islands (February).

Egg dates.—Athabasca, Mackenzie region: Nineteen records, May 28 to July 5; ten records, June 15 to 21. Alaska: Thirteen records, May 30 to July 5; seven records, June 16 to 20.

LARUS CANUS Linnaeus.

MEW GULL.

HABITS.

Contributed by Charles Wendell Townsend.

This gull, also called sea-mew or common gull, is a native of northern Europe and Asia, and is given a doubtful place in the Check List of the American Ornithologists' Union by the statement that it is "accidental in Labrador (?)". In Birds of Labrador, by Townsend and Allen (1907), the whole matter was carefully investigated, and as no new light has been thrown, it seems worth while to quote the results here:

The following is from Audubon's Labrador "Journal," under date of June 18, 1833. "John & Co. found an island (near Little Mecattina) with upwards of 200 nests of the *Larus canus*, all with eggs, but not a young hatched. The nests were placed on the bare rock; formed of seaweed, about 6 inches in diameter within and a foot without; some were much thicker and larger than others; in many instances only a foot apart, in others a greater distance was found. The eggs are much smaller than those of *Larus marinus*." Elliott Coues adds the following note after *Larus canus:* "Common gull.—This record raises an interesting question, which can hardly be settled satisfactorily. *Larus canus*, the common gull of Europe, is given by various authors in Audubon's time, besides himself, as a bird of the Atlantic Coast of North America, from Labrador southward. But it is not known as such to ornithologists of the present day." In his Notes on the Ornithology of Labrador (in Proc. Acad. Nat. Sci. Phila., 1861, p. 246) Dr. Coues gives *L. delawarensis*, the ring-billed gull, three speciments of which he procured at Henley Harbor, August 21, 1860. These were birds of the year, and one of them, afterwards sent to England, was identified by Mr. Howard Saunders as *L. canus* (P. Z. S., 1877, p. 178; Cat. B. Brit. Mus., XXV, 1896, p. 281). This would seem to bear out Audubon's Journal; but the "common American gull" of his published works is the one he calls *L. zonorhynchus* (i. e., *L. delawarensis*); and on page 155 of the Birds of Am., 8vo ed., he gives the very incident here narrated in his journal as pertaining to the latter species. The probabilities are that, notwithstanding Dr. Coues's finding of the supposed *L. canus* in Labrador, the whole Audubonian record really belongs to *L. delawarensis*.

The mew gull, although common during the migrations on the English coasts, does not breed south of the Scottish border, according to Saunders (1889), who says that its trivial name, "common gull," has led to many errors. In Scotland, the Hebrides, Orkneys, and Shetland it breeds in abundance, and a few breeding haunts are to be found in Ireland. It also breeds in Norway and Sweden and northern Russia and Siberia. In winter, according to Saunders (1889), "it occurs on the shores, lakes, and rivers of the rest of Europe down to the Mediterranean; also on the African side of the latter as far as the Suez Canal."

Nesting.—This gull breeds in colonies on the shores of lakes or of the sea not far above the water. It is especially fond of grassy islands, and often makes its nest among the wrack thrown up on the shore. It has been found in Norway breeding on the shores of lakes 4,000 feet above the sea. Instances are on record where it has occupied the deserted nest of a crow in bushes or trees. The nest is generally rather large, and is made up of seaweed, grass, weed stalks, bits of heather, etc.

Eggs—Three eggs constitute a set. They are olive brown to straw color in color, or even pale blue or light green, spotted and streaked with brown and black. The average measurements are 2.25 by 1.50 inches.

Young.—The downy young are of a yellowish gray color, lighter on the face, throat, and abdomen. The upper parts and throat are marked with large blackish spots. One of these spots always touches the base of the upper mandible.

Behavior.—Saunders (1889) says:

As a rule this gull does not go far from land, and owing to its being one of the first to seek the shore on the approach of coarse weather, it has been made the subject of many rhymes and poetical allusions. It feeds on small fish, mollusks, crustaceans, etc., and may frequently be seen picking up grubs on the furrows in company with rooks, while it will sometimes eat grain.

Macgillivray (1852) says:

The fields having been cleared of their produce and partially plowed, to prepare them for another crop, the " sea mews," deserting the coasts, appear in large flocks, which find subsistence in picking up the worms and larvae that have been exposed. These flocks may be met with here and there at long intervals in all the agricultural districts, not only in the neighborhood of the sea, but in the parts most remote from it. Although they are most numerous in stormy weather, it is not the tempest alone that induces them to advance inland; for in the finest days of winter and spring they attend upon the plow, or search the grass fields as assiduously as at any other time.

This gull also picks up floating offal from the surface of the water, and catches small fish, such as sand eels and young herring. From the beaches and rocks on the shore it picks up crustacea, mollusks, echinoderms, etc. In general habits it closely resembles the ringbilled gull. Its flight is light and buoyant and it dips down to the water gracefully, rarely if ever plunging below the surface. Its cry is shrill and somewhat harsh.

DISTRIBUTION.

Breeding range.—Northern Europe and Asia. East to northeastern Siberia (Gichiga and Marcova, Anadyr District) and Kamchatka. South to latitude 53° N. West to the British Isles. North to the Arctic coast of Europe and Asia.

Winter range.—From the British Isles south to the Canary Islands, the Mediterranean Sea, northern Africa, the Nile Valley, and the Persian Gulf, and on the Asiatic side to Japan and China.

Casual records.—Has been taken once in North America (Henley Harbor, Labrador), a young bird of doubtful identity. Records from California refer to other species.

Egg dates.—Great Britain: Twenty-two records, May 6 to July 18; eleven records, May 16 to June 1.

LARUS HEERMANNI Cassin.

HEERMANN'S GULL.

HABITS.

Among the mixed flocks of large gulls which frequent the beaches of southern California we frequently see a few and sometimes many smaller gulls conspicuous by their dark color and long legs. Some seem to be wholly black or dark brown; these are the young birds, which are present more or less all the year round. Others, with conspicuous white heads, are the adults; these are absent during the later part of the spring and early summer, while on their breeding grounds farther south. The species is very well marked and entirely unlike any other species of *Larus*. It has even been placed by some writers in another genus, *Blasipus*, together with two or three other species found in other parts of the Pacific Ocean, which its general appearance seems to warrant. It is different from other gulls also in its migrations, being the only one of our gulls which migrates southward to breed and northward again to spend the fall and winter.

Courtship.—Mr. Wilmot W. Brown jr., has given us the only account we have of the courtship of this species. He was fortunate enough to arrive on the Island of Ildefonso, in the Gulf of California, early enough to see it. I quote from his notes, published by Col. John E. Thayer (1911), as follows:

When I first arrived (March 24) there were an immense number of birds. The males were constantly seen fluttering over the females on the ground, near their nests; but no eggs were laid until April 2. It seems they spend some time in courtship before settling down to their matrimonial duties. The female when in passion emits a peculiar squeaky sound as she coaxes the male by squatting down and going through the most ludicrous motions. I have also seen a pair holding on to each other's bills, a kind of tug-of-war affair; then they would back away and go through a suggestion of a dance, but all the time talking to each other in low love tones. The appearance of a duck-hawk would send them all flying to sea. They would return, however, very quickly.

On the southeastern end of the island, facing the sea, there is a large semicircular shaped depression, which covers about 5 acres. It is quite level on the bottom and covered with gravel, with here and there blocks of lava scattered about.

It is well protected from the northwest wind, which prevails here in March and April. At the time I arrived on the island immense numbers of these gulls had congregated. They literally covered the ground. They were so occupied in their love making that they paid very little attention to us. Their cries deadened the cries of all the other birds, and they kept it up all through the night.

Nesting.—The nest in all cases was simply a well-formed depression in the ground with no lining whatsoever. There must have been over 15,000 Heermann gulls nesting on this island.

Mr. Pingree I. Osburn (1909) found a colony of Heermann's gulls breeding " on a remote rock off the coast of the State of Jalisco, Mexico, in about the parallel 18° N." He writes:

The rock was about 25 feet high and 50 by 150 feet across, with a plat of coarse bunch grass a foot high in the center, and along the edge a barren strip of white rock, broken up here and there with crevices and bowlders. The rock contained 31 pairs of breeding birds, ascertained after a careful count. The birds in the nesting grounds behaved in much the same manner as the western gulls, but were tamer, swooping down within a foot of my head and alighting nearby while I was photographing in the colony.

A cursory survey of the rock showed that it was steep on all sides. The birds undoubtedly preferred the level ground for a nesting place, as only one set was found on this cliff. The nests were located usually between bowlders or nestled down in the bunch grass in the center of the rock. Those in the grass were usually well made of sticks, dry grass, and weeds, and sometimes with a slight lining of feathers. They were much better made and more compact than those of the western gull. Several nests in my collection still show their original shape and construction; also retain the strong odor peculiar to these birds on their nesting grounds. A few sets were found with almost no nest; simply a cup-shaped cavity scantily lined with shells and a stick or two. The nests were well scattered about over the rock, no close grouping being evident. The measurements of the nests average, in inches—outside width, 10; depth, 2¼. No other species of gull was seen in company with the Heermann gulls, and none within hundreds of miles of these islands.

The first visit to the rock was on April 11. At this time about one-third of the eggs were heavily incubated. The remainder were in all the lesser stages. The sets contain two and three eggs in about equal numbers, with a possible majority of three.

Eggs.—The eggs show the greatest variation in color. The general ground color is pearl gray with a very slight creamy tinge. In some the ground color is ashy gray and in others light bluish gray. All the eggs are spotted and blotched, the markings showing no particular rule for location at one end or the other. They have faint lavender spots, which are covered with smaller but more distinct spots of grayish brown, umber, grayish blue, and dark lavender. They are very rarely scratched with fine lines, but occasionally the spots and splashes show a trend to a lengthwise direction. A few examples also have faint wreaths about the large end. Where this occurs the area inside the wreath is usually void of heavy markings and decorated only with faint irregular lavender spots. In extreme examples the eggs range from one egg, which is indistinctly specked with cinnamon brown and marked evenly with faint lavender, to an egg which has a ground color twice as deep as the egg just mentioned, and heavily splotched with dark olive and dark lavender. There is also one set of three which is especially unlike the others, in that the eggs are smaller and more elongated, both ends of the egg being almost identical in shape. This set is differently marked also. The spots are dingy and not clearly defined as in the remainder of the series. In all, they are the handsomest eggs of any species of this genus which I have ever seen.

The measurements of 52 eggs, in various collections, average 59.2 by 42.7 millimeters; the eggs showing the four extremes measure **64** by **45** and **53** by **37.5** millimeters.

Plumages.—The downy young is covered with short, thick down, which on the head, throat, breast and flanks is "pinkish buff" or "pale pinkish buff," becoming paler toward the belly, which is pure white. The back is grayish white, mottled with dusky, and there are a few dusky spots on the top of the head. I have seen no specimens illustrating the change into the first plumage.

Coues (1903) says of the young of the year:

Entire plumage deep sooty or fuliginous-blackish; all the feathers, but especially those of back and upper wing coverts, edged with grayish-white. Primaries and secondaries black, as in adults, with only traces of white tips on the former. Tail black, very narrowly tipped with dull white.

Birds that I have seen in what I call the juvenal plumage have the greater and lesser wing-coverts and the feather edgings "olive brown." They apparently change, by a partial and gradual molt, from this into the first winter plumage between June and October, the wing-coverts becoming grayer, the light edgings of the feathers disappearing by wear, and more or less white appearing on the throat and chin. During the first spring the wholly black bill of the young bird becomes dull reddish on the basal half. This plumage is worn until the next summer, the first postnuptial molt, if it may be so called, beginning in June. This complete molt produces the second winter plumage, which is similar to the first winter, except that the primaries and rectrices are blacker and very narrowly edged with pale brown; the upper tail-coverts are more slaty; the head and nape are clear slate-black, the mantle is darker slate-black and the bill is practically like the adult.

A year later the young bird assumes a third winter plumage, similar to that of the winter adult, except that the dark mottling on the head is more extensive, including the whole head and throat, and all the colors are darker. The white predominates on the throat, but the rest of the head is very dark. The wings and tail of the adult plumage are assumed, but there is great individual variation in the extent of the white tips of the primaries and the rectrices, though the latter are always broadly tipped with white. At the next prenuptial molt, which is only partial, including mainly the head and neck, young birds become indistinguishable from adults; they are then nearly 3 years old.

The postnuptial molt of adults, which is complete, occurs mainly in July and August, though it is often prolonged into September. Adults in the fall may be distinguished from young birds by being somewhat lighter in color both above and below, with the gray of the body plumage shading off gradually into the white of the head and neck; in young birds this change is much more abrupt. The head and neck are much whiter in old birds, with much less dusky mottling, confined principally to the top and sides of the head. The partial prenuptial molt begins in December, and by January or February the pure white head of the nuptial plumage has been acquired. The white tips of the primaries wear away partially or wholly before spring, and the white tips of the rectrices also disappear before the postnuptial molt.

Food.—Although the food of Heermann's gull consists largely of fish and other sea food, which it obtains offshore, it also indulges freely in a great variety of other foods and does its part as a scavenger along the shores and on the beaches with the other gulls, where it does not seem to be at all fastidious as to its diet. Dr. George Suckley (1860), however, says:

This species, unlike the ring-billed and many other gulls, does not seem to be fond of feeding on the shores and bare flats, but is almost always (in that vicinity at least) found on the kelp beds floating in the deep water some distance from shore. Whether they are attracted to these kelp beds by the hopes of finding small shellfish in the upturned and netlike roots of such plants as, detached from their fastenings on the bottom, have become entangled together and with others in situ, or because these floating islands afford a convenient resting place where they can rest to a great extent secure from their enemies of the land, I can not say; but presume that the presence of a supply of food must be a great inducement.

Mr. A. W. Anthony (1906) describes their method of catching fish as follows:

When herring are swimming in compact schools near the surface both Heermann's and western gulls secure them by approaching the school from behind and flying near the surface of the water, making repeated, quick dips into the school. The fish seek safety in the depths the instant anything occurs to alarm them, but soon return to the surface, so that the gulls by stalking them from the rear are enabled to approach quite near before the fish are alarmed. As soon as the limits of the school have been passed the gull, rising higher in the air, returns by a wide circuit and again passes over the school from the rear. As the fish all swim in one direction, in a compact mass, these tactics afford the gulls a decided advantage, which seems to be thoroughly understood. I think that the Heermann's gull secures about one out of five fish that are snapped at and the western half as many. Royal tern and the other gulls employ these same methods but to a less extent.

They have also been found to feed on shrimps and other crustaceans and mollusca.

Behavior.—I have never noticed anything peculiar or distinctive in the flight of this species, which is very much like that of the larger gulls; nor can I find anything of interest in regard to it in print. The species is, of course, easily recognized in life by its very distinctive colors in all plumages.

Mr. Anthony (1906) refers to its voice as a " whining catlike cry " while attacking the pelicans to rob them of their food.   Mr. Osburn (1909) says:

Their cry was an oft-repeated " cow-auk," " cow-eek," given when high in the air, and a rapid guttural " caw-ca-ca-ca " when hovering near the nest.

Mr. W. L. Dawson (1909) writes that, if disturbed in their summer loafing places, " they suddenly take to wing and fill the air with low-pitched mellow cries of strange quality and sweetness, as they make off to some distant rendezvous."

Though not so much of an egg thief as some other gulls, it is somewhat of a pilferer of food and quite bold in attacking species larger than itself which are too stupid to resist its persecution.   Mr. Anthony (1906) has given us the following interesting account of its method of robbing the pelicans:

Heermann's gull is by far the most active and successful in catching small fish from the surface; but as a rule will seldom attempt to catch his own dinner if there are any pelicans among the delegates to the convention. There are times when the herring are so thick and so driven from below by the large fish that the pelicans will sit on the surface and snap them up without plunging, as is their normal method, from a height of from 10 to 30 feet in the air. If the fish are swimming the deep plunge often carries the bird completely under the surface, and when a second later he bobs up like a cork he is sure of finding at least one, often two Heermann's gulls expectantly awaiting the result. If there are two they will usually take up stations on each side and but a foot in front of the pelican, which still holds its huge bill and pouch under the water. It may be that the pelican does not yet know the result of his efforts, for in plunging the pouch is used as a dip net and, if nothing else, it is full of water, which is allowed to escape past the loosely closed mandibles until, perhaps 5 or 10 seconds after the bird made his plunge, a flutter is seen in the pouch, announcing one or more struggling victims. It is still an open question, however, whether they will be eaten by the gull or the pelican, and the latter is seemingly well aware that a herring in the gullet is worth two in the pouch, for it will often wait several seconds for a favorable opportunity for disposing of the catch; the gulls meantime constantly uttering their nasal whining note and keeping well within reaching distance of the pouch. When the critical moment arrives the pelican throws the bill up and attempts to swallow the fish, but, with cat-like quickness, one or both gulls make a similar effort, and should the fish in its struggles have thrust its tail or head past the edges of the mandibles, as very often happens, it is an even chance that the gull gets the prize; in fact, I have often seen a Heermann gull reach well into the pouch and get away with a fish in the very act of slipping down the throat of the pelican.

I remember a very amusing incident of this nature I once witnessed on the coast of Lower California. The pelican, after securing a herring, " backed water" until it was supposed to be far enough from its parasite to venture swallowing it, but as the huge bill was tipped up and opened the gull plunged forward and thrust its entire head and neck into the pouch; the pelican, somewhat quicker than most of its kind, closed down with a snap and caught the intruder, which in turn had caught the fish; neither would yield any advantages gained, and for perhaps half a minute the pelican towed the gull about by the head, amid most violent protest from a hundred or more gulls assembled, while other pelicans sat like solemn judges, perhaps offering to arbitrate the question. At last a more violent twist than usual on the part of the gull freed him from limbo, minus a few feathers, but in no manner daunted, for a moment later it was following closely in the wake of the same pelican, waiting for it to plunge for another fish, and I never did learn which really swallowed the one in controversy.

Dr. E. W. Nelson (1899) observed that " these gulls are bold and noisy aggressors when they wish to take advantage of the gannets, and about the breeding places of the latter they feed largely at the public expense." One that he shot on Isabel Island, off the west coast of Mexico, had in company with its mate " harried a blue-footed gannet into disgorging a number of small fish upon a rock at the edge of the water, and was picking up the spoils by a series of little downward swoops and hoverings." Mr. Harold H. Bailey (1906) in the same region, noted similar behavior toward the boobies. He also mentions the following incident:

One day while sitting on a rock in front of camp at White Rock waiting for lunch, I saw one of a pair of great rufous-bellied kingfishers fishing from a rock about 20 feet farther on. As it returned to its perch from one of its little plunges a Heermann's gull swooped down and tried to get its food before it could be swallowed. The kingfisher dove to the water and at each descent of the gull, dove below, these tactics being kept up until the gull got disgusted and left.

Winter.—At the close of the breeding season the Heermann's gulls migrate northward along the coast of California and as far north as British Columbia. They have been seen flying north along the coast of Washington as early as July. Adults become abundant on the California coast in July and young birds in August. They are common all winter on the coast of southern California, both adults and young, until the adults migrate south again in the spring to breed.

DISTRIBUTION.

Breeding range.—Pacific coast of Mexico. Known to breed in the Gulf of California (Isla Raza and Ildefonso Island), Lower California (Magdalena Bay), on the Tres Marias Islands, and at Mazatlan.

Winter range.—Northward in summer along the Pacific coast to northern Washington (Puget Sound), and occasionally to northern Vancouver Island. Southward along the Central American coast to Guatemala (Chiapam and San José).

Spring migration.—Adults return to their breeding grounds from both northern and southern winter ranges in March.

Fall migration.—Northward movement begins in May, reaching southern California about June 1; Monterey, June and July; Farallones, May 20 to June 3; British Columbia, Vancouver Island, June 28. Southward retirement again begins in August, or even July, but last birds do not leave Puget Sound until October, and few remain in Washington until November. Bulk of the flight passes Monterey in November, but a few birds winter there.

Egg dates.—Mexico, west coast: Fifteen records, April 8 to June 17; fourteen records, April 8 to 11.

LARUS ATRICILLA Linnaeus.

LAUGHING GULL.

HABITS.

High above the gleaming sands of Muskeget Island, amid the whirling maze of hovering terns that swarm up into the blue ether until the uppermost are nearly lost to vision, may be seen some larger birds, conspicuous by their size, by their black heads and black-tipped wings, soaring at ease among their lesser companions. In the ceaseless din of strident cries may be heard occasionally the hoarse notes of this larger bird—notes which, from their peculiar character, give the bird the fitting name of laughing gull. Although larger and stronger than the terns the laughing gulls are much shyer and less aggressive on their breeding grounds; the observer must remain concealed for some time under a well-made blind before they will return to their nests in his vicinity.

The Muskeget Island colony is certainly the largest breeding colony of laughing gulls north of Virginia; it is therefore worthy of description, as typical of the numerous colonies which formerly existed all along the coast from Maine southward. Much has been written about this interesting island, and I have given a brief description of it under the head of the common tern. These gulls formerly bred here abundantly, but constant persecution reduced their numbers until they became very scarce about 1880, and would have been extirpated except for the protection afforded them by the passage of suitable laws and by the personal efforts of Mr. George H. Mackay in seeing that the laws were enforced. They increased slowly during the next 10 years, but after 1890 their increase was more encouraging. In 1894 the colony nearly doubled in numbers and it continued to flourish, increasing a little each year, until, at the time of my last visit (in 1919) it consisted of several thousand pairs.

Nesting.—The laughing gulls usually arrive at Muskeget during the second week in May, the date of arrival varying from May 7 to 17, according to the weather conditions. A period of warm weather with strong southerly winds in the first part of May is likely to bring them early, flying high in the air with the terns. Mating and nest building soon begin and the first eggs are laid during the first or second week in June. They build their nests in a compact colony, among the sand dunes, near the center of the island, where the beach grass grows long and thick on the sandy slopes and in the hollows between the dunes. Usually the nests are, at least partially, concealed in the beach grass, which grows 2 feet high or more, but often they are in plain sight. When the nest is placed in the thick grass, a well-trodden path over-arched with grass leads up to it on one side and away from it on the other, so that the bird may enter and leave the nest without turning around at the risk of ruffling its immaculate plumage. The nests are frequently placed among the beach peas, which grow in great profusion in the hollows among the sand dunes, or, again, they are found under bayberry bushes that are scattered all over the island—sometimes in the center of a clump. The nest is sometimes merely a hollow in the sand among the beach grass, lined with dry grasses, bits of sticks and rubbish; but usually it is a well-made structure of various coarse, dry grasses, firmly interwoven and built up a few inches above the sand among clumps of beach grass, beach peas, or poison-ivy vines. The interior of the nest is carefully rounded and neatly lined with fine dry beach grass. By the middle of June most of the nests contain full sets of eggs, though egg laying is continued more or less all through the month. Very few chicks are hatched before July, but during the first week in that month the majority of the young birds appear and may be found hiding in the beach grass or running about so nimbly that it is difficult to catch them.

Similar colonies formerly existed along the Long Island coast, where in Giraud's day the laughing gull was a common summer resident. It occurs there now chiefly as a migrant, and I doubt if there are any breeding colonies left. According to Mr. William Dutcher's notes it bred at South Oyster Bay up to 1884, at Amityville until 1887, and at Cedar Island as late as 1888.

Dr. Witmer Stone (1908) says of its status in 1908 in New Jersey:

Formerly an abundant summer resident on the salt meadows along the coast, it is now restricted to two colonies—one at Brigantine and the other on Gull Island, Hereford Inlet—both under the protection of the National Association of Audubon Societies. The birds arrive April 4 to 20, and have mostly departed by October 1. The first sets of eggs are laid in May.

On Cobb's Island, Virginia, and on the surrounding islands we found the laughing gulls still abundant in 1907, though considerably reduced in numbers by many years of persecution. Their eggs were persistently collected daily by the oystermen all through the breeding season up to July 4, after which date they were protected by law and the birds were allowed to raise their broods. Such treatment must prove discouraging to the less vigorous birds and probably will eventually drive many of them away, but the oystermen claim the right to collect the eggs as a legitimate food supply, and it would be difficult to enforce any more stringent laws for their protection. The establishment of reservations under the constant guardianship of resident wardens is the only practical solution of the difficulty. Their favorite breeding grounds in this region are on the salt meadows, which are partially covered with shallow water at the highest tides. There are numerous small islands in this vicinity known as " marshes," which form their principal breeding grounds. These are flat and muddy, only a foot or two above the ordinary high tides and covered with short salt meadow grass. The nests are well made, bulky structures of dead grasses and sedges, firmly interwoven and neatly lined with finer grasses. They are built up high enough to be above the reach of the spring tides.

The largest and most prosperous colonies of laughing gulls that I have ever seen were in the reservations off the coast of Louisiana, where, under rigid protection, the seabird colonies are still flourishing. Between June 16 and 24, 1910, I made the circuit of the islands with Warden W. M. Sprinkle, on his weekly patrol, visiting all of the more important colonies. The largest colony was on Battledore Island, where a resident warden was protecting the birds most successfully. I spent the whole of a long day on this little island and estimated that there were fully 5,000 pairs of laughing gulls breeding here, as well as 1,000 pair of black skimmers, 50 pairs of Lousiana herons, 30 pairs of Forster's terns, 25 pairs of common terns, one pair each of Caspian and royal terns, and a few pairs of Florida redwings, all of which seemed to be living together in perfect harmony. The island was formerly much larger, but had been reduced in size by the washing away of its shelly and sandy beaches, leaving broad stretches of sand and mud flats around it, bare at low tide. We had to walk at least half a mile over these flats to reach the dry portion of the island, which was not over 4 acres in extent. In the center was a flat and almost dry marsh, largely overgrown with small black mangrove bushes, in which the Louisiana herons were nesting. Surrounding this, and partly inclosing a shallow muddy bay, were high ridges of finely broken oyster shells sloping down to the sandy beaches. The laughing gulls' nests were thickly scattered over nearly all of the island, principally among the clumps of grass and coarse weeds or under small bushes, on and behind the shell ridges, but also on the marsh and on the muddy flats and sandy beaches, which were partially covered with grass and weeds. The nests on the dry ground or among thick vegetation were not so elaborately built as those on the open marsh. At this date (June 21) most of the eggs were heavily incubated, pipped, or hatched. According to Captain Sprinkle's records the majority of the eggs are laid during the last week in May and hatched about three weeks later. The gulls on this island were particularly tame, being accustomed to the daily visits of the warden. They alighted on their nests readily within 10 feet of my blind, and even in the open, if I sat down quietly, they would soon settle on the ground within easy reach of my camera.

On the outermost island in this reservation, Grand Cochere, a low flat sand bar, we found a few pairs of laughing gulls with nests scattered over the island somewhat apart from the large breeding colonies of royal and Cabot's terns, with which the island was chiefly populated. The nests were poorly made of the scant supply of grasses, seaweed, and rubbish available. As there was absolutely no vegetation on this bare sand bar, the nesting material must have been brought from a distance. In marked contrast to our experience elsewhere we found many broken eggs of the terns which had apparently been eaten by the gulls; we therefore thought it wise to discourage their nesting here and broke up all the nests we could find, about 10, and shot several of the birds.

Among the numerous small islands in the western part of the reservation, near the delta of the Mississippi River, we found a large number of breeding colonies of laughing gulls varying in size from 50 or 100 pairs up to 1,000 or 2,000 pairs. Some of the larger islands were of the same type as Battledore Island, but more of them were of the marshy type, locally known as "mud lumps," overgrown with rank grasses, low mangrove bushes, and other vegetation. Wherever there were shell or sand beaches black skimmers were nesting. There were numerous breeding colonies of Louisiana and black-crowned night herons in the red mangrove thickets; a few colonies of Forster's terns were breeding on the marshes; and there were a few scattering pairs of Caspian terns; but everywhere the laughing gulls predominated and apparently lived peacefully with their neighbors.

Eggs.—Three eggs usually constitute the full set, though four eggs are frequently laid, and sometimes only two. Mr. George H. Mackay (1893) speaks of finding a number of nests with five eggs each, and suggests the possibility that these may have been laid by more than one bird. The eggs vary in shape from ovate, or slightly elongated ovate, to short ovate, the prevailing shape being typical ovate. The ground color varies from "Isabella color" or "wood brown" in the darkest specimens to "olive buff" or "cream buff" in the lightest specimens, both of which extremes are unusual. The prevailing types show various intermediate shades of "olive buff" or "olive brown," or, more rarely, a pale olive greenish tinge. I have one set in which the ground color is very pale "pea green" and is almost immaculate. The markings consist of spots and blotches, or more rarely irregular scrawls, scattered more or less evenly over the egg, but often more thickly about the large end. These vary in color from "seal brown" or "clove brown" to "Mars brown" or "raw umber." In many specimens there are underlying spots or blotches of "drab gray" or "olive gray." The measurements of 69 eggs in the United States National Museum collection average 53.5 by 38.5 millimeters; the eggs showing the four extremes measure **62** by 37, 52 by **42, 48.5** by 37, and 52.5 by **30.5** millimeters.

Young.—The period of incubation is about 20 days. The young when first hatched are carefully brooded by their parents, who stand over them to protect them in wet weather or to shield them from the rays of the hot sun. They are fed at first on half-digested soft food, which they take from the open bill of the old bird, but later on are weaned and taught to feed on solid food. They remain in the nest for a few days, but soon learn to run about and hide in the grass or under herbage. For the next month or six weeks they lead an inactive life during the period of growth-feeding, resting and sleeping most of the time. They are fed by their parents until they are able to fly and for some little time thereafter. The flight stage is reached, on Muskeget, during the last week of July or the first week of August, at which time the adults, still in full nuptial plumage, may be seen hovering over the little grassy meadows, where young birds of various sizes may be found hidden in the long thick grass, so well concealed that one must be careful not to walk on them. Here they remain motionless until disturbed, often until touched, when they run nimbly or fly away. Comparatively few young birds may be seen exercising in the open sandy spaces or on the beaches, running about on their long legs almost as fast as a man can run, or learning to make short flights from the high spots.

Plumages.—The young are thickly covered with long, soft down. The prevailing color above is "wood brown" or "drab," which is often more or less extensively tinged with "tawny olive" or "cinnamon,' and the under parts show paler shades of the same colors tinged with "tawny ochraceous" on the breast or throat. There is no white below. The head, neck, and throat are clearly spotted or striped with dull black, dusky, or very dark brown; and the back is more or less heavily mottled or clouded with the same dark colors.

The juvenal plumage is complete before the young bird is fully grown. In the fresh juvenal plumage the upper parts are largely dusky drab, but the feathers of the back, scapulars, and lesser wing-coverts are broadly tipped and margined with "cinnamon buff" or "pinkish buff." The head, neck, and chest are heavily clouded with dusky, the sides of the head being nearly clear dusky, darkest on the lores, and the feathers of the neck and chest are narrowly tipped with pale buff. The throat is partially white, and the under parts are whitish, clouded with drab on the sides. The greater wing-coverts are dusky, broadly edged with gray, and white tipped. The remiges are black; the tertials and secondaries broadly and the inner primaries narrowly tipped with white. The tail is basally pearl gray, the outer third or more black, and is tipped with white. As the season advances buffy edgings on the upper parts wear away and fade out to whitish. A gradual postjuvenal molt also takes place during the fall and winter with the growth of new "gull gray" feathers in the back and new white feathers in the head, neck, and breast. This molt is practically continuous with the first prenuptial molt, which produces further advance toward maturity; the head becomes largely white, the under parts wholly so, the scapulars and lesser wing-coverts become "gull gray," and sometimes some, or even all, of the tail feathers are replaced by new pure white feathers; but usually the rectrices, the remiges, and the greater wing-coverts remain as in the juvenal plumage.

I can not find any evidence that the slate-colored head of the adult nuptial plumage is even partially assumed at this age.

At the first postnuptial molt, when the bird is a little over a year old, the adult winter plumage is assumed by a complete molt, but a few individuals may still retain traces of the black subterminal bar in the tail, or other signs of immaturity. In the adult winter plumage the dark hood of the adult nuptial plumage is replaced by a white head, mottled with dusky on the occiput, cervix, and auriculars; the inner primaries are conspicuously white tipped, decreasingly so outwards until the outer is entirely black; these white tips wear away during the winter. The complete postnuptial molt begins in July and is usually completed in September, but sometimes not until October; the outer primaries are the last feathers to be renewed. Apparently young birds molt earlier in the summer than adults, beginning sometimes as early as May. The partial prenuptial molt occurs mainly in March, and involves the contour feathers and the lesser wing-coverts. Dr. Elliot Coues (1877) gives a striking account of the changes which take place at this season:

Another change heightens the beauty of the birds when they are to be decked for their nuptials in full attire. They gain a rich rosy tint over all the white plumage of the under part; then few birds are of more delicate hues than these.

Nature blushes, filling the bird's breast with amorous imagery, till the feathers catch a glow and reflect the blush. Burning with inward fire, the whole frame thrills with the enthusiasm of sexual vigor. The dark glittering eye is encircled with a fiery ring; now it flashes defiance at a rival, now tenderly melts at sight of his mate, soon to be sacrificed to masculine zeal. The breath of desire seems to influence the mouth till it shares the carmine hue that tinges other parts. The birds speed on high with vigorous pinion, making haste to the wedding with joyful cries till the shores resound. But such ardor is too consuming to last; with the touch of a moment the life current flies like an electric shock, lighting a fire in another organism, only to be subdued in the travail of maternity; not only once, but often, till the tide ebbs that at its flood transfigured the bird. Its force all spent the change comes; the red mouth pales again; the glowing plumage fades to white; the bird is but the shadow of his former self, dull-colored, ragged, without ambition beyond the satisfaction of a gluttonous appetite. He loiters southward, recruiting an enervated frame with plenteous fare in this season of idleness, till the warm rays of another spring restore him.

Food.—The food of the laughing gull is quite varied. It consists largely of small fish or fry which it catches for itself on the surface or steals from the brown pelican. This latter performance is quite interesting. Wherever a number of pelicans are diving and feeding these gulls are apt to gather in large numbers, and with their warning cries of " *half, half, half,*" to share in the feast. As soon as a pelican appears above the surface with a pouch full of small fry one or another of the gulls attempts and often succeeds in alighting on the pelican's head and helping itself to the bountiful supply in the capacious pouch. Other gulls hover about and pick up the pieces that fall to the water. Audubon (1840) states that they eat the eggs and sometimes the small young of the noddies and sooty terns on the Dry Tortugas. I have seen some evidence of their egg-eating habits, but I think they are not nearly as bad in this respect as the larger gulls. Mr. Stanley C. Arthur writes me:

The laughing gull takes a heavy toll of the eggs of the Cabot and royal terns every year; of this there is no doubt; and it seems to favor the royal tern in this matter of egg breaking. While I have seen a number of Cabot tern eggs broken open by laughing gulls, there is no doubt that the royal tern suffers the most.

Mr. John G. Wells (1902) says:

As these gulls can not dive they have to depend for their food on the shoals of sprats and fry that come up to the surface, and they have been known to take large bites from the backs of a fish called corvally which swims near the surface in large numbers. After heavy falls of rain, when the pastures are covered with numerous rain pools, these gulls resort to them in numbers and feed on the earthworms which swarm in the pools. This may often be seen, especially in the Beausejour pasture.

Although not such scavengers as the larger gulls, the laughing gulls are not above eating quite a variety of garbage, and I have known them to follow our boat for long distances, while we were cruising in the Gulf of Mexico, to pick up the few scraps that were thrown overboard. Laughing gulls are frequently pursued by jaegers, and in tropical waters by man-o'-war birds, and after much darting, twisting, and turning they are finally forced to disgorge their food.

Behavior.—The characteristic notes of the laughing gull have been well described by Mr. J. H. Langille (1884), from which I quote as follows:

From the hoarse clatter of the terns one could distinguish its long-drawn, clear note, on a high key, sounding not unlike the more excited call note of the domestic goose; and every now and then it would give its prolonged, weird laughter, which has given rise to its common name. To one who has heard it it might be imitated by the syllables, *hah-ha-ha-ha-ha-hah-hah-hah*, all of which are uttered on a high, clear tone, the last three or four syllables, and especially the last one, being drawn out with peculiar and prolonged effect; the whole sounding like the odd and excited laughter of an Indian squaw, and giving marked propriety to the name of the bird.

The flight of the laughing gull is light and graceful, yet strong and well-sustained. When migrating or flying long distances in pleasant weather, they usually fly high in the air, but in stormy weather or when flying against a strong wind they fly close to the water or low over the land. In pleasant weather large numbers of them leave their breeding places soon after sunrise, flying in flocks or long lines to their feeding grounds, and return before sunset, flying low in broadly extended formations.

The laughing gulls on Muskeget Island seem to live in perfect harmony with their neighbors, the common and roseate terns. I have never found any positive evidence of their eating the eggs of these terns, although they eat the eggs of other species elsewhere. They seem to be shyer or more timid here than at other places, and perhaps they have learned that it is not safe to molest the more aggressive terns. Mr. Mackay (1893) says:

I shall not call them courageous birds, as far as I have observed them, for I have frequently seen a single *Sterna hirundo* chase or put one to flight, which would endeavor to escape without offering any resistance. I have also seen four or five laughing gulls concertedly chase and put to flight a single *Sterna hirundo*, which offered no resistance to such odds.

These observations tend to show that the terns are the masters of the situation and that the gulls simply have to respect their rights. After the breeding season is over the old and young birds wander about our coasts until they finally disappear on their southward migration about October 1.

Winter.—The fall migration begins in August, and by the end of September most of the laughing gulls have disappeared from the New England coast. Many linger on the North Carolina coast through November, and from South Carolina southward they are abundant all winter, frequenting the bays and tidal estuaries in large flocks. They are strictly maritime at all seasons and seldom wander inland or up the rivers beyond tidewater. Their winter range extends to the west coast of Mexico, Peru, and Brazil, where they associate with royal terns, brown pelicans, and man-o'-war birds on relations which are often more intimate than friendly.

Mr. G. K. Noble (1916) has recently called attention to the fact that the laughing gulls of the North American coasts are larger than those of the West Indies and has given the former a new name, *Larus atricilla megalopterus* (Bruch).

DISTRIBUTION.

Breeding range.—Along the Atlantic and Gulf coasts (formerly at many localities now deserted) from central Maine (Lincoln County) to southern Texas (Cameron County). Principal colonies are in Massachusetts (Muskeget Island), Virginia (Northampton County), Louisiana (various islands), and Texas (Padre and Bird Islands). Birds breeding in the Bahamas and West Indies have been separated as a smaller subspecies, to which probably belong the birds breeding on the coastal islands of Venezuela and Honduras.

Breeding grounds protected in the following national reservations: In Florida, Passage Key; in Louisiana, Breton Island, and Shell Keys.

Winter range.—From the Bahamas, coasts of South Carolina, Mississippi, and Louisiana southward, mainly in the Gulf of Mexico and the Caribbean Sea. It is impossible to separate the winter ranges of the two subspecies, but the species has been taken in winter as far south as Brazil (Cajutuba), and on the Pacific coast from central Mexico (Mazatlan) to Peru (Santa Lucia) and coast of Chile.

Spring migration.—Migrants arrive in North Carolina in April and May; Virginia, about April 1; New Jersey, April 6 to May 1; Massachusetts, Muskeget Island, April 12.

Fall migration.—Late dates of departure: Massachusetts, Nantucket, October 8; New York, Long Island, October 28; New Jersey, September 20 to October 1; South Carolina, Weston, October 20.

Casual records.—There are numerous inland records of stragglers, as far north as Quebec (Montreal, October 24, 1888), and Ontario (Toronto, May 23, 1890), and as far west as Iowa (Blencoe, October 10, 1894), Colorado (near Denver, December, 1889), and New Mexico (Fort Wingate). Accidental in Bermuda (winter of 1881–82), Lower California (San José del Cabo, September 6 and November 9, 1887), Great Britain (several old records), France (Le Crotay, June 29, 1877), and Austria (near Trieste, winter).

Egg dates.—Virginia: Forty-eight records, May 25 to July 19; twenty-four records, June 9 to 26. Louisiana and Texas: Thirty-three records, April 8 to June 21; seventeen records, May 21 to June 4.

LARUS FRANKLINI Richardson.

FRANKLIN'S GULL.

HABITS.

Spring.—In late April or early May, when the rich black soil has thawed to the surface, the settler of the northwest prairies goes forth to plow. The warm season is short and his tillage vast, so he delays not for wind or storm. One day he is dark as a coal heaver, when the strong winds which sweep almost ceaselessly over the prairie hurl upon him avalanches of black dust. Next day, perchance, in a driving storm of wet snow, he turns black furrows in the interminable white expanse, his shaggy fur coat buttoned close around him. Then comes a day of warm sunshine, when, as he plows, he is followed by a troop of handsome birds which some might mistake for white doves. Without sign of fear they alight in the furrow close behind him, and, with graceful carriage, hurry about to pick up the worms and grubs which the plow has just unearthed. Often have I watched the plowman and his snowy retinue, and it appeals to me as one of the prettiest sights which the wide prairies can afford. No wonder that the lonely settler likes the dainty, familiar bird, and in friendly spirit calls it his "prairie pigeon" or "prairie dove."

The above quotation, from Mr. H. K. Job (1910), furnishes a vivid picture of this useful prairie bird and its arrival in the spring, which occurs at about the time that the last of the ice goes out of the lakes. The beautiful Franklin's gull, or Franklin's rosy gull, as it was first called, is both useful and ornamental throughout the whole summer, and is justly popular in consequence. Although it was described by Swainson and Richardson in Fauna Boreali-Americana, it seems to have been almost wholly unknown by the earlier writers on American birds, and was for many years considered a rare bird. It was not until the great western plains began to be settled and cultivated that we began to realize the astonishing abundance of this species and its importance to the agriculturist.

Nesting.—A breeding colony of Franklin's gulls is one of the most spectacular, most interesting, and most beautiful sights in the realm of North American ornithology. The man who has never seen one has something yet to live for—a sight which once seen is never to be forgotten. No written words can convey any adequate idea of the beautiful picture presented by countless thousands of exquisite birds, of such delicate hues and gentle habits, in all the activities of their closely populated communities. For parts of two seasons we had followed their elusive lines of flight over many miles of prairie and plain. We had seen them flying out in loose straggling flocks in the morning as they scattered over the prairies to feed and seen them flying back again at night to some mysterious point which we could never find; whence they came and whither they went we never knew, but somewhere in the great beyond we knew that they had established a populous city. Like the Indians of the plains, they are a wandering, nomadic race, and for some mysterious reason, unknown to any but themselves, they move about from place to place, choosing each season the locality which suits their fancy.

At last our efforts were rewarded on June 9, 1905, for after driving for miles over the rolling plains of southwestern Saskatchewan and exploring many lakes and sloughs in vain we discovered a splendid colony of these elusive birds. As we drove over the crest of a bil- lowy ridge among roving bands of grazing cattle we saw a broad level grassy plain spread out before us, and beyond it in the dis- tance a lake fringed with marshes. With the aid of our glasses we could barely make out a cloud of white specks hovering over the marsh, and we knew at once that we had won the long-sought prize. Another mile of rapid driving brought us to the marshy shore, where scores, yes hundreds, of the dainty birds began flying out to meet us with a chorus of shrill screams and harsh cries of protest. We tethered our horse and waded out into the marsh, where the reeds or bullrushes (*Scirpus lacustris*) grew for a distance of 200 or 300 yards out from the shore and for half or three quarters of a mile along that side of the lake. The water was not over knee-deep anywhere, except on the outer edge, and usually much less than that; perhaps a foot deep on the average. The reeds were 3 or 4 feet high and were not very thick except on the outer edge, where they grew in thick clusters, dense and tall. Most of the reeds were of last year's growth, dead and more or less flattened down, with scattering tall, straight, green reeds growing up through them.

As we waded out toward the colony, clouds of gulls began to rise and circle over us, cackling and screaming, but it was not until we were 100 yards from the shore that we began to find nests. When we were fairly in the midst of the colony the excitement grew intense; clouds and clouds of the beautiful birds were rising all around us, and the din of their voices was terrific, as they hovered over, circled around, and darted down at us in bewildering multi- tudes. If we kept still they would gradually settle down all around us, but if we gave a shout the result would be startling as the whole surrounding marsh would seem to rise in a dense white cloud, and the roar of their wings mingled with the grand chorus of cries would be almost deafening. But they were very tame and we had plenty of opportunities to admire the exquisite beauty of their plumage, seldom surpassed in any bird; pearl gray mantles, delicate rosy breasts, black heads, and claret-colored bills and feet. We could form no very definite idea of their numbers, but there were certainly a mighty host of them; to say that there were thousands would be putting it mildly, for their nests were as thick as they could be over a large area.   Assuming that there were from 15 to 20 nests in an area 10 yards square, or in 100 square yards, which is certainly a conservative estimate, I figured that there were at least from 15,000 to 20,000 nests in the colony, meaning a population of from 30,000 to 40,000 birds.

As we stood wondering and admiring them, they grew more confident and gradually settled down on their nests all around us, and sometimes within 10 yards of us.   They seemed less afraid of us than of the cameras, for they would not alight on their nests very near the latter.   We got the best results with the Reflex cameras.   They had many a little squabble among themselves; they seemed to be disputing the ownership of the nests, fighting over it in the air, or if one alighted on the wrong nest a quarrel would arise with the rightful owner; but as a rule each bird returned to its own nest with remarkable accuracy, and it is a wonder that mistakes were not more often made amid such a vast confusion of nests and birds.   They frequently alighted in the little open pond holes among the reeds, where they floated lightly on the surface, swimming about in graceful elegance.   Many of them alighted on the lake out beyond the reeds, where they swam about with the eared grebes, scaups, and canvasbacks.   There was quite a large colony of the grebes nesting among the reeds with the gulls.

The gulls' nests began about 100 yards from shore and extended uniformly over all the reedy area to the outer edge, where they were, if anything, more abundant than elsewhere.   It seems as if a nest had been placed in every available spot, and it was difficult to walk without stepping on or overturning them.   They were in the open places and in the thick places as well.   The nests were generally large floating masses of dead reeds, but sometimes they were well built up among the green standing reeds and well secured.   In the latter case the nests were smaller.   They varied greatly in size and manner of construction.   A few that I measured, representing a fair average, were from 12 to 30 inches in diameter, and were built up from 4 to 8 inches above the water; the inner cavity, which was but slightly hollowed, was usually about 5 inches across.   The nests on the outer edge of the reeds seemed to have been occupied first, as it was here that we found most of the young.   Practically all of the eggs collected here were heavily incubated, whereas in the nests farther inland we found many fresh eggs and incomplete sets, but no young.   Three eggs were the usual number, though complete sets of two were very common.   We found in all four sets of four, but in these some of the eggs were fresh and some heavily incubated, showing that they were probably laid by two birds. After collecting a few sets of eggs and exposing a lot of plates we reluctantly came away, not having fired a gun among the beautiful and confiding birds. We even refrained from killing one which had become tangled in the reeds and was easily caught. We visited this locality again the following year, but were disappointed to find it entirely abandoned by the gulls, which was probably due to the fact that the lake had been very dry earlier in the season when they were beginning to nest.

The colony described above was undoubtedly unusual, as this species generally nests in a more open marsh in deeper water and often in quite exposed situations in marshy lakes. In the three other colonies that I have seen the nests have been floating in water which was waist deep, or deeper, and many of the nests could not be reached without a boat. Dr. Thomas S. Roberts (1900) describes a typical deep-water colony in his account of the nesting habits of this species at Heron Lake, Minnesota, in 1899. He says:

At a distance of about an eighth of a mile from the marshy, reed-grown shore, the little floating mounds dotted thickly a great crescent-shaped area some three-fourths of a mile in length by 300 or 400 yards in the widest part. The nests were irregularly distributed. In some places there were many close together, and again they were scattered yards apart, while now and then there were large spaces where there were none at all.

Under ordinary conditions the water over all this area would have been 2 or 3, nowhere over 4 feet deep, with a thick growth of bullrushes (*Scirpus*) standing well above the surface. But heavy rains had raised the lake until the water was in many places fully 6 feet deep and only the tops of the tallest rushes came into view; thus changing a large part of the nesting ground from a dense tangled bed of rushes into almost open water. Upon this condition of things the birds, of course, had not reckoned when they chose the site, and in consequence many of the nests were now torn from their moorings, having been lifted by the rising water, and were unprotected save by the weak tops of the submerged rushes. Thus free to drift, they were floating hither and thither at the mercy of the winds, but, strange to say, this state of things did not appear to greatly disconcert the owners. Here and there a number of nests had caught against some firm anchorage, and, receiving new additions with each favorable breeze, a windrow, or island, of these stray nests was soon formed. Nest touching nest in this manner resulted in a promiscuous crowding of families that must have tested the good nature and forbearance of the occupants not a little, and probably led to some vagaries in the care of the young described further on. A few nests had gone adrift entirely, and floating far out into the open water had been abandoned. But luckily a considerable part of the colony, wiser than their fellows, escaped this dire confusion of disaster as the result of having located their nests where shallower water and stronger growth of rushes provided protection and safe anchorage even when the flood was at its height. From nest-building operations still in progress at the late date of our visit (June 16) we inferred that a few at least of the gulls that had lost their homes were reestablishing themselves in safer retreats farther back, having perhaps learned a lesson against future similar mishaps.

The nests were all built of the same material—old water-soaked bullrushes—with sometimes a few fresh stems worked into the upper part. A heavy foundation of the thickest and longest rushes is first laid, forming a partly submerged platform held in place by the standing rushes about it, the whole being 2 to 3 feet across at the water line. Upon this the rather well-made superstructure of finer material is constructed, with a long slope from the water's edge up to the rim of the nest, which is raised 8 inches to a foot above the water. The cavity is 8 to 10 inches in diameter and 3 to 4 in depth, and is rudely lined with bits of fine rush tops and coarse grass. The inside is always perfectly dry, being several inches above the water. The variation in the nests was not very great, being merely as to general bulk and height. Much of the material of which the nests were constructed had been carried from a distance, probably from the neighboring shore, where the rushes, loosened by the ice, had been cast up in heaps. The gulls carry with apparent ease these great heavy rushes, and were often to be seen flying about for a considerable time with the long stems dangling from their bills. The nests were kept in good repair, and as they became trampled down or the rim disarranged the owners were to be seen putting things to rights or adding a new rush here and there as it was needed. At the time of our visit many young were already out of the shell, but there were also many sets of eggs in all stages of incubation, the result probably of second nest building.

Eggs.—As with most gulls the normal set of eggs is three; sets of four are rare, and often such sets are apparently the product of two birds; two eggs sometimes constitute a full set. The eggs show an interesting series of variations. In shape they are usually ovate, with some variation toward elliptical ovate. The shell is thin and almost lusterless. The ground color shows a great variety of buffy and greenish buffy shades, from "buffy brown" or "deep olive buff" to "cream buff," and from "ecru olive" or "water green" to "vetiver green" or "pale olive buff." Some eggs are sparingly spotted and others are quite heavily marked with large and small spots, blotches, or irregular scrawls, which sometimes are confluent into rings, of various shades of brown, such as "seal brown," "sepia," "bister," "Vandyke brown," and "burnt umber." Some eggs have a few spots of "lilac gray." The measurements of 48 eggs, in the United States National Museum collection, average 52 by 36 millimeters; the eggs showing the four extremes measure **56.5** by 37, 53.5 by **38.5, 47.5** by 35.5 and 49.5 by **34** millimeters.

Young.—I am inclined to think that both sexes incubate, for they are apparently affectionate and devoted to each other, both birds being often seen standing side by side on the nest. I believe that the male stands beside his sitting mate much of the time and relieves her by taking his turn on the nest. Dr. Roberts (1900) says that the period of incubation is "probably 18 or 20 days." He gives the following interesting account of the behavior of the young:

These pink-footed, pale-billed little balls of down now and then remain quietly in the home nest, basking in the warm sunshine, but more frequently they are no sooner dry from the egg than they start to wander. A few are content to go no farther than the broad sloping sides of the nest, and there they may be seen quietly dozing or tumbling about among the stems of the rushes as they explore the intricacies of their little island. The greater number, however, put boldly out to sea and drift away with the chance breeze, their tiny paddles of little avail as they pursue their now enforced journey. A gust of wind a trifle harder than usual, or a bump against a floating reed stem, and over they go bottomside up, only to come quickly right again, dry and fluffy as ever. Having, after many failures, crawled over the tiny obstruction, they sail contentedly on. Now and then they get out to sea in earnest and disappear, and are probably lost in the rough waters of the open lake. Their departure from the nests was apparently ever against the will of the old birds, and many were the scoldings and severe the punishments meted out to these venturesome offspring. A glance in the direction of some local outburst of furious cries would reveal a bevy of gulls crowded close together, beating the air and the water over a particular spot, where on closer inspection might be seen one or more of these hapless truants. The frenzy of the old birds as the chicks neared the open lake was pitiful to behold. With might and main they endeavored to turn them back, seeming not to realize their utter inability to stem the breeze even had they the inclination to make the attempt. At last, their protests of no avail, a resort is had to still more vigorous measures, and seizing the drifting chicks by the nape of the neck with the powerful beak they are jerked bodily and roughly out of the water, and from a height of 3 or 4 feet thrown as far as possible in the desired direction. This being repeated time and again—often several old birds taking part in the performance—until the youngsters are at last flung into some nest, exhausted and bleeding from the blows and pinches inflicted by the sharp bills of the parent birds.

This strange spectacle was of common occurrence, and these vigorous nursery duties seemed to occupy much of the attention of a goodly part of the members of this colony. Probably under ordinary conditions of water and protection such disturbances are less frequent. So far as the disciplining and care of the young went there existed a curious spirit of communisms among these gulls. An old gull cared for whatever young gulls fell in its way, and when the stray chicks chanced to clamber up into a strange nest, against which they happened to drift, they were, after a few admonishing squawks, welcomed as one of the household, and scolded, pecked, and fed just as though the foster parent had laid the eggs from which they were hatched. Now and then an entire brood would escape in a body, and crawling up beside some incubating bird on a neighboring windward nest would cuddle close about the old bird, who, to all appearances, was perfectly willing to adopt them in advance of the appearance of her own infants.

Occasionally we saw old gulls already in possession of a family twice the size to which they were entitled, rushing out and pouncing upon other fresh arrivals, who were quickly hustled and jerked up among the others until not infrequently 10 or a dozen of these tiny balls filled the nest to overflowing, and in the diversity of coloration presented plainly indicated their varied parentage.

Most jealously were these foundling asylums watched over and many were the fierce encounters in midair that resulted when some marauding band dared to interfere. A single gull, aided it might be by some accepted neighbor, fed apparently without distinction all these youngsters, and time and again we saw some little chap, just fished out of the water and still sore from the rough usage to which he had been subjected, fed to repletion by his captor, who disgorged into the tiny maw a juicy mass of dragon-fly nymphs brought from the meadows a mile away.

Plumages.—The downy young exhibit two color phases, with considerable variation in each. In the brown phase the upper parts are "wood brown" anteriorly, becoming "Isabella color" posteriorly; the throat and chest are "ochraceous buff," shading off to white on the belly. The back is heavily spotted or variegated with dusky, and the head is mottled with the same; there is a frontal black space at the base of the bill and usually a few dusky spots on the throat. In the gray phase the buff and brown tints are entirely replaced by light shades of "neutral gray" or "mouse gray," darker above and lighter below, the dusky markings on the upper parts being as described above.

The juvenal, or first plumage is acquired during July, previous to the flight stage. The back, scapulars, and lesser wing-coverts are "hair brown" and "drab"; the feathers edged with "wood brown;" the greater wing-coverts are gray; the primaries are dusky black tipped with white; the secondaries are centrally black, basally gray, broadly tipped, and edged with white; the tertials are dusky, broadly edged with white; the head is mottled with dusky and whitish above, white below, with a black crescentic spot in front of the eye and a white spot below it, the upper tail-coverts are white; the tail is light gray, with a broad subterminal band of dusky; the under parts are pure white, or rarely tinged with rosy.

The postjuvenal molt begins early in September and by November or December the first winter plumage is fully acquired by a partial molt, which involves everything but the wings and tail. The forehead is now largely white and the under parts are entirely so. The crown and occiput are mottled with dusky, the markings coalescing into a solid, slate-colored, nuchal collar, including the orbital and auricular regions; and the back is clear "gull-gray." This plumage is worn all winter until a *complete* molt occurs in May or earlier, which is practically a prenuptial and a postnuptial molt combined. This is a very peculiar molt, for, so far as I know, no other gull molts its wings and tail so early in the spring. I have seen at least six birds with the primaries in full molt in May, and fully as many in fresh plumage that had completed the molt in June. Although the birds do not breed in this plumage, I suppose we may as well call it a first-nuptial plumage. It is characterized by a partial, black hood, the head being mottled black and white. There is much individual variation, but usually the black predominates above and the white below; the outer primary is black, with a broad whitish wedge extending more than halfway up the inner web. The black decreases on each succeeding primary inwardly until it nearly or quite disappears on the innermost, which is largely "gull-gray." All the primaries are white-tipped; the tail is usually like the adult, but sometimes has a few dusky shaft streaks near the end. There is a slight roseate suffusion on the breast in this plumage. Perhaps the flight feathers are not molted again that year, but undoubtedly the plumage of the head is replaced by the winter plumage like that of the adult, and perhaps the wings may also be molted again during the late summer or fall. I have been unable to trace into subsequent plumages the peculiar wing acquired during the first spring, nor do I know when it is replaced.

The next step toward maturity we find in birds in both nuptial and winter plumages in which the plumage is fully adult except the primaries. This is undoubtedly the second year plumage, and the inference is that it is acquired at a complete postnuptial molt when the bird is a little over a year old, which means that the two complete molts are only about six months apart. In this plumage the primaries are black for a distance of about 3 inches from the tip on the outer and for a decreasing distance on each succeeding primary. The tips of all the primaries are white, sometimes for an inch or so on the outer, and sometimes there is an indistinct white spot in the black of the outer primary. At each succeeding molt the black in the primaries decreases and the white increases until only a small black area remains on each primary. There is apparently much individual variation in the extent and rapidity of this change.

The complete postnuptial molt of adults occurs mainly in August and September, but it is often not completed until October. The outer primaries are the last to be renewed. Winter adults have the forehead, lores, and throat white, and the occiput, cervix, loral, and auricular regions densely mottled or washed with slate gray. The beautiful nuptial plumage is acquired by a partial or perhaps a complete prenuptial molt in April and May.

Food.—The food and feeding habits of the Franklin's gull demonstrate its value to the agricultural interests of the west, and prove that it is almost wholly, if not entirely, beneficial to mankind. During the nesting season, at least, its food is almost wholly insectivorous.

Doctor Roberts (1900) says of its food at this season:

The stomachs and gullets of several birds collected by the writer and kindly examined by Professor Beal, of the Biological Survey at Washington, contained a mass of insect débris to the exclusion of all else. One stomach alone furnished some 15 different species, among them several varieties injurious to the interests of man. The chief part of the food, however, during the time of our visit to the colony, and that on which the young were largely fed, was the nymphs of dragon flies, which were then to be found in immense numbers in the meadows near by. The writer counted no less than 327 of these insects in a single stomach.

Early in the spring, when the farmers are plowing, these gulls follow the plow in large numbers, contending with the blackbirds and other birds in picking up from the freshly turned furrows quantities of angleworms, cutworms, and other grubs and larvae. Later in the season they resort to the prairies and grass fields to feed on grasshoppers and locusts, many of which are caught on the wing. I have seen them hovering over the water in open sloughs and small ponds and daintily gathering bits of food from the surface which probably consisted of aquatic insects or their larvae, and possibly a few small fish. I have also seen them coursing low over the meadows like large swallows, catching mosquitos and other small insects in the air. I once saw a great cloud of them flying over a large marshy area in the interior of an island in Lake Winnipegosis. They were so thick and so much excited that I thought it must be a nesting colony, but on investigation I found that they were feeding on the swarms of gnats, flies, and other minute insects that were rising from the bushes in long swaying columns like clouds of smoke. The air was full of dragon flies which were preying on the same insects, and probably the gulls were feeding on them also.

Mr. John F. Ferry (1910) states that the stomachs of three birds taken in Saskatchewan contained remains of numerous midges and Acrididae, a spider, a small mole cricket, a water beetle, and several large dragon-flies.

Behavior.—In flight the Franklin's gull is as light and graceful as at other times. When traveling long distances, as it does regularly, to and from its feeding grounds, it proceeds rather swiftly, with constant flappings in widely scattered and open flocks at a moderate height. When rising from or alighting on the water or ground its feet are allowed to dangle, but ordinarily they are stretched out behind and partly or wholly concealed under the feathers. At times small parties indulge in aerial exercise or sport by soaring upward in spiral curves, sailing on outstretched, motionless wings, mounting higher and higher, until almost lost to sight. Large numbers gather regularly at certain spots apparently for the sole purpose of performing these aerial evolutions, and after an hour or so of such exercise they suddenly disappear, as mysteriously as they came, drifting aimlessly about in roving bands. If one of their number is shot they gather immediately into a dense, hovering screaming flock, darting down toward their fallen companion, but if no more are killed they soon lose interest and silently drift away.

The Franklin's gull swims with exquisite grace and buoyancy, floating lightly on the surface. About its breeding grounds it is very tame and many a beautiful picture is seen of a party of these lovely birds, resting on the placid water of some small marshy pool, the delicate colors of their spotless plumage clearly reflected in its glassy surface and offset by a background of dark green reeds.

My field notes describe the ordinary note of this gull as a soft "Krrruk" or a low clucking call. This is sometimes varied with a louder and more plaintive cry, sounding like "pway" or "pwa-ay," which is rather musical; and when much excited or alarmed, as on their breeding grounds, it utters loud, shrill, piercing screams. Mr. Thomas Miller, in a letter to Major Bendire, described its notes as follows:

While feeding, their call is a shrill "Kuk Kuk Kuk Kuk" repeated incessantly, varied at times with their characteristic "Weeh-a Weeh-a," the first syllable prolonged and uttered with the rising inflection. This is the call most commonly heard, and while flying home from feeding about the only one they use. In visiting the breeding place they hover over you and repeat this call with a mournful cadence, as if imploring you not to molest their nests. Then their cries are incessant and can be heard a long way off. On bright sunny days in May and June they soar in the air to a great height, so high as to be scarcely visible, when they swoop back and forth crying "Weeh-a Weeh-a Weeh-a Po-lee Po-lee Po-lee Po-lee." The last notes are invariably uttered shorter and quicker than the first. They will fly thus all day long and the note "Po-lee Po-lee" is only heard when they are soaring at a great height during fine weather. This note is not unlike that heard on the Scottish moorlands while the whaup or sickle bill curlew is circling around the lonely traveler.

Mr. J. W. Preston (1886) says that "at intervals they utter a shill, clear cry much resembling the call of the marbled godwit. Their ordinary note is a loud, mewing cry, uttered in a short, jerky, impatient manner, somewhat resembling the mewing of a cat. This call is constantly kept up, and when they congregate at their rookery in the evening the din is deafening, and may be heard all night during the mating season, which begins about May 1 and lasts until the 15th of the month. Regularly at dark a large portion of the flock took their noisy way to the open lake, where they remained on the water until light."

Franklin's gulls are not only highly gregarious among themselves, nesting in compact colonies of immense numbers, but they are decidedly sociable toward other species, especially on their breeding grounds. In the sloughs where they breed they have for intimate neighbors large numbers of yellow-headed blackbirds, black terns, coots, rails, grebes, canvasbacks, redheads, and ruddy ducks, with all of whom they seem to be on good terms. They seem to be particularly intimately associated with eared grebes. There is almost always a colony of these grebes in or near every Franklin's gull colony, and often the nests of the two species are closely intermingled. Mr. Herbert K. Job has a photograph of a Franklin's gull eating the eggs in an eared grebe's nest, but I doubt if they regularly disturb the nests of their neighbors to any great extent, although nest-robbing is a trait peculiar to almost all gulls. Mr. Preston (1886) says of their behavior:

While defending their nests they evince great courage and spirit, successfully routing the Canada goose (*Bernicla canadensis*), white pelican (*Pelecanus erythrorhynchus*), and other large birds which chanced to molest them. A most distressing sight was the determined but unsuccessful attempt of a dozen frightened gulls to chase a large snapping turtle from a nest on which it had killed the mother bird and was leisurely devouring her eggs. When I approached the nest the owners, with a few others, hovered about crying piteously, almost striking me with their wings.

Fall.—After the breeding season is over these gulls gather into immense flocks and wander about in search of suitable feeding grounds, where they must prove of great benefit in destroying vast hordes of injurious insects, such as locusts and grasshoppers, which are swarming on the prairies during the latter half of the summer. Mr. George Atkinson, according to Macoun (1909), says of their abundance at that season:

While driving into the Eagle hills, about 40 miles west of Saskatoon, on July 30, 1906, we passed an extensive mud flat and salty slough, on which rested between four and five solid acres of gulls. I fired a shot into the air to note the effect and they rose as one bird in such a cloud that their wings clashed together in a frantic flapping and their discordant cries were almost deafening. It would be entirely impossible to estimate the number of birds in this flock.

Dr. Thomas S. Roberts has sent me the following interesting extracts from his field notes on the behavior of Franklin's gulls in the great autumnal gatherings of this species in Minnesota:

Immense numbers of these gulls spend the nights out in the open lake, congregating to form one or two or sometimes three flocks, 600 or 800 feet long and 200 or 300 feet wide. The gulls sit close on the water, so that from a distance they look like vast "banks" of ducks, except when the sun strikes them just right, then they show white. During the day the gulls feed on the fields and prairies at some distance from the lake, returning toward evening in various sized flocks and assembling out in the lake for the night. About sunrise in the morning they begin to stir, and for a time there is great commotion among them. Soon they get up in a body and the air is filled with them. As the slanting sun strikes their snowy bodies and slowly moving wings it is a curious and beautiful sight, appearing as though the air were filled with huge snowflakes or eddying bits of silver tinsel. Rising to some distance above the water they start for their feeding grounds in a great straggling company, the head of the flock soon becoming V-shaped as geese fly. Later they break up into numerous smaller flocks, each flying in more or less perfect V-shaped formation. They return at night in the same way or in broad straight-fronted flocks, and when the light makes them appear dark the inexperienced sportsman is apt to think a tempting flock of small geese is approaching. They fly too slowly for ducks.

On October 4 at 5 p. m. the gulls came from the north at a great height, circling around against the blue sky, appearing like shining white specks as the sun struck their white bodies. The wings were invisible, but their movements caused a flickering or twinkling, causing the gulls to look like stars in the deep blue sky; as they darted about or dropped suddenly the effect was that of shooting stars. I lay on my back on the bank for some time watching them. As they reached a point over the lake they descended by a series of sudden downward shoots or more frequently by a gentle spiral.

From the southeast the gulls came in immense flocks, low down, larger than I have seen before. At times the stream seemed to extend for what appeared about a mile and was at places dense and broad, at others thin. But the number of gulls was something beyond calculation; it reminded one of the way wild pigeons used to fly. As they approached the water they dropped near the surface and swept up the lake in great clouds to join the great concourse already assembled. This flight of gulls is something that never ceases to interest me; they are in such vast numbers, so regular in their habits, and so beautiful.

October 5. The gulls left the lake this morning going northward between 9 and 10. Many flew out in flocks directly, but I noticed a new performance. Over the lake a hundred or more gulls would get together and begin to fly about rapidly in a circle, and, others joining them, there was soon formed a great whirling mass of gulls, the birds moving in all directions within the globe, but turning about when reaching its limits. It was a curious sight, especially as at times five or six of these great whirligigs would be in view at the same time. It was a great game and presented a spectacle of perfect abandon. Fresh flocks encountering one of these merry-go-rounds either passed directly through it or more often joined at once in the sport. Round and round and up and down they went, forming a great whirling mass, which, as a whole, wound slowly onward away from the lake. Sometimes two of these eddying groups encountered each other, and then they merged to form a single one. They broke up finally by the gulls that tired first steering away in the direction of the flight until all had gone. I lay beside a haystack in the warm sun for an hour watching this gull play. The masses formed directly in front of me and passed over and by me at a height of 75 to 100 feet. It reminded me most of the revolving balls of gnats or other insects one sometimes sees on still evenings. The morning was clear, warm, and only a moderate breeze blowing from the north.

DISTRIBUTION.

Breeding range.—Prairie regions of the northern interior. East to central Manitoba (Shoal Lake) and western Minnesota (Becker and Jackson Counties, Heron Lake). South to northwestern Iowa (Dickinson County, formerly), northeastern South Dakota (Brookings, Clark, and Marshall Counties), southwestern Saskatchewan (Crane Lake region), and northern Utah (Bear River). West to southeastern Alberta (Many Island Lake). North to central Saskatchewan (south and east of the Saskatchewan River) and central Manitoba (Waterhen Lake).

Winter range.—A few birds winter in the Gulf of Mexico from the coast of Louisiana to Panama, on the west coast of Mexico (Mazatlan) and Guatemala (Chiapam); but the main winter range is on the west coast of South America, from northern Peru (Payta) to Patagonia and southern Chile (Magellan).

Spring migration.—Northward by the most direct route. Dates of arrival: Minnesota, Heron Lake, average April 4 and earliest March

27; Manitoba, Aweme, average April 25 and earliest April 8; Saskatchewan, Indian Head, average May 3 and earliest April 25. Transient dates: Missouri, April 20 to May 15; Kansas, April 10 to June 9; Iowa, April 6 to June 27. Late dates of departure: Peru, Callao Bay, April 11; Guatemala, Champerico, May 30; Texas, Kerrville, May 17 and Aransas Bay, June.

Fall migration—A reversal of the spring route, but more erratic. First arrivals reach Chile, Valparaiso, in September. Late dates of departure; Minnesota, Madison, October 8; Iowa, November 6; Nebraska, Lincoln, November 17; Texas, Brownsville, November 10.

Casual records.—Has wandered on migrations to Hudson Bay (specimen in British Museum from Hayes River); Pennsylvania (Philadelphia, October 22, 1911); Virginia (Blacksburg, October 24, 1898); the West Indies (St. Bartholomew Island); California (Hyperion, October 17 and November 24, 1914); and many other inland localities. Accidental in Hawaiian Islands (Mauai, winter).

Egg dates.—Minnesota and North Dakota: Forty-two records, May 3 to June 26; twenty-one records, May 18 to June 4. Manitoba and Saskatchewan: Twenty-one records, June 5 to 16; eleven records, June 6 to 11.

LARUS PHILADELPHIA (Ord).

BONAPARTE'S GULL.

HABITS.

This widely distributed American species is found at some season of the year in nearly all parts of our continent. As it retires to the northern wooded regions of Canada to breed, it is familiar to most of us only as a migrant or a winter visitor, and few naturalists have studied it on its breeding grounds. During the first warm weather in April, when the shad and herring are beginning to run up our rivers, we begin to see the migrating flocks of this pretty little gull moving northward along our coasts or up the valleys of our great rivers in the interior. They proceed in a leisurely manner, drifting along in loose flocks, as if aimlessly wandering, stopping to dip down and occasionally pick some morsel of food from the surface of the water, chattering to each other in soft conversational notes, or coursing over the meadows and marshes to catch the first flying insects of spring. The black-headed adults make up the vanguard of the migrating hosts, followed later by the immature birds; flocks of young birds, however, often have one or two adults with them as leaders. Sir John Richardson (1851) says:

This species arrives very early in the season, before the ground is denuded of snow, and seeks its food in the first pools of water which form on the borders of Great Bear Lake, and wherein it finds multitudes of minute crustacean animals and larvae of insects.

Nesting.—I have never succeeded in finding its breeding grounds and must quote from what scanty accounts of its nesting habits have been published. Mr. Roderick MacFarlane (1891) writes:

Thirty-seven nests are recorded as having been taken, with eggs in them, between 10th June and 10th July, in the wooded country in the neighborhood of Fort Anderson and on Lower Anderson River. They were all built on trees at various heights (from 4 to 15 and even 20 feet) from the ground, and, with one exception, which was composed of down and velvety leaves held together by some stringy turf, they were made of small sticks and twigs lined with hay and mosses, etc. The parents always fly about in close proximity to the nest, and scream vehemently when explorers, in the interests of science, are obliged to deprive them of their eggs or young, and not infrequently shoot one of them. They seldom lay more than three eggs.

The following account is published by Baird, Brewer, and Ridgway (1884):

Mr. Kennicott found this gull nesting in the neighborhood of Fort Yukon, and describes the nest as being of about the size of that of *Zenaidura carolinensis;* but the cavity is rather deeper. It was placed on the side branch of a green spruce, several feet from the trunk, and about 20 feet from the ground, near a lake. Mr. Kennicott saw several nests near this one, all alike and in similar positions, except that some were not over 10 feet from the ground, and were on smaller trees; but all were on spruce trees. One nest which he examined contained three young birds of a dirty yellowish color, thickly spotted with dark brown. He saw between 25 and 50 gulls about that breeding place, but he found only a few of their nests. These birds were said by the Indians always to breed in similar situations.

This species apparently bred formerly as far south as Michigan and Wisconsin, in the region of the Great Lakes. Mr. W. H. Collins (1880) was told by hunters living at St. Clair Flats that Bonaparte's gulls bred " in Baltimore Bay and the North Channel, and that they lay their eggs on old logs with no signs of a nest." Kumlien and Hollister (1903) write:

In 1880 a few were said to breed on Chambers Island, Green Bay, and we saw on some small islands in Big Bay de Noquet, Michigan, a number of nests like pigeons' nests on the flat branches of low coniferous trees that without question had been used by these birds.

Eggs.—The Bonaparte's gull lays from two to four eggs, ordinarily three, frequently only two, and rarely four. The eggs somewhat resemble those of the Franklin's gull, but are considerably smaller. In shape they are ovate, pointed ovate, or pointed elongate ovate. The ground color varies from " buffy citrine " or " Dresden brown " to " dark olive buff " or " deep olive buff." They are more or less evenly spotted or irregularly blotched, rarely scrawled, with various shades of brown, " brownish olive," and " brownish drab," too numerous and variable to be definitely named. The measurements of eggs, in various collections, average 49.5 by 34.9 millimeters; the eggs showing the four extremes measure **54** by 37, 50.6 by **38.2, 44.5** by 35, and 47 by **32.5** millimeters.

Plumages.—I have never seen the downy young of the Bonaparte's gull, but Dr. Jonathan Dwight (1901) describes it as " much like that of *Sterna hirundo*, yellowish with dusky mottling above." He describes the juvenal plumage as follows:

> The upper surface is decidedly brown, with paler edgings; a blackish brown band extends along the cubital border of the wing into the tertiaries; the secondaries have dusky markings; the primaries show little white, their coverts being partly black, and the tail is white with a broad subterminal black band, the rectrices being tipped with buff. The sides of the head are white with a dull black auricular patch and an anteorbital spot, and the rest of the lower parts are white with a brownish wash on the sides of the neck and breast. The bill and feet are black.

This plumage is partially replaced, in September and October, by the first winter plumage, the molt involving only the contour feathers. " A blue-gray mantle and paler head are assumed," but the wings and tail of the juvenal plumage are retained. A partial prenuptial molt, involving mainly the head and neck, possibly some of the body plumage, takes place during March and April. At this molt most specimens merely renew the first winter plumage on the head, but some birds acquire a partially black head. In some birds the head is only slightly mottled above, but in others the deep plumbeous hood of the adult nuptial is more or less complete. Young birds can always be readily distinguished, even at a distance, by the broad, dusky, subterminal band on the tail and by the color pattern of the wings. The dusky cubital band is always in evidence, though often much faded, in the lesser wing-coverts. The scapulars are largely dusky, the greater wing-coverts partly so, and all the remiges are broadly tipped with dusky. The three outer primaries are also dusky on the outer web and for a narrow space on the inner web, next to the shaft, on the outer two.

A complete postnuptial molt occurs in summer, beginning in July or August and lasting sometimes until October, at which the adult winter plumage is assumed, with the pure white tail and the white, black-tipped primaries. Adults have a partial prenuptial molt, as in young birds, and a complete postnuptial molt in summer. I have examined adults in full winter plumage as late as March 17 and molting into nuptial plumage at various dates from March 30 to May 15. I have seen specimens taken on the Pacific coast in full nuptial plumage on November 6 and December 2, but ordinarily the postnuptial molt begins in August and is completed in October; usually the flight feathers are molted last.

Food.—Like its larger relative, the Franklin's gull, the Bonaparte's gull is largely insectivorous. Over the marshy ponds of the interior

flocks of these pretty birds are frequently seen beating back and
forth, adroitly catching insects on the wing, and their stomachs are
often packed full of such food. Many insects are gleaned from the
surface of still pools or picked up from the drift rows of decaying
vegetation along the shores. Mr. Arthur H. Norton (1909) says that
in Maine it "has been found feeding over rafts of drifting seaweeds, when its diet was found to consist of maggots, probably
Coleopa frigida—a fly that breeds at high-water mark in decaying
seaweeds (*Algae* and *Zostera*)." Nuttall (1834) examined two that
" were gorged with ants and their eggs, and some larvae of moths in
their pupa state." On the seacoast they live on small fish, shrimps,
and other surface-swimming crustaceans, marine worms, and other
small aquatic animals. Apparently very little, if any, vegetable
food is taken.

Behavior.—The flight of this species is very light and buoyant, as
well as active and graceful. It is more tern-like than gull-like, and
it might easily be overlooked in a flock of loitering terns. When
moving about looking for food its flight seems listless and desultory;
every stroke of its long wings lifts its light body perceptibly, as
it drives it along much faster than it seems. Like snowflakes
wafted by the wind the loose flock drifts along; one hardly realizes
that it has come before it has swept away beyond our vision. Yet
with all this apparent listlessness there is no lack of the power of
control; it can breast the heaviest storms, it can rise and fall over
the crests of the largest waves, and can go whither it will with the
utmost ease and grace. It swims with equal buoyancy and grace,
resting on the surface as lightly as an eggshell. I have sometimes
seen it dive, though its food is often picked up while it is swimming
on the surface; but more often it drops lightly down in the air, picking the morsel from the water with its bill and perhaps touching
the surface with its feet.

Its voice is not powerful, but when feeding in flocks it is often
quite talkative. Doctor Townsend (1905) says that " occasionally
it emits a harsh, rasping cry, but as a rule it is silent." Neltje
Blanchan (1898) describes its note as " a plaintive shrill, but rather
feeble cry, that was almost a whistle."

Fall.—Of the fall migration of this gull in Ohio, Prof. Lynds
Jones (1909) writes:

In my experience this gull is far more numerous on both sides of Cedar Point
sand spit than elsewhere along the lake, and the times of maximum numbers
occur between November 1 and December 30. During the last three winters I
have found a flock of from 50 to 500 birds ranging along the shore of the sand
spit as long as there remained open water, which was well into January. They
act much like terns diving headlong into the water for fish, but can always be
readily distinguished from them by the almost sparrow-like conversational notes
instead of the harsh ter-r-r of the terns. They seem to prefer the vicinity of

the lake beach to the marshes for feeding grounds, possibly because small fish are more numerous there. On the occasions when the pent-up swamp waters at Rye Beach have broken through into the lake carrying all sorts of débris upon their floods, these gulls have collected at the place in great numbers, feeding.

Winter.—Bonaparte's gull also winters to some extent along the whole of both coasts of the United States, though rather rarely northward and much more abundantly southward, where it is associated with nearly all of the other common species. At this season it frequents the bays, harbors, and tidal estuaries, where it can find small fry to feed upon. I know of no prettier, winter, seashore scene than a flock of these exquisite little gulls hovering over some favorite feeding place, plunging into the cold gray water, unmindful of the chilly blasts and the swirling snow squalls.

DISTRIBUTION.

Breeding range.—Known to breed at only a few localities in the timbered regions of the northwest. East in Mackenzie to the Anderson River, Great Bear Lake (Fort Franklin) and Great Slave Lake (Forts Fae and Resolution) and on Southampton Island. South in British Columbia to the Cariboo District (Quesnelle Lake). West in Alaska nearly to the northwest coast (Nulato and Kowak River). North to the limit of trees. Adults, in breeding plumage, occur in summer more or less regularly as far south as the Gulf of St. Lawrence (Cape Breton and Magdalen Islands), some of the Great Lakes (Lake Michigan), and Saskatchewan (Quill Lake), which suggests that they probably breed far south and east of the known breeding places.

Winter range.—On the Atlantic coast regularly from South Carolina southward, more rarely farther north, straggling as far north as Maine. Frequently in Bermuda. On the Gulf coast from Alabama and Louisiana southward to Yucatan (Progreso). On the Pacific coast from Washington (Gray's Harbor) southward as far as central Mexico (Jalisco), rarely to Peru.

Spring migration.—Northwestward from the Atlantic coast to the interior. Early dates of arrival: Pennsylvania, Erie, April 13; New York, April 21; Prince Edward Island, May 10; Quebec, Godbout, April 27. Late dates of departure: Florida, Coronado, April 9; South Carolina, Charleston, May 15; District of Columbia, May 30; Pennsylvania, Erie, May 25; New York, June 14; Massachusetts, June 9. Dates for the interior: Louisiana, New Orleans (latest), March 25; Kansas (average), April 21; Michigan, Ann Arbor (average), April 19; Manitoba (average), April 24; Mackenzie, Fort Resolution (average arrival), May 14, and Fort Simpson,

May 12 to 22; California, Monterey, rare after May 18, latest June 2; British Columbia, transients passing from April 11 to May 24.

Fall migration.—Southeastward to the Atlantic coast *via* James Bay and the Great Lakes. Early dates of arrival: Gulf of St. Lawrence, August 4; Massachusetts, August 13; South Carolina, Charleston, August 20; Florida, Coronado, September 16. Late dates of departure: Quebec, Montreal, October 1; Gulf of St. Lawrence, November 25; Massachusetts, December 23. Late dates of departure in the interior: Manitoba, October 24; Minnesota, Aitkin, November 2; Nebraska, Lincoln, November 3; Missouri, Jackson County, December 8. On the Pacific coast early arrivals reach California, Los Angeles County, August 20. Late birds recorded in Alaska, Unalaska, October 5.

Casual records.—Accidental on Laysan Island (December 27, 1912), on Heligoland (winter, 1845), and in Great Britain (8 or 10 records).

Egg dates.—Anderson River region: Twenty records, June 10 to July 5; ten records, June 17 to 23.

LARUS MINUTUS Pallas.

LITTLE GULL.

HABITS.

Contributed by Charles Wendell Townsend.

The little gull is appropriately named, for it is the smallest of all gulls, being but 11 inches in length. Bonaparte's gull, one of the next smallest gulls, averages 3 inches longer. Although a native of Europe and Asia, breeding in the northern parts and wintering as far south as the Mediterranean, it deserves a secure place in the American avifauna, as there are several authentic records of its occurence in this country and others which are reasonably certain. The first is mentioned by Swainson and Richardson (1831), who say:

A specimen obtained on Sir John Franklin's first expedition was determined by Mr. Sabine to be a young bird of the first year of this species, exactly according to M. Temminck's description.

According to Baird, Brewer, and Ridgway (1884), one was obtained at Bermuda on January 22, 1849, by Major Wedderburn, and another one was killed in the following month; also specimens were obtained near Mazatlan, on the western coast of Mexico, in 1868 by Colonel Grayson. The first thoroughly authentic specimen is recorded by Dutcher (1888) of a bird shot by Robert Powell at Fire Island, Long Island, New York, about September 15, 1887. The specimen is now in the American Museum of Natural History. A second specimen, now in the Museum of the Brooklyn Institute of Arts and Sciences, was shot by Mr. Robert L. Peavey in a flock of Bonaparte's gulls at Rockaway Beach, Long Island, on May 10, 1902, and recorded by Braislin (1903). The last recorded specimen is one taken at Pine Point, Scarborough, Maine, on July 20, 1910, that fortunately fell into the hands of Mr. Arthur H. Norton (1910), who has also brought together all the evidence for its occurence in America.

Nesting.—In the neighborhood of the Baltic this gull breeds in marshes and nests on grassy knolls and floating islets of tangled plants. The nest is made of leaves and grass. Three eggs constitute a set, although sometimes four and rarely five are laid. The eggs vary in color from yellowish-brown and olive brown to greenish-gray, marked with spots and blotches of reddish brown and gray. They are considerably smaller than those of the Bonaparte's gull and measure 1.66 by 1.25 inches Meves, quoted by Dresser (1871), says that both the nest and eggs resemble closely those of *Sterna hirundo* that nested among them. He found, however, that the yolk of the little gull's egg was of an orange-red color, while that of the common tern was ocher-yellow. Both parents incubate.

Plumages.—In the juvenal plumage the upper parts are mottled with dark brown, and there is a band of the same color at the tip of the tail; the bill is blackish and the feet yellow. In the adult nuptial dress this bird, like the Bonaparte's gull, has a black hood. The mantle is pale gray, the underparts suffused with pink. The primaries are tipped with white, dark below; bill reddish brown, feet vermillion. The adult in winter loses the black hood and the head and neck are white, brownish gray on the occiput; there is a dusky spot in the auricular region. In many ways it resembles Bonaparte's gull, but lacks the broad black anterior and posterior margin to the wings. Norton (1910) sums ᵘp the distinctive marks of its plumage as follows:

> The adults are distinguished at once by the broad white posterior border of the wing without black, the pale pearl gray mantle, and the slaty lower surface of the wings. The young, by the inner vanes of the outer primaries being chiefly white; the inner primaries with both webs gray, their tips white, the white increasing in length as it proceeds in, and without black subterminal areas. Moreover, it is the smallest known gull.

Food.—Dresser (1871) quotes Meves as to their feeding habits, as follows:

> I found in the stomachs of many of the little gulls I examined not only insects but chiefly small fishes, which they are continually catching in the lake. Very few had insects in their stomachs; but it is probable that later, when the *Neuroptera*, *Phryganiae*, and *Ephemera* are more abundant, they feed on these in preference, as is the case with the black-headed gull (*Larus ridibundus*). Others have found *Neuroptera* in their stomachs.

Behavior.—In flight and general habits the little gull is said to closely resemble the black-headed gull. They are very tame and fearless of danger. Their flight is graceful and active, and it is said at times to be butterfly-like or to resemble that of swallows. Professor Liljeborg, quoted by Dresser, says that their graceful and quick evolutions in pursuit of insects "almost surpass goatsuckers." In a word, these gulls resemble terns in flight rather than the larger gulls.

Fall.—Gätke (1895), at Heligoland, says:

All the gulls leave their northern breeding stations before the approach of winter in order to betake themselves to more temperate latitudes. In the case of none, however, does this movement so much partake of the nature of a true migration as in that of the present species. Long-extending flights of these pretty little birds may be seen traveling over the sea past the island at the close of September and during the first half of October. Their movements, however, are quite different from what one is accustomed to see in the case of most migrants. Companies of from 100 to 200 individuals travel in motley throng quite low over the sea, continuously dropping to the surface to pick up food. All the time, however, they rigidly maintain their western course of flight, and speeding along with great rapidity are very soon lost to sight. Moreover, considerable quantities of these gulls, intermingled with the larger species, are met with here all the winter months during violent westerly and northwesterly gales, when they seek a temporary shelter on the lee side of the island. While roving over the sea in all directions in search of food they execute many rapid beats with their wings.

Winter.—Canon Tristram writes to Dresser (1871) that "*Larus minutus* abounds in winter on all the shallow lagoons of the North-African coast, especially between Tunis and Carthage, where it is extremely tame, flying and dipping after small fish like a tern."

DISTRIBUTION.

Breeding range.—Iceland, Northern Europe, and Asia, from Jutland, Prussia, Gothland, and the northern half of Russia, eastward across Siberia to the Sea of Okhotsk, and northward to Archangel and to the Arctic Circle on the Obi River.

Winter range.—South to north Africa coasts, the Mediterranean Sea, and inland waters of southern Europe; occasional in Great Britain.

Casual records.—Two records for Long Island, New York (Fire Island, September 15, 1887, and Rockaway Beach, May 10, 1902); two for Maine (St. George, August 12, 1904, and Scarborough, July 20, 1910); and two for Bermuda (January 22 and February, 1849). Accidental in northern India and in Faroe Islands.

Egg dates.—Northern Europe: Nine records, May 23 to June 16; five records, June 4 to 11.

The rosy gull is not only the most beautiful of the gulls but it is the most strictly Arctic, one of the rarest in collections and, to all but a favored few, the least known. Owing to its restricted habitat in an inaccessible region, few of us may ever expect to see it. As its wanderings carry it over a wide area in Arctic regions, a few specimens have been picked up by Arctic explorers. For nearly all that we know of its habits we are indebted to the Russian explorer and good ornithologist, Dr. Sergius A. Buturlin (1906), who, during his visit to the Kolyma delta, on the Arctic coast of eastern Siberia, in 1905, collected 38 skins and 36 eggs of this beautiful bird. Fortunately he has given us a very full and interesting life history of this species, from which I shall quote freely.

The delta of the Kolyma, which is the easternmost of the great rivers of the North Polar basin, lies, roughly speaking, between 68½° and 69¾° N. lat. and from 159° to 161½° E. long. This vast area, at least 15,000 square kilometers in extent, consists of a liberal admixture of lakes, lagoons, channels, rivulets (" viska "), swamps, moors, and damp ground of every description, with dry places only at intervals. The southern part of this delta, some one-third or even less of the whole, is covered by forests. The other parts stretch beyond the northern limit of the forests, but are for the most part covered by extremely dense and well-grown bushes of *Alnus incana* (ordinarily 5 to 10 feet high, but occasionally reaching a height of 15 feet with a thickness of from 5 to 6 inches), and by various species of *Salix*. The traveler must go some 20 kilometers from the main channels of the great river, and then perhaps 2 or 3 kilometers from the rivulet or "viska " along which he is advancing, to find a little piece of true "tundra " such as I have seen on Kolguev Island, with lichens covering the ground, tiny bushes of *Betula nana*, and different *Salices* studded over the drier spots, and mosses and *Carices* clothing the damp portions.

Spring.—After a period of very cold weather during the first half of May he describes the breaking up of winter, the coming of the earliest birds, and the arrival of the Ross's gulls on their breeding grounds, as follows:

Toward the middle of May the weather became somewhat better, and the snow melted at midday (freezing again, of course, in the shade), so that on the southern slopes and sandy islands the soil made its appearance. At this time the first specimens of geese (*Anser serrirostris, A. gambeli*, and in small numbers *A. rhodorhynchus*), and even swans (*Cygnus bewicki*) made their appearance, migrating down the river; while about May 20 small parties of them passed. *Linota exilipes, Plectrophenax nivalis, Corvus orientalis*, the white-tailed eagle, and *Lagopus albus* (partly wintering in the district) had of course long been present. Then migration stopped, and snowstorms began again until May 27. That day was fine, with only some 3°-6° cels. of frost, so that the snow melted in the hot sun, and on this and the following days geese, swan, ducks, gulls (*Larus vegae* and (?) *L. glaucescens*), and waders (especially *Tringa maculata, T. subarquata, T. sakhalina, Phalaropus fulicarius,* and *Charadrius fulvus*) migrated in great numbers. At last, on May 30, it rained, while the thermometer varied between 16° cels. above zero and as much below; snow became scanty on the open places, and the first rosy gull was reported. On the morning of May 31 one of my men saw a pair, and during the day I went on the river, where the fathom-thick ice was still quite safe, and came across several dozens. The sun was shining brightly, and in the distance each pair appeared like so many roseate points on the bluish ice of the great stream. I say "pair," as from their first arrival the birds were constantly seen in pairs. They had evidently just finished their migration and were tired after their exertions, for they sat very quietly on the ice, and though all attempts to stalk them were unavailing, they would not fly far, but only shifted from place to place with a lazy and somewhat uneasy motion of their wings, which made me jot down in my notebook on the spur of the moment that the flight was more fulmar-like than gull-like.

Courtship.—Although most of the birds seemed to be paired on their arrival, he noted some squabbles with unmated males and the following courtship performance:

Every now and then the male tried to express his feelings to his mate by pecking her curiously, as if trying to kiss her, with his open beak on her head or neck, or made a few steps round her to one side or the other, showing off as some pigeons do; then with a sound like *trrrrr* lowered his neck and breast to the ground, and in this position, with all the hinder part of the body, the tail, and the ends of the folded wings high up in the air, continued for some seconds his little promenade before the female, who very rarely engaged in such antics.

Nesting.—He

found the rosy gull nesting in little colonies of from 2 or 3 to 10 or 15 pairs, in company with the common black-capped tern of the delta, which, however, in nearly every case exceeds it in numbers. A pair or two of *Totanus fuscus* nearly always breed with them, and not unfrequently *Colymbus arcticus* and *Fuligula glacialis,* sometimes accompanied by the white-winged gull (*Larus Glaucescens*), and a pair or two of *Squatarola helvetica.* A little low island in a lake is usually selected for the breeding place, and this made the nests very difficult of access, as until the last days of June a boat can only be used near the banks and must be then dragged over the ice, which is exceedingly slippery and generally unsafe after June comes in, especially near the islands, as I found to my cost. One of the colonies, however, was on a piece of wet tundra near two lakes, a square kilometer in extent, covered with a labyrinth of pools of snow water from 2 to 6 or even 10 inches deep, but practicable in wading boots, thanks to its floor of everlasting ice beneath the underlying mud. Between these pools, which were from 15 to 50 feet in diameter, were pieces of very wet ground covered with *Carices,* damp mossy spots, and even tiny patches of comparatively dry bog covered with lichens or *Betula nana.*

In this colony I found 10 nests of *Rhodostethia,* placed, among those of the tern, on little mossy swamps almost bare of grass, evidently because the more grassy places were too wet and unsafe. But in the remaining colonies the state of affairs was otherwise; there the tern nested on the moss (sometimes making no nest at all), and laid its one or two eggs much nearer to the dry parts of the little islands, which were perhaps a hundred yards long and from 10 to 20 yards wide, while the rosy gulls made their nests on wet grassy spots or bogs much nearer to the water, and these nests rose from 4 to 10 inches, generally from 5 to 8 inches, above the surface. The hollow formed in the grass (dead grass, of course, as green grass is hardly seen even by the 20th of June) is about 6 or 7 inches in diameter; but the nest proper is a shallow cup only about 4 or 4½ inches in diameter. It is composed of dry grass and *Carices*, sometimes with the addition of a few dry *Betula* or *Salix* leaves, while I once saw one made of white reindeer moss. The cup of the nest is from ⅛ to ¼ inch, generally ¼ inch thick.

The eggs which he collected were taken between June 13 and 26, those taken on the latter date being nearly ready to hatch.

Later on (July 6 and 7) he discovered two more colonies, which he describes as follows:

Here we were clear of the *Salix* and *Alnus* thickets and were on the true tundra, which afforded a welcome relief to both eyes and limbs. After the delay caused by a long and heavy snowstorm I discovered two new breeding colonies of this gull—one on the wet grassy border of a lake about a kilometer in diameter, the other in the middle of a somewhat larger lake, furnished with many tiny islands, spacious bogs, and shallow grassy areas. Both colonies contained from 10 to 12 pairs of *Rhodostethia*, accompanied by five or six pairs of terns, considerable numbers of *Limosa uropygialis*, *Phalaropus fulicarius*, *P. lobatus*, *Tringa maculata*, *Pavoncella pugnax*, *Harelda glacialis*, and a pair or two of *Scolopax gallinula*, *Colymbus arcticus*, *Squatarola helvetica*, *Charadrius fulvus*, and *Totanus fuscus*.

Mr. John H. Dalgleish (1886) reports the finding of a nest of Ross's gull by Mr. Paul Müller near Christianshaab, Greenland, on June 15, 1885. The nest "was situated in the midst of the nests of a colony of *Sterna macroura*. The female bird was shot off the nest, which, when found, contained two eggs."

Eggs.—There are four eggs of this species in the United States National Museum, which bear a decided resemblance to eggs of the Sabine's gull. They are pointed in shape and have a uniform ground color of "ecru-olive." They are rather faintly marked with irregular and indistinct spots and blotches of "Saccardo's umber." The measurements of 31 eggs, in various collections, average 43.6 by 32 millimeters; the eggs showing the four extremes measure **46.6** by 32.7, 43 by **34, 39** by 31.5, and 44.4 by **30.3** millimeters.

Of the eggs Buturlin (1906) says:

The rosy gull lays sometimes two, but nearly always three, eggs; four are said to be found not uncommonly, but I doubt the fact. The eggs, as might be expected from so beautiful a bird, are very handsome and, happily for the collector, are quite unlike those of the black-capped tern.

The eggs of the rosy gull are not only larger and in particular broader than those of its neighbor, but are of quite a different shape, being extremely round for gulls' eggs, with the small end by no means pronounced. They are much darker and more evenly colored than any other eggs of the order known to me, being of a beautiful deep rich olive-green, without any of the grayish or sandy shade so common in eggs of *Sterna* and other members of the order. They are spotted, especially near the larger end, with chocolate-brown (not earthy brown), the somewhat clouded spots being generally some 3–5 mm. in diameter, and not so sharply defined on the dark ground color as is usual in gavian eggs. The spots are of unequal intensity, some darker, some paler, with every intergradation; they can not be divided into two sharply defined groups as in other gavian eggs, perhaps because the dark markings do not stand out very clearly on the deep olive-green ground color.

During the daytime even the female readily leaves the nest, and flies about the pools of water or walks over the melting ice, picking up insects and often slipping in a curious way on the surface. But in the night—the sunny Arctic night—the rosy gulls which mob you at some distance from the colony are invariably males. When an intruder visits the colony the gulls fly overhead and scream, but are far less noisy and anxious than the terns. If he sits down they very soon become quiet, and the female settles down on her eggs even within 30 or 40 yards, and so betrays their position. If the nest is approached both parents hover overhead persistently, but do not venture nearer than 15 or 25 yards, the male being usually silent, but the female screaming and uttering cries of various description—now the regular note of "kiaoo, kiaoo, kiaoo; miaw, miaw, viaw, viaw; trrrrr"; now the true Larine "kwa, kwa, kwa," or even a ternlike "ee, ee, ee-kwa, iew," all with very varied intonation. When the nest has been passed some 20 or 30 paces the female settles down and looks to see if the eggs are still there. On one occasion only, after I had taken the eggs, did she pursue me angrily at close quarters, until I had left the colony; this was an intensely colored, and evidently a very old, bird.

Young.—Young rosy gulls are very lively and clever little creatures. As soon as they see an intruder they try to creep through the grass to the water, and swim away to some distance, even if the waves are comparatively heavy. More readily still they swim to the places where tufts of *Carex* and other plants, old and dry, stand up here and there in the water, and then lie on the surface, quite still, close by one of these tufts, as if conscious that their grayish-marked dirty-yellow garb corresponds so closely with the spots and strips of light and shadow playing on the dirty-yellow dead grass as to be practically invisible even at a distance of a few yards, especially if the wind, which is nearly always blowing here, is ruffling the surface. If you lie well hidden, after several minutes the little creature begins to swim about, returning to the ground or wet grass whence you disturbed it, and uttering cries as it searches for its mother. When caught it pecks your fingers, peeps and quacks, but is not much frightened.

The parents, especially the females, make a great noise around an intruder in the colony, varying their voices and notes even more than when there are eggs; "kliaw, kliaw, kliaw; kwiaoo, a-wa, a-wa, a-wa, trrrrr . . . ; pioo, kwee-kwoo, a-dak, a-dak, a-dak; kliaw, kliaw, eea, eea; kwa-kwa-kwa, pee-kwa, kakee-a," are heard all the time in various modulations. Near its eggs the rosy gull might appear somewhat foolish, but now all is changed. The female flies slowly just above the ground or wet grass, or partly swims, partly flutters, over the surface of the plant-covered water, settles down again, looking here and there, gently uttering her "a-wa, a-wa," and makes you feel certain that she is trying her utmost to draw attention away from her young. But if you follow her, and then suddenly stop and look back, you will often see the little one hurrying from the place where you were just searching; while in any case you will find nothing at the place where the female appeared so busy. One female insisted upon fluttering about and sitting down so long at a certain place on an island where the colony of rosy gulls and terns was situated that I carefully marked the spot and examined it, but only a tern's nest was there. I thought at first that this was only an accidental occurrence, but immediately afterwards the same female rosy gull tried to attract my attention as persistently to another spot, lying still more out of my way, and another tern's nest was there. The terns understood these treacherous tactics quite well, and at the last nest the female with angry screams engaged in a short battle with the gull.

Plumages.—The newly hatched gulls in down are some 13 or 13½ centimetres in length, but they grow quickly and measure from 18 to 20 centimetres by the time that the feathers appear on the back and flanks. Eyes dark blackish brown; legs and feet intense fleshy, tinged with gray, or fleshy gray, with brownish claws; bill grayish fleshy with brownish tip. The ground color of the downy dress is dusty yellow, varying in tinge irrespective of growth; in some examples it is pale sulphur-yellow, in others a somewhat burnt wood-yellow, occasionally, with a rusty tinge. This ground color is densely covered with numerous irregular and ill-defined blackish-gray markings, taking up at least as much space as the yellow ground color itself. They are pale and quite ill-defined on the flanks, while the middle of the breast and belly is without them and whitish. They are sharply defined and nearly black on the head, where they are narrower. The markings vary in detail in different specimens, but in all the pattern is somewhat longitudinal on the body, transverse on the nape, and wedge shaped on the crown. This pattern is much obscured, especially on the body, as the markings are so much broken up and wavy. The sides of the throat, the eyebrows, and the down which covers the uppper mandible nearly to the nostrils, are marked with dark color.

The feathers begin to appear first on the wings, and nearly at the same time on the scapulars and tail; next on the upper part of back and on the flanks, and then on the uropygium. So far as can be seen the new primaries are blackish; the secondaries and tail feathers white; the tertiaries, wing coverts, scapulars, and back feathers brownish black, with wide rusty-yellow ends, as are also upper tail coverts. Flank feathers and those of the uropygium white rusty ends and blackish-gray subapical portions.

The sequence of plumages to maturity can be only provisionally inferred from the limited amount of material available for study. Doctor Buturlin (1906) gives us a very satisfactory and detailed description of the first or juvenal plumage, the principal characters of which are: " White under parts, tinged on the chest and breast with pale grayish cinnamon buff; upper parts dark brown, barred with ochraceous on the ends of the feathers; lesser wing-coverts of the foremost and inner half of the wing white, with narrow, ochraceous tips; all the primary coverts blackish brown; the three inner primaries practically blackish brown with the inner half of the inner web (excluding the end) white; remaining primaries outwardly edged with blackish brown, decreasing inwardly; and tail white, with a narrow ochraceous tip and a blackish brown apical band."

This plumage is well illustrated in Nansen's (1899) colored plate of this species, based on specimens collected by his expedition near

Franz Josef Land, in August. The white lesser wing-coverts show very plainly in this plate, but apparently these are molted before October, as they do not show at all in Nelson's (1887) plate.

Nelson's bird, taken October 10 at St. Michael, illustrates the change into the first winter plumage, which differs from the foregoing in having the under parts pure white and having lost all traces of the white lesser wing-coverts, the ochraceous barring on the back and the ochraceous tip of the tail. Some of this may be accounted for by wear or fading, but the appearance of a few " mantle blue " feathers in the back indicates a partial molt, including, at least, the back and lesser wing-coverts.

The young bird figured in P. H. Ray's (1885) report, a bird in its first autumn, is considerably more advanced, as it has a pink breast and a blue mantle, the wings being practically the same as in Nelson's (1887) bird. This specimen illustrates the first winter plumage, which is worn with little change until spring. A partial molt, involving nearly, if not quite, all the contour feathers and the tail, takes place in the spring. This first nuptial plumage is illustrated by a bird in the author's collection, taken on the Kolyma River on June 2. In this the wings, including all the coverts, are as in the first winter plumage. The remainder of the plumage is fresh; the mantle is clear blue; the underparts are decidedly rosy; the tail is pure white; and the black neck ring is indicated by scattering black feathers. At a complete postnuptial molt, the following summer, the young bird would probably assume the adult winter plumage.

Adults apparently have a complete postnuptial molt and an incomplete prenuptial molt of the contour feathers. The black ring on the neck is characteristic of the nuptial plumage, but the pink underparts and the pure white tail are present at all seasons.

Food.—Buturlin (1906) noted the Ross's gulls chasing insects, and the stomachs which he examined contained " only fragments of coleoptera, gnats, and other insects;" therefore, on their breeding grounds, at least, their food seems to be wholly insectivorous.

Behavior.—Although he first noted the flight of this species as " more Fulmar-like," Buturlin (1906) finally concluded that it

was really much more tern-like * * *. The rosy gull swims easily, and sometimes I saw it taking a regular bath. It dipped its head under, while sitting deep in the ice-cold lake, and, throwing the water over its back, moved its wings quickly below the surface, holding itself almost clear, and threw itself forcibly head downward into the water. Once a rosy gull flew over the surface of the lake with a cry of " carvac-wa " and took up water with its beak on the wing, as swallows do, but subsequently it settled on the surface for some two or three-seconds without folding its wings, which were elevated over the back, and drank after the usual fashion.

The note of *Rhodostethia* is peculiar, being high and more melodious than that of gulls in general, and very variable. The cries that I most often heard resembled "a-wo, a-wo, a-wo" and "claw, claw, claw" (or "cliaw, cliaw"). When disturbed the birds have a short cry of "via, via, via," and if much disappointed a longer "kiaw, kiaw" or "kiaoo; kiaoo, viaw." When quarreling they utter "miaw, miaw, miaw" and "a-dac, a-dac, a-dac," as already mentioned.

The rosy gull can hardly be called a peaceful bird, though the terns, comparatively weak as they are, generally begin the trouble, for it is quite prepared to fight, if challenged. Usually the tern distances its rival in the air, but I have seen the gull catch it on the wing and give it a good shake. I once saw a female rosy gull pounce ferociously on an innocent *Calcarius lapponicus* which was passing, but she was in a very nervous state owing to my examination of her nest, which was going on.

The rosy gull and its eggs are too small to be hunted up by the Lamuts or Chukchas of the delta, and rapacious birds proper are scarce there; but the eggs are often destroyed by the numerous *Stercorarii*, and I have to-day seen (June 30) two Buffon's skuas trying to catch the bird itself.

Fall.—When Doctor Buturlin (1906) visited their breeding grounds on July 22 the Ross's gulls "were nowhere to be seen; only some shells of their pretty eggs and a wing of a young bird were found near the nest of one of those greedy robbers of the tundra, *Larus vegae*." But he "observed three small gulls flying silently about with uneasy strokes of the wing, in a somewhat owl-like manner, and their silence reminded him of *Xema sabinii* during the spring migration." All of these he shot and they proved to be "young *Rhodostethia rosea*, easily identified by the form of the tail, and only one was without the remains of down on the head." These were the last rosy gulls that he saw alive; evidently they had deserted their breeding grounds and started in their fall migration as soon as the young were able to fly. They sometimes move off their breeding grounds even before the young are able to fly; for "on July 7, having disturbed a colony with the young in down, he "noticed a few hours later that the colony was deserted, and that, partly swimming, partly on foot, they had gone to the other end of the lake (or rather a chain of swampy lakes), nearly a mile distant." This exceedingly early northward migration in the half-downy stage of plumage explains why both young and old *Rhodostethia rosea* have been observed during August, or even seen after the middle of July, far away from their breeding grounds.

Nelson (1887) took a specimen of this rare gull in immature plumage near St. Michael, Alaska, on October 10, 1879. The International Point Barrow Expedition in 1881, 1882, and 1883, under Lieut. P. H. Ray, obtained a fine series of this rare bird, and I quote from Mr. John Murdoch's notes in regard to it, in Ray's (1885) report, as follows:

In 1881, from September 28 to October 22, there were days when they were exceedingly abundant in small flocks, generally moving toward the northeast, either flying over the sea or making short excursions inshore. Not a single one was seen during the spring migrations or in the summer, but two or three stragglers were noticed early in September—a few out among the loose pack ice; and on September 21, 1882, they were again abundant, apparently almost all young birds. They appeared in large, loose flocks, coming in from the sea and from the southwest, all apparently traveling to the northeast. Most of the flocks whirled in at the mouth of our lagoon and circled around the station with a peculiarly graceful, wavering flight, and many were shot close to the house. A cold easterly wind was blowing at the time. They continued plentiful for several days, while the east wind blew, all following the same track, moving up the shore, and making short excursions inland at each of all beach lagoons. After September 28 they disappeared until October 6, when for several days there was a large flight. On October 9, in particular, there was a continuous stream of them all day long moving up the shore a short distance from the beach, and occasionally swinging in over the land. None were seen to return.

It is difficult to form any idea of what becomes of the thousands that pass Point Barrow to the northeast in the autumn. It is certain that they do not return along the shore as they went. Nevertheless, at that season of the year they must of necessity soon seek lower latitudes. Perhaps the most plausible supposition is that soon after leaving Point Barrow, perhaps when they first encounter the main ice pack, they turn and retrace their steps so far out at sea as to be unnoticed from the land, and pass the winter at the edge of the ice field, proceeding north to their breeding ground, as the pack travels north in the spring. Capt. Everett Smith, of the steam whaler *Bowhead*, who is a trustworthy witness, reports that when he was in the loose ice, 70 miles northwest of Point Hope, on June 10, 1883, he saw large numbers of these birds.

Nansen's (1899) discovery of Ross's gulls in large numbers near Franz Josef Land in August, would seem to indicate that there are other breeding grounds farther west along the Siberian coast, or that there is a westward as well as an eastward migration after the breeding season. After August 23, when the channels and lanes about the ship froze up, these gulls disappeared. What becomes of these birds in winter, when it is impossible for them to obtain food in the Arctic Ocean, is a question which still remains to be answered. A specimen is recorded by Dr. B. W. Evermann (1913) as taken on St. George Island, Pribilof Islands, on May 25, 1911, which suggests the possibility that Ross's gull may winter in the open waters of the North Pacific Ocean; but, if so, it is strange that no specimens have been recorded from that region.

I would refer the reader also to Mr. Murdoch's (1899) excellent historical account of this species, telling us practically all that was known about it at that time.

DISTRIBUTION.

Breeding range.—Probably circumpolar, but erratic and irregular. Known to have bred on the Arctic coast of northeastern Siberia (Kolyma Delta) and on the Indigirka River from its mouth to 300 miles inland. Said to have bred once in western Greenland (Disco

Bay), but the record is open to some doubt. Taken in summer, and perhaps was breeding near Spitzbergen (82° N.), Franz Josef Land (Hvidtenland) near the Bennett Islands, near Wrangel Island, in northeastern Siberia (Pitlekaj), and on Melville Peninsula (Alagnak).

Winter range.—Unknown. Taken at Bering Island, December 10; Heligoland, February 5; Faroe Islands, February 1; France (coast of Verdée), December 22; and Italy (Sardinian Sea), January.

Spring migration.—Taken in the Pribilof Islands (St. George). May 25, probably a straggler.

Fall migration.—Birds leave their breeding grounds in northeastern Siberia about July 20 and are abundant at Point Barrow, flying east, between September 10 and October 9. Taken at St. Michael, Alaska, October 10; at Heligoland, October 25 to November 10; and at New Siberia Islands in September.

Casual records.—Accidental in England (Yorkshire), in France (Verdée, December 22, 1913), and in Italy (Cagliari Bay, January, 1906).

Egg dates.—Kolyma Delta: Three records, June 9, 10, and 11.

XEMA SABINI (J. Sabine).

SABINE'S GULL.

HABITS.

This beautiful little gull was named for its discoverer, Capt. Edward Sabine, who first saw it on its breeding grounds on some low rocky islands off the west coast of Greenland, where it was associated and breeding with a number of Arctic terns. It is not an abundant bird, however, on the Greenland coast, but it has been found breeding at widely scattered points in the Arctic regions of both hemispheres. Its center of abundance during the breeding season seems to be in the vicinity of Bering Sea. Dr. E. W. Nelson (1887) says:

All the marshy coast districts on both shores of Bering Sea are chosen resorts for this beautiful gull during the breeding season. It is especially numerous along the Alaskan coast from the Kuskoquim mouth to Kotzebue Sound and on the Siberian side from Plover Bay to beyond the Straits, but they occur more as birds of passage along the latter coast than as summer residents.

In the vicinity of St. Michael he

found these birds to be among the most numerous of the gulls, and the main body of arrivals came in the spring, as the ponds and small tide creeks were nearly free from snow and ice, dating from the 15th to 25th of May. At this season they wander in company with the Arctic tern, but the last of May or 1st of June they congregate about the parts of the marshes selected for their nesting ground.

Nesting.—The same author gives the following interesting account of his experience with a nesting colony:

On June 13, 1880, about 20 miles from St. Michael, while egging in company with some Eskimo, we found a pond, some 200 yards across, in the middle of which were two small islands. A gunshot caused at least 100 of these gulls to rise like a white cloud over the islet, and showed us that we had found a breeding place. As we stood on the shore a few birds came off, and circling close about us for a few moments, but rarely making any outcry, returned to the island, where the others had already settled again and appeared to be sitting upon the ground. The water of the lake we found to be about waist-deep, under which lay a solid bed of ice of unknown depth.

The smallest island lay nearest, and sending one of my men out to it he found a set of two eggs of the black-throated loon, one set of the arctic tern's eggs, and two of Sabine's gull. Proceeding to the next island he found a set of *Aythya marila nearctica* eggs as he stepped ashore, and a moment later cried out that the ground was covered with gulls' eggs. At the same time he answered with chattering teeth that the water in the lake was very cold. Having never seen the nest of this gull I called my man back and he transported me upon his back to the island after narrowly escaping several falls on the way. The island was very low, and the driest spots were but little above the water. Built on the driest places were 27 nests, containing from one to three eggs each, and as many others just ready for occupancy. Four or five nests were frequently placed within two or three feet of each other. In about one-half the cases the eggs were laid upon a few grass blades the spot afforded with no alteration save a slight depression made by the bird's body. In the majority of the other nests a few grass blades and stems had been arranged circularly about the eggs, and in the remainder only enough material had been added to afford the merest apology for a nest.

While I was securing my prizes the birds hovered overhead in great anxiety, although they rarely uttered their grating cry, and in the very few instances when a bird darted down at us it was in perfect silence. While we were on the island several glaucous gulls and jaegers passed by, and in every case they were attacked by several of the Xemas and driven hastily away. Two nests had been despoiled either by these birds or a muskrat, as the broken shells showed. When the eggs were secured a large and fine lot of gulls were obtained, and we then made our way back to camp heavily laden with spoils. Solitary nests were afterwards found either on islands like the last or on the border of a pond. In one instance the female left her eggs when I was over 100 yards away and flew directly away until she was lost to sight.

Thirty-five years later Mr. Hersey visited the same locality to gather information for this work. On June 19, 1915, he found a colony of about six nests that had been completely washed out by a recent heavy storm accompanied by unusually high tides. The nests were all mere hollows in the wet ground with hardly any lining. Broken eggshells were lying all about and a few dead young were seen. In other places he found other similar nests containing broken eggs—about 15 in all. This disaster evidently discouraged the gulls, for, although he visited the locality later, they apparently did not attempt to lay again. A typical nest of this species containing three eggs was found on June 5, 1915; his notes describe it as located on a

narrow tongue of land projecting into a small pond among a net-
work of ponds on the tundra. The nest was a slight hollow in the
wet ground, 5 inches in diameter and 2 inches deep, lined with a few
dry grass stalks. The nest cavity was wet and the eggs were covered
with a coating of mud. Both of the parent birds showed anxiety
while he was some distance from the nest, but kept quiet when he was
near it. After he had taken the eggs the birds followed him for
half a mile, darting about his head.

The Canadian Neptune Expedition to Hudson Bay, according to
Rev. C. W. G. Eifrig (1905), found the Sabine's gull "common on
Southampton and other islands, breeding there along the shores and
the banks of small ponds, in company with the Arctic tern. They
make no nest but deposit their eggs in the sand. Two eggs were
taken at Southampton, June 28, 1904."

Eggs.—Three eggs, or often only two, constitute a full set. They
are ovate or pointed ovate in shape. The ground color is " Dresden
brown," " Isabella color," " ecru olive," or " deep olive-buff." They
are seldom conspicuously marked, but are usually faintly and irregularly spotted and blotched with " Saccardo's umber " or " sepia."
Sometimes they are more clearly and boldly marked with " sepia,"
" bister," or " warm sepia;" occasionally an egg is marked with a
few bold markings of " blackish brown;" and sometimes the markings
are concentrated in a ring around the larger end. The measurements of 56 eggs, in the United States National Museum, average
45.5 by 32 millimeters; the eggs showing the four extremes measure
49.5 by 31.5, 47 by **34**, and **39.5** by **30** millimeters.

Young.—Nothing seems to be known about the period of incubation, but both birds apparently incubate and are very devoted in the
care of the young. Mr. Hersey noted that when the birds were hiding
in his vicinity the parents frequently alighted on the ground near
him and ran back and forth with trailing wings after the manner of
shore birds, but unlike other gulls or terns.

The young are less active than most young gulls; at the approach of danger
they either sit perfectly still with half-closed eyes or march slowly away in
the dignified manner of adult gulls. They have a note like the adults, but it
is not so sharp and is lacking in strength. While in the downy stage they
hide in the grass, but when about two weeks old and nearly fledged they begin
to frequent the small ponds when they swim about; if danger threatens they
swim ashore and hide. Even at this age the old birds watch them constantly,
and any glaucous or short-billed gull that comes near is promptly driven away,
several Sabine's gulls uniting in the pursuit to protect the helpless young.

Plumages.—The downy young is dark colored, from " ochraceous
tawny " to " tawny olive " on the upper parts and throat, paler on the
chin, fading off to " pale pinkish buff " or paler on the belly. The
crown and sides of the head are distinctly spotted or streaked with

black and the rest of the upper parts are thickly but indistinctly mottled with " fuscous black "; the under parts are immaculate. The young bird grows rapidly and the juvenal plumage soon appears; the down is retained on the tips of the feathers until the bird is nearly fully grown, wearing away or dropping off gradually, until the last of it finally disappears from the head, neck, flanks, and rump. In this plumage the crown and the sides of the head and neck are clouded or washed with different shades of " mouse gray "; the throat and under parts are pure white, and the upper parts are mainly dusky or " fuscous." The feathers on the anterior gray portions are narrowly edged with pale buff; these edgings increase in breadth, extent, and intensity of color on the back, wing-coverts, and scapulars, becoming " clay color " or " tawny olive " on the latter feathers. The wings and tail are as described in the next plumage. The first winter plumage is but a continuation of the juvenal; the buffy edgings described above fade out or wear away during August and September, leaving the plumage of the upper parts more uniform " fuscous " or pale grayish brown. The primaries are dull black without the conspicuous white tips of the adult wing, but the secondaries are white, producing the large white wing patch so characteristic of the species. The tail is white, broadly tipped with black, especially on the central rectrices; the bill is wholly dusky. A partial prenuptial molt takes place in the spring, at which the gray hood and black collar of the nuptial plumage are partially assumed, the amount of white remaining on the throat and head varying greatly in different individuals. At the next complete molt, the first postnuptial, in August and September, the adult winter plumage is assumed, and young birds become indistinguishable from adults.

Adults have a partial prenuptial molt, at which the gray hood and black collar are acquired before May, and a complete postnuptial molt in August and September. The latter is very variable in time and often very late; it is often completed in August and sometimes does not begin until nearly the middle of September; the black collar is the last to go. The winter plumage is similar to the spring dress except that the head is white, heavily clouded with dusky on the occiput, and hind neck; the bill becomes black.

Food.—On their breeding grounds, the Sabine's gulls feed in the small ponds and pools on the tundra, where they find small fishes, aquatic worms, insects, and larvae, and small crustaceans. They hover over the pools, daintily picking up their food from the surface, but apparently never diving for it. Mr. Hersey says in his notes:

These gulls spend much time, when the tide is out, feeding about the mud flats, where they run about like shore birds; so much do they resemble them that I have repeatedly mistaken them for plover when the light was poor and I could not easily make out their markings. The young, with their white breasts and dark backs, even more closely resemble birds of this family.

Behavior.—On the wing this species bears a closer resemblance to a tern than it does to the other gulls. It flies with continuous wing beats, seldom, so far as I have observed, sailing, and its flight is direct though not straight. It may swoop to the earth to pick up a bit of food or hover a moment if something attracts its attention, but only for an instant does it delay before resuming its onward flight in the direction it was going. It seems almost devoid of curiosity. I have never had one fly about me when walking over the tundra, as the short-billed gulls and Arctic terns frequently do, and unless I am directly in its path I have never seen one turn aside in its flight to look at me. If one of their own species or another bird is shot they pay no attention to the fallen comrade, even if it be only wounded. They attend strictly to their own business. They usually fly singly or with one or more short-billed gulls, but sometimes two are seen together, rarely three. Except on their breeding grounds they are not social and are generally silent. At St. Michael I have seen as many as six birds together on the bay, but on land they are usually solitary. When a number do come together on the water it appears to be the presence of food that attracts them rather than a desire for the society of their own or other species. When a half dozen birds are resting on the water it is usual to see them scattered about, each 30 or 100 yards from his nearest neighbor and not close together, as other gulls generally are.

Doctor Nelson (1887) says of the notes of this species:

Sabine's gull has a single harsh, grating, but not loud note, very similar to the grating cry of the Arctic tern, but somewhat harsher and shorter. When wounded and pursued or captured it utters the same note in a much higher and louder key, with such a grating file-like intensity that one feels like stopping his ears. It has the same peculiar clicking interruptions which are so characteristic of the cry of a small bat held in the hand. A low, chattering modification of this is heard at times as the birds gather about the border of a favorite pool, or float gracefully in company over the surface of some grassy bordered pond. The same note, in a higher key, serves as a note of alarm and curiosity as they circle overhead or fly off when disturbed. When one of these gulls is brought down the others of its kind hover over it, but show less devotion than is usually exhibited by the terns.

Fall.—Nelson (1887) says further:

As August draws to a close, young and old forsake the marshes to a great extent, and the rest of the season are found scattered along the coast feeding at the water line on the beeches. Toward the end of September they become more and more scarce until only a comparatively small number are found at the beginning of October; but the last ones remain until the 8th or 10th of this month, and these birds are usually the young of the year.

Winter.—On the southward migration the Sabine's gull has occurred on both coasts of North America, probably migrants from different breeding stations, and at many points in the interior. Prof. W. W. Cooke (1915) says that "the only place where Sabine's gull has been found in winter is on the coast of Peru. Here it is common in Callao Bay from December to April." He also suggests that

" whenever the winter home of Ross's gull is discovered, Sabine's gull will probably be found there also, for the two species arrived together at the mouth of the Kolyma River, Siberia, the 1st of June, 1905, and were together when seen in migration in May several hundred miles west of that district."

DISTRIBUTION.

Breeding range.—Arctic coasts of both hemispheres. In the Western Hemisphere, east to northeastern Greenland (Cape Bismarck). South to central western Greenland (Upernavik), northern Hudson Bay (Southampton Island), Boothia Peninsula, Victoria Land (Cambridge Bay), northern Mackenzie (Franklin and Liverpool Bays), northern Alaska (Point Barrow and from Norton Sound to Hooper Bay), and St. Lawrence Island, Bering Sea. In the Eastern Hemisphere it is known to breed in northeastern Siberia (near Bering Strait), in northwestern Siberia (Taimyr Peninsula) and on Spitzbergen. The northernmost breeding record is at Thank God Harbor, northern Greenland, 81° 40′ North.

Winter range.—The only known winter range seems to be on the coast of Peru from Tumbez to Callao Bay.

Spring migration.—Northward along both coasts and in the interior of North America. Dates of arrival: Maine, Scarborough, May 31; Cumberland Gulf, June 15; Melville Peninsula, Winter Island, June 29; Ellesmere Land, Fort Conger, July 6; Illinois, Chicago, April 1; Manitoba, Norway House, June 11; California, Monterey, April 9 to May 21; British Columbia, Bell Bella, May 24; Yukon, Chilkat Inlet, June 1; Alaska, St. Michael, May 7 to 25, Point Barrow, June 2 to 6, and Demarcation Point, May 28. Some birds remain in Peru until April.

Fall migration.—Southward by same routes. Dates of arrival: Maine, Portland, September 22; Massachusetts, August 21 to September 27; New York, Long Island, October 7; Iowa, Burlington, October 12 to 15; Nebraska, September 2 to 30; Washington, Shoalwater Bay, September 24; California, Monterey, July 22. Dates of departure: Melville Peninsula, Igloolik, August 13; Greenland, Kikkerton Island, October 6; Alaska, Point Barrow, September 17 to October 22; California, Monterey, October 28.

Casual records.—Accidental in Bermuda, Switzerland, and Austria-Hungary. Occasional in winter in British Islands and northern France.

Egg dates.—Northern Alaska: Eight records, May 28 to July 6; four records, June 8 to 28. Northern Mackenzie: Seven records, June 20 to July 10; four records, July 5 to 7.

GELOCHELIDON NILOTICA (Linnaeus).

GULL-BILLED TERN.

HABITS.

This species was referred to by the earlier writers as the marsh tern, on account of its preference for the salt marshes as a feeding ground, and in many places as a breeding ground also; but, based on my limited experience with it on the Atlantic coast, I should say that it hardly deserves that name, for, at the present time, on the coasts of Virginia and the Carolinas, it seems to prefer to nest on the sandy beaches. But, as it is a cosmopolitan species of wide distribution, its habits differ in different localities. It was formerly much more abundant and more widely distributed on our Atlantic coast than it is to-day, where it is now one of the rarest of the terns. The reduction in its numbers and the restriction of its breeding range may have resulted, by natural selection, in the survival of those individuals which chose to breed on the beaches, where their eggs were not so easily found, and the annihilation of those which nested in the marshes. In support of this theory Mr. H. H. Bailey (1913) says of its breeding habits on the Virginia coast:

The nest location of the few remaining pair has changed from the inner side of the island sand dunes and marsh edges to the open beach, but now well concealed amongst the oyster shells, rocks, and pebbles, not an unsimilar location from that of the oystercatcher.

Doctor Stone (1908) regards it as " a rare straggler " on the New Jersey coast to-day. He says:

Formerly it bred rather commonly on the marshes of Cape May County, where it was discovered by Wilson about 1813. In 1869 Turnbull regarded it as rare. In 1886 Mr. H. G. Parker reported it still nesting at the lower end of Seven Mile Beach, and M·. C. S. Shick spoke of it as still present in 1890, associating with the laughing gulls. We have no subsequent record for the State.

On the Virginia coast Doctor Rives (1890) referred to it as " common at Cobb's Island, and breeds, formerly in great abundance," indicating that, even at that date, it had begun to decrease. He says further:

I have been informed that great numbers of the eggs have formerly been taken from the north end of Hog Island, adjoining Cobb's.

Ten years later, in 1900, Captain Andrews reported to Mr. Dutcher (1901) that the gull-billed terns on Cobb's Island had been reduced to about a thousand. The following year, according to the same authority, their number had been reduced to 300. In 1903, Doctor Chapman (1903) found only eight pairs there; and when Doctor Bishop and I visited Virginia in 1907 we saw only two pairs on Cobb's Island, and perhaps 8 or 10 pairs on Wreck Island, a few miles distant. Mr. A. B. Howell (1911) visited Cobb's Island in 1909 and recorded eight pairs. This record shows clearly the results of the same causes which annihilated the least terns in this region—the demands of the millinery trade for the decoration of women's hats and the zeal with which a lucrative trade was pushed by local gunners. Apparently the few survivors are holding their ground and perhaps increasing under adequate protection.

Spring.—From its winter quarters in Central and South America the gull-billed tern makes it spring migration along the coast in March and April. Audubon (1840) gives the following account of it:

The marsh tern is pretty abundant about the salt marshes of the mouths of the Mississippi in the beginning of April; and by following the shores of the Gulf of Mexico you will find that it comes to us from beyond Texas, as many make their appearance along that coast in a straggling manner during spring, there being seldom more than half a dozen together, and generally only two. Their journeys are performed over the waters of the sea, a few hundred yards from the shore; and when in want of food they diverge from their ordinary course, and ranging over the land satisfy their hunger, when they resume their route.

Wayne (1910) says that it arrives in South Carolina "about the middle of April and is sometimes common up to May 10, but does not breed. It does not frequent the salt marshes while on this coast, but prefers the sandy beaches."

Courtship.—Audubon (1840) has given us the only account of what might be considered a nuptial flight. He says:

Excepting the Cayenne tern, I know no American species that has so powerful a flight as the present. To this power is added an elegant lightness that renders it most conspicuous and pleasing during the love season. Then "the happy pair" are seen to rise in elegant circling sweeps, almost in the manner of hawks, and only a few feet apart, until they attain a height of about 200 yards, when they come close together, and then glide with extended pinions through the air, the male over the female, both emitting tender and plaintive notes, while they vary their evolutions at the same height for five or six minutes. After this the winged lovers separate, plunge toward the earth with wonderful rapidity, resume their ordinary notes, and seek for food in concert.

Nesting.—On Cobb's Island and Wreck Island, Virginia, we found four nests on June 26 and 28, 1907. These were all placed on the high, dry sand flats, back of the beaches, beyond the reach of the ordinary tides, but where the spring tides had deposited large quantities of oyster, clam, and scallop shells, with numerous small stones scattered over the sand. These were excellent places for the concealment of the eggs, which so closely resembled small spotted stones that it was very difficult to find them. The nests were quite characteristic and entirely different from other terns' nests; three of them were merely slight hollows in the sand, among the clam and oyster shells, lined with a few small pieces of shells and bits of straw. The other was a very elaborate structure—a large pile of dead sedge stems, gathered from a neighboring marsh, and the shells of oysters, clams, and scallops. It was lined with small clam and oyster shells, making quite a pretty picture. I measured this nest and found it to be about 18 inches in diameter externally and 4 inches internally. All of these nests were in or near breeding colonies of black skimmers, among which a few pairs of common terns were also nesting.

Dr. Paul Bartsch writes to me as follows regarding a breeding colony of this species that he found in the Bahama Islands:

On May 23, 1912, we visited Little Golden Key, which is listed as Middle High Key on the Andros Island chart. The northwest corner of this island consists of a sand spit, the edge of which has been worn off by strong tidal currents. Here we found a large flock of gull-billed and least terns. I crawled up to the edge of the sand bar from the rear and found myself face to face with them, almost too close to them to take a picture, but succeeded in capturing several snapshots, one of which I send to you herewith. On the northeast side of this same island we found the gull-billed terns breeding. I should say that the colony probably embraced 25 pairs. It seemed rather remarkable to find gull-billed terns assembled in a colony, for my experience heretofore had been to find them nesting scattered among colonies of the common tern; at least this has been the case wherever I have observed them breeding on our Atlantic coast.

I have no recent information about its nesting habits in Texas, but Davie (1889) says:

Dr. James C. Merrill and George B. Sennett found a colony of this species, in company with *Sterna forsteri*, breeding on a grassy island among lagoons and marshes near Fort Brown, Tex., May 16, 1877. The nests were slight depressions among the short grass, and the eggs were frequently wet.

It also breeds on the sandy islands on the coast of Texas, depositing its eggs in slight hollows in the sand.

Eggs.—The gull-billed tern raises but one brood in a season and lays ordinarily two or three eggs; sets of four eggs are occasionally laid, but they are uncommon. The eggs are characteristic and are easily recognized by their size and shape. In general appearance they are rounder and lighter colored than the eggs of any of the medium-sized terns. In shape they are usually ovate or short ovate, well rounded at the small end. The ground color varies from " warm buff " or " pinkish buff " in the darkest eggs to " cartridge buff " or " ivory yellow " in the lightest eggs; the prevailing colors are the lighter shades of buff. The markings consist of spots and blotches of various sizes and shapes scattered irregularly over the egg in varying amounts, but a majority of the eggs are not very heavily marked. The underlying spots show all five shades of " brownish drab," and the heavier markings are in various shades of the darker browns, such as " Vandyke brown," " bister," and " sepia." The measurements of 47 eggs in the United States National Museum average 47 by 34 millimeters; the eggs showing the four extremes measure **51** by 35.5, 49 by **36, 44** by 33.5, and 46 by **32.5** millimeters.

Plumages.—The downy young is "pinkish buff" or "cream buff" on the upper parts, shading off to white on the breast and belly; sometimes it is almost unspotted, but usually it is more or less mottled, streaked or spotted with black on the back and on the head. The juvenal plumage is acquired first on the wings, then on the scapulars, back and breast. This plumage is largely "pale gull gray" on the back, with a decided brownish suffusion, which is due to broad edgings of "snuff brown" and "clay color," deepest on the back and most extensive on the scapulars. These browns gradually fade out, before the bird is fully grown, to produce a soft mottled effect on the upper parts, pale buffy tints on a pale gray ground color. The partial postjuvenal molt begins early in September, and the change into the first winter plumage is rapid. The mottled or dusky marked feathers of the upper parts are replaced by the "pale gull gray" feathers of the adult and the heads become whiter. The young bird in its first winter plumage is much like the winter adult, but can be recognized by its slightly smaller bill and by having more dusky streaks on the crown and cervix, as well as traces of dusky in the tail. I have not been able to trace the first prenuptial molt, but infer that it is complete, and that it probably produces a plumage indistinguishable from the adult. I have not been able to find any spring birds showing any signs of immaturity.

Adults probably have two complete molts each year, as in the other terns. They are in full nuptial plumage when they arrive in March; the postnuptial molt occurs in August and September. The adult winter plumage is like the nuptial, except that the head is wholly white, with more or less slaty-gray in the orbital and auricular regions.

Food.—All observers seem to agree that the gull-billed tern is mainly, if not wholly, insectivorous in its feeding habits. Wilson (1832) says:

This new species I first met on the shores of Cape May, particularly over the salt marshes, and darting down after a kind of large black spider, plenty in such places. This spider can travel under water, as well as above, and during summer at least, seems to constitute the principal food of the present tern. In several which I opened the stomach was crammed with a mass of these spiders alone. These they frequently pick up from the pools as well as from the grass, dashing down on them in the manner of their tribe.

Audubon's (1840) spirited drawing illustrates this species in pursuit of an insect. He says:

I believe that these birds never immerse themselves in the water, as other terns are wont to do; nor do I think that they procure fish, as, on examining a number of individuals, I never found any other food in their stomachs than insects of various kinds.

Gätke (1895) notes similar habits for the species in Heligoland, in the following words:

Anyone who, day after day, has watched the terns darting down into the sea from great heights, so that the foam spurts high into the air must feel particularly surprised to see a bird so similar in appearance roving about over the fields, suddenly dropping among the long stalks of the potatoes and disappearing from sight. Such, however, is the only way in which the bird seeks its food on this island; for it has never been seen fishing on the sea like the other members of the genus.

Yarrell (1871) credits it with eating other food to some extent, as follows:

The food of this species is somewhat varied. In Ceylon Col. W. V. Legge found it to consist of frogs, crabs, and fish; in Egypt, Von Heuglin observed the bird darting into the dense smoke of a prairie fire in pursuit of locusts; and in Algeria Mr. Salvin noticed it hovering over grass fields and pouncing upon grasshoppers and beetles. It also captures many species of insects on the wing.

Behavior.—The flight of the gull-billed tern is slightly heavier and steadier than that of the other small terns, but it is strong and at times very swift; it seems to have better command of itself on the wing. When traveling it usually flies at a considerable height with rapid wing beats and with steady and direct purpose. When in pursuit of its insect prey its plunges are exceedingly swift and daring. It shows also much of the skill of a swallow in making quick turns or in darting about with great velocity. It shows its command of its movements in its sudden plunges to the ground or to the surface of the water, where it secures its food, as it checks its descent, and darts away again, all of which is done with the grace and ease of an expert. I believe that it never dives and seldom swims, though, of course, it can do both.

I know of no very distinctive field mark by which the gull-billed tern may be easily recognized, although its flight is characteristic, its tail is shorter and less deeply forked than that of the common tern, and, if near enough, its heavy black bill will identify it.

The hoarse voice of this species and its characteristic notes will serve to identify it with certainty. On its breeding grounds its notes sounded to me like " Katydid, Katydid," or " Kadid," accented on the last syllable, or sometimes like " Killy " or " Killy-Kadid," all quickly uttered, loud, and rasping. Mr. Montague Chamberlain (1891) describes the notes " by the syllables *Kay-wek, Kay-wek.*" Yarrell (1871) says:

During the breeding season its note resembles the syllables *che-ah*, and, at other times it utters a laughing *af, af, af*, like a gull.

Its behavior with relation to other species seems to be above reproach. It associates freely on its breeding grounds with common terns, Forster's terns, laughing gulls, and black skimmers. Reports

that it destroys the eggs of other birds seem to have no foundation
in fact. Audubon (1840) says that he has seen "this species mas-
tered and driven from its feeding grounds by the kingbirds and the
martins," which would seem to indicate that it is a gentle bird and
far from quarrelsome.

Winter.—The winter home of the gull-billed tern is far beyond
our borders in southern Mexico and South America. Very little
seems to be known, or to have been published, regarding its winter
habits.

DISTRIBUTION.

Breeding range.—The American form breeds on the Atlantic and
Gulf coasts, formerly from New Jersey, now from Virginia (Northampton County) southward to southern Texas (Nueces and Cameron
Counties) and Mexico (Tamaulipas). On the Bahama Islands
(Andros, Eleuthera, Inagua, Long Island, etc.) and Cuba. Closely
allied forms breed in other parts of the world, making the species
cosmopolitan.

Winter range.—Mainly in South America, southern Brazil, Argentina, Patagonia, and Chile. A few winter as far north as Guatemala
(Chiapam), Mexico (Tehuantepec) and even Texas and Louisiana.

Spring migration.—Early dates of arrival: Bahama Islands, May
5; Bermuda, April 29; Virginia, Cobb's Island, May 10.

Fall migration.—Southward along both coasts of South America,
arriving in Argentina, September 18, and Ecuador in September.
Recorded at Barbados, October 7.

Casual records.—Stragglers have been taken at various points
along the coast as far east as New Brunswick (Grand Manan, August, 1879).

Egg dates.—Virginia: Forty records, June 2 to July 8; twenty
records, June 12 to 26. Texas: Nineteen records, May 3 to June 10;
ten records, May 6 to 28.

STERNA CASPIA Pallas.

CASPIAN TERN.

HABITS.

Among the vast hordes of sea birds nesting in the great colonies
of the southern Atlantic and Gulf coasts, this king of all the terns
may be seen climbing into the air on its long, strong wings, its big
red bill wide open, yelling out its loud raucous cry of defiance. As
the dominant, ruling spirit in the colonies it scorns the companion-
ship of humbler fowl, holds itself aloof, and lives a little apart from
the others. The largest, the strongest and the fiercest of the terns, it

well deserves the name, imperial tern.   It was christened Caspian
tern by Pallas, because it was first described from a specimen taken
near the Caspian Sea.   It is a cosmopolitan species of wide palae-
arctic and nearctic distribution.

Spring.—Although resident throughout the year on our southern
coasts, it is a summer visitor only to all of its northern breeding
grounds.   On the New England coast it occurs as a migrant to and
from its summer home in Labrador.   Mr. William Brewster (1879)
evidently found it quite common here at one time, for he says:

During the first week of May, 1875, I found them quite numerous at Chatham,
Massachusetts.   They frequented the sand bars near the shore, and kept apart
from the herring and black-backed gulls, the only other species of Laridae
present at the time.

I have always considered the species rare here during recent years,
and it is by no means abundant in Labrador.   Of its spring migration in Minnesota Dr. P. L. Hatch (1892) says: " Usually, about the
1st of May, or possibly a little earlier, the Caspian tern makes its
appearance, and for only a short time is seen passing rapidly from
lake to lake in search of its favorite food, the fresh-water mussels,
with which the margins of the marshland streams and lakes abound.
The flight is a marvel of gracefulness, ease, and unwearied main-
tenance, never failing to arrest the attention of anyone at all interested in the birds."

Nesting.—The breeding range of the Caspian tern in North
America includes a number of widely scattered localities, in which
it nests under widely different conditions.

Audubon (1840) was the first to record the breeding of this species
on the south coast of Labrador.   He evidently did not recognize the
difference between this and the royal tern, for he referred to both
under the name, Cayenne tern.   On June 18, 1833, he " found it
sitting on two eggs deposited in a nest neatly formed of moss and
placed on the rocks, and this on a small island, in a bay more than
12 miles from our harbor, which itself was at some distance from the
open gulf.   On another sequestered islet some were found amidst a
number of nests of our common gull " (ring-billed gull).   We saw
only a single Caspian tern on the south coast of Labrador, near
Natashquan, in 1909; but Mr. M. Abbott Frazar (1887) found a
colony " about 20 miles to the westward of Cape Whittle," consisting
" of some 200 pair, mixed with a larger settlement of ring-billed and
a few herring gulls.   Their nests were built upon the ground, and
generally contained two eggs, never more."

On the Virginia coast, according to Mr. H. H. Bailey (1913), " a
few pairs still breed on one of our coastal islands."   The Caspian tern
was never abundant there, but one or two pairs have several times

been found breeding there, laying two eggs in a hollow scooped in the sand. We did not see any Caspian terns in our visit to these islands in 1907.

My only experience with the nesting habits of this fine species was in 1910, in the Breton Island reservation, off the coast of Louisiana. Here, on June 18, on Grand Cochere Island, a low, flat, sandy island, a hundred miles offshore, we found about 40 pairs of Caspian terns breeding. The island is more fully described under the royal tern, which was breeding here in immense numbers. The Caspian terns did not mingle with the large colonies of royal and Cabot's terns, but had selected the extreme eastern end of the island entirely apart from the others, where they had placed their nests in a fairly compact colony among the scattered rows of driftwood and rubbish, which offered some slight concealment. The nests were large, deep hollows, lined with sticks, coarse straws, bits of shell and other rubbish picked up in the vicinity; the rim of the nest was usually built up, more or less, elaborately like a gull's nest. The nests were almost always decorated with shells and often with feathers. Numerous pellets of fishbones, evidently cast up by the birds, were scattered about the nests. In marked contrast with the royal and Cabot's terns, the Caspian terns were very shy; they left their nests long before we reached them and flew about overhead, screaming loudly. They never offered to attack us and barely came within gunshot. I was told by my boatmen that I could not shoot any, as they were very shy and extremely hard to kill. I succeeded, however, in bringing down four, all I wanted, with five shots from my heavy 10-bore gun. We found several other scattering pairs on the other islands in the reservation, among the colonies of other sea birds, but usually the Caspian terns nested singly and a little apart from the others. Larger colonies, containing from 75 to 200 birds, have been found on some of these islands.

Mr. Stanley C. Arthur writes me that he found a colony of 119 pairs of Caspian terns breeding on a small islet, about an acre in extent, near Alexander Island, on the Louisiana coast, on July 3, 1918. The interior of the island was low and covered with marsh grass, but it was surrounded by a horseshoe-like rim of shells and sand, principally old oyster shells, on which the terns were nesting. Their nesting habits here were exceedingly primitive, for in no case did he find any evidence of nest building. Many eggs were merely lying on the shells; others were in slight depressions or hollows, which may have been made by the birds or may have been found already made. No nesting material had been brought in. The number of eggs in a nest was never more than two and often only one.

On the Texas coast large colonies are found. Capt. B. F. Goss, in a letter to Major Bendire, says:

We found the Caspian tern breeding only in Nueces Bay, and, although we examined 150 miles of coast, did not see a bird of this species more than a mile or two from the mouth of the bay. They breed on some small, low sandy islands near the middle of the bay. We took about 60 sets of eggs in all, mostly on one island not larger than 4 by 6 rods. As we approached this spot in a boat the birds rose about 8 feet and hovered a few moments, looking like a white cloud; then commenced circling, doubling, and turning in the most remarkable manner. It was a beautiful sight. As we approached they began plunging at the ground in great apparent excitement. My companion shouted, "They are breaking their eggs," and we hastened with all speed to the spot; found about 40 sets, a few of one, but mostly of two eggs. These lay on the bare sand without any attempt at a nest. At least one-quarter of the eggs had been broken by the birds in their frantic plunges, some only marked, in others the bill had passed clear through the egg. My companion said they had done the same thing in former years when he was collecting the eggs for culinary purposes, and thought they did it to prevent the eggs falling into our hands. It seemed to me like a frantic attempt to remove or conceal the eggs, but will not attempt to account for the actions of the birds, but deem the fact worth recording.

Some fine breeding colonies still exist in Michigan, of which Prof. W. B. Barrows (1912) writes:

A few are seen, spring and fall, on Lakes Erie, Huron, and Michigan, and colonies of the birds have long been known to nest on certain islands belonging to Delta County, Michigan, lying in the entrance from Lake Michigan to Green Bay, and also on certain of the Beaver Islands, belonging to Charlevoix County, Michigan. At both these places the birds have been persecuted from time immemorial by fishermen and Indians, who use their eggs as well as those of other terns and gulls for food; and unless better protection is afforded, the extinctiou of the colonies can not be long postponed. The nests are placed on gravelly or shingly islands, are usually pebble-lined, and the two or three eggs (rarely four) are very variable in ground color, ranging from grayish white to pale olive, and more or less thickly spotted with brown and black, the spots commonly small and distinct." Mr. C. A. Reed (1904) refers to a colony on Hat Island, Lake Michigan, found by Mr. Charles L. Cass, on July 1, 1896, where "fully a thousand terns" were "nesting on about one acre." They had built no nests, but the two eggs were "laid in a hollow in the gravel."

A distinctly different style of nesting is found in the big colonies of the Klamath Lake region of Oregon. Messrs. Finley (1907) and Bohlman have illustrated these colonies very fully in the numerous excellent photographs which they have taken. In one case they found as many as 500 nests of Caspian terns in a single colony. Here these terns nest in closely grouped colonies often in proximity with other species, such as California gulls, Forster's terns, Farallon cormorants, and white pelicans, on the floating masses of dead tules. The nests are merely hollows in the dead and decaying vegetation, lined with small broken bits of the same material. The birds seem to be much tamer here than elsewhere.

Eggs.—The Caspian tern raises but one brood in a season and lays from two to four eggs; two seems to be the commonest number, especially so in southern colonies; three eggs are commoner in northern colonies, where this number seems to prevail; four eggs are very rarely found. The eggs are distinctive and are more like gulls' eggs than other terns' eggs. In shape they are ovate or elliptical ovate. The shell is lusterless and sometimes rather rough. The ground color varies from " pinkish buff " or pale " warm buff " to very " light buff " or " cartridge buff." They are usually rather sparingly marked, sometimes evenly with small spots, sometimes with scattering large spots or irregular blotches, and occasionally with a few fantastic scrawls. The markings are in the darker shades of brown, " raw umber," " auburn," " mummy brown," or dark " sepia." The lighter types are often indistinctly spotted with " pale violet gray," or " lilac gray." The difference between these eggs and those of the royal tern is more easily seen than described. I think I could pick them out every time. The measurements of 48 eggs, in the United States National Museum and in the writer's collections, average 64.5 by 45 millimeters; the four extremes measure **73** by 44.5, 62.5 by **48, 58.5** by 45.5, and 64.5 by **42** millimeters.

About 20 days is said to be the period of incubation. Probably both sexes incubate, as is commonly the case with related species. Perhaps under favorable conditions, when the sun is not too hot, the eggs may safely be left for a time to be kept warm by the sun; the birds are sufficiently sensitive to changes in temperature to recognize such conditions.

Young.—Mr. Arthur has sent me some very interesting notes on the behavior of young Caspian terns in the colony referred to above, from which I quote as follows:

Before the motor boat reached the shore it was quite evident that there were a number of young on this island, as the noisy approach of our boat caused the little ones to take to the water and swim rapidly away. In their aquatic journey the young terns were followed by their perturbed parents, who hovered in the air uttering hoarse cries. I landed and discovered a few of the smaller terns hiding in the grass and a number of eggs scattered on the rim of the shell. The Caspian terns who had eggs on the island were the first to return, soon followed by those parent birds whose young had taken to the grass for the purpose of concealment. While it is true that the majority of the small Caspian terns had taken to the open gulf and the distracted parents still hovered over them, I noted with my glasses that they were now guiding their babies back to the oyster shells that the little ones called home. The larger of the small terns showed in no little way their adaptitude for swimming, for a number of them were from one-fourth to one-half mile away, and I could see them being tossed up and down upon the salt waters, as there was a good breeze blowing. They were stout little swimmers and soon paddled back to land.

With the return of the main colony of Caspian terns I had exceptional opportunities to watch the feeding of the young. The adult Caspians carry fish food to the island directly from the sea. The single fish was carried crosswise in the bill and seemed to be about from 2 to 3 inches in length. The fish are minnows of different species, and at no time did they seem to swallow this food before allowing the young to have the food; that is, the parent bird did not first eat and partially digest the finny delicacies. The male (?) wings his way in from the adjacent waters with the fish crosswise in his bill. The moment he lands on the island there is a commotion among all the young terns. As a rule the rightful heir would seize the fish before it would leave the parent's bill and unhesitatingly get the fish by the head; then with one or two gulps it would disappear head first, and nine times out of ten if the fish was of considerable length, say about 3 or 4 inches, the youngster would keel over on its back, with its little red feet frantically waving in the air, the fish's tail also waving about (for the caudal fin and that end of the fish protruded about three-quarters of an inch), while the process of digestion started. However, this display on the part of the little tern lasted only about three or four minutes, and while the little fellow was lying on its back it displayed the writhings of a person suffering from suffocation; but once back on its feet the little Caspian would besiege the parent bird for more fish.

The adult Caspian has a very decided note, and while I fully appreciate no bird's call or cry can be properly imitated by the printed word, to me they called " ca-arr, ca-arr, ca-arr, ca-arrrrrrrr." The young know the call of its parents. I was very much amused in watching a little fellow that had selected a slight hole within 2 feet of my blind to take a sun bath. Here it would lie as still as death until it would hear the particular " ca-arr " of its own ma or pa. Then it would suddenly come to life, and, opening wide its little red beak, would chirp loudly in reply and rush about waving its little wing stumps in a most grotesque manner. The parents would make a few circles above their little one and alight or fly off after seeing it was safe. An incident that would frequently happen in the afternoon was that a little fellow would seek its hole and lie still until the " ca-arr " cry which it knew best would again be heard, then it would suddenly be galvanized into instant action. The young, when frightened, utter a peculiar whistling note.

Toward their own young the Caspian terns are very tender. However tender they are toward their own offspring they are extremely brutal toward the young of others, and I frequently saw the young ones mauled and flung about by the parent birds of other young. The young Caspians have no recreation save that of eating and sleeping. They do not flock together save when common danger threatens. In fact, according to my observations, it is extremely dangerous for little Billy Caspian to play with a little Charlie Caspian next door, for as sure as he does Charlie's ma is quite likely to knock the visitor down and jump on him with black feet, to say nothing of the thrashing she gives with the elbows of her wings. Such treatment arouses the parents of little Billy Caspian, who rush to the rescue with hoarse cries and there is much ado in the ternnery, in which red bills and white wings play a prominent part, and black crests pointed straight out behind.

Plumages.—The downy young varies on the upper parts from dark grayish buff or " vinaceous buff " to " cartridge buff " or pale grayish white. The throat is very pale dusky and the remainder of the under parts are white. There are sometimes no dark markings, but usually the upper parts are more or less heavily spotted or mottled with dusky. As the young bird grows the color on the upper parts fades to almost white. The first plumage appears on the scapulars and back. In the juvenal plumage the young Caspian tern is distinctively marked, differing from all other young terns in corresponding plumages. The most striking character is the black crown, which in all other terns is largely white; in the young Caspian the entire upper half, or more, of the head is black, including the lores and cheeks, down to a line running from the commissure straight back to the occiput; the black is more or less relieved on the forehead and crown by whitish or grayish streaks. The feathers of the upper parts, back, scapulars, and wing-coverts are basally " light gull gray," but they are so broadly edged or tipped with pale buffy shades, " cartridge buff," or " tilleul buff," that they impart this color to the upper parts. The scapulars are broadly banded with black, two bands on each feather, and the feathers of the back and coverts are more or less barred or spotted with black. The under parts are white.

When the young bird attains its full growth, a partial molt, involving most of the contour feathers, begins early in September. The feathers of the fore back are now heavily tipped with dusky, forming an interscapular dusky patch; the scapulars are variegated with hastate dusky markings and the tertials are doubly banded with dusky near the tips; the rectrices are mottled with dusky near the tips, more so centrally and less so laterally; and the lesser wing coverts are mottled with dusky. This might be considered the first winter plumage though it is more properly a transition stage from the juvenal plumage for it soon disappears by wear, fading, or molt. Later in the fall young birds assume the pearl gray mantle and can be distinguished from adults only by the dusky in the lesser wing-coverts and the mottled tails. A complete molt in early spring renders old and young indistinguishable in March. Some birds retain the mottled crown until May.

Adults have two complete molts—the prenuptial in February and March, producing the full nuptial plumage, and the postnuptial in August and September, producing the adult winter plumage with the white-streaked crown, the pearl gray mantle and wing-coverts, and the pure gray tail. Adults usually have white foreheads and more white in the crown than young birds; they also have larger bills. The postnuptial molt of adults begins before the end of the breeding season, sometimes as early as June, with the appearance of white feathers in the black crown. The outer primaries are molted last.

Food.—The Caspian tern secures its main food supply, which consists almost wholly of small fish, by plunging headlong into the water, often disappearing entirely under the surface. It probably feeds to some extent on shrimps and other forms of surface swimming aquatic life. Dr. P. L. Hatch (1892) says that its favorite food is "the fresh-water mussels, with which the margins of the marshland streams and lakes abound," while on its spring migration in Minnesota. Several writers have stated that it feeds on the eggs and young of other birds, a gull-like trait not shared by the other terns.

Behavior.—The flight of the Caspian tern is strong, swift, and graceful, but heavier and more gull-like than that of the smaller terns. Its general manner of flight is, however, decidedly tern-like, as it flies along in search of food, with its bill pointed downward, pausing to hover for an instant and then plunging vigorously down into the water. When fishing it usually flies only a few yards above the water, but when traveling it flies at a great height, with its bill pointing straight forward, making rapid progress, even against a strong wind. It has a broad expanse of wing, and is more given to soaring than the other terns. I have seen it soaring in great circles, mounting higher and higher in the air, as the gulls are wont to do. It so closely resembles the royal tern that the illustrious Audubon never detected the difference, but it can be recognized by its heavier, more stocky build, by its heavier flight, by its shorter and less deeply forked tail, and by the larger amount of black in the primaries, which look wholly black when seen from below, whereas those of the royal tern seem to be largely white or grayish.

The cry of the Caspian tern is entirely unlike that of the royal tern and quite different from that of any of the Laridae. Its ordinary note is a hoarse, croaking "kraaa" on a low key, loud, harsh, and grating. A shorter note sounding like "kow" or "kowk" is often heard on its breeding grounds, where it also utters, when angry, a loud, vehement, rasping cry of attack.

On its southern breeding grounds, where it is usually larger and stronger than its associates, it has few enemies. It has been said to eat the eggs and young of other birds, but I have never seen any evidence of this habit, and I believe that it seldom, if ever, attacks them. Audubon (1840), however, saw some evidence of its pugnacity on the Labrador coast. He says:

Until that period I was not aware that any tern could master the *Lestris Pomarinus*, to which, however, I there saw the Cayenne tern give chase, driving it away from the islands on which it has its eggs. On such occasions I observed that the tern's power of flight greatly exceeded that of the jager; but the appearance of the great black-backed gull never failed to fill it with dismay, for, although of quicker flight, none of the terns dared to encounter that bird any more than they would venture to attack the frigate pelican in the Floridas.

The Caspian tern has suffered but little from the hand of man; it is too shy, too hard to kill and not sufficiently abundant to tempt the plumage hunter. Some of the northern colonies, particularly those in Lake Michigan, have been regularly and persistently robbed of their eggs for food until some of them have been materially reduced in numbers.

Fall.—The Caspian terns leave their northern breeding grounds during the latter part of September or the first half of October. During recent years they have been growing scarcer on the New England coast, probably because their numbers have been decreasing on their Labrador breeding grounds. They were evidently more regular in their appearance formerly, for Mr. Brewster (1879) wrote:

They come down from their northern breeding-grounds during the latter part of September and for several weeks, at least, are to be found in moderate numbers all along our seaboard. I have observed them at various points from Ipswich to Nantucket. At the latter place, upon one occasion, six individuals were seen fishing in the harbor near the town. As to their wintering within New England limits, I can offer only negative evidence, but that points to the inference that they pass farther south with the approach of severe weather.

Winter.—The Caspian tern winters, more or less regularly, as far north as South Carolina, but it is more abundant in the Gulf of Mexico in winter. Messrs. Beyer, Allison, and Kopman (1906) say of its winter habits on the coast of Louisiana that " it occurs singly or in flocks of two or three, and associates freely with other gulls and terns, often congregating about the oyster and shrimp canneries. It never occurs far from the coast."

On the California coast it seems to be rare in winter.

DISTRIBUTION.

Breeding range.—In North America in widely scattered localities, mainly on the coasts or large lakes. East to southern Labrador (near Cape Whittle), Virginia (Northampton County), and South Carolina (Bulls Bay). South to the coast of Louisiana (numerous islands) and southern Texas (Cameron County). West to central California (Sutter Basin) and southern Oregon (Klamath Lakes). North to Great Slave Lake (Fort Rae), central Manitoba (Lakes Winnepegosis and Winnipeg), and Lake Michigan (Green Bay). Eastern Hemisphere birds have been separated as distinct subspecies.

Breeding grounds protected in the following national reservations: In Oregon, Klamath Lake and Malheur Lake; in Wisconsin, formerly Green Bay (Gravel Island, 1905 and earlier).[1]

---

[1] See Ward, Bull. Wis. Nat. Hist. Soc., vol. 4, 1906, p. 113.

Winter range.—South Atlantic and Gulf coasts, from South Carolina to Texas and Mexico. Pacific coast, from San Francisco Bay to Lower California (La Paz) and western Mexico (Manzanillo).

Spring migration.—Early dates of arrival: Pennsylvania, Erie, April 26; New York, Canandaigua, April 28; Rhode Island, Ocean View, May 10; Prince Edward Island, May 13; southern Labrador, Natashquan, May 31; Nebraska, Lincoln, May 2; Iowa, March 10; Michigan, Lake St. Clair, April 25; Wisconsin, Milwaukee, April 10; California, Fresno, April 3 to May 6.

Fall migration.—Transient dates: Massachusetts, September 6 to 20; New York, Long Island, September 7 to 13; Pennsylvania, Marietta, September 21; Virginia, Four-Mile Run, October 4; Michigan, Ann Arbor, September 5; Wisconsin, Delavan Lake, September 19; Iowa, September 9 to October 15; California, Madera County, September 28 to October 2, and Stanislaus County, September 4 to October 6.

Casual records.—Recorded in summer east to Newfoundland (said to have bred at Sandy Lake in 1912) and north to the mouth of the Mackenzie River (Harrison Island, August 1, 1848). Taken in fall in Washington (Westport, October 5, 1917).

Egg dates.—Lake Michigan: Twenty-eight records, May 25 to July 1; fourteen records, June 5 to 22. Texas: Fifteen records, April 8 to June 18; eight records, May 6 to 30. California: Eight records, May 20 to 25.

STERNA MAXIMA Boddaert.

ROYAL TERN.

HABITS.

Although the royal tern is a splendid bird it seems to me that the name "royal," as well as the specific name *maxima*, should have been applied to its near relative, the Caspian tern, which is both larger and more aggressive, a real king among the terns. The two species so closely resemble each other that so good a naturalist as Audubon did not recognize them as distinct, confusing the two under the name, Cayenne tern.

Throughout the southern portion of its range, from Florida and the Gulf of Mexico southward, the royal tern is resident throughout the year. Northward to Virginia it occurs as a summer resident only, and beyond that merely as a straggler. In former years royal terns bred abundantly on the coast of Virginia. Mr. Robert Ridgway (1880) in the summer of 1880 found and reported a breeding colony of some 500 nests, but in the persecution which followed during the next 20 years this species suffered with the other terns which were slaughtered for the millinery trade. On account of their large size royal terns were not in demand for ladies' hats, but their eggs, being large and palatable, were collected for food in great quantities. Persistent nest robbing and constant shooting near their breeding grounds discouraged the birds and frightened them away. The reports of the wardens in 1901 and 1902 indicated that the colonies were much depleted until, in 1903, Capt. N. B. Rich stated, in Mr. Dutcher's (1903) report, that he " did not see any royal terns, so they probably have been exterminated so far as Virginia is concerned." During my visit to Cobb's Island in 1907 I did not see any royal terns, but was told by the fisherman that a few are seen occasionally. Since that time conditions have evidently improved under protection, for Mr. Harold H. Bailey (1913) says:

The royal terns are much more numerous, a large colony still breeding on one of our coastal islands. They did, however, for a number of years during the overwhelming destruction of some of the following species for millinery trade, desert our coast entirely, but it has only been within the last few years that they have become established as breeding birds once more.

Spring.—On its spring migration the royal tern, according to Bailey (1913), reaches Virginia "the last week in May," although, according to Coues (1877), it arrives in North Carolina "early in April." Its migration is so limited that its movements are probably very deliberate and perhaps quite erratic or variable. I have never seen its courtship performance and can find nothing about it in print.

Nesting.—An old-time colony on the Virginia coast is described by Ridgway (1880) as follows:

Allowing the birds sufficient time to deposit their eggs, we visited the locality two days afterwards, and found an area of perhaps one-eighth of an acre completely covered by their eggs, it being impossible to walk through the nesting site without crushing a greater or less number, many eggs having been covered by drifting sand. Comparatively few pairs had deposited their full complement, a large majority of the nests containing but a single egg. Still, more than 500 nests were counted, while our man declared that not one-third the number of birds seen by him on his former visit were there, the greater part having been frightened away by the shots which he had fired at them two days before.

In Virginia, the bird is known as the "gannet striker" or "gannet."

Mr. B. S. Bowdish (1910) and Mr. P. B. Philipp discovered four breeding colonies of royal terns on the coasts of the Carolinas in 1909, as follows:

The first was situated on Vessel Reef, a low sand key in Bulls Bay, South Carolina, visited on June 12. About 75 birds were seen there and nesting had just begun, three fresh eggs being found. The second colony was on Royal Shoal, Pamlico Sound, North Carolina. Here, instead of the enormous numbers of the preceding season, estimated at some 7,000 birds, only 50 were found. On

June 24 one fresh egg was noted. The third and largest colony was found on June 26, on Miller Lump, a small, low sand bar in Pamlico Sound, lying in a broad expanse of very shallow water. This colony comprised 1,000 adult birds. The nesting was advanced; some 258 good eggs were counted, usually one egg to a set, though a few doubles were found. There were also many young, some of which were able to run about. All the eggs were advanced in incubation. The fourth breeding colony visited was on Davis Lump, a small sand bar near Miller Lump. Here about 60 pairs of birds were breeding. Thirty-two eggs were counted, for the most part advanced in incubation. Half a dozen newly hatched young were also seen.

My own experience with the nesting habits of the royal tern was gained in the large protected colonies of the Breton Island reservation, off the coast of Louisiana, where the birds have certainly flourished during the recent years. They are now safe from the depredations of man, but they still suffer occasionally from the destruction of their breeding colonies by the elements. The combination of high winds or storms with a high course of tides often results in the flooding of the low sandy islands on which they breed and the washing away of the eggs or young; but such wholsesale damage is generally repaired by a second attempt at nesting.

On June 18, 1910, with Warden W. M. Sprinkle, in his patrol boat, I visited one of these colonies. Sailing due south from what seemed to be the outer islands, we headed straight out to sea and were soon out of sight of land. After several hours of apparently aimless sailing Captain Sprinkle pointed out on the horizon a distant sand bar, and as we drew nearer we could see with our glasses a cloud of white specks hovering over it, so we knew that the terns were nesting there as expected. They had been washed off one of the other islands earlier in the season and had come here to make their second attempt at nesting. The island, which is known as Grand Cochere, was merely a low, flat sand bar, with no vegetation on it whatever, only 2 or 3 feet above high-water mark at its highest part. It was nearly triangular in shape, perhaps half a mile long, and surrounded by dangerous sandy shoals. On an old wreck at one end 30 or 40 man-o'-war birds were perched in a long black row; a large flock of brown pelicans were resting on one of the sand bars; and at night thousands of black terns came in to roost on the beaches. There were several small nesting colonies of black skimmers, and three or four small mixed groups of royal and Cabot's terns, scattered over the island with their eggs lying in the dry, hot sand, as well as a few scattering pairs of laughing gulls and a little colonly of 40 nests of Caspian terns at the eastern end. But the main population of the island was concentrated in an immense, closely packed nesting colony of royal and Cabot's terns on the south side. As I approached this colony, over the level sandy plain on which it was spread out, the birds all arose at once, as if impelled by a common impulse, with a great roar of thousands of wings, a dense cloud of screaming birds, and a bewildering moving picture of flashing black and white. As the birds were shy my attempts at photography resulted in only a few distant snapshots of the colony as a whole; so I set up my blind in the midst of the colony and left it overnight for the birds to get accustomed to it.

On my return the next morning I was delighted to find that the terns had learned to regard my blind as harmless and had settled down on their nests all around it. Walking up to the blind, with two companions, I concealed myself inside of it with my cameras, and the other two men walked away. The birds, thinking that all of us had gone, immediately returned and assumed their regular vocations. For two or three hours I sat there unobserved and watched the activities of that populous colony. All around me the flat sandy plain was dotted with eggs, a single egg in each little hollow in the sand at regular distances, just far enough apart so that the birds could not touch each other when sitting. It was a hot, sunny day, probably too hot for the eggs to be left uncovered, so the birds spent most of their time incubating; but there were many birds standing beside their sitting mates. There was not sufficient difference between the sexes for me to determine whether both sexes incubate or not, but probably they relieve each other occasionally. There were no young in the colony, so I could not study their method of feeding them. Life is never dull in a large bird colony and the birds are never still; some were coming and some were going all the time; there was a constant babel of voices and numerous little squabbles occurred, if an incoming bird alighted too near its neighbor. They were so close together that they could hardly spread their wings without interfering. An air of nervous excitement seemed to pervade the colony all the time, as in a crowd of women at an afternoon tea, and at frequent intervals, without any apparent cause, a large portion of the colony would rise suddenly and simultaneously, as if frightened, fly around for a minute or two, all screaming excitedly, and then all would settle down again as if nothing had happened.

I counted the nests in a measured area and then roughly measured the whole colony, from which I estimated that it contained, at least, 3,500 nests. There were a hundred nests in a space four yards square; certainly this was a densely packed colony of a highly gregarious species.

The colony described above may be considered as typical of the species, which almost always nests in similar situations in closely populated colonies. The nest is nothing more than a slight hollow in the sand, without any attempt at a lining. I believe that the normal set consists of two eggs; very rarely three are found and four eggs have been recorded, though these were probably laid by two birds. Often only one egg is laid, and where the first set has been destroyed, only a single egg is laid for the second set. Two eggs are more often found in northern colonies, but in the southern portion of its range this tern usually, or at least frequently, lays only one egg for the first set. Only one brood is raised in a season, so far as I know.

Eggs.—The eggs of the royal tern are usually quite characteristic and are not likely to be mistaken for anything else. They are quite different from those of the Caspian tern. In shape they vary from ovate to elongate ovate or even cylindrical ovate, but average about elongate ovate. The shell is smooth but without luster until it becomes worn by incubation. The common types have a very light ground color, practically white, varying from "light buff" or "ivory yellow" to pure dull white. Darker shades are rare, but I have a few in my collection which vary from "clay color" or "cinnamon buff" to "light buff." The greener types, "olive buff" or "yellowish glaucous," are still rarer. The eggs are usually quite evenly spotted with small, dark-colored spots, sometimes with fine dots and sometimes with large, bold, heavy blotches; very rarely they are marked with irregular scrawls. The markings include only the darkest shades of brown, "chestnut brown," "bister," or "clove brown," and often they are practically black. The spots have a washed-out appearance on the edges. On many eggs there are underlying spots of "lavender gray" or "pale violet gray," often in washed-out splashes. Sparingly spotted or even immaculate eggs are occasionally found. The measurements of 54 eggs, in the United States National Museum, average 63 by 44.5 milimeters; the eggs showing the four extremes measure **74.5** by **48.5**, **57.5** by 43, and 63.5 by **40.5** millimeters.

Plumages.—In a series of 10 downy young royal terns, in the author's collection, no two are alike, and there are, at least, three distinct types of coloration. In the palest type the color of the upper parts varies from "light pinkish cinnamon" to "pale pinkish buff," which becomes paler on the throat and sides and almost white on the belly. Some specimens are nearly immaculate, but there are always a few small black-tipped filaments of down on the rump and often a few on the head. The character of the down is peculiar; on the head is rather stiff and hair-like, but on the back and flanks each filament stands out by itself, round and soft like chenille at the base and tapering to a fine point at the end. The bill and feet are light yellowish flesh color in the dried skin.

In the mottled type the color varies from "light pinkish cinnamon" to "cartridge buff" above, shading off to the latter or to nearly white below. This is more or less heavily spotted with black, more or less evenly, over all the upper parts, including the sides of the head, throat, and flanks. The spots are very distinct and include either the tip or the whole of the filament. The bill is light colored, and the feet may be light colored, as in the preceding type, or grayish or nearly black.

In the dusky type the ground colors are as described above, but they are largely, and sometimes almost wholly, concealed on the head, throat, back, wings, rump, and flanks with black or dusky filaments. Often the forehead and lores are solid black. The bill in this type has a subterminal black tip on one or both mandibles. The feet show both light and dark phases without any correlation with the other colors; in fact, my darkest specimens have the lightest feet. A larger series would probably show a great variety of intermediates between these three types and perhaps other types.

The juvenal plumage is fully acquired before the young bird is fully grown. It is entirely unlike that of the Caspian tern; the upper parts are mainly white with a faint creamy tinge, the feathers centrally tinged with light gray and with many narrow, dusky shaft-streaks; the primaries and secondaries are "slate gray" or lighter, edged with white and the tail feathers are chiefly dusky, with white tips and white toward base of inner web; the underparts are pure white; the feathers of the crown have narrow, blackish shaft-streaks, becoming broader on the nape and auriculars, forming a dusky collar. This plumage is worn until about the last of August, when the post-juvenal molt begins. The wings and tail are retained and will serve to distinguish the young bird, but otherwise the first winter plumage is the same as the adult, the contour feathers being molted during the fall. A complete prenuptial molt occurs in March, at which the adult nuptial plumage is apparently assumed, but perhaps young birds do not acquire such a completely black pileum as adults.

Adults have two complete molts, the prenuptial in March or earlier and the postnuptial mainly in August and September, but often prolonged into October or even November, the outer primaries being molted last. The prenuptial molt, which produces the clear black pileum, is usually but not always soon followed by a partial molt on the head, which produces the white forehead, more or less variable in extent. The full black pileum seems to be the courtship plumage, and the white forehead the prevailing nesting plumage. Only a very small percentage of incubating birds have the pileum wholly black. In the adult winter plumage the forehead is white, the crown mainly so, but streaked with black, and only the occipital crest is mainly black. The tail is shorter and more tinged with gray than in spring.

Food.—The food of the royal tern consists almost wholly of small fish, up to 4 inches in length, which it catches by plunging down into the water, in much the same way as the smaller terns. Mr. Philip H. Gosse (1847) thus describes the process:

High above the water we discern a bird, the snowy whiteness of whose plumage contrasts with the blue sky. He flies rapidly round and round in a large circle, quickly flapping his wings without intermission. Suddenly he arrests his flight, flutters his wings in rapid vibration, as he looks downwards, but in a moment proceeds as before. It was doubtless a fish near the surface, but which disappeared before he could descend. Presently he again stops short, flutters; then bringing the elbow of the wings to a right angle, descends perpendicularly, but with a singular turning of the body, so as to present now the back, now the belly, alternately, to the observer; not, however, by a rotation, but irregularly, and as if by jerks. But his purpose is again frustrated; for on nearly reaching the surface he recovers himself with a graceful sweep and remounts on flagging wing. Again he circles, and again, and again stops; at length, down he swoops, disappears with a splash, and in a moment breaks, struggling, from the wave, and, as if to rise burdened with prey were difficult, flags heavily near the surface, and circling slowly round, gradually regains his former altitude.

Audubon (1840) says:

They alight on the banks of raccoon oysters, so abundant in the inlets, and are seen in company with the semipalmated snipe and the American oyster-catcher, searching for food like these birds, and devouring crabs and such fishes as are confined in small shallow pools. These they catch with considerable agility, in a manner not employed by any of our other terns.

Mr. A. W. Anthony (1906) says that they feed on herring " swimming in compact flocks near the surface," and " secure them by approaching the school from behind and flying near the surface of the water, making repeated, quick dips into the school." They also eat shrimps.

Behavior.—The flight of the royal tern is much like that of the common tern, but somewhat less bouyant, as might be expected in a larger and heavier bird. On the wing it is lighter in appearance than the Caspian tern, as it is more slender, and it has a longer and more deeply forked tail, with less black in the outer end of the wing. Audubon (1840) says:

When traveling, these birds generally proceed in lines; and it requires the power of a strong gale to force them back, or even to impede their progress, for they beat to windward with remarkable vigor, rising, falling, and tacking to right and left, so as to seize every possible opportunity of making their way. In calm and pleasant weather they pass at a great height, with strong unremitted flappings.

Though webfooted and perfectly capable of swimming, these and other terns seldom alight on the water and are very poor swimmers. Their feet are rather small and weak, as they depend almost entirely on their long wings for locomotion.

The voice of the royal tern is not so loud and raucous as that of the Caspian and is pitched on a higher key. The note most often heard, when disturbed on its breeding grounds, is a loud penetrating squawking cry, audible for a long distance, like the syllables, "quak," "kak," or "kowk." Another note on a lower key sounds like the bleating cry of a sheep. It also has a very musical, rolling call, a soft liquid whistle, "tourrrreee," suggestive of the melodious rolling whistle of the upland plover.

This highly gregarious species is a sociable and harmless neighbor on its breeding grounds, where it is intimately associated with Cabot's terns, black skimmers, and laughing gulls, which it apparently never molests. Its nests are preyed upon to some extent by the laughing gulls, though I believe that the royal tern is more than a match for the gull, as a rule. The royal tern is frequently seen fishing in company with the brown pelican, which it is said to rob occasionally by seizing the fish from its capacious pouch. The robber often pays the penalty for his crime by giving up his ill-gotten booty to the man-of-war bird, that arch robber of the southern seas, ever ready to pounce upon any bird weaker than itself and make it drop its catch.

Fall.—In September the short migration flight begins, which is hardly more than a withdrawal from the northern portions of its breeding range, though its winter wanderings carry it to the Bahamas and the West Indies. The southward movement is deliberate. It leaves the coast of Virginia about the middle of September and lingers on the coasts of the Carolinas until the end of November. In its winter quarters, from Florida and the Gulf States southward, it prefers to frequent the harbors, estuaries, mouths of rivers, and the vicinity of sand shoals, where it may be seen fishing in company with brown pelicans, man-o-war birds, laughing gulls, and other terns, or perched on convenient spar buoys, or resting and dozing on the warm bare sand bars. It also roams inland to some extent in winter, visiting fresh water lakes and ponds. It is common along the Pacific coast in winter from Monterey Bay southward, in the harbors and about the islands, as well as in some of the lakes near the coast.

DISTRIBUTION.

Breeding range.—South Atlantic and Gulf coasts, from Virginia (Northampton County) to southern Texas (Cameron County). Some of the Bahamas (Berry and Ragged Islands, etc.); and many of the West Indies (Isle of Pines, Porto Rico, Dominica, Grenada, Carriacou, etc.). Pacific coast of Lower California (Natividad Island) and Mexico (Isabella Island).

Breeding grounds protected in the following national reservations: In Louisiana, Breton Island, Shell Keys, and Tern Islands.

Winter range.—From central Florida (Micco) and from the coast of Louisiana southward, including the Bahamas and West Indies, along the east coasts of Central and South America to Patagonia. On the Pacific coast, from central California (San Francisco Bay) southward to Peru. Also on the west coast of Africa, from Gibraltar to Angola.

Spring migration.—First arrivals reach North Carolina early in April, and Virginia during the last week in May.

Fall migration.—Last birds leave Virginia about the middle of September, but they linger in North Carolina until late in November.

Casual records.—Stragglers in summer wander northward along the Atlantic coast, sometimes as far as Massachusetts (Nantucket Island, July 1, 1874).

Egg dates.—North and South Carolina: Thirty records, May 15 to June 28; fifteen records, June 20 to 26. Texas: Sixteen records, April 8 to June 18; eight records, May 13 to 20. Mississippi and Louisiana: Eight records, May 18 to June 19; four records, May 19 to 29.

STERNA ELEGANS Gambel.

ELEGANT TERN.

HABITS.

This beautiful tern well deserves its name, for in color, form, and behavior it is certainly one of the most elegant of our sea birds, the most exquisite member of the charming group of "sea swallows." Unfortunately, owing to its remote habitat, it has been seen in life by very few ornithologists. Many handsome specimens have found their way into collections, but the dried skin can give but a faint impression of the grace and beauty of the living bird. Not all of the few collectors who have explored the coasts of the peninsula of Lower California have succeeded in finding it, and still fewer have seen it on its breeding grounds. Consequently very little is known of its life history and habits. Probably Mr. Wilmot W. Brown, jr., has been more successful than anyone else in the pursuit of this rare species, and we are indebted to him for practically all that we know in regard to its nesting habits.

Nesting.—Mr. Brown obtained a fine series of the eggs of this species for Col. John E. Thayer (1911a), who published a brief account of its nesting habits on Cerralvo Island, Lower California. He says:

The nests were slight depressions in the sand on the beach about 20 yards from the surf on the protected or land side of the island.

The eggs "were taken April 9 and 15, 1910. Most of the eggs were slightly incubated. One egg is generally what they lay, sometimes two, but only rarely."

Eggs.—Mr. Thayer's beautiful series of 18 sets, of one egg each, makes an attractive display of striking variations. The eggs suggest those of the Cabot's tern rather than those of the royal tern. They vary in shape from ovate to elongate ovate. The ground color is very light, varying from "pinkish buff" or pale "pinkish buff" to pure white, with a decided tendency toward the latter. The commoner types are spotted like eggs of the royal tern, but more sparingly. Some are very heavily and boldly marked with great irregular blotches of various shades of the darker browns, often almost black. These dark markings frequently have the appearance of having been washed out on the edges. One pink egg is uniformly covered with small spots of very dark brown and pale shades of "violet gray."

Another pink egg is blotched with "pale violet gray," overlaid with large handsome blotches of "chestnut," "chocolate brown," and "chestnut brown"—a beautiful egg. The measurements of 27 eggs, in various collections, average 53.5 by 38 millimeters; the eggs showing the four extremes, measure **57** by 39, 55 by **40.5,** and **51** by **35.5** millimeters.

Plumages.—As I have never seen a specimen of the downy young or any birds in the immature plumages, I can not say much in regard to the sequence of plumages to maturity, but it seems reasonable to assume that all the plumage changes are similar to those of the closely related royal tern.

Behavior.—I have never seen the elegant tern in life and can not find anything in print regarding its habits, but probably its behavior is not very different from that of the royal tern, which it so closely resembles in appearance.

Fall.—The elegant tern is another one of the Lower California species, which has adopted the peculiar habit of migrating northward at the close of the breeding season, wandering occasionally as far as Monterey or San Francisco.

DISTRIBUTION.

Breeding range.—So far as known only in the Gulf of California, Mexico (San Pedro Martir, and Cerralvo Islands, and near Guaymas).

Winter range.—From central California (San Francisco Bay) southward along the coast to Chile (Coquimbo Bay, Valdivia, and near Valparaiso).

Spring migration.—Returns to its breeding range in March and April. Lower California, La Paz, April 12 to 27.

Fall migration.—Southward to Peru (Callao Bay) in September. Northward to California at about the same time: San Francisco Bay, September 17; Monterey Bay, September 22 to October 29; Point Pinos, September and October.

Casual records.—Accidental in Texas (Corpus Christi).

Egg dates.—Gulf of California: Seven records, April 1 to May 1; four records, April 9 to May 1.

STERNA SANDVICENSIS ACUFLAVIDA Cabot.

CABOT'S TERN.

HABITS.

Among the sandy islands and shoals of our southern Atlantic and Gulf coasts we find this fine tern, everywhere intimately associated with its larger relative, the royal tern; like Damon and Pythias, they are always together and seldom is one found without the other. The same resorts seem to be congenial to both, but there is probably some stronger bond of friendship which we do not understand. Our American bird is only subspecifically distinct from the Sandwich or Boy's tern of the Eastern Hemisphere, differing from it in the color pattern of the primaries. This makes the species cosmopolitan and gives it a wide range. The European bird ranges farther north in summer than ours, which may be due to the difference in climate.

What little evidence we have on the subject seems to indicate that this species has extended, and is perhaps still extending, its breeding range northward along our Atlantic coast. This, if it is a fact, is both interesting and remarkable when compared with the histories of other species, nearly all of which have been reduced in numbers and restricted in range. In Audubon's time, Cabot's tern was not supposed to breed north of Florida. Royal Shoal Island, in Pamlico Sound, North Carolina, had been protected and watched carefully, as a sea-bird breeding resort, for five years before Mr. T. Gilbert Pearson (1908) discovered the first breeding colony, over 20 pairs, of Cabot's terns on this island on June 25, 1907. Mr. Pearson says, in reporting the incident:

This bird has not previously been noticed breeding among the protected colonies in the State, and in fact, so far as I am aware, there have been no records of its occurrence in North Carolina, except one reported by Dr. Louis B. Bishop (MS.), from Pea Island, August 22, 1904.

Since that time I believe that Cabot's tern has bred regularly on the North Carolina coast and in larger numbers. And now comes the latest news from Mr. Harold H. Bailey (1913), telling of the extension of its breeding range into Virginia. He says:

This is an extremely rare bird on our coast, and it was not until the summer of 1912 that a set of two eggs of this species was secured from one of our coastal islands. As there has been a small colony of these birds breeding on the North Carolina coast for the last few years, the birds with us are probably stragglers from that colony.

Spring.—North of Florida this species is only a summer resident, the northward migration starting in Florida about the 1st of May. It is rather a late breeder. Even on the Gulf coast egg laying does not begin until the last of May, and farther north it is two or three weeks later.

Nesting.—The only breeding colony of this species that I have ever seen was on Grand Cochere Island, in the Breton Island reservation. This was a low, flat sandy island, hardly more than a sand bar, 114 miles offshore, south of Pass Christian, Mississippi. I have given a fuller description of it under the royal tern. When I visited this island on June 18 and 19, 1910, I estimated that its bird population consisted of about 7,000 royal terns, 2,000 Cabot's terns, 600 black skimmers, 80 Caspian terns, and 20 laughing gulls. These estimates were arrived at by counting the nests in a measured area and then roughly measuring the total area occupied by the colonies.

There were several small mixed colonies of royal and Cabot's terns, but the bulk of the population was concentrated in one vast colony of approximately 3,500 nests. In this and in the smaller colonies the Cabot's terns were grouped together in certain sections by themselves, though not in any way separated from the general continuity of the colony; but their nests were seldom, if ever, scattered singly among the royal terns. The nests of both species were evenly spread out over a level, sandy plain, above the ordinary hightide mark, in the central portion of the island, which was entirely devoid of vegetation—a hot, dry waste of sand. They were apparently placed at measured distances, just far enough apart for each sitting bird to be beyond the reach of its neighbor; probably the distances were actually measured by the birds when the eggs were laid, each bird choosing a spot as close to its neighbor as seemed safe from the jabs of a long, sharp bill. The nests were hardly worthy of the name, for they were never more than slight hollows in the sand, with no attempt at lining whatever, and often the eggs seemed to have been dropped on the smooth, flat sand without even a pretense at a hollow. Nearly all of the nests held one egg each, but a few held two. This colony had been washed off another island earlier in the season and had come here for a second attempt at nesting. Captain Sprinkle told me that both of these terns usually lay two eggs at the first laying and only one at the second. The Cabot's terns in this colony were very tame, even tamer than the royal terns. After they became accustomed to my presence I had no difficulty in photographing them at short range without the use of a blind. I was disappointed to find no young in the colony, which would have given me an opportunity to study their home life even better.

From what I can learn from the writings of others this colony was fairly typical of the species and descriptions of other breeding colonies, all of which seem to be on low sandy islands on the sea-coast, would be useless repetitions. On the other side of the Atlantic, however, the nesting habits of the species may differ, as several writers speak of nests among the beach grass and nests lined with dry grass. References to such nesting habits by American writers are probably based on the statements of foreign writers.

Mr. W. E. D. Scott (1888) took some young birds on September 20, 1886, " not quite fully grown, indicating that probably more than one brood is raised, and showing how late in the summer the last broods are hatched out." If this species raises two broods it is a notable exception to the rule among the terns; probably Mr. Scott's birds were hatched out late in the season, because earlier attempts were frustrated by storms or other destructive agencies. Cabot's tern has been said to lay as many as three or four eggs to a set, but I believe that such large numbers are exceedingly rare, on this side of the Atlantic at least. Two eggs seem to be the normal number, with occasionally three. One egg to a nest is the rule on second and subsequent layings.

Mr. Stanley C. Arthur writes me regarding his observations on this species:

There was very little opportunity given me at this time to study the Cabot tern and its young, as what little ones were there were absolutely in the downy stage and evidently too young to eat, for at no time did I see a young Cabot being fed by its parent. I did, however, see the male (?) bringing the female (?) fish food while she was engaged in incubating a single speckled egg which she covered. Here I had an excellent opportunity to learn that the Cabot tern incubated but one egg. While it is true that in one or two instances there were two eggs, so close to make it appear they belonged to a single clutch, yet when the mother bird settled on them she threw her breast feathers over one egg, to the other paying not the slightest concern. In fact, at one time I saw a Cabot tern cover a single egg and with her bill roll the other some inches away from the hollow in which she had deposited her own.

At this time I made an experiment, contemplated for the past several years. I had often wondered why it is, where there are several thousand single speckled eggs, such as the Cabot terns deposit on the beaches, one particular egg can be singled out by the parent as her own private and individual property, and have often wondered whether or not they can, with certainty, know their own egg. I have often been asked : " How does the tern know its own eggs?" and have always facetiously answered: " By counting the spots." As I was studying the birds I selected two Cabots, one on the left and the other on my right, that were marked quite distinctly—one having a wholly black crest and one having its crest speckled with a few white feathers which heralded the coming of the winter plumage.

At 11.15 I left the blind, which naturally scared off the birds, and changed the egg on my left, which had been covered by the pure black-headed tern, and moved it several feet away, exchanging it for the egg that had been covered by the Cabot with white feathers in its crest. This egg was placed on the spot belonging to the black-headed tern. At 11.18 the circling and frantically crying birds commenced resettling on their eggs, and showing not the slightest concern each tern sought its own egg despite the fact that it had been moved several feet and placed in a different nest. After allowing each bird to remain on its egg for 15 minutes, I again left the blind and retransferred the eggs with the same result as before. Each parent bird settled on its own egg without hesitation, and, as before, not evidencing any surprise over the change of the location.

The eggs of Cabot's tern are certainly beautiful and subject to great variation; they make one of the prettiest series in the egg collector's cabinet. The ground color on the prettiest eggs varies from "seashell pink " to " pale cinnamon pink," or from " pale pinkish buff " to " pale ochraceous buff." Some show various olive shades, from " olive buff " to " light buff; " others vary from creamy white to pure dull white. The markings vary endlessly in size, shape, and extent. Some eggs are uniformly covered with small spots, densely or sparingly; others are boldly marked with large heavy blotches or irregular, fantastic scrawls. These markings may be confluent in a ring at either end. The markings are usually in the darkest shades of " blackish brown " or black; occasionally they are more or less washed out on the edges, as in the royal tern's eggs; occasionally blotches or scrawls of " burnt umber " or " russet " are overlaid with darker shades; spots, blotches, and scrawls of " pale lavender gray " are seen under the bolder markings. Often both fine spots and bold scrawls are seen on the same egg. When these include two shades of brown and the lavender gray on a pink background the effect is beautiful. One odd egg in my collection has the pink ground color nearly concealed by fine scrawls of several shades of reddish brown, suggesting certain types of falcon's eggs. The shell is smooth, but without luster. The shape varies from ovate to elongate ovate. The measurements of 41 eggs, in the United States National Museum and the writer's collections, average 51.1 by 36 millimeters; the eggs showing the four extremes measure **57** by 37.5, 51.5 by **38.5** and **46** by **33** millimeters.

Young.—Incubation seems to be shared by both sexes and lasts for about three weeks. Morris (1903) quotes Selby as saying:

As soon as the young birds become tolerably fledged, but before they are altogether able to fly, they frequently take to the water, swimming off to the smaller rocks, where they continue to be fed by the parents until capable of joining them in their fishing excursions.

Plumages.—Downy young Cabot's terns do not show so much variation as young royal terns and will average much lighter in color. They are seldom much darker than " cartridge buff " on the upper parts and are usually buffy white or white. They are also usually immaculate; often a few small dusky tips are seen on the down of the back, and occasionally an individual is uniformly mottled with such dusky tips over the entire back and pileum. The bill is light yellowish flesh-color, and the feet either the same or dull grayish in the dried skin. The juvenal plumage appears first on the scapulars, back, and wings. In the juvenal plumage the forehead and crown are white, the latter streaked with black, which increases on the occiput and auriculars to nearly solid black; the back and scapulars are boldly marked with black spots and V-shaped markings, which are largest and most prominent on the scapulars; the remiges are slaty gray with white edges; the rectrices are grayish white with dusky subterminal areas or black-spotted near the tips; there is a grayish cubital band on the lesser wing-coverts and the greater coverts are washed with pale gray; the under parts are white. A partial postjuvenal molt begins in September, at which the dark markings disappear and the first winter plumage is assumed. This is similar to the adult winter plumage except that the wings and tail of the juvenal plumage are retained. This plumage is worn all winter until the first complete prenuptial molt in the early spring, at which probably most young birds assume a plumage practically indistinguishable from the adult.

Adults have two complete molts each year. The prenuptial molt occurs between March and May, producing the well-known breeding plumage. The postnuptial begins early in July and often lasts through August and September. In winter adults the yellow tip of the bill is duller and more restricted; the forehead is white, the crown narrowly streaked with black, and the occipital crest is brownish black; the tail is shorter than in the spring and shows some gray near the end.

Food.—The food of Cabot's tern consists almost wholly of small fish, such as small mullets, sand launces, and young garfish, which it obtains by making vigorous plunges into the water much after the manner of other terns; but it also eats shrimps and squids. It is more of a sea bird than the smaller terns, and is more often seen feeding out on the open sea or among the breakers than in the quiet tidal estuaries. Audubon (1840) thus describes its feeding habits:

While plunging after the small mullets and other diminutive fishes that form the principal part of its food, it darts perpendicularly downward with all the agility and force of the common and arctic terns, nearly immersing its whole body at times, but rising instantly after, and quickly regaining a position from which it can advantageously descend anew. Should the fish disappear as the bird is descending the latter instantly recovers itself without plunging into the water.

Behavior.—In flight this is one of the swiftest and most skillful of the terns. Its long, slender, pointed form is highly specialized for speed and ease in cutting the air.   Mr. Montague Chamberlain (1891) says:

Its strength of wing and skill enable it to outride the severest storms, and flocks of these birds may be seen dipping into crested waves or skimming over angry breakers to seize the prey that may be brought to the surface by the gale.

Intermediate in size between the two large terns and the several smaller species, it seems to combine the strength and vigor of the former with the activity of the latter.   It may be distinguished from either by its shape and by its long, slender bill.   The yellow tip of its bill is quite conspicuous at short range.

Its cry is short, sharp, loud, and shrill.   Audubon (1840) refers to it as " sharp, grating, and loud enough to be heard at the distance of half a mile."   Morris (1903) calls it " a loud, hoarse, and grating cry or scream, likened to the syllables ' pink' or ' cree.' "   Yarrell (1871) noted the syllables " kirhitt, kirhitt."   When disturbed on its breeding grounds, or when feeding in flocks, it is very noisy.

Winter.—Throughout the southern portions of its breeding range in this country, on the southern Florida and Gulf coasts, Cabot's tern is a permanent resident, its numbers being increased by the addition of migrants from more northern points.   The species withdraws in the fall from its summer resorts, on the coast of Virginia, the Carolinas, and northern Florida, to its winter home in the Bahamas, the Gulf of Mexico, and the coasts of Central and South America.   Here it spends the winter roaming about the outer islands and sand bars in company with other terns and gulls, following schools of fish or resting in flocks on the sand.   At this season it is highly gregarious and quite shy.

DISTRIBUTION.

Breeding range.—Atlantic and Gulf coasts from Virginia (Northampton County) to British Honduras (Saddle Cay).   Some of the Bahamas (Acklin and Ragged Islands, Samana Keys, etc.), and West Indies (from Cuba to Dominica).

Winter range.—From the Bahamas and Florida southward through the West Indies and along the Atlantic coast of South America to southern Brazil (Iguape).   From the coasts of Louisiana and Texas southward, along the Central American coast to Colombia (Cartagena).   And on the Pacific coasts of Oaxaca (San Mateo) and Guatemala (Chiapam).

Spring migration.—Birds depart from coast of Brazil during March and April and first arrivals reach South Carolina, Capers Island, April 9.

Fall migration.—Apparently in September, but data is very scanty.

Casual records.—Stragglers have wandered in summer as far north as Massachusetts (Chatham, August, 1865). Three specimens taken in spring of 1882 in Lucknow, Ontario. A few remain in Brazil in summer (Iguape, June, and Rio Janeiro, August).

Egg dates.—Texas: Eighteen records, April 25 to June 14; nine records, May 17 to 28. Bahamas: Twelve records, May 14 to June 20; six records, May 16 to 22.

STERNA TRUDEAUI Audubon.

TRUDEAU'S TERN.

HABITS.

This unique and well-marked species belongs to the South American fauna and is a very rare straggler to North America. The only record for North America is that of Audubon (1840), who first described the species and says of it:

This beautiful tern, which has not hitherto been described, was procured at Great Egg Harbor, in New Jersey, by my much esteemed and talented friend, J. Trudeau, Esq., of Louisiana, to whom I have great pleasure in dedicating it. Nothing is known as to its range, or even the particular habits in which it may differ from other species. The individual obtained was in company of a few others of the same kind. I have received from Mr. Trudeau an intimation of the occurrence of several individuals on Long Island.

Nesting.—Mr. A. H. Holland (1890) has studied Trudeau's tern in its native haunts in Argentina in the region of Estancia Espartilla. He says:

This tern is rare with us, excepting in the breeding season, when it appears suddenly and in numbers, either single or in pairs.

While hunting through a large gullery of *Larus maculipennis* early in November I came upon a corner of the lagoon entirely occupied by these pretty terns. There was little shelter for the nests, a few scattered willow stumps, but no rushes or flags, and the water was some 4½ feet deep. The nests were all placed together, as the gulls' nests were, 30 or 40 of them, each a foot or two from its neighbor, and so on. They were very shallow structures, composed of green water grasses (very succulent ones and wet), with no lining, and supported on the water by the thick growth of grass underneath. The eggs were three to four in number, of the usual tern type, varying from the dark, thickly spotted, and blotched varieties to the thinly spotted pale ones. In no two nests were the eggs similar. As I approached the ternery (if there is such an expression) the birds became very anxious, darting down close to my head as I stood over a nest and uttering shrill cries. The sight was a beautiful one, with thousands of gulls and these graceful terns as well, all showing beautifully against a blue sky.

Eggs.—There are three sets of eggs of this rare species in the collection of Col. John E. Thayer, which were collected by Mr. Herbert Ozan on St. Ambrose Island, in the St. Felix group, off the coast of Chile, on December 17, 1907. The nests were mere hollows scraped in the sand among bowlders without any material of any kind or any lining in the nests. The "birds were close sitters, perching on rocks only 10 feet away while the eggs were secured. The male bird was killed by a stone thrown by a companion," according to the collector's notes. There are seven eggs in the series—one set of three and two sets of two. The eggs are not distinguishable from certain types of common tern's eggs. The ground color varies from "Isabella color" to "deep olive buff." Some are uniformly spotted or blotched with dark browns, and some are more heavily blotched at the larger end. One set is spotted with the lighter shades of brown and olive. Some of the eggs show underlying spots of drab or lilac. The shape is ovate. The measurements of these eggs and of three furnished by Rev. F. C. R. Jourdain, 10 in all, average 41.7 by 30.6 millimeters; the eggs showing the four extremes measure **46.4** by 30.4, 44.7 by **31, 39** by 30.5, and 39.5 by **30** millimeters.

Plumages.—Nothing seems to be known about the downy young or the immature plumages. The full nuptial plumage is well illustrated in Audubon's plate. Two birds in my collection taken in Argentina on October 17 and 27 are just completing the molt of the primaries, but otherwise are in full fresh winter plumage; probably they are young birds, for adults should be molting into the nuptial plumage at this time. Dr. L. C. Sanford, from whom I obtained my specimens, has quite a series in this plumage collected by Mr. R. H. Beck in the same locality at about the same time, but there are no adults in nuptial plumage among them. The winter plumage is strikingly like that of Forster's tern, but Trudeau's tern may be distinguished by the much shorter and much less deeply forked tail, the long streamers of the outer rectrices being very conspicuous in the Forster's tern. The bill in Trudeau's tern, especially in adults, is also longer and slenderer than in the commoner species, and it is tipped with yellow.

Behavior.—As to the habits, behavior, and life history of Trudeau's tern there is nothing more to be said at present.

DISTRIBUTION.

Breeding range.—Known to breed only in Argentina (Estancia Espartilla, Ajó district, etc.) and off the coast of Chile (St. Ambrose Island).

Winter range.—Unknown.

Migrations.—Not definitely known. Argentina records: Estancia Espartilla, September to February; La Plata River, March; Mar del Plata, October 17 to 27; Punta Lara, October; Buenos Aires, September, November, and January. Brazil records: Rio Janeiro, August; Santa Catharina, February and August. Straits of Magellan, Punta Arenas, November 19 and 20. Chile, Arica Bay, August.

Casual record.—Accidental in North America. New Jersey (Great Egg Harbor).

Egg dates.—St. Ambrose Island, Chile: One record, December 17.

STERNA FORSTERI Nuttall.

FORSTER'S TERN.

HABITS.

Although differing from the common tern in several details and in its habits, the Forster's tern so closely resembles it in general appearance that it is not to be wondered at that the species remained so long unrecognized, and that, even after its discovery, its distribution and habits were so little understood. Audubon (1840) described and figured this species, in its winter plumage under the name *Sterna havelli*, but apparently never recognized it in its spring plumage. Doctor Coues (1877) says of it:

Swainson and Richardson described it as the common tern; Wilson did not know it at all; and Audubon only became aware of it in the imperfect plumage which he described as "*havelli*." Nuttall doubtingly gave it a name upon the strength of Richardson's description. Mr. Lawrence, in 1858, was the first to elucidate its characters satisfactorily, while it was not until the appearance of my paper that its changes of plumage became known.

But even he, with all his wide field experience, was entirely ignorant of its breeding range, saying:

It breeds in the interior of British America, and very abundantly, to judge from the great numbers of eggs from that region I have seen. It may yet be found to nest on or near the northern tier of States.

It is now known, of course, to have a very wide breeding range, as far east as Virginia, as far south as Texas, and as far west as California.

It seems to me that the name marsh tern might much more properly have been applied to this species than to the gull-billed tern, for Forster's tern is, during the breeding season at least, essentially a bird of the marshes, whereas the gull-billed tern shows a decided preference for sandy beaches.

Spring.—Rev. P. B. Peabody (1896) says that these terns arrive on their breeding grounds at Heron Lake, Minnesota "about April 7," and describes their behavior as follows:

Terns creep, scout-like, on the wing, along the thawing shores. Then, as heat and wind wave melt and crush the ice bonds of the lake, the tern speedily assumes the hawk-like (or swallow-like) habit, wandering fitfully over the newly released waters, with eye alert, beak pointing downward, and with many a

shrill but cheery cry of self-gratification or of brotherly good will. He knows
not fear. As one rows among the innumerable " copes " of rush and flag, bent
on reaching the Mallard's feeding ground, a skirmish line of terns will wander
by, 20, 15, 10 feet overhead, furiously, without swerving a wing breadth from
their course. The one or two that are passing eye curiously the dumb decoys
in the boat's belly, and then saunter on with a rattling " jeer " of derision at
the hunter who toils at the oar, and who, unlike the tern, is never quite sure
of his game. But, then, our black-capped jaeger hunts all day.

Nesting.—I first found this species breeding on Wreck Island, off
the coast of Virginia, on June 28, 1907, where we discovered a colony
of about 50 pairs. This and the other large islands in the group are
much like Cobb's Island, consisting of long, wide beaches on the outer,
or ocean, side, flat and sandy in some places or piled high with accumulated oyster shells in others. Back of the beaches, on the shore
side, are extensive salt meadows or marshes, intersected by numerous
creeks and dotted with small ponds or mud holes. On the outer
beaches we found breeding colonies of black skimmers, common and
gull-billed terns, and over the marshes were scattered nests of laughing gulls and clapper rails. Our attention was first attracted to the
Forster's terns by their harsh grating cries, as they flew out to meet
us while exploring one of the creeks in our skiff. We finally located
the colony, by the actions of the birds, just beyond the long grass,
which grew thickly along the banks of the creek, and found the nests
thickly scattered along the drifted piles of dead sedges, which the
high tides had floated off the marsh and deposited in long rows close
to the tall-growing sedges. The nests were so close together that I
counted 12 nests in a space about 10 yards long by 3 yards wide. One
nest was placed within 3 feet of a clapper rail's nest. The nests were
mostly large and elaborate structures, remarkably well built, and reminding me of the nests of Franklin's gulls. They consisted of large
piles of dead sedges and grasses, surmounted by neat little nests,
deeply hollowed, with well-rounded and compactly woven rims. They
usually measured between 20 and 30 inches in diameter, the smallest
one measured being 16 inches at the base; the cup-shaped portion, or
nest proper, measured from 7 to 8 inches outside and from 4 to 5
inches inside in diameter; the inner cavity was from 1 to 1½ inches
deep and was neatly lined with split reeds and grasses. On the whole,
the nests looked like works of art when compared with the slovenly
nests built by other species of terns. Most of the nests contained
three or four eggs, but many sets of five were found and a few nests
held newly hatched young.

In the Breton Island reservation, off the coast of Louisiana, I
found two breeding colonies of Forster's terns. On Battledore
Island a colony of about 30 pairs were nesting in a compact group
on a strip of drift seaweed which had washed up over a marsh and
lodged against the tall grass and " black mangrove " bushes sur-

rounding it. Numerous Louisiana herons were nesting in the "mangroves" and vast colonies of breeding, laughing gulls and black skimmers occupied the remainder of the island. The terns' nests were similar to those seen on the Virginia coast, described above, and the eggs were nearly all hatched. The following day (June 22, 1910) I found a much larger colony of this species, consisting of about a thousand pairs, on Hog Island, a few miles distant. This island had been broken up into several sections by the washing away of beaches and soil, leaving large areas of swampy salt meadows, overgrown with long grass and extensive thickets of "black mangrove" bushes. Louisiana herons were breeding in the "mangroves" and laughing gulls and Forster's terns on the marshes. Most of the tern's eggs had hatched and some of the young were nearly grown.

In Texas the nesting habits of this species seem to be entirely different. Mr. George B. Sennett (1878) on May 16 found it breeding in the salt marshes on the Rio Grande.

On the same low and nearly submerged island where we found the eggs of stilt, *Himantopus nigricollis*, and some hundred yards or more distant, was a group of these terns upon the ground near their eggs. When we approached them they commenced screaming and flying about in great distress. They had only fairly begun to lay, as no set was complete. One or two eggs were all that any nest contained, and some were not occupied. The nests were situated farther away from the water than the stilts, but still where the mud was wet, and consisted simply of a patting-down of grasses and soil into a shallow, saucer-shaped depression.

Mr. N. S. Goss (1891) found them "breeding in numbers on the small islands in Nueces Bay, Texas, as early as the 1st of April. The birds at such times are very noisy, and, as their nesting places are approached, their hoarse notes as they circle close overhead are almost deafening. Nest, a hollow, worked out in the sand, and broken shells, and lined with grasses."

Still another style of nesting seems to prevail in the western States. Mr. Robert B. Rockwell (1911) gives an interesting account of a colony of Forster's terns in the Barr Lake region of Colorado, saying:

On May 24, 1907, a week after the first eggs were found, the breeding colony was in full swing, and we were surprised to find a number of nests containing complete sets, which had been built by the birds upon floating masses of decaying cat-tails. These structures were all made entirely of dead cat-tail stalks, and while they varied greatly in size and bulk, the general plan of construction was the same in all, being a compact pile of material of irregular outline, apparently floating on the surface of the water (although in reality the nests were supported by masses of dead cat-tails beneath the surface of the water), and were very conspicuous owing to the lack of concealing vegetation. The eggs were deposited in the center of the pile in a neat depression, which was lined with small bits of the same material. The bottom of the cavity was, in every instance, well above the surface of the water (usually from 2 to

6 inches), and the nest cavities were entirely free from moisture. Most of these nests were built in comparatively open water almost waist deep, and about 30 yards from shore. On the date mentioned (May 24) 15 nests were examined, about a third of which were constructed by the birds as described, while the remaining two-thirds were the usual depressions in muskrat houses. The majority of these nests contained three eggs, but a few of them held only one and two, and one nest contained five.

The habit of nesting on old and partially dilapidated muskrat houses seems to be common at many places throughout the lakes and swamps of the interior. In such situations little, if any, nest is built, and sometimes two, or even three, sets of eggs are found on one house. Usually the nest consists merely of a hollow excavated in the half-decayed vegetable rubbish, but sometimes a few reeds, rushes, or bits of grass, brought from a distance, are added to line the cavity or build up a slight rim around it.

Mr. Milton S. Ray (1903) describes a breeding colony of this species in Lake Valley, California, in which—

the nests were built in various situations. The majority were built up of dry tules where the water is about 5 feet deep. When freshly built of green tules the nest formed a pretty picture. They were placed among tall, thick tules or marsh grass and pond lilies at their edge. Great difference existed in the nests, some being elaborate structures, while others were scantily made and placed on soggy masses of dead tules or floating logs.

In Washington, according to Dawson (1909), these terns make use of the old nests of the western grebe and sometimes even appropriate an occupied nest of the latter. He shows a photograph of such an occupied nest, and says he has " seen others in which the eggs of the rightful owner were nearly buried under a little turret of dried reeds, upon which the tern had been allowed to place her full complement of eggs."

Eggs.—In spite of the fact that the breeding season is much prolonged, and that early and late sets of eggs are often found, the Forster's tern doubtless raises only one brood in a season. The normal set consists of three eggs, sometimes only two; sets of four eggs are common, sets of five are not rare, and even sets of six have been reported. These larger sets usually, if not always, show evidences of having been laid by more than one female, either in the shape, color, or extent of incubation in the eggs.

The eggs of Forster's tern are practically indistinguishable from those of the common tern. In shape they are ovate, short ovate, or elongate ovate. The shell is thin, smooth, and without luster. The ground color varies from ' tawny olive " or " cinnamon buff " to " cartridge buff " or " pale olive buff." The markings are usually rather small spots, more or less evenly distributed, but often these are congregated to form a ring on or near the larger end; many eggs are boldly and handsomely marked with large blotches or irregular scrawls. These markings are in the darker shades of brown, such as "chestnut brown," "burnt umber," or "seal brown." Some eggs have underlying blotches of lighter shades, such as "tawny russet" or "hazel." Nearly all eggs, especially the lighter types, show spots or blotches of various shades of lilac or lavender grays. Where there are markings of several different colors on the same egg the effect is often very pretty. The measurements of 65 eggs, in the United States National Museum, average 43 by 31 millimeters; the eggs showing the four extremes measure **48** by 29.5, 43 by **32.5, 39** by 31 and 42 by **28.5** millimeters.

Young.—The period of incubation is 23 days, and probably both sexes incubate. The young remain in the nest for a few days, until they are strong enough to run about or swim, when they become very lively and pugnacious. They take to the water readily and soon become expert at running or swimming about the marsh and hiding in the grass. They are fed by their devoted parents until fully grown and able to fly.

Plumage.—The downy young is quite different from that of the common tern. The upper parts vary from light "clay color," through "cinnamon buff" to "pinkish buff," shading off to paler shades of the same color below, paling on the breast and belly almost to white, and darkest on the throat, which is "wood brown" or "drab" in some specimens, but never so dark as in the common tern. The upper parts are heavily spotted or streaked with black or "blackish brown," less heavily on the head and more heavily on the back, where these markings are confluent into great blotches or longitudinal bands. This color pattern is well adapted to conceal the chick among the lights and shadows of the marsh grass where it hides.

The juvenal plumage, which is acquired by the time that the young bird has attained its growth, is also quite distinctive and matches the surroundings in which the young bird lives with a heavy suffusion of dark browns on the upper parts. In this plumage the pearl gray of the back and scapulars is almost wholly concealed by the brown terminal portions of the feathers, which are "clay color" or "cinnamon buff," centrally clouded or barred with "snuff brown," or "burnt umber"; the top of the head is nearly uniform "snuff brown"; the sides of the neck are heavily clouded, and the forebreast and rump are lightly clouded with the same color, which also shows on the tips of the lesser wing-coverts, some of the greater wing-coverts, and the rectrices; a conspicuous black patch surrounds the eyes and covers the auriculars. As the season advances all these brown markings fade or wear off to produce the first winter plumage; in this plumage the rump and breast become pure white, the browns on the upper parts gradually disappear or leave only traces of the buffy edgings in the shape of transverse bars; a partial molt of the body plumage also takes place at this time. Young birds, in their first winter plumage, may be distinguished from adults by their shorter and less deeply forked tails with some brownish mottling, and by their darker primaries, which are less silvery and have the white spaces more sharply contrasted with the black.

A complete prenuptial molt in February and March produces the first nuptial plumage, which is usually indistinguishable from the adult. Some young birds in nuptial plumage have wings somewhat like those of the first winter plumage; others renew the first winter plumage of the head; but, as a rule, young birds become indistinguishable from adults when 9 or 10 months old.

Adults have two complete molts—a prenuptial in February and March and a postnuptial in August—and two distinct plumages. The adult winter plumage, which Audubon described as *Sterna havelli*, is quite different from the well-known spring plumage. The crown is usually largely and sometimes wholly white, though dusky spots are often scattered through it, and there is a more or less distinct nuchal crescent of dusky tipped feathers; there is a distinct black space, including the eye and the ear coverts; the lateral tail feathers are shorter than in the spring, and the primaries, when freshly grown, are beautifully silvered.

Food.—Being so largely a bird of the marshes, Forster's tern feeds less on fish and has a more varied bill of fare than the other terns. It may be seen catching insects on the wing, as well as hovering over the pools, its bill pointing straight downward, looking for tiny morsels of food on the surface. It sometimes makes a diving plunge into the water, but more often it drops down lightly or swoops gracefully along the surface, picking up its food without wetting its plumage. Rev. P. B. Peabody (1896) notes that " the first apparent spring-time food consists of dead fish and frogs and other *aquatica* that have perished in the winter ice, and are being revealed as the latter melts beneath the sun." Mr. W. L. Dawson (1909) says:

When the insects are flying well the terns prefer to hawk. Dragon flies and caddis flies are favorite quarry, and in pursuit of the latter the birds will often rise to a height of several hundred feet.

The birds shot in Louisiana by Audubon (1840) " were engaged in picking up floating coleopterous insects."

Behavior.—I have never been able to discover anything distinctive in the flight of Forster's tern; it is as light and graceful as that of the common tern, which it closely resembles in every particular. Although quite different in the fall, the two species can not be easily distinguished in the spring; the white breast of the former is often obscured by shadow, the slight difference in size inappreciable, and the only field mark of consequence is the slightly longer tail of *forsteri*, which is not very conspicuous.

The voice, however, is quite distinctive and usually makes identification easy and certain. The cry of the young bird in juvenal plumage, as we heard it in the Manitoba marshes, is a shrill, high-pitched squeal, quite different from the notes of other terns or gulls. I noted at the same time the call of the adult as harsh and grating, on a low key and sounding like "tza-a-ap." Elsewhere in my notes I find that I have described the same note as "zreep" or "zrurrrr"— a rasping, nasal, buzzing sound, suggesting the well-known note of the nighthawk. It also utters on rare occasions a soft "wheat, wheat," like the common tern. On the Virginia coast the prevailing notes were the characteristic, harsh, grating cries described above; but I also heard here a shrill, peeping note, "pip, pip, pip, pip, pip," rapidly given.

Mr. Peabody (1896) condemns Forster's tern as a "mis-avian spirit," saying:

While sociable among his kind, and, to them, moderately good-tempered (except in the breeding time), he is radically hostile to all other birds. A veritable Ishmael among the waterfowl, his spirit, both of courage and of mean cowardice, is never so clearly portrayed as when, by mutual encroachment upon favorable waters, many species other than those of *his* feather flock together.

Evidently the tern has many foes. The Franklin's gull is his arch enemy; the muskrat and the mink undoubtedly do away with many eggs, while the character of this tern himself inclines me to think that he occasionally plays the cannibal.

Mr. Rockwell (1911) cites the following incident:

A few black-crowned night herons were nesting among the terns, and one unfortunate youngster, unable to fly, who deserted his nest at our approach, took refuge on a tern's nest, where he was promptly attacked by half a dozen of the birds, and although twice as large as his assailants, was knocked down repeatedly by well-directed blows of the birds' wings, until he finally sought safety in the water.

Winter.—As Forster's tern is somewhat hardier than others of its genus, the fall migration is more prolonged and it winters farther north. Migrants begin to arrive on the Carolina coasts as early as August and linger until late in the fall, wintering regularly in South Carolina and occasionally farther north. In Florida it is a very common winter resident on inland waters and on the coast.

DISTRIBUTION.

Breeding range.—Temperate North America, mainly within the United States, at widely scattered localities. East to western Ontario (Port Maitland, near the east end of Lake Erie) and the coast of

Virginia (Northampton County). South to the coast of Louisiana (various islands), southern coast of Texas (Refugio to Cameron counties), central Colorado (Barr Lake region), northern Utah (Great Salt Lake region) and central California (Merced County). West to the central valleys of California (San Joaquin and Sacramento Valleys), central southern Oregon (Klamath Lakes), and central Washington (Douglas County). North to central Alberta (60 miles southeast of Edmonton), and central Manitoba (Lake Winnipegosis).

Breeding grounds protected in the following national reservations: In Louisiana, Breton Island and Shell Keys; in Oregon, Klamath Lake and Malheur Lake.

Winter range.—From the coast of South Carolina and the Gulf coasts of Florida, Louisiana, and Texas southward to Brazil (Pernambuco. From southern California (San Diego region) southward along the west coast of Mexico to Guatemala.

Spring migration.—Early dates of arrival: Virginia, Smith's Island, May 10; New Jersey, Five Mile Beach, April 26, and Long Beach, May 14; Ohio, Cincinnati, May 4; Ontario, May 22; Kansas, Emporia, April 18; Illinois, Chicago, May 6; Minnesota, Heron Lake, April 7; Manitoba, Oak Point, May 17; California, Stockton, April 17, and Monterey, May 10.

Fall migration.—Early dates of arrival: Lower California, San José del Cabo, September 29; Guatemala, Lake Duenas, October 28. Late dates of departure: Ontario, Toronto, October 19; Minnesota, Heron Lake, October 14; California, Monterey, September 23.

Casual records.—Stragglers in summer and fall have been taken as far east as Massachusetts (Ipswich, September, 1870, and Monomoy Island, October 2, 1880).

Egg dates.—Virginia: Twenty-eight records, May 30 to July 12; fourteen records, June 5 to 28. Manitoba: Twenty-one records, June 7 to July 12; eleven records, June 8 to 21. Utah: Nineteen records, June 5 to July 3; ten records, June 11 to 20. California: Fifteen records, May 26 to July 12; eight records, May 27 to June 15.

STERNA HIRUNDO Linnaeus.

COMMON TERN.

HABITS.

One of the most charming features of our eastern seacoast is this graceful little " sea swallow." The most attractive combination of summer sea, sky, and sandy beach would be but an empty, lifeless scene without the little " mackerel gull," such a fitting accompaniment of its gentle surroundings and so suggestive of summer sunshine and cooling sea breezes. One can not help admiring such an elegant and dainty creature, its spotless and delicate plumage and its buoyant, graceful flight, as it flies listlessly up the beach until the discovery of some school of small fry, on which it feeds, causes it to pause, hover for an instant, and plunge headlong into the water for some tiny minnow.

We came near losing this beautiful bird a few years ago, because its exquisite plumage was so much in demand for feminine decoration that, before we realized it, collectors for the millinery trade had alarmingly reduced its numbers. Stringent laws, however, were passed for its protection and it has now practically regained its former abundance. The most important breeding colony in Massachusetts is on Muskeget Island, between Nantucket and Marthas Vineyard, which has been rigidly protected for a number of years and contains the largest sea-bird colonies on the New England coast south of Maine. Mr. George H. Mackay kept very close watch over it during its most critical period, and the keeper of the life-saving station has guarded it ever since. That the terns prospered under protection is clearly shown by Mr. Mackay's records, covering a period of five years from 1894 to 1898, inclusive, during which time they nearly doubled in number.

When Mr. William Brewster first visited Muskeget in 1870 the terns were astonishingly abundant though he was told by the fishermen that they had been diminishing for years. Four years later he found their numbers sadly depleted by the depredations of fishermen who landed there regularly to collect their eggs, through June, July, and August, keeping the poor terns laying like hens, so that very few of them succeeded in raising broods. I made five visits to Muskeget in 1885, 1889, 1890, 1892, and 1903. Between my first two visits they continued to decrease in spite of the new laws enacted for their protection, but between 1890 and 1902 they increased again and are now probably as abundant as they ever were within my memory. Mr. Mackay's record show a very satisfactory increase between 1894 and 1898. Egging operations and shooting for millinery purposes have been effectively stopped.

Muskeget Island is the largest of a group of small, low sandy islands forming a part of the southern boundary of Nantucket Sound. It is a little more than an elevated sand bar raised above the level of the numerous sand shoals so dreaded by sailors in that region, which are usually invisible at high tide, but in rough weather are white with combing breakers. A life-saving station has been established there for the rescue of unfortunate mariners. A few fishermen's and gunners' shanties are the only other buildings on the island. It is approximately crescent shaped, though its outline changes frequently, and is about 3 miles long and a mile wide. Several small islands near it are practically a part of it. In the central portion of the island are low rolling sand hills and small sand dunes; the beaches are mostly flat and sandy, though in some places stony. Vegetation is scarce over most of the island, consisting of a sparse growth of beach grass (*Ammophila arundinaca*) and a low-growing poison ivy (*Rhus radicans*), with scattering patches, some of them quite extensive, of bayberry (*Myrica carolinensis*) and beach plum (*Prunus maritima*) bushes. In some places the beach grass grows tall and thick or in dense clumps or tufts. The isolation of this island, the variety of nesting sites offered, and the abundant food supply to be obtained in the adjacent shoals and tide rips make Muskeget an ideal breeding ground for common and roseate terns and laughing gulls. I know of no more extensive or interesting colony of these two terns on the American coast. A visit to Muskeget Island in June or July, the height of the breeding season, is an experience never to be forgotten. As we approach it in our little sailboat a cloud of minute white specks is seen hovering over it and the air is full of birds coming and going, for not all of this vast multitude can find food enough in the immediate vicinity; hence they wander far to the shores of Martha's Vineyard and Cape Cod.

As we land and walk out among the sand hills the terns rise from the ground on all sides and circle about us overhead in an ever-increasing cloud. Some are darting down at our heads with harsh and grating cries of protest, others are drifting around us closely at hand. If we look up into the air we are made fairly dizzy; for as far as we can see, extending up into the deep blue sky, is a bewildering maze of whirling birds, flying in every direction and at varying heights in countless thousands. Their plaintive notes when heard singly are nearly musical, but the combined din of such a multitude of voices is almost deafening in its effect, and for days afterwards we can hear the rhythmic chorus ringing in our ears. If we shoot down one of them every voice is hushed; the silence is appalling as they come gliding in from every side in sympathetic horror to hover over their fallen companion and try to encourage him to rise again. Some observers have attributed this action to another motive—the desire to kill and remove a useless member of their society—but I have never seen any evidence to support this theory. Now is the greedy murderer's chance, as the plume hunters have learned to their advantage, for as fast as the terns are shot down others will hurry in, and, as if at a given signal, all will burst out again into an excited chorus of angry cries of protest, hovering over and darting down at their dead companions in confusion and despair; but if no more are shot they seem soon to forget, the crowd gradually disperses and all goes on as if nothing had happened. Perhaps a marsh hawk may appear upon the scene quartering over the low ground in search of mice. The din suddenly ceases, every voice is still; the silence is so striking that we look up to see the cause, as thousands of white wings are diving after him in an angry mob, and he is forced to beat a hasty retreat, leaving the terns free to renew their attacks on us.

Spring.—The terns arrive at Muskeget usually about the 8th or 10th of May, but sometimes as early as the 1st, their time of arrival depending somewhat on the weather conditions prevailing at the time, mild weather with strong southwest wind being favorable for their migration, and cold northerly winds retarding it. When first seen they are usually flying high in the air in small numbers, but they soon settle down onto the island as their numbers increase.

Courtship.—Soon after their arrival they may be seen indulging in their simple courtship performances. Gathered in a small party on the beach, resting and sunning themselves, the male begins strutting about before and around the females. His neck is stretched upwards to its fullest extent with his bill pointing to the sky, his chest is thrown out, and his tail is held at a steep angle as he waddles about on his short legs. Soon he flies away and brings his lady love a peace offering, a sand eel, curving in a circle around his bill like an engagement ring. As he struts around her with it she seems to beg for it with open mouth, waddling up to him with half-raised wings. Finally he offers it to her and she accepts it; perhaps they pass it back and forth again before she swallows it; but at length the conjugal pack seems sealed and they fly away. Sometimes this little ceremony is interrupted by the arrival of a second male with another sand eel which he offers to the same female. She seems willing to accept the offering from either suitor until a fight ensues and one of the males is driven away.

Nesting.—Nest building for the common tern is not an elaborate operation, for many of them build no nest at all, merely excavating a slight hollow in the sand or on a pebbly beach. The windrows of seaweed or dry eelgrass, just above high-water mark, are favorite nesting sites, and here the bird makes a small cavity by beating down the soft mass with a circular movement of its body. On Muskeget Island nests are scattered everywhere over the sand hills, among the beach grass or ivy, along the higher portions of the beaches, about pieces of driftwood and in entirely open situations. Generally some nesting material is brought in—seaweed, grasses, bits of twigs, and other rubbish. These the bird molds into a circular hollow with its body, and in this way elaborate nests are sometimes built, but they always harmonize with their surroundings.

The first eggs are laid on Muskeget between the middle and end of May, the date of laying being more dependent on the weather than on the date of the arrival of the terns. Comparatively few eggs are laid in May, the greater portion being laid during the first two weeks in June and plenty of fresh eggs may be found up to the Fourth of July. Formerly, when much disturbed, egg laying was prolonged through August, but now only a few belated sets are to be found in that month. One egg is laid each day until the set is complete, which normally consists of three eggs, often four, sometimes five, and very rarely six. Frequently, sets of four, and usually the larger sets, show evidence of having been laid by two birds, either by marked difference in color, shape, or size, or by different degrees of incubation. Many eggs are dropped indiscriminately anywhere, probably by birds unable to reach their nests in time, and left to bleach in the sun. Such eggs are often broken, as if dropped by birds in the air.

On the islands near Penobscot Bay, Maine, which are mostly high and rocky or covered with grass, I have examined a number of small breeding colonies of common terns. The nests were on the higher portions of the islands in open situations, either on bare rocky or stony ground or in the short grass, frequently near or even on pieces of driftwood or bunches of seaweed. They were merely slight hollows in the ground, carelessly lined with bits of straw, grass, or rubbish. Once I saw a broken sea-urchin's shell half inclosing one of the eggs. There are numerous small and several large breeding colonies scattered along the New England coast where the terns adapt their nest building to the conditions existing. These are almost invariably on islands, and generally on small islands, which are inaccessible to predatory animals. Notable among these are Penikese and Weepecket Islands, south of Buzzards Bay, Massachusetts, where both the common and roseate terns breed in large numbers, nesting among the stones and rocks on the beaches or on the grassy uplands. Occasionally a nest is found lined with small stones, as if collected for that purpose. On Cobb's Island, Virginia, and on the adjacent islands, we found a few small colonies of common terns, nesting on the beaches with the gull-billed terns and black skimmers, and on drift seaweed in the marshes. Mr. B. S. Bowdish (1910) mentions a colony of 250 common terns breeding on Royal Shoals, a low sand spit on the coast of North Carolina, together with least terns, black skimmers, and laughing gulls. The most southern breeding colony I have ever seen was in the Breton Island reservation off the coast of Louisiana, a small colony of about 25 pairs on Battledore Island scattered among the large breeding colonies of laughing gulls and black skimmers.

In Lake Winnipegosis we found a number of large colonies, on small rocky or stony islands, breeding in company with ring-billed gulls, double-crested cormorants, and white pelicans. Some of these colonies contained over 1,000 pairs of terns, nesting in dense groups on the pebbly beaches. Often the nests were not over 2 or 3 feet apart and often within that distance of the gulls' nests.

Eggs.—The eggs of the common tern vary in shape from ovate or short ovate to elongate ovate. The ground color varies from " pale buff " or " olive buff " in the lightest eggs to shades of " wood brown," " cinnamon," or " Isabella color " in the darkest eggs. I have one egg in my collection which is " pale turquoise green "—a rare type of coloration. There is a great diversity of color patterns in the markings, but most of the eggs are quite heavily spotted with various shades of dark brown and drab, " hair brown," " Vandyke brown," " seal brown," or " clove brown." Some eggs are sparingly spotted and others quite densely covered with small spots or dots; some are boldly marked with large blotches of dark colors or heavily splashed with lighter shades; many have underlying splashes or blotches of " olive gray " or " lilac gray," producing handsome effects. The measurements of 82 eggs, in the United States National Museum, average 41.5 by 30 millimeters; the eggs showing the four extremes measure 45 by 31.5, 44 by 32.5, 35.5 by 28.5 and 41 by 27.5 millimeters.

Young.—I believe that only one brood is normally raised in a season, although it frequently happens that the first set of eggs or young is destroyed, making a second attempt necessary; but Prof. Lynds Jones (1906), who has made a careful study of this species, has produced some evidence to indicate that two broods are often raised. It does not seem to me, however, that his evidence is conclusive. He has worked out the period of incubation as 21 days and has given a very accurate account of the development of the embryo. I can hardly spare the space to quote from his excellent paper on the subject as freely as it deserves, but the following two passages are well worth repeating:

Both male and female take regular turns sitting, but my observations indicate that the female spends more time on the nest than the male. In the cases studied, a bird, later found to be the female, approached the nest abruptly and settled upon the eggs without any preliminaries. She remained quiet 40 minutes, when she uttered a peculiar call, which was repeated at short intervals, until a bird separated itself from the hovering cloud or company at the water's edge, when she stood up, took a few steps, and flew away. The male alighted on the sand several rods to leeward of the nest and approached it gradually, simulated feeding, and called loudly at intervals. When he reached the nest he merely stood over the eggs to protect them from the scorching rays of the sun and kept calling at intervals. In 20 minutes he became more restless, called more frequently, and soon ran some distance to windward of the nest and took wing. Within a few minutes the female alighted on the sand near the nest and went abruptly to it and settled upon the eggs. This maneuver was repeated many times, with slight modifications.

How do the old birds recognize their own young among the multitude of young birds congregated on the beach? was a question which occupied a good deal of my attention and interest. After the young leave the nest and its vicinity they wander about aimlessly and may be at widely different places at two visits of the old birds. Hence it is often a serious question on the part of the parent how to find its offspring. Abundant opportunity was afforded for studying this question. Old birds with young which had left the nest, when coming in with a fish, stooped to examine each group of young in turn until a young bird, apparently its own, was found, when the old bird alighted. Immediately the youngster began to dance and call vociferously, but not until the old one had touched the young one with its forehead was the question decided. Often this minute inspection was immediately followed by the departure of the old bird without delivering the fish, the quest for its own young being renewed. It thus became clear that sight alone was not depended upon for recognition, but that the final decision rested upon the sense of smell. Sometimes the quest resulted in failure, when the old bird swallowed the fish. The evidence seemed to indicate that these terns feed only their own young.

By the 1st of July on Muskeget probably the majority of the young terns have hatched in nests which have not been disturbed. Under favorable weather conditions the eggs are often left uncovered, the sun and the warm sand supplying the proper amount of heat; but the birds seem to be able to judge these conditions quite accurately, for in cold, cloudy, or rainy weather, when the eggs might become chilled, or, on the other hand, when the sun is too hot for them, I have always found the birds anxious to return to their nests and protect their eggs. I think they always incubate at night. Terns are seldom seen on their nests because they are timid and restless, but they will soon return to them if the intruder remains quietly concealed at a safe distance. The hatching process is often slow and laborious, a day or more intervening between the time when the horny tip of the bill makes a small hole near the larger end of the egg and the actual hatching time, when the weak, wet little chick emerges from the shell. It dries off within a few hours and remains in the nest for two or three days. Its eyes are open at birth, but it is not fed until the second day. It is fed on small fish from the very first, which it swallows head first. When three or four days old the young chick becomes very lively, running about rapidly, hiding in the grass or between stones, or even lying flat on the sand, where its protective coloring helps to conceal it. It seems to realize this fact, for I have often seen one remain perfectly motionless until it felt sure it was discovered, after which its capture was far from easy. Parents must experience considerable difficulty in finding their own young, and still more trouble in protecting them against inclement weather. On July 4, 1903, I noticed evidences of great mortality among the very young chicks on Muskeget; I found hundreds of their little dead bodies scattered over the island, drying in the sun, sometimes two or three in one nest, and once I saw the dead body of an adult tern covering the bodies of two young in the nest. Captain Gibbs, of the life-saving station, thought that they were killed by exposure to prolonged, cold, easterly rainstorms which prevailed during the previous month. Probably the older young were able to run to shelter under the ivy vines, bushes, and thick grass, and thus survived. On certain portions of the island, where the grass grew tall and thick, the mortality was much less noticeable.

The young are fed by their parents until they are fully grown and well able to fly and have been taught to fish for themselves. I have seen young birds fully as large as their parents and in the first winter plumage fed in this way while standing on a sand bar or sitting on the water. As the old bird approaches with a small fish held crosswise in its bill the youngster shows its excitement by fluttering its wings rapidly, screaming and throwing back its head, with open mouth ready to receive the coveted morsel, while the parent hovers over it and feeds it. I have never seen the feeding process performed on the wing.

Dr. Charles W. Townsend contributes the following notes on the feeding of the young:

The full-grown young appear to be always hungry and call in a monotonous, beseeching way whenever an adult appears with a fish. There are three methods of receiving the fish from the parent—either in the air, on the sand, or on the water. There can be no doubt that the hungry and clamorous young will take food from any adult. Whether the adults feed any but their own young and whether they are able to recognize their own is of course a question. I am inclined to think that, although an adult may occasionally feed a clamorous youngster not its own, as a rule it refuses to feed any but its own legitimate offspring, which it is perfectly able to recognize. As the sexes of the adults are alike in plumage it is difficult to tell whether only one or both parents feed the young.

In the air the feeding of the young is often a graceful and interesting performance. By a series of aerial evolutions the adult and young reach a point where the transference of the fish directly from bill to bill is made so quickly that one often can not be sure whether the fish was thrown or dropped or actually passed from mouth to mouth. I am inclined to think all methods are used.

On the sand the young sometimes collect in numbers while the adults fish for them. Although the young, easily recognized by their white foreheads and black bills, generally stand motionless, they sometimes walk about, often more rapidly than adults are in the habit of doing. When an adult flies toward a group with food the young all clamor at once, opening their black bills and displaying their crimson gapes, and crowding up toward the food-bearing adult. On one occasion at Ipswich I saw an adult with a fish in its bill alight on the beach near two immature birds, who both clamored loudly to be fed. Disregarding their cries it flew to a third immature bird, but was soon off and alighted near an adult, to whom it delivered the fish, which was swallowed. The young either swallow the fish at once on the beach or sometimes rise in the air and fly about until the fish disappears down the throat. If the fish is large the swallowing may be a slow process. One young bird after swallowing the fish alighted on the water a moment and appeared to take a drink before rejoining its companions on the beach.

The process of feeding the young bird on the surface of the water is perhaps the most interesting, and points to the former more aquatic ancestry of the terns. An adult flies screaming with a fish in its bill; the young responds by a beseeching call and flight toward the parent, and alights on the water still calling. The old one flies down and delivers the fish without alighting, or doing so but for a brief moment. The thing is done so quickly that it is often impossible to know what happens. The young one as soon as it receives the fish flies up into the air.

Plumages.—Several very distinct color phases may be found in the downy young of the common tern, each having numerous variations. The commonest type is " cream buff," " ochraceous buff," or " clay colored " above, irregularly mottled with " sepia " or " seal brown; " the throat is sometimes " smoke gray," but more often " drab " or " sepia; " and the under parts are pure white. There is a gray phase in which the back is " pale neutral gray " and the crown " cartridge buff " or " pale olive buff; " it is spotted with black on the upper parts; and the throat is " bone brown." A much rarer type is plainly colored and entirely unspotted. In this type the color of the upper parts varies from " clay color " to " pinkish cinnamon " or " cinnamon buff," shading off to paler tints on the sides and to white on the breast. This type intergrades with the common type, and there is much individual variation in the extent of the dusky throat and its color, which varies from " smoke gray " to " brownish black."

Dr. Jonathan Dwight (1901) describes the molts and plumages of the first year as follows:

Juvenal plumage acquired by a complete post-natal moult shortly after leaving the egg. Dusky markings and buff edgings are conspicuous above, the lower parts being a clear white. The forehead is pale brown, blending into a dull black occiput. Buffs and browns later become dull white by fading and the blacks become brownish. The forking of the tail is much less than that of adults, and the rectrices are more rounded, darker, and tipped with dusky or buff markings which become largely lost by wear. A couple of rows of lesser coverts along the cubital border of the wing form a dull black band. The flesh-colored bill and feet, after first brightening, begin to darken.

First winter plumage acquired by a partial post-juvenal moult, limited to the body feathers, and sometimes a few of the lesser wing coverts. The new mantle is gray except for the dusky cubital bands. The forehead is white and the occiput black, with some tendency to streaking on the crown. The bill and feet become wholly black. Save for the less forked, darker tail, and traces of buff on the retained wing coverts, young birds closely resemble adults. The change to this plumage is not apt to begin before the end of September on the Atlantic coast.

First nuptial plumage acquired by a complete first prenuptial moult, which explains the freshness of all the feathers of breeding birds. The lateness of this moult in some birds is indicated by over 50 specimens (some of which appear to be adults) taken in Florida between May 28 and June 3, which vary from birds with the first primary barely grown to those still retaining two or three of the old primaries and a number of old rectrices and body feathers. The black cap is now assumed, the dusky cubital bands disappear, and the bill and feet become chiefly coral red.

Occasionally in young birds the first nuptial plumage, described above, is not assumed, but instead a plumage like the adult winter plumage is acquired by a late prenuptial or an early postnuptial molt. This plumage is worn throughout the spring and summer, probably by the less vigorous birds which do not breed. It is the plumage which was once described as a species under the name *Sterna portlandica*.

Adults have two complete molts each year, a prenuptial early in the spring, before their arrival on their breeding grounds, and a postnuptial in September or later. The adult winter plumage is similar to the first winter except for the wings and tail; the latter is shorter than in spring.

Food.—The food of the common tern consists almost wholly of small fish, not over 3 or 4 inches long, such as the sand launce (*Ammodytes americanus*) and the pipe fish (*Siphonostoma fuscum*), and probably the young fry of larger species. Shrimp and aquatic insects are eaten to some extent. Mr. Ora W. Knight (1908) speaks of seeing a tern chase, catch, and devour a yellow swallow-tail butterfly (*Papilio turnus*). The fishermen about Nantucket find the terns very useful in helping them to locate a school of bluefish, for a hovering, diving flock of terns is almost sure to indicate the presence of the fish. The small fry on which the bluefish feed are driven to the surface in dense schools to escape from their enemies below only to be pounced upon by their enemies in the air. It is remarkable to see how quickly the terns will gather, from far and near, as soon as one of their number has discovered such a school. It is an exciting scene, for the water fairly boils with rushing, plunging fish, and the air is full of screaming, fluttering, diving birds; but for the poor fry it is a strenuous struggle for existence.

Doctor Townsend describes its feeding habits as follows:

The plunge of the common tern resembles in miniature that of the gannet. Down they drop like winged arrows, folding their wings as their bodies enter the water. Often they disappear entirely under the water to emerge victorious, with the fish in the bill, or prepared to try again. They scream their triumph or failure, for they can scream even with a fish in the bill. Sometimes a fish is difficult to swallow, and it is dropped to be caught again before it strikes the water. As the terns leave the water they generally shiver violently, probably to shake off the water. At times they fly down at the beach for a small crustacean or a sea worm. Off the southern Labrador coast I have seen flocks of terns follow small whales and dart down screaming at the water, after the whale had broached and gone down. It is probable that the whale and tern both relish the same small fry.

During the month of August one of this tern's favorite food fishes, the sand eel or sand launce (*Ammodytes americanus*), abounds in the shallow waters about the beaches and inlets at Ipswich, Massachusetts, and thither the terns flock in large numbers from distant breeding places. These fish are 3 or 4 inches long and swim in compact schools of many hundreds. Where they abound the terns congregate and busily bombard the water, disappearing completely below the surface in order to capture their prey. As the bird rises from the water, with the fish hanging from its bill, it occasionally throws it into the air either from pure fun or to get a better hold on the fish. Sometimes a bird drops a fish, but catches it again before it has fallen more than a yard or two. The presence of the fish in the mouth never interferes with the capacity of the bird to scream or cry out. In fact, the fish bearer generally screams constantly, as if to announce its success in the chase or the fact of food to its young.

Behavior.—The flight of the common tern, like that of all of its congeners, is light, airy, and graceful. At times it seems listless and desultory, as it flits along the shore looking for its prey, the slow beats of its long wings lifting its light body at every stroke; but again it is swift and direct when traveling high in the air or when hurrying to join a bevy of its fellows hovering over a school of fish; but always the bird has better control of its movements than it appears to have. Its diving habits have been described above. It seldom indulges in swimming, though it can do so if necessary. On hot days large numbers may sometimes be seen swimming and bathing.

In life the common tern can not be easily distinguished from the Forster's tern, and it still more closely resembles the Arctic tern; the movements of all three are almost exactly alike, and the common tern is intermediate in color between the other two. Its voice will distinguish it from the former, but not from the latter. Its somewhat harsh rolling call, " tee ar-r-r-r-r," is almost musical at times and has a decidedly pleasing cadence, a tinge of wildness, associated with the poetry of summer seas. There is a delightful variety in its notes, with the repetition of the same theme, varying in rapidity and tone, expressive of its various moods. Doctor Townsend writes to me in regard to it:

I have had them fly directly at my head to within a few feet, when they suddenly swerve upward. As they dart down they emit in their rage a rapidly repeated and vibratory tut tut or kik kik kik, followed by a piercing, screaming tear. These sharp rapidly repeated notes are sometimes followed by a loud rattling sound, as if the mandibles were vibrated in anger.

The Muskeget terns have suffered seriously at times by the introduction of cats, kept by the life-saving people, which also nearly exterminated a local species of field mouse (*Microtus breweri*). Perhaps their worst enemy, next to man, has been the short-eared owl. A colony of these owls lived on the island, making their home on some high grassy knolls, about which hundreds of dead terns lay, partly eaten and drying in the sun. Mr. William Brewster (1879) has thus described their destructive work:

Every day at a certain time these owls sallied forth in search of fresh prey. We used regularly to see them about sunset, sailing in circles over the island or beating along the crests of the sand hills. They were invariably followed by vast mobs of enraged terns, which dived angrily down over the spot where the owl had alighted, or strung out in the wake of his flight like the tail of a comet. The owl commonly paid little attention to this unbidden following, apparently never tried to seize his persecutors while on the wing, but on several occasions we saw a sitting bird pounced upon and borne off. Sometimes in the middle of the night a great outcry among the terns told where a tragedy was being enacted.

Fortunately for the terns, but unfortunately for the cause of science—for the owls were supposed to be approaching subspecific distinction—this little colony of interesting owls was entirely wiped out during the summer of 1896, through the misdirected ardor of a bird protectionist. Furthermore, as the owls destroyed large numbers of the mice, which probably destroyed many of the eggs of the terns, perhaps it would have been better to have left nature's balance undisturbed.

A very large colony of terns at Chatham, Massachusetts, was practically exterminated by a colony of skunks in 1917 and 1918.

Dr. Townsend writes:

The common tern appears to be one of the favorite victims of jaegers, but the worm sometimes turns and chases the jaeger in return. Once in mid-August, on the Maine coast, I found a common tern chasing a male sharp-shinned hawk. The latter twisted and turned, but was unable to escape his adversary until he took refuge in an alder thicket, around which the tern flew screaming in anger.

Dr. Louis B. Bishop sends me the following interesting notes on the behavior of terns on an island in Stump Lake, North Dakota. He says:

On the third island we found the terns killing the young ring-billed gulls by chasing them till they took to the water, then descending on their heads in a perfect shower, striking at the back of their heads until they had pierced their brains. We saw three killed in this manner in less than half an hour, two more before we left, and many bodies of those killed before. The old gulls seemed to pay no attention to them.

I remember it as if it were yesterday. Eastgate and I had seated ourselves on the bank of the high island, and the adult gulls had gone offshore. Suddenly we noticed the terns screaming loudly and diving at something in the high weeds. Wondering what was the matter we watched, and soon saw a young gull make its way to the water with the terns diving at it. When it swam from shore the terns simply rained on it. The gull was, I think, just out of down. As the terns descended, the little gull tried to strike back, but presently a tern struck it on the back of the head, and its head fell to one side. Soon it came to life again, when the terns again descended until its head fell to rise no more. Then the terns left it to chase up others. We tried to save some of these young gulls by shooting the terns that were attacking them, but to no avail; the other terns paid no attention to those who were killed, or to the reports of the gun. They were more anxious to kill the young gulls than to save their own lives. We picked up several of the young gulls thus killed, and the backs of their heads, where merely a membrane covers the brain at this age, looked like pincushions. The only explanation I could think of was that the adult gulls ate the terns' eggs and young, and the later were taking their first chance to retaliate. This theory was strengthened by the fact that we did not find nearly as many young terns as there ought to have been with a colony as large as this.

Fall.—As soon as the young are able to fly, usually in August, many of the terns desert their breeding grounds and wander about the shores in loose scattering flocks, free from the arduous cares of reproduction, to spend the remainder of the season in rest and recreation. They are still largely gregarious and may be seen resting on the sand bars or sandy beaches in large compact flocks, all facing the wind. Some may be bathing in the shallow waters or preening their immaculate plumage, while others stand and sleep with bills buried under the scapulars. As the rising tide encroaches on their roosting ground those nearest the water are forced to rise, and flying over their fellows, to alight above them on the sand. Birds are constantly coming and going, making an animated scene of lively interest. Their summer wanderings are often extended over long distances in search of food. Large numbers of terns are seen daily, flying high in the air over Cape Cod to their favorite feeding grounds in Massachusetts Bay, spending the day on the sandy beaches near Plymouth and returning each night to their breeding grounds south of Cape Cod, 25 or 30 miles distant. The fall migration begins on the coast of Maine by the middle or last of September. In Massachusetts there are a few scattering winter records, but as a rule they begin to leave early in October, and by the end of that month nearly all of the common terns are gone. Winter records along the Atlantic coast seem to be scarce north of Florida, and probably most of the common terns spend the winter from the Gulf of Mexico southward.

DISTRIBUTION.

Breeding range.—Along the Atlantic coast of North America from northern Nova Scotia (Cape Breton) south to North Carolina (Pamlico Sound); and in the interior, south to the Gulf of St. Lawrence, the St. Lawrence River, northern Ohio (Oberlin and islands in western Lake Erie), southeastern Michigan (St. Clair Flats), southern Minnesota (Heron Lake), northern North Dakota (Devil's Lake region), and southwestern Saskatchewan (Crane Lake region). West to southeastern Alberta (Many Island Lake) and central Alberta (near Edmonton). North nearly, if not quite, to the Arctic coast of Mackenzie, certainly to Great Slave Lake (Fort Providence) and the west coast of Hudson Bay. A few birds breed in Bermuda, the Bahamas, and the Florida keys, on the coast of Venezuela (Aruba and Bonaire Islands) and on the coasts of Alabama, Louisiana, and Texas (Matagorda). In Europe, from Norway to the Mediterranean, Black, and Caspian Seas, in the Azores.

Canary, and Madeira Islands; in northern Africa and in temperate Asia, from Turkestan to Lake Baikal.

Winter range.—A few birds winter as far north as Florida (St. Johns River), but the main winter range is in South America, all along both coasts, as far south as the Straits of Magellan. In the Eastern Hemisphere, Africa, ranging to the Cape, and southern Asia.

Spring migration.—Early dates of arrival: Masaschusetts, April 20 to 25; St. Lawrence River, May 20; Pennsylvania, Erie, April 26; Ohio, Columbus, April 4; South Dakota, April 20; Colorado, New Windsor, May 14; California, Point Pinos, April 29. Late dates of departure: Brazil, Barra, May 1; Chile, Valparaiso, April 23; Peru, Ancon, May 10.

Fall migration.—Early dates of arrival: Argentina, Mar del Plata, September 18; Chile, Valparaiso, September 17; Straits of Magellan, Punta Arenas, November 19. Late dates of departure: Massachusetts, Barnstable, November 14, and Woods Hole, December 2; Pennsylvania, Erie, September 26; Ohio, Cincinnati, November 11; British Columbia, Comox, September 24; California, Point Pinos, October 17; Lower California, San José del Cabo, September 30.

Egg dates.—North Dakota, Saskatchewan, and Manitoba: Thirty-six records, May 31 to July 15; eighteen records, June 11 to 21. Virginia: Thirty-five records, May 27 to July 19; eighteen records, June 11 to 27. Maine: Twenty-one records, May 29 to July 26; eleven records, June 14 to July 4.

STERNA PARADISAEA Brünnich.

ARCTIC TERN.

HABITS.

Contributed by Charles Wendell Townsend.

The casual observer, fascinated by the sight of a flock of graceful terns diving for fish on the New England coast, naturally supposes they are all of one kind, and is told they are mackerel gulls. The ornithologist enjoys the same esthetic charm in the sight, but has often the added intellectual pleasure of discovering several distinct species in the flock. Common terns are generally in the majority but arctic and roseate terns may also be seen, as well as least and black terns. It would be difficult to point out to the untrained observer the differences between the common and arctic terns, but they can be recognized with a little practice and without the use of the gun. The feeding and nesting habits, mode of flight, size, and general appearance of these two species are, however, very much alike.

The Arctic tern breeds throughout the entire circumpolar regions as far north as it can find land, and south in this country to northern

British Columbia, Great Slave Lake, Central Keewatin, Maine, and Muskegat Island, Massachusetts. It is credited by Cook (1911) with being "the world's migration champion." After the breeding season is over the bird repairs from the Arctic to the Antarctic regions. "What their track is over that 11,000 miles of intervening space no one knows," says Cooke (1911).

A few scattered individuals have been noted along the United States coast south to Long Island, but the great flocks of thousands and thousands of these terns which alternate from one pole to the other have never been met by any trained ornithologist competent to learn their preferred path and their time schedule. The Arctic terns arrive in the far north about June 15 and leave about August 25, thus staying 14 weeks at the nesting site. They probably spend a few weeks longer in the winter than in the summer home and, if so, this leaves them scarcely 20 weeks for the round trip of 22,000 miles. Not less than 150 miles in a straight line must be their daily task, and this is undoubtedly multiplied several times by their zigzag twisting and turning in pursuit of food.

The Arctic terns have more hours of daylight and sunlight than any other animal on the globe. At their most northern nesting site the midnight sun has already appeared before their arrival, and it never sets during their entire stay at the breeding grounds. During two months of their sojourn in the Antarctic they do not see a sunset, and for the rest of the time the sun dips only a little way below the horizon and broad daylight continues all night. The birds therefore, have 24 hours of daylight for at least eight months in the year, and during the other four months have considerably more daylight than darkness.

Spring.—The most southern breeding place of the Arctic tern seems to have been Muskegat Isle, off Nantucket. Mackay (1897) gives the earliest date for the arrival of terns at this island as May 3, in 1897. The day before no terns were to be seen, while on the third they arrived "in large flocks, thousands dropping from the sky when they were first observed." The larger part of these were common and roseate terns, but he found a few Arctic terns breeding. When I visited this island in 1913 about 20,000 common terns, 1,000 roseate terns, and 3,000 laughing gulls were breeding, and I feel fairly sure that I saw a couple of Arctic terns, so there is a possibility that they still breed there. They were found breeding at Beverly in 1846 by Cabot (1846) and at Ipswich between 1868 and 1870 by Maynard (1870). They no longer breed there. On the Maine coast the Arctic tern, like the common tern, has steadily increased in numbers under protection since its low ebb due to the war of the milliners in the late nineties. Its chief breeding grounds there, according to Knight (1908), are Metinic, Green, Machias Seal Islands, and Matinicus Rock, where it nests with the common tern. It arrives from the south from the middle to the last of May. Its arrival on the southern coast of Labrador is at about the same time. Turner

(1886) says that this tern is one of the earliest birds to arrive at St. Michael, Alaska.

The earliest date recorded was April 25,, a very early season, showing that the terns only await the movement of the sea ice to appear in any locality. They become very abundant by the middle of May.

Murdoch (1885) reports that the tern arrives at Point Barrow, Alaska, about June 10.

Nesting.—The Arctic tern prefers to breed in colonies of its own species, but it is not rare to find a few common terns in these colonies or to find a colony composed largely of common terns with a few arctic terns. In Alaska they are often associated with Aleutian terns. Turner (1886) says their nests are sometimes placed within 2 feet of each other, and apparently without causing animosity between the species. Sandy or rocky islands are usually chosen, and the nests are scattered more or less thickly over the ground. Grinnell (1900) states that in Alaska he did not find the bird in colonies, as two nests were seldom within a hundred yards of each other; usually only one pair were found at a pond. Small islets were often selected, but he occasionally found this species nesting on the tundra a quarter of a mile from the nearest lake.

Nelson (1883) says:

Along both shores of Bering Sea and upon both shores of the adjoining Arctic waters this bird is very common. It nests wherever found in this region, and occurs indifferently either in the interior along the courses of the rivers, or on the salt marshes and barren islands on the seacoast. * * * It nests on some of the sterile islands of the North, in flocks, upon the bare sandy or pebbly ground, with no trace of any artificial nest. * * * On the eastern shore of Bering Sea I have only found it nesting singly, in pairs scattered here and there over the marshes, and in one instance three pairs were found occupying the same small island in a lake, which is the largest number I found nesting in close proximity.

This goes to show, as he says, "that the birds' habits vary greatly with the locality." Hinckley (1900) found the Arctic tern nesting along the Sushitna and Kuskokwim Rivers "even in high mountain valleys." Turner (1886) says:

They breed in the low grounds, preferably a low, damp island, such as those at the northern end of the canal. At this place hundreds of nests were discovered in 1876.

Feilden (1877) found several pairs of Arctic terns breeding in latitude 81° 44' on Bellots Island, on August 21. The land was covered with snow, and from one nest, in which was a newly hatched tern, the parents had thrown out the snow so that the nest was surrounded by a border marked by their feet 2 inches above the general level.

The Arctic tern is more inclined to omit nesting material than is the common tern, and its nest is generally merely a hollow in the sand, gravel, or moss or in the rocks. Occasionally a thin lining of dry grasses is used, but an elaborate nest is rarely or never seen. Turner (1886) says:

> The nest is merely a bare spot on the ground. Sometimes a few blades of grass surround the margin of the nest, but these seem to be more the result of cleaning off a bare spot than an attempt to construct a nest.

Palmer (1890), who found this the only species of tern at Funk Island, says that the eggs were laid on the bare rocks, often with broken pieces of granite or pebbles sometimes gathered from a distance arranged about them in a circle. In some cases he found bones of the great auk used in the same manner. Occasionally the eggs were laid in depressions in the gravel, among mussel shells, in crevices, amid tangled masses of chickweed 6 inches high that was dead, in a circle 5 inches about; also in depressions in dead grass as if a mouse's nest had been appropriated. McGregor (1902) says:

> A typical nest was a depression 1 inch deep by 5 inches in diameter, lined with dry grass and weed stalks.

Parry (1824) says:

> The nest in which the eggs are deposited, and each of which generally contained two, consisted merely of a small indentation in the ground, without any downy feathers or other material.

[AUTHOR'S NOTE: *Eggs.*—The Arctic tern raises only one brood in a season and the set usually consists of two eggs; three eggs are often laid, but larger numbers are very rare. A very large majority, or nearly all, of the sets collected in the far north consist of two eggs. The eggs can not be distinguished from those of the common tern by any constant or even prevailing character, though they seem to average a trifle darker in color and more rounded in shape, which varies from ovate to rounded ovate. The ground color varies greatly; in the darkest eggs it is " Brussels brown " or " Dresden brown "; in others it is " Saccardo's olive," " écru olive," or " dark olive buff "; and in the lightest egg " water green " or " pale olive buff." The eggs are more or less irregularly spotted or blotched with the darker shades of brown, such as " chaetura black," " bone brown," or " chestnut brown," and often there are underlying spots of various shades of " brownish drab " or " écru drab." The measurements of 123 eggs in the United States National Museum average 41 by 29.5 millimeters; the eggs showing the four extremes measure **46 by 32** and **37 by 27** millimeters.

Plumages.—The period of incubation is probably about 21 days. Both sexes incubate. The downy young of the Arctic tern may be distinguished from that of any other American tern by the black or dusky frontal space, which includes the lores and extends across the base of the bill. This dark area matches in color the dark-colored throat, which varies from "dusky drab" to nearly black. The breast is pure white, becoming more grayish posteriorly. The upper parts show at least two distinct color phases, both of which are sometimes found in one brood. In the brown phase the head, back, and wings vary from "cinnamon" to "pinkish buff." In the gray phase these parts are "pale drab gray" or "pale smoke gray," shading off gradually into the white or paler color of the under parts. In both phases the head is distinctly spotted and the back is heavily mottled or variegated with "fuscous" or black; the markings are usually blacker in the brown phase than in the gray. The plumage appears first on the wings and scapulars, then on the sides of the breast, and the last of the down is seen on the head.

The juvenal plumage is fully acquired by the time the young bird is fully grown. In this plumage the forehead and crown are grayish, the latter mottled with black, which increases on the auriculars and occiput to practically solid black. The back and wings are "deep gull gray," each feather of the back, scapulars, and wing-coverts being edged with pale buffy, with a subterminal dusky band and fine dusky sprinkling; these markings are most conspicuous on the scapulars. The tertials, secondaries, and inner primaries are broadly edged with white. There is considerable dusky and some pale buff near the ends of the tail feathers. The under parts are white, washed with pale brownish tints on the throat, breast, and sides. This plumage seems to be worn until the birds leave in September, but it is probably partially molted in the fall to produce the first winter plumage, which is similar to the adult. Subsequent molts and plumages are apparently similar to those of the common tern, including the *portlandica* plumage.]

Food.—The food of the arctic tern is the same as that of the other terns found in the same region, and consists chiefly of small fish, such as capelins, and sand eels or sand launces, and the fry of larger fish. Small crustaceans are also eaten. The method of capture is the same as in the case of the other terns. Scanning the water with down-turned head and bill from a height of 30 or 40 feet, this little tern falls with the speed of an arrow, strikes the water with a splash, and often disappears completely below the surface in order to capture its prey. As it rises from the water it shakes its plumage vigorously, and the fish may be seen hanging from the bill. Occasionally it throws the fish into the air either for pure fun or to get a better hold. Sometimes the tern drops the fish but catches it again before it has fallen more than a yard or two. The presence of the fish in the bill never interferes with the capacity of the bird to scream or cry out. In fact the fish bearer generally screams constantly as if to announce its success in the chase.

Behavior.—I have known them to fly directly at my head to within a few feet, when they suddenly swerve upwards. As they dart down they emit in their rage a rapidly repeated and vibratory *tut tut* or *kik, kik, kik,* followed by a piercing, screaming *tearr,* which is shriller than that of the common terns and ends in a rising inflection, which has been well characterized by Brewster (1883) as " sounding very like the squeal of a pig." He says " the bird also has a short, harsh note similar to that of Forster's tern." Grinnell (1900) says that the teasing cries of the young " closely resemble the usual note of the white-throated swift in California."

The Arctic tern, like the common tern, kittiwake, and others, is frequently harassed by the various species of jaegers, and after much twisting and turning is forced to drop the fish, which is at once snapped up by its pursuer. Although terns frequently quarrel among themselves, the various species often rest peaceably together. The former pernicious practices which led to the almost complete annihilation of terns for millinery purposes have already been described at length under the common tern. It is fortunate that these days of slaughter are passed. The increase of terns along the New England coast in the last 10 or 15 years has been very marked. In regions where game laws are but little understood or regarded the killing of such easy victims as terns still goes on. I have seen on the Labrador coast both common and Arctic terns that had been shot to feed captive black foxes.

Dutcher (1903) quotes Norton in regard to mortality among the young of the Arctic tern on the Maine coast as follows:

Abundant as they were living, I noticed quite an extensive mortality among the downy young, and their decaying bodies were scattered over the island. There was no visible cause, but two things suggested themselves—one an epidemic; the other that the damp, cold summer just passed had not supplied sufficient warmth and sunlight to keep them from being chilled.

In another place (1905) he quotes Capt. James Hall, of Matinicus Rock, Maine, as expressing " the belief that food is scarce and starvation is the cause of much death late in the summer." Palmer (1890) says:

In no other species of bird with whose breeding habits I am familiar has nature been so prodigal of life as in the case of the young terns on Funk Island. The surface of the granite rock of the island has been corroded by time and the elements to such a degree that many shallow depressions have been rotted as it were. These have been filled with water by the abundant rain and form veritable death traps to the young terns. Many of them leave the nest when a few days old and wander about. Numbers are thus lost among the rocks and drowned while trying to get back to their parents. This explanation seems to me to account for the numbers of dead young found in the pools.

It is possible, however, there may be some other explanation, for young terns are expert swimmers.

Breeding range.—Circumpolar. In North America, south on the Atlantic coast to Massachusetts (Muskeget Island); in the interior south to the Gulf of St. Lawrence (Magdalen Islands), southern Quebec (Point de Monts), southern Mackenzie (Great Slave Lake), southern Yukon (Pelly Lakes and Lake Tagish), and southeastern Alaska (Taku Inlet). The coasts and islands of Bering Sea south to the Aleutian and Commander Islands. North to the Arctic coasts of North America and in the Arctic Archipelago north to 82° north latitude in King Oscar Land, Grant Land, and northern Greenland. In the Eastern Hemisphere, north to 82° north latitude. South in Europe to 50° north latitude; and in Asia to 52° north latitude.

Breeding grounds protected in the following national reservations: In Alaska, Aleutian Islands, as Amchitka, Near Islands, Range Island, Semichi.

Winter range.—Antarctic Ocean, south to 74° south latitude, Weddell Sea, and probably Ross's Sea (off Victoria Land, 76° 52' S). Northern limit of winter range unknown.

Spring migration.—Northward along both coasts, often well out at sea. Early dates of arrival: Massachusetts, March 20 to 31; Davis Strait, 66° north, April 12; Wellington Channel, June 13; Greenland, 81° 30' north, June 16; Washington, Crescent Lake, April 15; Alaska, St. Michael, April 25 to May 16, and Demarcation Point, May 31.

Fall migration.—Southward over same routes. Early dates of arrival: California, Point Pinos, August 4; Peru, Santa Lucia, September 19; Chile, Arica, October 4; Argentina, Mar del Plata, October 21. Late dates of departure: Greenland, 81° 30' north, August 26, and Disco, September 5; Wellington Channel, August 29; Franklin, Winter Harbor, September 5; Keewatin, York Factory, August 28; Ungava, Koksoak River, September 15; New York, Saratoga, October 8; Massachusetts, Cape Cod, October 24 to November 9; Alaska, Point Barrow, September 9; British Columbia, Okanagan Landing, October.

Casual records.—Accidental in the interior, where records are none too well established. Wisconsin records (Lake Koshkonong, breeding, June 1891; Kelley Brook, September 21, 1897, and Milton, May 27, 1899) seem to be authentic. Recorded twice in Hawaii (May 9, 1891, and April 30, 1902).

Egg dates.—Northern Mackenzie: Thirty-two records, June 14 to July 16; sixteen records, June 23 to July 5. Maine and Nova Scotia: Twenty-six records, June 8 to July 21; thirteen records, June 15 to 23. Alaska: Twenty-two records, May 4 to July 1; eleven records, June 14 to 27.

STERNA DOUGALLI Montagu.

ROSEATE TERN.

HABITS.

I shall never forget the thrill of pleasure I experienced when I held in my hand, for the first time, a freshly killed roseate tern and admired with deepest reverence the delicate refinement of one of nature's loveliest productions. The softest colors of the summer sky were reflected on its back and pointed wings, while its breast glowed with the faint blush of some rare seashell. The graceful outlines, the spotless purity of its delicate plumage, and the long tapering tail feathers made it seem like some ethereal spirit of the heavens which it was sacrilege for human hands to touch.

Having been always intimately associated on our Atlantic coast with the common tern, it has suffered with that species in the persecution inflicted on these birds by hunters for the millinery trade. It was everywhere threatened with extermination, and became extirpated in many localities until its range was much restricted. It formerly bred as far east as Maine, and even Nova Scotia, as recently as in 1912, but I believe it is no longer common north of Cape Cod. It seems to have disappeared soon after 1890 from the coasts of New Jersey and Virginia, where it was once abundant. It has profited, however, from the protection afforded the terns in favored localities, and is now increasing on the Massachusetts coast and elsewhere.

Spring.—Audubon (1840) first saw this species in the Florida Keys, where he was told that it arrives about the 10th of April. Baird, Brewer, and Ridgway (1884) give the following interesting account of its arrival on Faulkner's Island in Long Island Sound:

It makes its appearance about the 15th of May, seldom varying three days from this date. At first six or eight of these birds are seen well up in the air. These hover over the island a while and then disappear. The next day the same individuals return, with an addition of 12 or more to their number; but none of them alight on the island until the third or fourth day. After this, if nothing disturbs them, their number increases very fast.

Its arrival on Muskeget Island, Massachusetts, is thus described by Mr. George H. Mackay (1895):

As far as I am aware *Sterna hirundo* and *S. dougalli* first make their appearance in Muskeget waters any time after the first week in May, and they are remarkably constant in the time of appearing. In 1892 they arrived on May 10, in flocks of fifty or more, drifting sideways before a heavy southeast rainstorm. In 1893 they arrived on May 8, with light air from the west-northwest and clear weather. Twenty were first observed hovering over South Point, Muskeget Island, very high in the air. About 5 o'clock p. m. two were observed to come quite low down. The next day they were arriving in considerable numbers, flying high during the day time and settling down after sunset. The weather was clear, with a light southwest wind. On the 10th, at sunrise, the Wilson's and roseate terns were rising in very large numbers from the northern-middle part of Muskeget proper, the weather being clear, with a strong southwest wind. On the 11th they continued to increase. There was a strong southwest gale during the night, dying out in the forenoon.

Courtship.—During the last week in May, while the countless hordes of terns are gathering on these breeding grounds, the roseate terns may be seen flying about in pairs or chasing each other in the air, with their long slender tail feathers streaming behind; or, in the dense flocks, resting and sunning themselves on the beach, their simple courtship may be seen. Both birds show their interest in each other by stretching their necks upward and strutting about with drooping wings and elevated tails; or standing side by side they exchange greetings. Finally the accepted suitor mounts his mate and stands squarely upon her back for a long time, with frequent interlocking of bills. The nuptial caress is most deliberate; and after it is over they stand close together, billing and cooing and preening each other's plumage.

Nesting.—The finest breeding colonies of roseate terns, so far as I know, are at Chatham and on Muskeget Island, Massachusetts. The most important of these is on Muskeget Island, a low sandy island lying between Nantucket and Marthas Vineyard, which has been more fully described under the common tern. On my various visits to this island I have always found roseate terns nesting here abundantly, although they have always been far outnumbered by the common tern. The nests of the common tern were scattered in various situations all over the island, and occasionally a few nests of roseate terns were found among them, but the main stronghold of the roseate terns was on the southern extremity of the island, separated from the main island by a long, narrow beach; here, except for a few scattering pairs of common terns, the whole population was made up of roseates. We determined this fact to our own satisfaction by trapping nine of the birds on their nests in snares made of very fine steel wire. This usually did not injure the birds at all, as we soon released them. The nests were closely congregated on the highest part of the point, particularly along the crest of a little ridge which rose abruptly from the beach. They were mostly well concealed in the thick growth of tall beach grass (*Ammophila arundinacea*), which grew luxuriantly at this end of the island. Some of the nests were hidden among the poison-ivy vines (*Rhus radicans*), or under the shade of herbaceous plants. Often the nests were arched over with the tall grass, having pathways leading to them, and almost always they were more or less under cover, in marked contrast to the nests of the common tern, which were always in open places. In many cases the eggs were laid on the bare sand, but generally a scanty nest was formed by scraping together a few pieces of dry grass or rubbish to partially line a slight hollow in the sand. The method we employed for identifying the nests is the only sure way in a locality like this; it is seldom possible to see one of the birds sitting on its nest; for, as Mr. Mackay (1895) says:

The alarm is given from bird to bird until it reaches those at the farthest end, who hasten to lend their vocal aid in driving off their common enemy, thus rendering it impossible to come to any conclusion regarding any particular nest and eggs. I have had roseates dart down at me and show every demonstration of anger and solicitude when I have been examining a Wilson's tern's nest and eggs, the identification of which I felt sure. I have also had the same experience with Wilson's tern as the assailant when I have been busy over a roseate's nest and eggs. It must not therefore always be assumed that the solicitous bird is the owner. As far as my observation shows I should say that not only do roseate and Wilson's terns lay their eggs indiscriminately at times in each other's nests, but also care for each other's young and make united battle against intruders.

On Penikese and Weepecket Islands the roseate terns nest mostly in the beach grass, poison ivy, and rank herbage on the higher parts of the islands, where their nests are well hidden. In the summer of 1915 I visited a large and populous colony, consisting of many thousand pairs of common and roseate terns, which had recently been established near the extremity of Nauset Beach, on the mainland of Cape Cod, near Chatham, Mass. This is probably an overflow from the Muskeget colony. Here the roseate terns were nesting under similar conditions to those noted on Muskeget, mainly on the ridges or sand dunes heavily overgrown with beach grass, but surrounded by common terns nesting in the open. On Faulkner's Island, in Long Island Sound, Baird, Brewer, and Ridgway (1884) say:

While some gather a few dry weeds or a little dry seaweed, others make only a hollow in the sand; and some deposit their eggs on the stones without any nest at all.

Audubon (1840) found them breeding in considerable numbers along the shores of southern Florida. He writes:

At different times in the course of nearly three months which I spent among the keys I saw flocks of 20, 30, or more pairs, breeding on small detached rocky islands, scantily furnished with grass, and in the company of hundreds of Sandwich terns. The two species appeared to agree well together, and their nests were intermingled. The full number of eggs of the present species is three. * * * They were deposited on the bare rocks, among the roots of the grasses, and left in fair weather to the heat of the sun. Like those of the common tern and other species they are delicious eating. The eggs of the Sandwich tern were more attended to during the day, but toward night both species sat on their eggs.

In the Bahamas and West Indies they seem to nest in open situations, with Cabot's and Sooty terns, laying their eggs in hollows in the sand, on bare ground, or on rocks without any attempt at concealment or at nest building.

Eggs.—Some observers suggest that the roseate and common terns raise two broods in a season; fresh eggs are often found late in August, but these are probably laid by birds that have failed to raise their first broods. The usual set consists of two eggs; three are frequently found in a nest and rarely four. The larger sets often, though not always, show evidence of having been deposited by more than one bird.

The eggs of the roseate tern are similar to, and often indistinguishable from, those of the other small terns; but when a large series is compared with others the average difference is well marked. They will average a trifle longer and the markings are smaller and more evenly distributed, with fewer of the large bold markings when compared with a series of eggs of the common tern. There is less variation in the ground color, which ranges from " cream buff " to " cartridge buff " or " pale olive buff." The darker and richer colors of other terns' eggs are seldom, if ever, seen in this species. A majority of the eggs are evenly sprinkled with small spots or dots over the entire surface, either with or without an occasional larger spot; these spots are seldom large enough to be called blotches and never as large and conspicuous as they are on the eggs of the common tern. These markings are in the darker shades of brown from " warm sepia " to " dark clove brown." There are often numerous spots of various shades of violet, plumbeous or lavender gray, underlying the darker markings. In shape the eggs vary from ovate to elongate ovate, usually quite pointed. The shell is smooth, thin, and without luster. The measurements of 87 eggs, in the United States National Museum, average 42 by 30 millimeters; the eggs showing the four extremes measure **45.5** by 31, 43.5 by **32, 38** by 30, and 44 by **27.5** millimeters.

The exact period of incubation was found to be 21 days by Prof. Lynds Jones (1906), who has also given us (1903) a good account of the process, as follows:

In two cases that were under careful observation for some time both parents performed the office of incubation in regular turn. The one that I judged to be the female brooded the eggs, tucking them carefully under her feathers, but the male merely stood above them, apparently shielding them from the burning sun, while the female went for a lunch and bath. The incoming bird uttered a peculiar rattling sound just before alighting some 20 feet from the nest, when the brooding bird got up and immediately flew away. The relief carelessly sauntered toward the nest, made believe picking up food when it reached the nest, then stood over it a moment before settling down, if the female. Neither bird remained on the nest over an hour; the male usually less than 40 minutes, not waiting for the female to appear every time before leaving.

Young.—In the same paper Mr. Jones gives us the results of his observations on the behavior of the young terns in the following words:

There is no uniformity in the development of the instinct to assume protective attitudes. With some young there is no evidence of such an instinct while they remain in the nest, while with others there seems to be almost as soon as the shell is cast. All of the young from the beginning of the pinfeathers gave evidence of the instinct well developed. Some young left the nest two days after hatching; some remained for four days. When partly feathered birds on the uplands were taken from their hiding places in the grass or bushes their tendency was to try to run away instead of hiding again when replaced on the ground. Those on the beach treated the same way would invariably take to the water if not prevented. Even the young upon which the pinfeathers were barely showing frequently took to the water and swam readily. In hiding the birds were content to emulate the ostrich, hiding only the head and often leaving the whole body exposed. They were always careful, however, to keep the white underparts well concealed.

Unlike the gulls, the terns do not swallow the food and then regurgitate for the young, but carry the fish in the beak directly to the young. After studying the feeding process at close range for some time I became convinced that the old birds do not stuff the fish down the throat of the young, but only thrust its head into the mouth far enough for the throat muscles to grip it, when the young bird swallows for himself. The sand launce (*Ammodytes americanus*) was the chief fish food, probably because it is so soft and easily digested. A 4-inch fish could not manage to get wholly inside a 4-inch bird, so the tail was left sticking out for future consumption. Even with the young able to fly the fish's head rested in the primitive gizzard, while the tail was scarcely more than concealed in the throat. Mr. Field induced one Muskeget young common tern to part with his dinner of two young herrings and one sand launce. Usually but a single fish was found in the digestive tract of the young.

The downy young merely raised their heads and opened their mouths for food, when very hungry uttering a faint peep, but the young ones able to fly were made to dance for their dinner. With widely gaping mouth and wings held akimbo, they executed a surprisingly fine clog to their own piercing music. In one case a young bird called for lunch just 20 minutes after receiving a good-sized fish. He was not fed, however, until half an hour after his last lunch. I have repeatedly seen the old birds swallow three and four sand launces in rapid succession. This colony of 1,500 old birds and their 1,500 young must consume great quantities of the sand launce, yet the supply does not seem to diminish.

It was interesting to watch the old birds come in with a fish dangling from the beak. As it passed close along the beach each young bird in turn clamored for the morsel. When the old bird approached the place where its young had been last seen it skimmed above the stones, halting now and then before a particularly vociferous youngster, then either passed on or circled back to look farther, finally either finding its own young or going to another place where another young had been left. I was eager to know how the old birds could recognize their own offspring among the multitude which looked exactly alike to me. It seemed incredible that they depended upon sight, or why should they almost actually touch the young each time before deciding the matter? I was forced to the conclusion that the sense of smell must play an important part in the final determination.

Later in the season young birds were seen following the old birds to where they fished, all the while loudly calling for food. I was prepared to see the morsel delivered while the birds were still flying, after the manner of the swallow, but it was never so done. The young, at least, must first rest upon the water or land, then the old usually settled for the moment of the delivery, the young bird, first shaking his feathers well before rising and following. During the second week in August young birds were to be seen and heard about Great Harbor and Penzance, but none appeared to be fishing for themselves. Up to this time, there appeared no evidence that either the old or young had begun to molt.

Plumages.—The downy young of the roseate tern can be readily distinguished from the young of the other species, with which it is associated, by certain well-marked characters. Its general appearance is more grizzly, more finely and evenly sprinkled with smaller spots, whereas the young common and arctic terns are more boldly spotted with a more conspicuous pattern. The texture of the down is more hair-like, particularly on the heads, necks, and throats of the younger birds. In this respect and in the texture of the down on the back there is a striking resemblance to the young chick of the royal tern. In the newly hatched chick the downy feathers of the back and wings stand out separately, round and fluffy at the base, but tapering to a fine point at the tip. There are at least two distinct color phases in the downy young, brown and gray; in the brown phase the color varies from " pinkish buff " or " cream buff " in the youngest birds, to " cinnamon buff " or " chamois " in older birds; in the gray phase the color varies from " pallid neutral gray " to " pale neutral gray "; in both phases the upper parts, including the throat, sides of the neck, and flanks, are uniformly and thickly spotted with small spots of " dark neutral gray " or dull black. Only the central under parts are white. The dusky throat of the young common tern is replaced by a pale grayish area or one uniform in color with the upper parts. Another distinctive character is the color of the feet; whereas in young common and arctic terns these are in light shades of flesh color, reddish, or orange, in the young roseate they are much darker, " russet vinaceous " in the youngest, to " sorghum brown " or " Hay's brown " in older birds, and finally darkening to dull black in large downies and juvenals.

The first plumage appears on the scapulars when the young bird is half grown. In the brown phase this is a rich " clay color "; in the gray phase it is pale buff. The wings are the next to become feathered. The juvenal, or first, plumage is unlike that of the common tern; it is more boldly and conspicuously marked with black and white; the feathers of the back, scapulars, and tertials are subterminally barred with brownish black or heavily marked with U-shaped or V-shaped spots of the same; the scapulars and tertials have several such markings or a variegated pattern of them. When the plumage is fresh these feathers are broadly margined or tipped with "pinkish buff," but this color fades out to white. Often these buffy areas are finely sprinkled with dusky; the outer tail feather on each side is unmarked, but the others are more or less dusky near the tips. In the juvenal plumage young roseate terns have faintly rosy breasts and black or blackish feet, whereas in young common terns the breasts are white and the feet pale flesh color or dull reddish. The change into the first winter plumage, early in the fall, is accomplished by a partial molt of the body feathers. Early in the spring a complete prenuptial molt takes place, at which all of the mottled feathers disappear, the black cap is assumed, and most young birds become indistinguishable from adults. I have never seen a "*portlandica*" plumage in this species.

Adults have a complete postnuptial molt in August and September, or later, at which the adult winter plumage is acquired; the rosy breast is replaced by white and the white forehead is assumed. They also have a complete prenuptial molt in the early spring which produces the full nuptial plumage.

Food.—In the swift tide rips about the sandy shoals, where the voracious bluefish drive the small fry to the surface in great schools, the terns find a fruitful feeding ground, for the little fish in their attempts to escape from their enemies below only betray themselves to the hungry birds above as they huddle together and skip along the surface in their fright. Here the terns gather in excited throngs and turn the tables by showing the fishermen where to troll for bluefish. In return the fishermen shoot the birds for their plumage or rob them of their eggs. So the struggle for existence goes on, and the weakest individual—in this case the tiny minnow—always gets the worst of it, for at best he can only "jump from the frying pan into the fire." Mr. William Brewster (1879) has well described it as follows:

It is an interesting sight to watch the birds collect. A moment before perhaps only a few were to be seen, leisurely winnowing their way along the shore; but in an incredibly short space of time the lucky discoverer of a school is surrounded by hundreds of his fellows, and a perfect swarm of eager, hungry birds poises over the spot. Dozens dash down at once, cleaving the water like darts, and, rising again into the air, shake the salt spray from their feathers by a single energetic movement, and make ready for a fresh plunge. Every bird among them is screaming his shrillest, and the excitement waxes fast and furious. Beneath, the bluefish are making the water boil by their savage rushes, and there is fun and profit for all save the unfortunate prey.

The food of the roseate tern consists almost wholly of small fishes, but Audubon (1840) found them feeding also on "a kind of small molluscous animal which floats near the surface, and bears the name of ' sailor's button.' " Professor Jones (1903) identified the following species of fishes dropped on their breeding grounds:

Sand launce (*Ammodytes americanus*), cunner (*Tautogolabrus adsperus*), mullet (*Mugil curema*), pollock (*Pollachius virens*), flounder (*Pseudopleuronectes americanus*), and young herring (species not determined). Of all the food the sand launce comprised not less than 80 per cent.

Behavior.—The flight of the roseate tern is exceedingly light and graceful; it is the greyhound of its tribe, the longest, slenderest, and most highly specialized of the terns. As it floats along, with its long tail feathers streaming out behind, it seems to cleave the air with the greatest ease and swiftness, like a slender-pointed arrow. Its downward plunges into the water for its prey are swift and accurate; it often goes beneath the surface and generally emerges with a tiny minnow in its bill. Its shape and movements will generally serve to identify it, and if near enough, its black bill is a good field mark.

Its voice, however, is the surest means of identification, for it is entirely unlike that of the other terns with which it associates. Its alarm note seems entirely out of keeping with its grace and beauty of form and color, for it is harsh and grating, a prolonged rasping cry, like the syllables " kreck " or " crack " or " kraak," louder and on a lower key than the cries of other terns. Mr. Brewster (1879) has likened this note of excitement or anger to the sound made " by forcibly tearing a strong piece of cotton cloth." He also observes that its usual note is " a soft mellow hew-it, repeated at frequent intervals," which I have recorded in my notes as " kulick," a musical note heard on its breeding grounds when undisturbed. This is usually in soft conversational tones, mingled with a variety of cackling, chattering, and gurgling notes.

The roseate tern is intimately associated on its breeding grounds with the common tern, the laughing gull, the Cabot's tern, and the sooty tern in different portions of its range, all of which species seem to live with it in reasonable peace and harmony. It is generally a peaceful and harmless neighbor, even friendly and sympathetic at times in helping to care for the young of others. At other times it seems to be very pugnacious, attacking and severely mauling a strange young one which wanders too near its own young, or quarreling with other adults of its own or other species. On Muskeget its chief enemy used to be the short-eared owl, a pair of which lived on the island and raised havoc among the terns; the owls were finally killed, however, in the cause of bird protection. Cats have been brought to the island, where they did so much damage that they, too, were removed. Marsh hawks and crows occasionally visit the islands and probably kill some young terns.

Fall.—By the first or middle of August, when the young birds have been taught to fly and fish for themselves, both old and young birds begin to move away from their breeding grounds and wander about the coasts and islands in search of food, often straying far north of their breeding haunts at this season. They often congregate in large flocks, following the schools of small fish, resting and roosting on the sand beaches and sand bars. Their time for departure for the south depends on the food supply, but they usually begin to disappear in October and before the end of the month are all gone. They are said to follow the schools of bluefish, or, at least, to disappear with them. Their fall migration carries them beyond the limits of the United States to their winter quarters in the Bahamas, the West Indies, and the coasts of South America.

DISTRIBUTION.

Breeding range.—In North America, along the Atlantic coast from Nova Scotia (Sable and Noddy Islands) locally to New York (Long Island and vicinity); Florida (Tortugas); formerly in New Jersey and Virginia. Bermuda and Bahama Islands (Acklin, Eleuthera, etc.), the Lesser Antilles (Antigua, Guadeloupe, Dominica, Grenada, etc.), and westward to Venezuela (Aruba Island) and British Honduras. In the Eastern Hemisphere on the coasts of the North Sea and Atlantic Ocean from 57° north latitude to the Mediterranean, the Azores, Madeira, the coasts of Africa, Madagascar, Ceylon, and southern China. The Australian bird has been described as a distinct subspecies.

Breeding grounds protected in the following national reservation: In Florida, Tortugas Islands.

Winter range.—From the Bahama Islands, Cuba, and occasionally Louisiana, southward to Brazil; and from southern Mexico (Tehuantepec) to Chile.

Spring migration.—Arrives in Bermuda from April 29 to May 1; Massachusetts, Muskeget, May 8 to 10; Connecticut, Faulkner's Island, May 15.

Fall migration.—Leaves Bermuda in September and Massachusetts about October 1. Other migration data seems to be lacking; probably the migration occurs well off the coast.

Casual records.—Accidental inland as far north as New York (Youngstown, May 31, 1886) and as far west as Indiana (Millers, August 14, 1916).

Egg dates.—Massachusetts: Thirty-one records, June 2 to August 15; sixteen records, June 15 to July 6. Bahamas and Florida Keys: Eight records, April 30 to June 12; four records, May 16 to 21.

HABITS.

The type specimen of this unique species was secured by Bischoff, on Kodiak Island, on June 12, 1868, together with a single egg. It has apparently not been found breeding there since and has not even been seen there in recent years. The name Aleutian tern is a misnomer, based on an erroneous theory that it would be found breeding among those islands; but none of the various explorers who have visited that region have succeeded in finding it. It was not heard of again until Mr. L. M. Turner (1886) found it breeding near St. Michael, Alaska, in 1875 and 1876. Dr. E. W. Nelson (1887) was still more successful in adding to our knowledge of this rare species. During his "residence at St. Michael he found these birds to be regular and common summer residents in certain restricted localities where they nested. They extend their range to the head of Norton Bay, and also reach the Siberian coast of Bering Straits, as shown by their presence in St. Lawrence Bay, where Mr. R. L. Newcomb, naturalist of the *Jeannette*, found them in 1879." Practically nothing has been added since that time to our meager knowledge of the habits and distribution of this rare species, which seemed to have such a restricted habitat. Col. John E. Thayer has recently shown me 11 specimens of Aleutian terns collected on Sakhalin Island, on the east coast of Siberia, on June 23 and 24, 1914, which were probably breeding birds. This tends to confirm a theory which I have long held that the Aleutian tern is an Asiatic species which has extended its breeding range across Bering Straits, as several other species have done, and become temporarily or permanently established at a few isolated spots on the Alaskan coast. The Kodiak colony was evidently unsuccessful, but the two colonies near St. Michael have persisted up to the present day (1915) as permanent outposts, one containing about 20 pairs and one about 40 pairs of breeding birds.

Spring.—According to Doctor Nelson (1887), the Aleutian terns reach St. Michael from May 20 to 30, rarely earlier than the first date, and are found scattered along the coast, in company with the Arctic tern, for a short time, but early in June they gather about the islands where they nest. One of these islands is about a mile from St. Michael, in the mouth of a tide channel known as the "canal." This island is nearly half a mile across, rises about 30 feet from the beach in a sharp incline, and has a rather level top, covered with a thick mat of grass, moss, and other vegetation. The upland is dry, and here the birds breed, laying their eggs directly upon the moss, with no attempt at a lining, which would be entirely unnecessary there. Some 18 miles to the eastward, along the coast, and less than a mile from the Eskimo village of Kegikhtowik, is another island in a bay, presenting almost the same characteristics as the one first described, and upon the higher portions the birds nest even more commonly, for, as against the 20 pairs or so nesting on the first island, some 30 or 40 pairs occupied the latter island both seasons when it was visited by the writer. From the proximity of native villages, and owing to the persecution received at the hands of Turner and myself, the birds on these islands were very shy, and it was no easy task to secure specimens.

Nesting.—While passing through St. Michael on July 8, 1914, my assistant, Mr. Hersey, secured two specimens of Aleutian terns, and again on July 17, 1915, he succeeded in collecting a small series of these interesting birds near the island referred to above. I had sent him there again in 1915 to spend the whole summer in the vicinity of St. Michael. His several visits to the island at the mouth of the canal resulted in his securing several sets of eggs, mostly sets of two, taken on June 23 and 28 and July 3. His notes state:

The island where the Aleutian terns breed rises rather abruptly from the water to a height of about 25 feet and then spreads out broad and fairly level. At one end are several small ponds, and here it is lower than at other places. The higher parts are covered with a mat of dry grass of last year's growth, through which the new green blades are now appearing. In this matted grass the terns are now nesting, not in a compact colony, but scattered about in single pairs. Although apparently nesting anywhere over this space, the nests are in reality placed rather near the edge of the island, and in most cases the sitting bird could look out over the water. I found no nests in the center of the island. Among this tangle of dry grass are interspersed patches of a soft gray moss which grows close to the ground. These patches vary from 1 or 2 feet in diameter to several yards in size. In these patches of moss the nests are generally made, the small ones being selected as the near-by grass affords some concealment. None were found among the larger patches. One nest was found on a mound of rotten wood, where a log of driftwood had decayed. The nest is a depression in the moss 3 or 4 inches across and about 1½ inches deep, and is unlined. Two eggs appear to complete the set.

While walking over the island the birds circled high overhead, and nothing in their actions disclosed the location of any of their nests. They seldom came very near even when a nest was found, but one pair of birds darted down close to my head as I neared their nest. When I first landed on the island where the terns were nesting the birds began to fly up out of the grass, and by marking the spot from which they rose a nest could generally be found. Although but slightly concealed I found the nest exceedingly hard to find, and it took an average of an hour to locate each one.

Eggs.—Mr. Hersey's experience would seem to indicate that two eggs constitute the normal set; probably three eggs are rarely laid, and occasionally only one. Several sets of three eggs each, collected on Stuart Island by Capt. H. H. Bodfish, are probably eggs of the Arctic tern. Some of these that I have seen do not show any of the well-marked characteristics of Aleutian tern's eggs. Moreover, Mr. Hersey, who spent considerable time on Stuart Island, says that it is not at all suited for the breeding requirements of the Aleutian tern, and that none breed there, though the Arctic tern does breed there.

I believe that the series of eggs collected by Mr. Hersey are the only authentic eggs of the Aleutian tern in existence outside of those collected for the United States National Museum referred to above. These eggs vary in shape from ovate to elongate ovate, with a decided tendency toward the latter. The shell is thin, with very little luster. The ground color varies from "clay color" or "honey yellow" to "olive buff" or "Marguerite yellow." In a general way, they are not only more elongated, but darker and more richly colored than other tern's eggs. They are usually heavily marked with large blotches and smaller spots, scattered irregularly over the egg or coalesced into longitudinal splashes or in a wreath near the larger end. These markings consist of underlying spots or splashes of various shades of drab, from "deep brownish drab" to "pallid brownish drab," overlaid with bold and handsome blotches and spots of the darker and richer shades of brown, such as "Mars brown," "Vandyke brown," and "light seal brown." The measurements of 44 eggs, in the United States National Museum and the writer's collections, average 42 by 29 millimeters; the eggs showing the four extremes measure **46.7** by 30, 45 by **30.5**, and **40** by **27.5** millimeters.

Young.—Only one brood is raised in a season, and, according to Mr. Hersey's experience, no second attempt to raise a brood is made if the first eggs are taken. Mr. Turner (1886) gives the period of incubation as 17 days, but this is evidently an error, as the common and roseate terns are known to have an incubation period of 21 days. Doctor Nelson (1887) says:

The eggs are rarely laid before June 5 or 10, and I found one egg with an embryo two-third grown on September 1, but this is very unusual. The young of *aleutica* are hatched from the last of June until September, and the first ones are on the wing by the last of July.

Speaking of the second island, referred to above, near St. Michael, he writes:

On September 1, 1879, I visited the island near Kegikhtowik and found from 60 to 80 adults of this species haunting the vicinity and circling in graceful flight all about the island. When we landed and passed over the island the birds showed considerable anxiety and continually uttered a thin, clear, thrilling whistle. With the exception of some broken eggshells and the old depressions showing the nesting sites, nothing but a single egg was found there; but as we walked out on a low cape, covered with large scattered rocks, we put up, one after the other, a considerable number of young birds just able to fly, and a goodly number were secured. When they arose they had a queer, erratic, dazed kind of flight, reminding me of the flight of an owl suddenly disturbed in the daytime. The old birds kept flying in toward the point with small fishes in their beaks, but although we concealed ourselves in the rocks others of the party evidently warned them, so that only two or three of the adults were taken. One young bird was fired at and missed and flew wildly out to sea, when it was joined by an old bird, which kept close to it, and as the young bird became tired and turned toward shore the parent met it and forced it to turn back. This maneuver was repeated over a dozen times, until the young bird was forced off to sea out of sight. This was one of the most striking instances of bird sagacity I met with in the north.

Plumages.—Doctor Nelson (1887) describes the downy young as follows:

The downy young of this species appear to be distinguishable from the young of all other species. The color above is a grayish buff profusely blotched with black. The black of the chin and throat extends somewhat to the upper portion of the breast. The breast is pure white, shading into a very dark gray on the belly and sides. There is considerable difference in individual specimens, some being of a light buff above. As compared with the downy young of *paradisaea* from Labrador, these birds are darker above, buff instead of a light fulvous, and with more black blotching. The black of the under parts in *paradisaea* is limited to the chin and throat, while the belly is of a much lighter color.

He says further:

The young in any stage may be readily distinguished from the young of *paradisaea* by the deeply cleft toe-web, whereas the web of the latter is nearly full.

August birds, in fresh juvenal plumage, have the crown " fawn color" or " wood brown" mottled with blackish, more thickly posteriorly; the sides of the neck and chest are washed with paler shades of the same; the feathers of the back, scapulars, and lesser wing-coverts are dark " sepia," broadly edged with " cinnamon buff," which is most conspicuous and brightest on the larger scapulars; the secondaries are broadly tipped with white, making a conspicuous wing band; the rump is ashy, not white, as in the Arctic tern; the tail feathers are broadly tipped with " cinnamon buff" beyond a subterminal dusky area; the under parts are white. These colors become paler with age and probably the buff edgings fade out to white or wear away during the fall.

Unfortunately we have no material for study in our collections which illustrates anything but the juvenal and the fully adult breeding plumages, so we can only guess at the subsequent molts and plumages. No birds in immature spring plumage have ever been taken on the breeding grounds, which shows that the young birds do not breed during the first spring or that the full plumage is acquired by that time; probably the latter is the case.

Food.—There seems to be no data on the food or feeding habits of the Aleutian tern, but probably it does not differ materially in this respect from the Arctic tern with which it seems to be intimately associated.

Behavior.—Regarding the appearance of the Aleutian tern in life, Mr. Hersey says that it can be distinguished from the Arctic tern by its darker color, the under parts, including the wing linings, appearing lead-colored. The white forehead is seldom noticeable in flight, except at short range, when the black bill and black feet can be seen. The body appears to be heavier, the wing strokes slower, and the whole bird larger. It habitually flies at a higher elevation above the ground or water, usually above gun range. A wounded bird gives the characteristic, harsh tern cries which serves to draw its companions down nearer the ground. The birds thus attracted seldom hover over their fallen comrade, but swoop down near him, then pass and mount upward again.

Mr. Turner (1886) says:

The note of this bird differs from that of *S. paradisaea* in that the " squay " is weaker and squeaky. The other note is like *twe-e-e-e* prolonged, and is really distinguishable from the harsher " squay " of the *S. paradisaea*.

Mr. Hersey records the ordinary note as a three-syllable whistle, suggesting a shore-bird's call rather than the harsh, grating *tee-ar-r-r* so characteristic of other terns.

After collecting the eggs mentioned above, Mr. Hersey left the terns to lay again and hatch out broods of young, but evidently they did not do so, or, if they did, their plans for rearing young were frustrated by a short-eared owl which he found living on the island; whether the owl had destroyed the young or had so persecuted the old birds that they did not lay again is a question.

Fall.—Not much is known about the fall migration or the winter home of the Aleutian tern. Mr. Nelson (1887) says:

The old birds stray along the coast after the 1st of July and until about the middle of September, after which none are seen until the following season.

Where they go is a mystery, certainly not down the Pacific coast of North America; probably they retreat to their Asiatic home, whence they extended their range to Alaska and migrate down the coast to Japan, and perhaps much farther south or west.

DISTRIBUTION.

Breeding range.—Known to breed only on two small islands in Norton Sound, Alaska, near St. Michael and near Kegikhtowik. Probably breeds on or near Saghalin Island, in the Sea of Okhotsa, Siberia, where birds were taken in June. Once bred on Kodiak

Winter range.—Unknown. Recorded in northern Japan (off Island, Alaska.

Yezo).

Spring migration.—Arrives at St. Michael, May 20 to 30.

Fall migration.—Leaves St. Michael about the middle of September.

Eggs dates.—Alaska (St. Michael) : Five records, June 23 to 28.

STERNA ANTILLARUM (Lesson).

LEAST TERN.

HABITS.

Clearly impressed upon my mind is a vivid picture of a peaceful summer scene in a remote corner of Cape Cod; a broad, flat sandy point stretched for a mile or more out into the sea; the deep blue ocean with its cooling breezes made a pleasing contrast to the glaring white sands which reflected the heat of the midday sun; scattered about on the sandy plain around me were the little hollows containing the eggs of the least tern, almost invisible among the pebbles, bits of shells, and small stones, which they resembled so closely; and overhead the air was full of the graceful, flitting forms of this little " sea swallow," darting down at me, with sharp cries of anxiety, or soaring far aloft until they were lost to sight in the ethereal blue of a cloudless sky. Such a picture as this was a common sight, in those days, anywhere along the Atlantic coast from Massachusetts to Florida, where the least tern was widely distributed and very abundant in all suitable localities. But its graceful form and delicate plumage was so much in demand for the millinery trade that it was practically extirpated in nearly all places where it was easily accessible, leaving only a delightful memory of a joy that had passed. It was never particularly shy and was easily killed on its breeding grounds, its social and sympathetic habits making it a simple matter to practically annihilate a whole colony in a single season.

Numerous colonies formerly existed on the southern coasts of New England. Mr. William Brewster (1879) wrote that " formerly a small colony of least terns nested annually upon the Ipswich sand hills, but they have been entirely driven away by persecution," but since that time they have not been found breeding north of Cape Cod. Mr. John C. Cahoon (1890) wrote:

Not a day passes in the summer that the fishermen about this island do not patrol the beach in search of the tern's and piping plover's eggs. The birds have no chance to breed. When I first visited the island about six years ago there were several hundred pairs of least tern breeding, but they have now become reduced to less than 25 pair.

This and other Massachusetts colonies were practically annihilated during the next few years, but a few small colonies have always survived on the south coast of Martha's Vineyard, though they became much reduced in numbers. On the much-frequented beaches, near the summer resorts, the birds were shot and their eggs were picked up by boys; cats undoubtedly did their part in the extermination; and occasionally a whole colony was washed out by an extra high tide. During recent years, since 1905, the least terns have been slowly increasing in Massachusetts; they are now breeding again in several places where they had been entirely extirpated, on the mainland as well as on the islands.

In Wilson's time the least terns bred abundantly on the New Jersey coast. During his whole stay on the Cape May beaches they flew in clouds around him. Mr. G. S. Morris says, writing of the same spot in 1881, in some notes sent to Dr. Witmer Stone (1909):

The least terns bred in considerable numbers. and were equally vociferous in their protests against intruders. It is difficult, at this late date (1909), to give an estimate of numbers, but I can remember standing in one spot and seeing five or six nests within a radius of 15 or 20 feet; but my recollections are that these conditions only pertained to an acre or so of the beach. In the summer of 1884, in July, I could find no least tern's eggs, and natives told me they no longer found eggs on the beach. During the period 1881–1886 I saw a good deal of the slaughter of the birds in this region. I remember coming upon two professional millinery gunners, I think in the summer of 1885, who had two piles about knee-high of least and common terns, which they said they were sending to New York, my recollection being that they got 12 cents apiece for the birds.

Dr. Witmer Stone (1909), writing of the conditions in 1908, says:

Mr. H. G. Parker in 1888 estimated that there were only 30 pairs left on Seven Mile Beach, and Mr. Philip Laurent (1892) says that some still breed there. Since then we have no definite breeding record, but Mr. W. L. Baily saw two birds together at Stone Harbor, July 15, 1899, which he felt sure were nesting.

Since that time least terns have increased in numbers all along the coast where protected.

The most pitiful tale of destruction is the story of the Cobb's Island and other colonies on the coast of Virginia. Mr. H. B. Bailey (1876), in writing of the nesting habits of the least tern, or " little striker," on Cobb's Island in 1875, says:

Colonies of about 50 pairs each of this species extend the whole length of the island at about a distance of 1 mile apart.

Least terns were astonishingly abundant all along the Virginia coast at that time, but during the next decade their destruction was appalling. Professional collectors for the millinery trade spent the greater part of the breeding season on the islands and killed the innocent birds in almost incredible numbers. The resident fishermen and oystermen also found it a lucrative occupation. As many as 1,200 birds were often killed in a day, and one of the residents, who had taken part in the slaughter himself, told me that as many as 100,000 terns were sometimes killed in a season. Mr. William H. Fisher (1897), writing of conditions in 1891, says:

When I first went to the island about 28 years ago the least, common, and Forster's terns nested there in colonies of thousands, but now few of them breed and the least is seldom seen. During four days on the island in May, 1891, I only saw one of the latter, and it was as wild as an oystercatcher, which is a very wild bird. The royal tern also nested on the island at one time.

The least terns disappeared entirely during the next 10 years. Dr.
Frank M. Chapman (1903) visited Cobb's Island in 1902 to gather
material for his habitat group, and found them entirely gone. He
says of their destruction:

The former captain of the life-saving station told me of 1,400 least terns being
killed in one day; while the present captain of the station and Mr. E. B. Cobb,
owner of the island, informed me that when terns were first killed for millinery
purposes they, with another man, killed 2,800 birds in three days on and near
Cobb's Island. The birds were packed in cracked ice and shipped to New York
for skinning, 10 cents being paid for each one.

The least terns were reported as increasing again in 1905, but when
I visited the island during the height of the breeding season in 1907
I failed to see a single bird of this species.

The colonies on the coasts of North and South Carolina were not
completely annihilated, but they were greatly reduced in numbers.
Mr. Arthur T. Wayne (1910) says:

Hunters came from the north with regular outfits to wage war against these
poor, defenceless creatures, and in one season alone all of these terns breeding
on Bull's Island were killed.

In Florida the same cruel work of destruction was systematically
conducted. Mr. W. E. D. Scott (1887) thus describes the methods
employed:

About 4 o'clock this afternoon a "sharpie" schooner, some 45 feet in length,
came from the direction of Big Gasparilla Pass and anchored within 200 feet
of us. The crew to the number of four at once went on the beach, and from
the time they landed until dark there was a perfect fusilade. Going over to see
what they were doing I found that they were killing all kinds of shore birds
and least terns. One of the men told me that this was Mr. Batty's boat, and
that they were collecting birds for the "plume market"; that Mr. Batty was
down the beach shooting and would be back for supper. They had bunches of
Wilson's plover (breeding), least terns, and various kinds of sandpipers. These
birds are skinned, partly filled out with cotton, and at once wrapped up in
paper and packed away to be finished after reaching the north. They were
killing and preparing by these methods, during the time I was near Mr. Batty's
party, from 100 to 150 birds a day. I called on Mr. Batty later in the evening
and learned something of his work.

Spring.—Mr. William Brewster (1879) has written the following attractive account of the arrival of the terns on their breeding
grounds:

Spring comes over the sea later than upon the land, and fewer tokens are
given of its presence. There is no freshening grass; no budding foliage, nor
springing up of green things in sheltered places. Summer may be close at
hand, but as yet the sea gives no sign. When the wind is from the north the
waves in the bay have that steely glint that they have borne all winter. The
sand drifts drearily over the wind-swept beach ridges, and the marshes are
black and brown, while in the interior robins may be hopping about upon
green lawns and violets blooming in every woodland nook. The ducks and
geese, it is true, are marshaling their cohorts and stretching out in long lines

northward, but the breath of ocean is still chill and cold. Indeed, the season is commonly far advanced and the apple orchards in bloom inland ere the winter gulls are gone to their distant breeding grounds. Scarcely has the rear-guard of their legions departed, when the terns begin to appear.

The least terns, although the smallest and seemingly the most delicate of their tribe, arrive first. By the middle of May they appear in certain favored spots—for they are not anywhere very numerous—and small colonies of from 10 to 50 pairs are soon formed at various points along the shores of Cape Cod and upon some of the more sandy islands in the Vineyard Sound.

Nesting.—The localities usually selected by the least tern for nesting are broad, flat, open sand beaches, entirely devoid of vegetation, where there are more or less small stones and bits of shells scattered about, among which the eggs are quite difficult to detect. The eggs are usually laid well above the reach of the ordinary high tides, but occasionally the combination of a heavy gale with the spring tides will result in the washing out of a whole colony. This has occurred several times on the south shore of Marthas Vineyard, where the beaches are low and much exposed. Whereas other terns almost always nest on islands, the least tern frequently breeds on suitable beaches on the mainland if they are not too near human habitations. The depredations of cats, rats, or small boys will drive them away from much frequented beaches.

In the northern portion of its range, at least, these terns usually select a section of beach somewhat apart from other species, though they often associate to some extent with piping plovers. In the Carolinas they are found breeding among or near the common terns and black skimmers. The nest is merely a small hollow scooped in the sand, in which usually two eggs are laid, occasionally three, and very rarely four; the larger numbers are more frequent northward and less so southward.

On May 8, 1903, I found a small breeding colony of least terns on Lake Key, one of the Florida Keys, a low, flat island, with sandy or shelly beaches, frequented by migrating shore birds. Beyond a narrow strip of low mangroves, just above the beach, we came upon a small, shallow, muddy pond, where a small but very noisy colony of black-necked stilts were breeding. The least terns' nests, about 40 of them, were on a narrow strip of beach on the shore of this pond, and consisted of little hollows in the sand, or finely broken shells, of which the beach was composed. Most of the nests contained two eggs, some only one, and those that we collected were all fresh. The nests were strung along in a row a few feet apart. A few pairs of Wilson's plover were breeding on the beaches and among the small mangrove bushes. In the Florida Keys and West Indies the eggs of the least tern are gathered for food. The bird is locally known there by a variety of names, such as "killing peter," "kill-em polly," and "sand peter."

There are a few small breeding colonies of least terns in the reservations on the coast of Louisiana. In the lower Mississippi Valley there are a few colonies breeding on low, sandy islands in the Mississippi and Missouri Rivers, where their nesting is much delayed by high water in the spring. Mr. Gideon Mabbett, who has studied the breeding habits of this species on the sand bars of the Mississippi River, near Rodney, Mississippi, sent to Major Bendire the following notes:

On their first appearance they are generally resting on an old log or piece of drift-wood floating in the back water of the Mississippi River, and remain very quiet for sometimes for a day or two, as though they were tired from a long flight. In a few days they are here in great numbers, flying around and chasing each other as though making love to each other. As the waters recede they take themselves more to the river proper; when the high places are out of water they then prepare the nest, which is nothing more than a small depression scooped in the sand about the size of a half-closed hand.

Mr. F. W. Kelsey (1902) says of their nesting habits near San Diego, California:

In this section we seldom find a set of this species containing more than two eggs. The nesting places vary considerably, sometimes being merely a little wallow, 3 or 4 inches across, in the fine gray or black sand; at other times the eggs are deposited among coarse gravel and broken shells, while at others the nest is in the plain sand, but is more or less elaborately decorated with bits of rock, shell, or wood. In all cases, however, that have come to my notice, the nests have been on almost level ground, and entirely devoid of shelter.

Mr. A. I. McCormick (1899) describes their breeding grounds in Los Angeles County as follows:

The beaches of this county, from Santa Monica southward, afford excellent breeding grounds for numberless birds of this species. The coast consists mainly of low sandy beaches, extending back 100 to 200 feet from the water's edge. Back of the beach proper come low sand hills, interspersed with small valleys, and farthest from the ocean are the higher lands, covered with a thick growth of low sage and other shrubs, about 200 feet from the water's edge. Water on the one side and sage brush on the other mark the boundaries of the nesting grounds of least terns, most of which last year (1897) arrived from the south about May 10. For 10 days they remained, flying high over the sea, seldom if ever coming within gunshot range.

My second and last trip to the beach was made on June 5, when I was fortunate enough to take 15 sets of least tern's eggs. Six of them consisted of three eggs each. This is exceptional in the county. I have consulted several collectors who have had considerable experience with least terns in this locality, and with one or two exceptions two eggs has been the invariable complement found.

Judging from my own experience I should say that the least tern normally raises only one brood in a season, at least in the northern portions of its range. But Mr. W. Lee Chambers (1908), in speaking of a protected colony in southern California, says:

I should say that fully 75 per cent of the birds in this colony raised two or three broods.

Probably in warm climates, where the breeding season is more prolonged, second broods are more often raised.

Eggs.—The eggs of the least tern are good examples of protective coloration, for they match their surroundings remarkably well and can hardly be distinguished from mottled pebbles. The usual ground color varies from deep rich " cartridge buff " to very " pale olive buff," or to a color between " pale olive buff " and white. This is more or less unevenly sprinkled with small spots, and sometimes with a few large spots or blotches of dark shades of brown, such as " Mars brown," " sepia," or " mummy brown." Most eggs show some spots and many, particularly of the lighter types, show large underlying blotches of " Rood's lavender " or other shades of " lavender gray." Some eggs show very handsome patterns of bold dark markings over lighter shades. The shape varies from ovate to short ovate and the shell is thin and lusterless. The measurements of 63 eggs, in the United States National Museum, average 31 by 23.5 millimeters; the eggs showing the four extremes measure 37 by 24, 28.5 by 23 and 29.5 by 22 millimeters.

Young.—The period of incubation is said to be from 14 to 16 days. The young remain in the nest for a few days, but soon begin to develop powers of locomotion. They realize the value of the hiding pose and are well aware of their protective coloration; they lie prostrate on the sand, where they are nearly invisible, until almost touched, when they start up and run away with astonishing rapidity. When once started they seldom attempt to hide again and are very difficult to catch.

Mr. Edward H. Forbush has sent me the following interesting observations on the behavior of the young:

Near me were two little young, just hatched and their down hardly dry, yet they were able to run about a little. Near by were several other youngsters. As I lay there propped up on my elbows, awaiting the return of the mother birds, several of them flitted back and forth, and soon their cheeping cries changed to a musical metallic " pidink," which has something of the tinkling quality of the bobolink's note. Soon the mother of the two nearest little ones alighted, and, running to her charges, settled easily upon them, shading them from the hot sun's rays. Then she turned her gaze upward and called softly in reply to the tender notes of the male, which circled overhead. Soon he alighted and took the mother's place in shading the young, while she flew away, perhaps to fish and bathe. Soon she returned with a little sand eel, which she gave to one of the tiny ones, who ran to her for it. Then she flew again, descended into the sea and returned to her charges which the male relinquished to her care. She stood over them with ruffled feathers, and seemed to shake off some drops of water on their little panting forms, and then raised her wings a trifle to shade them from the hot sun. All this I saw at a distance of about 7 or 8 feet, and photographed some of it, the male meantime standing near by. He then took flight, and she nestled over the chick nearest me, coaxing him gently farther away by using her bill and calling the other, which finally followed to her new position and settled by her side.

Again the gentle twittering, and the father came down on the sand with a tiny, bright, silvery fish. A little one stuck its head out between the mother's wing and her body, the father courteously passed the fish to the mother, and she fed the chick, which begged for it with open mouth. Again the bread-winner winged his way over the sunny sea and returned with another fish. Now the little ones were asleep under the mother's breast. He offered her the fish. She refused it. He flew away, but soon alighted and proffered it again, only to be refused again. At last, having full assurance that his family did not need food, he swallowed it himself. Where shall we look to find a lovelier picture of happy, harmonious family relations than that shown here on this desolate beach, beside the roaring surf?

Plumages.—The colors of the downy young are very pale, to match their sandy surroundings. They are practically white, tinged locally above with "ivory yellow" or "pale olive buff," mainly on the crown and wings; they are spotted or mottled on the head and back with various shades of "mouse gray"; the under parts are pure white. When about half grown the juvenal plumage appears on the back and then on the head, "pinkish buff" on the back with U-shaped markings of "sepia" or "brownish olive," one on each feather. The pure white breast feathers appear at about this time, and the dusky wing quills are growing rapidly.

As the young bird attains its growth, in August, the colors become grayer, "pallid mouse gray," or "pallid neutral gray" on the back and wing-coverts; the forehead and crown "pale olive buff," with a dusky orbital and cervical crescent, and with numerous subapical, U-shaped spots of "brownish olive." The wing quills are gray, darker externally, and margined inwardly with white. The lesser wing-coverts, particularly on the bend of the wing, are mottled with dusky and the greater wing-coverts are white clouded with "pearl gray."

In the first winter plumage according to Coues (1877) the young bird begins to resemble the adult, but differs from it as follows:

It is somewhat smaller, with considerably weaker bill, the basal portions of which are still more or less dirty flesh color. The forehead and vertex are rather grayish-white than pure white, and the brownish-black of the nape is interrupted with light grayish. The uniformity of the colors of the upper parts is interfered with by the still remaining lighter tips of most of the feathers, while some may yet retain the brownish subapical spots of the *avis hornotina*. The tail has still some traces of dark subapical spots. It is only in early winter that this particular plumage can be seen, for toward spring the birds are hardly to be distinguished from the adults.

The distinguishing features of this plumage usually disappear at a complete prenuptial molt in the spring. At the first postnuptial molt, which occurs in July and August, the young birds become wholly indistinguishable from adults. The winter plumage of the adult is mainly characterized by the brownish black occiput and nape, by the grayish black on the bend of the wing, and by the black bill. The adult nuptial plumage is produced by a complete prenuptial molt in the spring. It is characterized by the glossy black pileum, the pure white forehead, the yellow, black-tipped bill, and other minor points in which its differs from the winter plumage.

Food.—The least tern does not differ materially in its feeding habits from other species of the genus. It obtains its food, which is mainly small fish, by skimming over the surface or by hovering in the air and plunging down into the water after its prey. This plunging habit has given it the name of "little striker." It is very active while feeding and light and graceful in its movements, darting down upon its quarry with speed and accuracy. Its food is generally swallowed on the wing, but if not properly adjusted in the bill it is sometimes dropped and caught again before it reaches the water. Occasionally a bird will alight on the ground to devour its food, and often it flies away with it to feed its mate or its young. Mr. Ora W. Knight (1908) saw them in southern California "lightly skimming over the surface of the water and feeding on the various small surface-swimming crustaceans and small fish or engaged in feeding on various species of beach insects." The examination of 75 stomachs of birds by Warren (1890) killed on the New Jersey coast in summer "showed that they had fed almost exclusively on little fish; not more than four or five had any traces of insects in their stomachs." Audubon (1840) refers to their feeding on "shrimps and prawns." Sand eels are also eaten.

Behavior.—The flight of this delicate little "sea swallow" is exceedingly light, graceful, and buoyant; it is at times swift and well sustained. Audubon (1840) has well described its movements as follows:

When you invade their breeding place they will sometimes sweep far away and suddenly return, coming so near as almost to strike you. While traveling their light but firm flight is wonderfully sustained, and on hearing and seeing them on such occasions one is tempted to believe them to be the happiest of the happy. They seem as if marshalled and proceeding to a merrymaking, so gaily do they dance along, as if to the music of their own lively cries. Now you see the whole group suddenly check their onward speed, hover over a deep eddy supplied with numberless shrimps, and dash headlong on their prey. Up rises the little thing with the shrimp in its bill, and again down it plunges, and its movements are so light and graceful that you look on with pleasure and are in no haste to depart. Should this scene be enacted while they have young in their company the latter await in the air the rise of their parents, meet them, and receive the food from them. When all are satiated they proceed on their journey, stopping at another similar but distant place.

When their breeding grounds are invaded these terns show their anxiety by hovering over the intruder or darting down at him with shrill, strident cries of protest. Wilson (1832) described their cries as sounding like the "squealing of young pigs." Their ordinary call note, the one most often heard on their breeding grounds, is a shrill, rasping cry, sounding like the syllables "zree ee eep." They also have a variety of cackling and whistling notes. When attacking an intruder, at which they are very bold, they utter a sharp "yip" or a series of vehement notes like "keck, keck, keck," rapidly repeated. While hovering over a school of small fish they become very much excited and noisy, indulging in a constant chorus of shrill cries.

Least terns are particularly gentle and harmless birds. They are not as sociable as some other species, but they live in perfect harmony with their neighbors on their breeding grounds. They seem to prefer the same localities, and become intimately associated with piping plovers, Wilson's plovers, and snowy plovers in their respective breeding ranges. Their chief enemies are human beings, who shoot them and destroy their eggs, and dogs, cats, and rats, which eat their eggs and young. Fortunately protection has come in time to save this beautiful species from complete extermination, with which it certainly was threatened.

Winter.—There is not much to be said about their winter habits, for most of them spend the winter south of our borders in warmer climes, though a few winter on our southern coasts. They are more given to wandering during the fall and winter, and are more often seen inland then than at other seasons.

DISTRIBUTION.

Breeding range.—All along the Atlantic coast, from Massachusetts (Chatham) to the Florida Keys, and along the Gulf coast to southern Texas (Cameron County). Islands in the Mississippi and Missouri Rivers; north, formerly at least, to southern South Dakota (Vermillion) and central northern Iowa (Clear Lake); and west to northern Nebraska (Niobrara River) and southwestern Kansas (Cimarron River). From the Bahamas (Andros, Abaco, Eleuthera, Watlings Island, etc.) and the Greater Antilles (Cuba, Porto Rico, Cayman Islands, etc.), southward throughout the Lesser Antilles to Venezuela (Aruba and Bonaire Islands), and westward to British Honduras. On the Pacific coast, from central California (Monterey Bay) southward to southern Mexico (Tehuantepec). Pacific coast birds are now considered subspecifically distinct.

Breeding grounds protected in the following national reservations: In Florida, Mosquito Inlet, Tortugas Islands.

Winter range.—From the Gulf of Mexico (Louisiana coast) south, along the east coasts of Central and South America, to Argentina (Corrientes); and from the Gulf of California, south, along the west coast to Peru (Sarayacu).

Spring migration.—Early dates of arrival: New Jersey, Long Beach, May 12; Rhode Island, Newport, May 15; Massachusetts, Chatham, May 2; Nebraska, April 2.

Fall migration.—Late dates of departure: New York, September 11; New Jersey, Long Beach, August 25; Maryland, Baltimore, September 4; Kansas, Emporia, August 12; Missouri, St. Louis, August 31; Texas, Bonham, August 20; Lower California, San José del Cabo, September 6.

Casual records.—Said to wander in summer north to Minnesota, Ontario, and Nova Scotia, but many of the records are doubtful. Labrador and Newfoundland records are very doubtful. Occurs occasionally in winter on Atlantic coasts of Africa.

Egg dates.—California: Eighty-nine records, May 20 to August 12; forty-five records, June 5 to 25. South Carolina and Georgia: Thirty-seven records, May 8 to July 20; nineteen records, May 21 to June 21. Florida: Fourteen records, May 3 to June 29; seven records, May 8 to 21. Massachusetts: Eleven records, May 29 to July 4; six records, June 2 to 29.

STERNA FUSCATA Linnaeus.

SOOTY TERN.

HABITS.

This wide ranging species, represented by different races in the two hemispheres, gathers for the purpose of breeding into numerous vast colonies on remote islands in the tropical waters of both oceans, where it is one of the best known sea birds and one of the most popular as a producer of eggs for food. Its most famous resort is probably Bird Key in the Dry Tortugas, near the Florida Keys, about which much has been written, beginning with Audubon's (1840) graphic account, from which I quote, as follows:

On landing I felt for a moment as if the birds would raise me from the ground, so thick were they all around and so quick the motion of their wings. Their cries were indeed deafening, yet not more than half of them took to wing on our arrival, those which rose being chiefly male birds, as we afterwards ascertained. We ran across the naked beach, and as we entered the thick cover before us, and spread in different directions, we might at every step have caught a sitting bird, or one scrambling through the bushes to escape from us. Some of the sailors, who had more than once been there before, had provided themselves with sticks, with which they knocked down the birds as they flew thick around and over them. In less than half an hour more than a hundred terns lay dead in a heap, and a number of baskets were filled to the brim with eggs.

It was curious to observe their actions whenever a large party landed on the island. All those not engaged in incubation would immediately rise in the air and scream aloud; those on the ground would then join them as quickly as they could, and the whole forming a vast mass, with a broad extended front, would as it were charge us, pass over for 50 yards or so, then suddenly wheel round and again renew their attack. This they would repeat six or eight times in succession. When the sailors, at our desire, all shouted as loud as they could, the phalanx would for an instant become perfectly silent, as if to gather our meaning; but the next moment, like a huge wave breaking on the beach, it would rush forward with deafening noise.

Spring.—A description of this island is given in the life history of the noddy. Dr. Joseph Thompson (1903) says that sooty terns arrive about a week after the coming of the noddies; they " arrive in larger flocks and they all seem to reach the breeding place within about four days. Within a week of the arrival of the first one their eggs are to be found."

Courtship.—Audubon (1840) witnessed the courtship of this species, of which he writes:

The male birds frequently threw their heads over their backs as it were, in the manner of several species of gulls; they also swelled out their throats, walked round the females, and ended by uttering a soft puffing sound as they caressed them. Then the pair for a moment or two walked round each other, and at length rose on wing and soon disappeared.

Nesting.—From Prof. John B. Watson's (1908) careful observations of this species and the noddy, made in this colony, we have learned much regarding their habits and characteristics. Some of this information I shall attempt to give in concise form or in exact quotations from his excellent paper, to which I would refer the reader for details. Regarding the nest-building activities he says:

The building of the sooty nest is quickly accomplished. The obtaining of a nest site is the difficult part of the reaction. As has been said, the sooties build their nests very near one another. For this reason it is extremely difficult to make complete observations. My observations began late one afternoon, before any eggs had been laid. Hundreds of the birds were grouped together, incessantly fighting and screaming. It quickly became apparent that most of them had chosen a nest site and were defending it against all late comers. Both male and female were present. Each pair in this particular locality defended a circular territory, roughly 14 inches to 2 feet in diameter. Other birds in wandering around would stumble into this sacred territory and a fight would ensue. The fights would often lead to encroachments upon the territory of still other birds. The number of those fighting would thus be constantly increased. I have seen as many as 14 sooties thus engaging in a fight. Birds 10 to 15 feet away would rush into the fight and the noise and confusion beggared description. Sometimes as many as 10 or 15 such fighting groups could be observed in the area of 1,000 square feet. Quiet would momentarily ensue and then be broken by another series of fights. During the choice of the nesting site the fights continue day and night, with only intermittent periods of quiet.

Within this charmed circle the two mated birds remain relatively quiet. At this time sexual activity is at its height. It frequently happened in the sexual process that the two birds would step ouside of their own territory and a general fight would ensue. When the sexual reaction is in progress it is a signal for the surrounding males to encroach. Coition is thus completed only after much fighting. I have seen the male attempt to mount the female 12 to 15 times, and at each attempt be interfered with by neighboring males.

The actual construction of the nest, when a nest structure is formed, begins after an undefended area has been found. The process of nest building is somewhat as follows: The bird puts the breast to the ground, thereby supporting the body and leaving the legs comparatively free. The feet are used as a combined scraper and shovel. A few backward strokes of the feet are made, which serve both to loosen the sand and to remove it from beneath the body. The bird then turns slightly and repeats the process. When it has turned 360°, or less, it begins to use the breast as a shaper. By continuing this process the depression is soon made to assume the required diameter and depth. My notes show that the bay-cedar leaves are often gathered up and placed around the rim of the nest as the hole is being dug. I can not say which sex does the work, but I believe that both male and female engage in it. As soon as the depression is made both birds begin to defend it. Naturally, where no nest is made, the nest site alone is chosen and defended as described above.

The nest of a sooty, when a nest is made, consists of a shallow oval depression in the sand. This depression varies greatly in depth, depending upon the nature of the surface. It is rarely over 5 centimeters in depth, even in loose sand.

The northern and northeastern sections of the island are free from bushes, but are covered by a shallow growth of Bermuda grass. These areas contain by far the largest number of nests. The eggs in these areas are laid literally on the grass and bare earth in no kind of nest structure. The eggs are often deposited in open sandy places, but nest depressions are not always made, even where the nature of the surface easily permits it.

A rather interesting variation in nest structure appears among certain nests which are built under the bay-cedar bushes. The leaves from the bushes sometimes form a carpet over the sand. The nesting sooties often gather up these leaves and place them around the rim of the depression. Under no circumstances are the leaves collected from a distance farther than the birds can reach with their beaks while remaining in a sitting posture in the nest.

Mr. B. S. Bowdish (1900) found a large colony of these terns breeding on Desecheo Island, near Porto Rico, under quite different conditions, which he describes as follows:

The nesting sites were ledges or shelves in the face of the rocky walls, ranging between 10 and 40 feet above the beach. Some were narrow and others wide. In one case the egg was laid underneath a cactus plant on top of the rocks. In some instances there seemed to be a slight gathering of rock chips and small pebbles about the eggs in the form of a ring, and in a very few one or two bits of twigs were added, but otherwise there was no nesting material, and often the egg laid on the bare rock.

The Pacific form of the sooty tern (*Sterna fuscata crissalis*) breeds on several islands on the west coast of Mexico and in the Hawaiian group, congregating in vast colonies, surpassing in extent and density any tern colonies that I have ever heard of elsewhere. Mr. E. W. Gifford (1913) says:

Messrs. Beck and Hunter reported sooty terns nesting by thousands on several low, flat islets in the brackish lagoon at Clipperton Island. On one islet, about 800 square feet in area and 10 inches in elevation above the water of the lagoon, there were over a thousand eggs. They were laid on the bare coral, with no semblance of a nest, and were so closely placed that it was necessary to step with extreme care to avoid crushing them. The owners were very fearless and allowed themselves to be handled freely. They were also very noisy and kept up a great din. On the 9th 400 eggs were collected by the two residents of the island from a space 20 by 20 feet, and by 11 a. m. on the 10th over 100 fresh ones had been laid in the same area.

The colony on Laysan Island is probably the largest, and it certainly is a wonder among wonders. Prof. Homer R. Dill (1912), reporting on the condition of this colony, states:

The first day of June we measured the rookeries of these birds and two days later we went over the same ground again. We found that in two days the rookeries on the west side had increased in area 3,600 square yards. The final estimate of the number of sooty terns was made June 4—333,900 for both rookeries. This species outnumbers any other on the island.

Dr. Walter K. Fisher (1906), writing of the same colony, says:

The sooty terns nest in among the tall grass, and the single egg is laid directly on the sand, with sometimes scarcely a hollow to suggest a nest. The eggs are placed very close together in many localities—so close that it is sometimes difficult to progress and not walk on them. The birds are very loath at times to leave their nest, and scold soundly before finally slipping off. When at last driven, they limp away, dragging their wings in a painful manner, just as our own birds do. Thus, here, on a little island, is this firmly implanted instinct strongly in evidence, and practiced where it can be of no possible advantage to the bird. Sometimes a dozen or more will struggle on ahead of the pedestrian, trampling over each other and crying incessantly, kicking eggs to the right and left in a mad endeavor to escape, while overhead their fellows keep up an incessant screaming. There is always a great cloud of these birds flying back and forth over the colony, even when no disturbing element is present. They seem to need the nervous excitement. Just at sunrise they are spontaneously most noisy, for they apparently are returning from the sea, where I have heard them at various times during the night.

Eggs.—The same writer gives a very good description of the eggs of the sooty tern, and I can not do better than quote his words, as follows:

The eggs of the sooty tern vary much in markings, but can usually be told from those of *Sterna lunata* by greater size and usually coarser spotting. The ground color is white or occasionally a cream buff. One type of marking consists of deep burnt sienna and grayish vinaceous spots, with occasional nearly black scrawls scattered rather evenly over the whole surface. The spots are 1, 2, and 3, mm. in diameter, with occasional larger and smaller ones. Another less prevalent variation consists of heavy, very deep burnt sienna blotches (5 mm. to 15 mm. in extent), congregated in a zone near the blunt end, and lesser pale grayish vinaceous and deep burnt sienna spots sparsely scattered over the rest of the egg. A very handsome type has the brown laid over the vinaceous, and occasionally the deep burnt sienna or chestnut shading off to one side into light, caused by the spiral twisting of the egg in the oviduct. One specimen shows this to a marked degree, having long chestnut daubs extending spirally from the big end. Still another type has fine brown and grayish vinaceous maculations scattered all over the egg, but more numerous at the blunt end. An abnormal specimen is entirely without markings, being pure white. The shape is ovate, either elongate or thick. An average specimen measures 53 mm. by 35 mm.

The measurements of 76 eggs, in the United States National Museum collection, average 50 by 35 millimeters; the eggs showing the four extremes measure **56** by 36, 54.5 by **37.5, 44.5** by 35 and 48.5 by **33** millimeters.

Young.—Both sexes incubate, and, according to Prof. Watson's observations, the shift is made during the night, each bird remaining on the nest 24 hours except for occasional short excursions for water. The incubating bird is evidently fed by its mate. Based on the study of 16 nests he determined that the period of incubation is 26 days. During the first three days after the young are hatched they are closely guarded by their parents, after which they learn to " run to the bushes, where they remain motionless after sticking their heads into the crotch of some bush or depressing the body against any convenient solid object." The parents soon learn to recognize their own young, and the young learn to respond to the calls of the parents. Each bird feeds it own young and attacks the young of any other bird which invades its territory. This leads to many fights among the adults and much mortality among the young. Professor Watson (1908) says:

The parents alternately feed the young, but instead of a diurnal period of feeding, such as the parents have before the appearance of the young, the intervals vary anywhere from four to seven hours. My observations are few on this point. Though the parents feed the young at any hour of the day, feeding can be most easily observed at dusk. It has already been mentioned that the sooties hurry home at nightfall in great numbers. From 4 until 8 p. m. this feeding process keeps the island in commotion. The feeding of the young birds has many interested spectators. While I have never seen the terns from the neighboring nests, which may be observing the process, attempt to rob the young bird, I judge from the actions of the feeding parent that such is occasionally the case. If the parent happens to disgorge more than the young tern can take into its beak, and the food is allowed to fall to the ground, it is ludicrous to watch the rapidity with which the parent picks up the food and reswallows it. Often times the mate of the feeding parent is near; its rôle is a purely passive one, except when the "spectators" attempt to approach too near. Its part is then to assist in warding them off.

The care of the young, especially from 20 days on, must be an exhausting process for the parents. They become emaciated and somewhat bedraggled in appearance. This is not to be wondered at when we consider that a healthy young sooty can eat anywhere from 20 to 40 minnows of no insignificant size

in a day. It may be of general interest to note that after the first few days
the parent always recognizes and feeds its own young and no other, and, furthermore, the young tern recognizes its own parents and attempts to feed only
from them. Never but once out of many thousands of observations did I see a
young tern begging food from a stranger.

Plumages.—I have seen two quite distinct types of downy young.
In one the upper parts are variegated with "chamois buff" and
black; in the other the upper parts are deep sooty or brownish black,
the down on the head and neck being tipped with "ochraceous
buff." These colors include the sides of the head, neck, and body,
in each case, and the under parts are pure white. Mr. Gifford (1913)
describes some downy young, collected on Clipperton Island, as
"streaked with grayish brown and dull white on the upper surface,
but the white down is tipped with rufous."

When about 30 days old the young bird is fairly well clothed in
its juvenal plumage. In this plumage the upper parts are "clove
brown"; the back, upper tail-coverts, and wing-coverts are narrowly
edged with buff; the scapulars are broadly tipped with buffy white;
and the under parts are uniform "olive brown," shading off to grayish white on the belly and crissum. The bill is small and the tail is
square, or nearly so. Probably the light edgings wear away during
the winter and apparently a complete prenuptial molt takes place
in the spring. I have seen birds in summer, apparently about a
year old, with long wings and forked tails, in which the crowns and
upper parts are "fuscous black," the foreheads white, and the under
parts white, heavily clouded with dusky. At the next molt, the first
postnuptial, the adult winter plumage is probably assumed. This
differs from the adult nuptial plumage only in having a few scattering white feathers in the crown and the lores. I have not seen sufficient material, collected at the proper seasons, to work out the seasonal molts of the adult.

Food.—The food of the sooty tern seems to consist almost entirely
of small fishes, which it picks up gracefully off the surface of the
sea without wetting its plumage. Audubon (1840) says:

Like some of the smaller gulls, this bird not infrequently hovers close to the
water to pick up floating objects, such as small bits of fat pork and greasy substances thrown overboard purposely for making the experiment.

Dr. E. W. Nelson (1899) says of the Pacific variety:

They feed well out at sea, and were not found anywhere along shore, except
when they came to their roosting place on Isabel Island. There were no signs
of their roosting about the Tres Marias, although they may roost on some of
the outlying rocky islets. Grayson found them in small numbers farther
west, about the Revillagigedo Islands. During our trip to the Tres Marias many
schools of large fish were encountered swimming close to the surface and constantly breaking, often with such force and rapidity that the water boiled and
foamed over considerable areas. These schools of fish were commonly accom-

panied by flocks of sooty terns and gannets, which appeared to be animated by the wildest excitement. The terns hovered over the foaming sea, uttering shrill cries and darting down into the water, evidently after food; and in the midst of the turmoil the blue-footed gannets swam about, beating the water with their wings and adding to the noise made by the terns and leaping fish. While on Maria Madre I saw a flock of terns some distance offshore, and, taking a canoe, managed to get out to them and directly in the course of the school of fish they were accompanying. Letting the boat drift I stood up and watched the swarm go by. Thousands of large fish and hundreds of terns and gannets passed the boat on every side, amid loud cries from the terns, a rushing sound from the fish and gannets, and a bewildering complexity of motion in sea and air that was intensely exciting. This novel sight was so interesting that I came near losing a chance to secure some of the birds.

Behavior.—Dr. Frank M. Chapman (1908) says of the flight of this species:

Sooty terns in flight are much like common terns, and, when alarmed, they have the common tern's habit of hanging in the air above their nests. Because of their comparative tameness and of the steadiness of the easterly trade wind, an admirable opportunity was presented to observe these birds in the air at close range. So even was the breeze that the birds, all facing it, seemed to be suspended and motionless. There was, in truth, but little change in their position, but it was maintained by constant adjustment to the slight variations in the force and direction of the wind. Wings were raised or lowered, widely spread, or partly closed; tails depressed or slightly elevated, and fan-like, opened or shut. In short, there was a ceaseless, if unconscious, effort on the part of the birds to maintain the balance between gravity acting in one direction, and air pressure in another, and so well did they succeed that it was a common sight to see one put its foot through its inner wing feathers and scratch its ear with as much ease as though it had been on its nest.

Professor Watson (1908) noted that the sooty tern seldom, if ever, perched upon the stakes, buoys, or other resting places, as the noddy does, but spends most of its time on the wing when away from its breeding place. He writes:

I think the sooty always leaves the island and returns to it without at any time having ceased its flight. This seems rather remarkable when we take into account the fact that the sooty leaves the island in the early morning and oftentimes does not return until toward nightfall.

The sooties often soar round and round, getting higher and higher until lost to sight. They usually join the frigate birds in this reaction. I am inclined to think that the sooty when sufficiently fed spends a large part of its time in such maneuvers.

Audubon (1840) also remarks that this " species rarely alights on the water, where it seems incommoded by its long tail; " also that it " never dives headlong and perpendicularly, as the smaller species are wont to do, but passes over its prey in a curved line, and picks it up. Nor is the flight of this tern characterized by the buoyancy and undecidedness, if I may so speak, of the other species mentioned above, it being as firm and steady as that of the Cayenne tern, excepting during the movements performed in procuring its food."

On its breeding grounds the sooty tern is not only a very active and nervous bird, but a very noisy one as well. Its shrill, piercing cries create an incessant din; it is almost never quiet, even at night. One can hardly make himself heard in the rookeries by day and it is difficult to sleep near them at night. Doctor Chapman (1908) describes the notes as follows:

The sooty's common flight note is a squeaky quack and a clearly enunciated, high-pitched ker-wacky-wack. Nesting birds when disturbed uttered a sharp barking note, changing to a long-drawn, aggressive squawk, suggesting the notes of an annoyed brooding hen. Indeed, as one crawled through the more or less open spaces beneath the bushes with birds protesting or retreating, one seemed to have invaded a densely populated hen yard.

Mr. C. J. Maynard's (1896) version is only slightly different. He says:

The ordinary notes of the sooty tern are extremely harsh, sounding like " Quanck," " quanck ; " but when disturbed on their breeding grounds they utter a double note like " qu-ank." They also, at such times, emit a snarling sound, when all the terns on the key will dive downward, and darting outward, fly over the surface of the water a short distance, scattering in every direction, but will immediately return, and gathering over the intruder, commence their noisy cries, continuing until another one of them chances to give this peculiar sound, when off they will go again, repeating the maneuver over and over again, as long as the object of their aversion remains on the key.

Winter.—After the breeding season is over and the young birds are able to fly the sooty terns leave their breeding grounds and wander about the neighboring seacoasts, sometimes much farthei north. Many of them winter in the Gulf of Mexico and among the West Indies, while others wander south along the tropical coasts of South America.

DISTRIBUTION.

Breeding range.—The Atlantic form breeds from the Florida Keys (Dry Tortugas) eastward throughout the Bahamas (Atwoods, Gauldings, and Ship Channel Keys, Acklin, Eleuthera, Watlings, and Berry Islands, etc.). Southward throughout the West Indies (Cuba, Jamaica, Porto Rico, Dominica, Guadeloupe, Carriacou, etc.) to Venezuela (Margarita Island). Westward to British Honduras (Belize). Northward, formerly at least, to southern Texas (Cameron and Nueces Counties). Also on tropical islands in the Atlantic Ocean at least as far south as equatorial Brazil (Fernando Noronha Island) and Ascension Island. Other forms are widely distributed in the Pacific Ocean and adjacent seas.

Breeding grounds protected in the following national reservations: In Florida, Tortugas Keys.

Winter range.—Practically resident throughout most of its breeding range. Winter range extends north to the Louisiana coast and south to Patagonia (Ascension), Tristan da Cunha, and the Falkland Islands.

Casual records.—Has wandered north (numerous records) as far as Maine (Piscataquis County, October 5, 1878), and New York (Lake Champlain, September 6, 1876). Several Bermuda and European records, such as England (near Wallingford, June 21, 1869), and France (near Verdun, June 15, 1854).

Egg dates.—Bahama Islands: Forty-eight records, May 6 to June 10; twenty-four records, May 18 to June 2. Texas: Eight records, May 10 to 22. Florida: Six records, April 10 to June 5; three records, May 2 to 21.

STERNA ANAETHETA Scopoli.

BRIDLED TERN.

HABITS.

The bridled tern so closely resembles its near relative, the sooty tern, that it can hardly be distinguished from it in life by the casual observer. The two species are intimately associated and very abundant among the tropical islands of the West Indies, although the sooty is much more abundant than the bridled tern in most localities and is more widely distributed. Owing to the difficulty in distinguishing the two in life very little comparative study of the two has been made, and very little has been published about the habits of the bridled tern, but probably most of its habits are similar to those of its better-known relative. Both species are known to the island natives as "egg birds," about which Dr. Frank M. Chapman (1908) says:

Throughout the Bahamas the name "Egg bird" is applied to the sooty, bridled, and noddy terns. The latter part of April these birds come in large numbers to certain regularly frequented keys to breed. If their resort be near a settlement, they are robbed of their eggs by its inhabitants. In Nassau I have seen many of them offered for sale on the street, each one with the shell punctured as a guarantee that one was not buying a tern. If they are remote from human habitation, they are generally preyed upon by the cruising spongers, to whose scanty bill of fare fresh eggs are an eagerly sought addition. Doubtless there are but few colonies of terns in the Bahamas that do not contribute to the food supply of the usually hungry native, hence the current name egg bird. Efforts to secure the passage of a law prohibiting the taking of the eggs of these birds has failed, and, sentiment aside, provided they are permitted to breed and their numbers therefore not decreased, there seems to be no reason why, in a country of such limited food products, this source of supply should not be drawn upon.

Nesting.—Although it often resorts to the same islands to breed, its nesting habits are somewhat different from those of the sooty tern, as the following brief accounts, selected from a large number, will show:

Mr. B. S. Bowdish (1900) found a small colony nesting on Desecheo Island, near Porto Rico, on June 23, of which he writes:

These birds are nothing like as common as the noddy. I think it doubtful if 50 pairs of birds were breeding on the entire island. They are also, I should judge, later in their breeding, the only three nesting sites which I found occupied containing a single egg in which incubation was only just commenced. Also I noted birds showing strong anxiety regarding certain nooks under the rocks, quite similar to those where eggs were found, and I have no doubt that these were nesting sites selected but not yet laid in. In one such case the native caught the male bird on the nest, or at least in the nook.

The first egg was found in a slightly hollowed spot on a flat rock and arched over by a small rock. No pretense at nesting material whatever. The second was in a sort of pocket in the face of the cliff at about 40 feet above beach. The third was under an overhanging rock about 10 feet above beach. From the small amount of data I should judge that the birds almost always select rather hidden and covered sites, and from this fact, and the further one that they do not sit nearly so close as the noddy, their nests are not so easily found, the noddy tern being usually easily seen in its nesting ledge, whereas the bridled leaves its nesting site with a dash often before you see it.

Dr. George W. Field (1894) gives a good account of a small colony near Kingston, Jamaica, as follows:

At the entrance to Kingston Harbor are several cays, varying in size from a mere sand bank to islands of an acre or more in area. The larger of these are dignified by names. Between South Cay and Drunkenman Cay there is a small island, composed entirely of broken coral rock; in reality it is merely a part of the barrier reef above water. Close by and to the southeast of this is a larger, sandy cay, with a few broken slabs of loose coral rock, the western end of which is covered with mangroves. Upon the former of these islands we found, June 15, about a dozen pairs of bridled terns, evidently breeding, but from the nature of the place we were able to find but a single young bird in the down, for the slabs piled in confusion furnished a labyrinth into which they beat a hasty retreat and from which they were not easily dislodged. Leaving the island we landed on the wooded island last mentioned and here we found three or more pairs breeding. Under a flat rock, supported at one end by another rock, we found the single egg laid as usual on the bare sand; the bird darting out at our approach betrayed the place.

Eggs.—The eggs of the bridled tern are somewhat similar to those of the sooty tern, and are nearly as handsome, but they do not show such a wide range of variation and are usually much more finely and evenly spotted, the bold, striking color patterns being seldom seen. The ground color is pinkish white, creamy white, or pure white, which is generally well covered with rather small spots of a great variety of shades of brown, from the darkest shades to bright reddish brown, also various shades of drab, gray, violet, and lavender; occasionally an egg is boldly splashed or blotched with violet-gray or lavender, overlaid with bold markings of brilliant shades of brown, and producing a very pretty effect. The measurements of 20 eggs in the United States National Museum average 46 by 33.2 millimeters; the eggs showing the four extremes measure **49.5** by 31.7, 47.5 by **35.5**, **40.6** by 31.7 and 43.1 by **31.2** millimeters.

Plumages.—The downy young bridled tern is gray, to match the rocks on which it is born. The color varies from very light gray to dark gray or drab-gray, and it is usually tinged with buff; the under parts are grayish white and the throat is dark gray; the upper parts are more or less mottled with dark brown. The young bird, in the juvenal plumage, has the forehead and the entire under parts pure white. The crown and hind neck is " light gull gray," lightly streaked on the crown and heavily streaked on the cervix with black. The feathers of the back, lesser wing-coverts, or scapulars, are edged with pale buff, which fades or wears away during the fall and winter, leaving the back " gull gray " and somewhat mottled. The sequence of plumages to maturity, so far as we can tell from the limited material available, is apparently similar to that of the other small species of the genus *Sterna*. The same is probably true of the molts and plumages of the adult. The adult in winter may be distinguished from the young of the year by having no buffy edgings on the upper parts, but the fresh feathers of the back are broadly tipped with very " pale gull gray," or whitish; and the head is more distinctly marked with black and white, though in a similar pattern to that of the young bird.

Food.—Dr. Alexander Wetmore (1916) says of the food of the bridled tern:

Of five stomachs examined one was entirely empty. Fish remains were present in all the other stomachs, and amounted to 70 per cent. One species was identified as a filefish (*Alutera*, species). Mollusks (25 per cent) were represented by a gastropod and a cephalopod (*Spirula australis*), the latter one of the few of that order bearing a shell that exist to-day. Miscellaneous matter (5 per cent) consisted of a moth and a small echinoderm. Fish and marine mollusks form the large bulk of the food, and under present conditions the birds are to be considered harmless, as the fish eaten are not of economic importance.

In its feeding habits, flight, vocal performances, and general behavior it is apparently similar to the sooty tern. I can not find that anyone has noted any special peculiarities of the bridled tern. On its breeding ground it is often intimately associated with other tropical terns in large colonies, also with boobies and other water birds, with all of whom it seems to live in perfect harmony. At the close of the breeding season, in August or September, it leaves with the others and wanders about over adjacent seas and coasts during the winter.

DISTRIBUTION.

Breeding range.—The American form breeds in the Bahamas (Acklin, Eleuthera, and Berry Islands, Atwoods, Samana, French, and Gauldings Keys, etc.). Southward throughout the West Indies (Dominica, Jamaica, Porto Rico, St. Thomas, etc.) to Venezuela (Aruba Island). Westward throughout the Caribbean Sea to

British Honduras (Saddle Cay). Other forms are found in the Eastern Hemisphere and in the Pacific Ocean.

Winter records.—Practically the same as the breeding range.

Casual records.—One record each for South Carolina (Frogmore, August 25, 1885), Georgia (coast, September, 1912), and Florida (Audubon's specimen, probably taken in Florida Keys).

Egg dates.—Bahama Islands: Thirty-three records, April 12 to June 26; seventeen records, May 16 to June 8.

CHLIDONIAS NIGRA SURINAMENSIS (Gmelin).

BLACK TERN.

HABITS.

A prairie slough, teeming with bird life is one of the most fascinating spots for an ornithologist, for nowhere else can he come in close touch with such a variety of species of interesting birds, with such a multitude of individuals crowded into a narrow space and under such favorable conditions for observation. I have never enjoyed anything more keenly than the long drives we used to take over the virgin prairies of North Dakota, drawn by a lively pair of unshod bronchos, unconfined by fences or roads, with nothing to guide us but the narrow wagon ruts which marked the section lines and served as the only highways. In those days the prairies were like a sea of grass, as boundless as the ocean and nearly as level, where only the distant horizon marked the limit of our view. The prairie birds were interesting but widely scattered over a vast area. In the timber belts along the streams the small land birds were swarming in the only available trees; but the real bird life of the region was to be seen in the thickly populated slough. We seemed to be driving on and on into limitless space until suddenly we came to a depression in the prairie marked by a steep embankment, and there, 10 feet below the level of the prairie, lay a great slough spread out before us. Various ducks—mallards, pintails, shovellers, and blue-winged teal—began rising from the surface as we appeared, and way out in the open water in the center of the slough we could see redheads, canvasbacks, and ruddy ducks swimming about in scattered flocks. An occasional pied-billed or horned grebe and scores of coots were scurrying in and out among the reeds, clucking and scolding or pattering away over the water. Ring-billed and Franklin's gulls and a few Forster's terns were floating overhead. The loud cries of marbled godwits, western willets, and killdeers betokened their anxiety as they flew about us. Dainty little Wilson's phalaropes were flitting about the edges of the marsh, and from the recesses of the reeds came the cackling notes of soras and Virginia rails. Blackbirds, redwings, and yellowheads fairly swarmed in the reeds, and the constant din of their rhythmic notes gave volume to the grand chorus of varied voices that were ringing in our ears. And last but not least, among all this great concourse of bird life, was the subject of this sketch, the black tern, flitting hither and thither, one of the most active and the most restless of the throng.

Nesting.—Among all the water birds of the middle west I suppose the black tern is the most widely distributed, the most universally common and the most characteristic summer resident of the sloughs, marshes, and wet meadows of the plains. The center of its abundance seems to be in the great, flat marsh country of Manitoba, where we found it everywhere the commonest and most conspicuous water bird in the extensive cane swamps about Lake Winnipegosis and Waterhen Lake, breeding anywhere in wet marshy situations. In the tall, thick growth of canes (*Phragmites communis*) their nests were widely scattered and hard to find, but wherever the canes were beaten down or partially open they had placed their frail nests on the dead and fallen canes of the previous year's growth, and about the little open marshy ponds we found them nesting in small colonies. If we did not find the nests it was not through any fault of the terns, for they did the best they could to show us by their actions where their treasures were hidden. There are few birds that are bolder, more solicitous or more aggressive than these little terns in the defense of their eggs, and even before the eggs are laid they will indicate by their actions the exact locality they have chosen. The short, sharp notes of protest come thicker and faster, as the intruder approaches, and when he is fairly among them their cries are prolonged into hard, shrill, angry screams, as the excited terns dart down upon his head, striking him again and again if he does not retreat. By making use of this telltale habit we were able to locate a number of nests in the hidden recesses of the tall canes, where they were sufficiently open for the bird to drop down upon the nest from above or to rise from it without becoming entangled in the canes. Some of these nests were quite elaborate and well made, resembling miniature nests of Forster's terns or Franklin's gulls, but more often they consisted of a few pieces of dead canes or reeds loosely arranged, and sometimes the eggs were laid in a mere depression in the prostrate and closely matted vegetation. In one little open slough hole we found four nests within a radius of 5 yards, but this is closer than they are usually placed. One of these was on the edge of a large muskrat house, just above the water level, and another was built on the remains of an old submerged muskrat nest.

In North Dakota in 1901 we found small colonies of black terns nesting in open situations in the sloughs, where the water was 1 or 2 feet deep and where numerous little piles of dead and partially rotted reeds and flags were floating. The nests were usually very flimsy affairs, a few loosely arranged bits of reeds and flags serving to raise the eggs an inch or so above the water. Often the eggs were laid in slight depressions in this floating rubbish, with no apparent attempt at nest building, where the eggs were wet and nearly awash. In Saskatchewan we found a small colony on June 24, 1906, breeding in a wet, grassy meadow where the water was only a few inches deep. The nests all contained fresh eggs and were merely small piles of rubbish floating among the scattered growth of short green meadow grass. I have several sets of eggs in my collection, taken by Mr. Gerald B. Thomas in Livermore, Iowa, during the last week in July. The nests were located in sunken muskrat houses, old grebe nests, and an old coot nest. Nests of the black tern often have substantial foundations of water mosses and other soft vegetable substances, which some writers seem to think are built by the birds. I think, however, that the black tern never gathers any such materials and that these foundations are either old grebes' nests, or merely floating masses of muck, selected by the terns, on which only the superstructure of the nest is built by them.

Mr. J. C. Knox (1899), who has seen the nest-building process, gives the following account of it:

I had always before believed that the black tern merely hollowed out a nest on a bog and deposited her eggs there, but I was now undeceived. As I was walking along I happened to glance upward and saw a black tern with something in her bill. She was coming directly toward me, so I dropped down out of sight in a clump of green rushes. Just in front of me was the remains of an old muskrat house, now little more than a bog—a capital place for a tern's nest. Here she alighted and deposited her weed stem on the edge of a little hollow near one edge of the bog; then she flew away again, but soon returned with another weed and deposited that. I watched her for half an hour, and during that time she made 14 trips to the nest, bringing material each time, and twice her mate came with her. When I left the nest was not completed, but I think she had quit nest building for that morning. Many of the eggs of this species are laid on a bare bog, with no nest at all, but in this instance a nest was made and the materials, which could have been had directly at hand, were brought from a distance.

Occasionally nests of this species are placed on pieces of driftwood or boards where they are very conspicuous, but usually they are very hard to see, as both nests and eggs match their surroundings perfectly.

Eggs.—The eggs of the black tern are very handsome and are subject to considerable variation. Many of these resemble the eggs of some of the Limicolae, as they are often somewhat pointed. The average shape is ovate, with a decided tendency in some specimens toward ovate pyriform. The shell is thin and has a dull luster.

The ground color shows a great variety of shades of olive and buff, from "Dresden brown" to "clay color," and from "deep olive buff" to "ivory yellow." The eggs are usually heavily marked with the darkest shades of brown, "blackish brown," "seal brown," "bister," and "mummy brown;" sometimes the eggs are evenly sprinkled all over with fine dots, but more often with larger spots and blotches unevenly arranged. Frequently the markings, of either type, become confluent in a ring around the larger end of the egg, and occasionally large bold markings of different shades of brown produce handsome effects. The measurements of 122 eggs, in the United States National Museum, average 34 by 24 millimeters; the eggs showing the four extremes measure 37 by 25.5, 35.5 by 26.5, 31.5 by 23 and 32 by 22.5 millimeters.

In the southern portions of its range the black tern apparently raises two broods, at least occasionally, for fresh eggs are frequently found in May and again in July. As very few, if any, of the water birds raise two broods in a season, it may be that these late sets may be second or third layings of pairs previously robbed of their eggs. Some good observers, however, seem to think that two broods are regularly raised in some localities. The full set is almost always three eggs, occasionally two, and very rarely four or even five. Personally I have never seen a set of four eggs, and think it is an exceedingly rare occurrence. Smaller sets than these are probably second layings. Dr. E. W. Nelson, according to Dr. T. S. Roberts (1877), says:

I have seen the eggs of *Sterna plumbea* deposited on masses of floating weeds in several instances, but only for the *third* brood, the bird having previously built two nests and deposited the eggs in both, which had been removed by myself to ascertain how many they would lay. The result was almost invariably as follows: First nest, three eggs; second nest, two eggs; and the third, one egg.

Dr. Frank M. Chapman (1904) has learned that the period of incubation is 17 days. Audubon (1840) states that both sexes incubate—a difficult matter to determine, as a black tern is seldom seen on its nest.

Young.—The young remain in the nest but a few days, and even before that time they will leave it on the approach of danger. Doctor Chapman (1904) gives an interesting illustration of this in his account of the home life of this species. He says:

Three days later we visited the nest, expecting to see a pair of downy young, but, to our surprise and disappointment, it was deserted. Evidently, however, there was something not far away in which the terns were greatly concerned. With piercing screams they darted at us, once actually hitting Mr. Seton's hat.

Search failing to reveal any sign of the young birds, the camera was left to play detective. Focusing it on the empty nest and surrounding it with "cattails," we attached some 70 feet of tubing and retired to the high grasses of a neighboring dry bank. But we were not hidden from the tern. She hovered over us, shrieking her disgust with scarcely a pause, turning her long beak to this side and that, as she brought each eye in turn to bear. Finally, her *craiks* grew softer, and, fluttering over the nest, she uttered a soft *wheent-wheent-wheent*, which probably meant to her downings "It's all right; come back home now." After half a minute of this calling she fluttered lower and dropped out of sight behind the reed barriers. Apparently, there could be little doubt that with her voice she had conjured the chicks back to the nest.

Acting on this belief, a dozen rapid strokes were given to the bicycle pump at the end of the tube, and the tern promptly flew up into the air, uttering her loud *craik-craik* in a way that plainly showed something had happened close by to alarm her, and thus plainly told us that the shutter on the camera had been sprung. Instantly we rushed through the mud and water to the nest, but only to find it as empty as before.

Inserting a fresh plate in the camera, we returned to our hiding place. Again the tern scolded us vigorously, but after a while, as before, her fears seemed to decrease; she gradually drew nearer to the nest and eventually dropped lightly down into the reeds, evidently on it. After waiting a moment for her to settle herself, the bicycle pump was again used, and at the twelfth plunge of the piston the tern shot upward as though she were blown from the end of the tube. We accepted her action as an unfailing indication that the shutter was properly released and once more splashed quickly through the water to see what we might see; but only an empty nest met our gaze, and we were as ignorant of the fate of the young terns as we had been in the beginning.

The continued anxiety of the parents, however, encouraged us to continue our efforts to solve the mysterious disappearance of their chicks, and, after several more attempts similar to those just related, we reached the nest just in time to see the two little ones paddling away into the surrounding reeds, like ducklings. This caused us to believe that on each occasion they had returned to the nest only to desert it again as the old bird left them; but it was not until the plates were developed, a month later, that we could really put together the whole story.

The young birds are fed by their parents until they are able to fly. Rev. W. F. Henninger writes to me that they seem to be fed on "spiders, water scorpions, flies, and perhaps other swamp-loving insects, fragments of the first three being found in the nests with young." Mr. Frank M. Woodruff has sent me a photograph showing a black tern alighting on its nest with a large dragon fly in its bill, presumably for its young. The young terns develop very fast and soon learn to fly, but their parents continue to feed them more or less, sitting in long rows on the fences about the marshes or on pieces of drift wood waiting to be fed. Audubon (1840) says that he has "seen the parent birds feed them on the wing in the manner of swallows."

Plumages.—The young of the black tern, when first hatched, is a swarthy individual, entirely different from the young of other terns. It is thickly covered with long, soft, silky down, "cinnamon drab' on the throat, neck, and sides, shading off to " pale drab gray " on the belly and cheeks; the upper parts are rich " cinnamon," heavily blotched with " fuscous black." When very young the sides of the head, including the orbital region, the cheeks, the lores, and sometimes a narrow frontal strip, are pure white. This feature becomes less conspicuous as the bird grows older. As the bird attains its full size the down is gradually replaced with feathers, beginning on the wings, scapulars, and the sides of the breast; but much of the cinnamon down remains on the head, neck, and crissum until the juvenal plumage replaces it at the flight stage in July.

By the time that the young bird has attained its full growth the juvenal plumage has been fully acquired and the flight stage reached. This plumage is worn through August and September, and perhaps later. The upper parts are decidedly brown and often the under parts are extensively washed with brownish, dusky, or drab on the sides of the neck and chest, on the flanks and sometimes on the entire belly. The feathers of the back and scapulars are broadly margined with " clove brown " and narrowly tipped with whitish. The forehead is dirty white, the crown and occiput are mainly black, and the auriculars, as well as a ring around the eye, are pure black. The browns gradually fade and the light edgings wear away during the fall, but there is probably also a partial postjuvenal molt of the contour feathers. The first winter plumage is then much like the adult, but young birds can be recognized by having smaller bills, more or less signs of light edgings in the wing-coverts and back, and tails which are much less deeply forked, the lateral rectrices being broader and more rounded at the tips. I have not been able to trace very clearly the first prenuptial molt, but apparently a majority of the young birds acquire at this molt a plumage which is exactly or nearly like the adult nuptial, with more or less white in the black areas. Many birds, however, seem to wear the first winter plumage or a new one closely resembling it, until the first postnuptial molt, which occurs in June and July. This molt produces the adult winter plumage.

Adults have two complete molts—the prenuptial early in the spring and the postnuptial in July, August, and September. The seasonal change is very striking. In the winter plumage the forehead, a nuchal collar, and the entire under parts are white; the auriculars and a narrow orbital space are black; the crown and occiput are mottled with gray and black; and the mantle, wings, and tail are much lighter gray than in the spring—" light neutral gray " or paler.

Food.—The black tern is credited with eating minnows or other small fry, but I believe that it rarely does so except when associated

with other terns on the coast.   Mr. William Brewster (1878) says
of their feeding habits in Massachusetts:

> They associated most commonly with the Wilson's and roseate terns, and
> procured their food in the same way, hovering over the schools of bluefish
> and pouncing upon the small fry which these voracious creatures drove to the
> surface.   The stomachs of all the specimens which were dissected contained
> the macerated remains of small fishes only.   In no case were any insects
> detected.

My own experience with the bird in this State is somewhat different, for I have seen large numbers of them hovering over the meadows
and grassy marshes, catching insects in the air and darting down to
pick them off the tall waving grasses, just as they do in the western
sloughs.   I have also seen them feeding with the common terns, but I
believe that they prefer insect food when they can find it.   In the
interior the black tern is almost wholly insectivorous; its food includes crayfish, small mollusks, dragon flies, moths, grasshoppers,
crickets, beetles, spiders, water scorpions, flies, and a great variety of
other insects, nearly all of which are caught on the wing.   Dr. R.
M. Anderson (1907) says:

> They evince little fear of man, and large numbers will often follow a man
> plowing, hovering over his head and looking for grubs turned up by the plow.
> They are often killed with a whip at such times.

In the South it has been seen capturing the moths of the cotton-
boll worm in flight over the fields of young plants.   Its ability to
catch dragon flies, one of the swiftest of insects, is sufficient proof
that the black tern is an expert flycatcher.   Mr. Ernest E. Thompson (1890) says in regard to this performance:

> Besides aquatic insects, the black tern feeds largely on dragon flies, which
> it adroitly captures on the wing.   The bird may frequently be seen dashing
> about in a zigzag manner so swiftly the eye can offer no explanation of its
> motive until, on the resumption of its ordinary flights, a large dragon fly is
> seen hanging from its bill and sufficiently accounts for the erratic movements of
> the bird.   After having captured its prey in this way I have frequently seen
> a tern apparently playing with its victim, letting it go and catching it again,
> or, if it is unable to fly, dropping it, and darting under it to seize it again and
> again before it touches the water.

I have watched black terns for hours beating the air over the
western sloughs, dipping down frequently to pick up some small
morsel of insect food from the surface of the water, but I have never
seen them plunge into the water, as they would do if they were after
minnows.   They glean much of their food from the tall, waving
grasses, reeds, flags, and bullrushes.   Their eyes must be very keen to
find the small insects and spiders which crawl up the stalks to hide,
and they are certainly expert at swooping down and catching them.
At certain times, especially when it is blowing hard or raining, countless millions of mosquitoes, flies, small dragon flies, and other small

insects seek shelter on the lee sides of the reeds, which means a bountiful harvest for the terns.

Behavior.—The black tern is a restless waif of the air, flitting about hither and thither with a wayward, desultory flight, light and buoyant as a butterfly. Its darting zigzag flight as it mounts into the air to chase a fluttering moth is suggestion of a flycatcher or a night-hawk; as it skims swiftly over the surface of the water it reminds me of a swallow; and its true relationship to the terns is shown as it hovers along over the billowy tops of a great sea of tall waving grass, dipping down occasionally to snatch an insect from the slender, swaying tops. When looking for food the bill is usually pointed downward, but in ordinary flight it points forward. Mr. Thompson (1890) made some calculations as to the speed at which this tern flies and arrived at the following conclusions:

A large number of observations resulted in an average of three wing beats per second, with the greatest of regularity; another series of observations, not so satisfactory, allowed a distance of 5 yards to be traversed at each beat. This gave only the disappointing rate of something over 30 miles per hour, but this was at the uncertain foraging flight. Once the mother tern has secured her load of provender a great change takes place, as already mentioned. She rises high in air, and I am sure she doubles her former rate of speed, and straight as a ray of light makes for home. It is said that many birds can not fly with the wind; not so the tern; for now, if there be a gale blowing her way, she mounts it like a steed and adds its swiftness to her own, till she seems to glance across the sky, and vanishes in the distance with a speed that would leave far behind even the eagle, so long the symbol of all that was dashing and swift.

The ordinary call note of the black tern, given in flight when not particularly disturbed, is a short, sharp, shrill, metallic "*krik.*" When much excited this is prolonged into a shrill scream like "*kreek*" or "*craik*," given with ear-piercing vehemence when attacking an intruder near its nest. Mr. Henninger, according to Doctor Chapman (1904), contributed the following interpretation of the notes:

Call note, "*kleeă*"; note of anger and anxiety, "*karr krr*"; ordinary note heard while on the wing, "*gik.*"

Doctor Chapman described the note used to call the young as a soft "*wheent-wheent-wheent.*"

With all the varied inhabitants of the sloughs, its bird neighbors, the black tern seems to live in peace and harmony. I have never known it to molest the eggs or young of other species, or to attack the adults, nor can I find in print any evidence of its hostility. It is not as sociable as some other species, and its nests are usually somewhat apart from others. As a species it is sociable and gregarious to a limited extent, and it shares with other terns the habit of gathering in flocks to hover over a fallen companion.

Fall.—By the middle or last of August, when the young birds have acquired their first winter plumage and most of the adults have completed their molt, the fall migration begins in a leisurely way, as the birds are in no hurry to reach their winter homes. Their wanderings are more extended at this season and more erratic. Generally a few, and sometimes large numbers, of black terns, mostly in immature plumage, are seen on the Atlantic coast from New England southward, sometimes in large flocks by themselves frequenting the marshes and wet meadows, but more often in small numbers mingled with other terns and gulls along the coast. Rev. M. B. Townsend writes to me that he has seen black terns flying over the waters of the Gulf of Mexico as early as August 1, some of which were still in full spring plumage, some were molting, and some had completed the molt into winter plumage. On June 16, 1910, while cruising off the coast of Louisiana, I saw a large number of black terns in small flocks; I counted 10 of them sitting on a stick of drift timber, equally spaced about a foot apart. They evidently thought that there was no more standing room, for they would not allow another bird to alight on the log, although several tried to do so. Capt. W. M. Sprinkle told me that they breed in the West Indies in February, appear here early in May, and remain all summer. I am more inclined to think that these were nonbreeding birds which failed to migrate northward in the spring.

DISTRIBUTION.

Breeding range.—Interior of North America. East to eastern Ontario (Kingston and Charleston Lake) and west central New York (Cayuga Lake). South to northern Ohio (Sandusky), northern Indiana (English Lake), northern Illinois (Cook, Putnam, and Henry Counties), central Iowa (Hamilton County), northern Nebraska (Holt and Cherry Counties), north central Colorado (Barr Lake region), north central Utah (Utah Lake), western Nevada (Washoe Lake), and southern California (Elsinore Lake). West to central California (San Joaquin and Sacramento Valleys), central southern Oregon (Klamath Lakes), east central Washington (Brook Lake), and central British Columbia (Chilcotin). North in the interior to central Alaska (Fort Yukon), Great Slave Lake, and central Manitoba (Lake Winnipegosis and Lake Winnipeg).

Breeding grounds protected in the following national reservations: In Oregon, Klamath Lake, and Malheur Lake.

Winter range.—From the Gulf of Mexico southward to northern South America (Surinam), and along the Pacific coasts of Mexico (Mazatlan), Panama, Peru, and Chile. Nonbreeding and young birds remain in the Gulf of Mexico all summer.

Spring migration.—A few birds migrate up the Atlantic coast and across the Great Lakes to the interior. Transient dates: Maryland, May 17 to 30; Pennsylvania, Erie, April 27; New York, Carmel, April 9; Massachusetts, Framingham, June 20; New Hampshire, Lake Winnipesaukee, June 10. The main flight is northward through the interior. Early dates of arrival: Missouri, St. Louis, April 29; Iowa, Floyd County, March 28; Wisconsin, Mayville, March 22; Minnesota, Heron Lake, May 1; Manitoba, Oak Lake, May 17; Great Slave Lake, Fort Resolution, June 5.

Fall migration.—Eastward, at irregular intervals, to the Atlantic coast from Nova Scotia southward and then down the coast to its winter range. Transient dates: Prince Edward Island, September 13; Nova Scotia, Sable Island, September 9; Massachusetts, August 7 to September 26; New Jersey, August 4 to October 20; North Carolina, July 28 to September 23; Florida, Tarpon Springs, September 15. Transient dates for the interior: Nebraska, August 8 to October 15; Kansas, July 25 to September 14; Missouri, up to October 21. Pacific coast dates: British Columbia, Sumas, up to September 1; Washington, Bellingham Bay, up to August 26; California, Point Pinos, August 2 to September 23; Lower California, San José del Cabo, September 6 and 7, and Cape San Lucas, September 16; Mexico, Mazatlan, arrives in October.

Casual records.—Accidental in Bermuda (October, 1876). The more northern Atlantic coast records might be classed as casual.

Egg dates.—Minnesota and North Dakota: Thirty-six records, May 25 to August 4; eighteen records, June 5 to 13. California: Twenty-six records, May 11 to July 2; thirteen records, May 19 to June 8. Illinois and Iowa: Twenty-four records, May 11 to July 28; twelve records, June 6 to 18. Manitoba and Saskatchewan: Nineteen records, May 28 to July 5; ten records, June 6 to 14.

CHLIDONIAS LEUCOPTERA (Temminck).

WHITE-WINGED BLACK TERN.

HABITS.

The following quotation from Kumlien and Hollister (1903) contains all we know of this beautiful Old World species as a bird of the North American Continent:

The only known instance of the occurrence of this species on the Western Continent is that of a breeding female shot by L. Kumlien in a large marsh near Black Hawk Island, Lake Koshkonong, July 5, 1873. The specimen was sent freshly skinned to Doctor Brewer and was presented by him to the United States National Museum. The partially denuded abdomen and well-formed ova prove that it would have bred, whether with its own kind or with the common species we know not, as no others were seen at the time nor since, although days have been spent in the tern colonies for almost no other purpose than the vain hope of seeing more of them. The bird was quite noticeable among the enormous numbers of black terns; so much so that there is no special need for any one to sacrifice the life of any of the common species under the delusion that it may prove to be *leucoptera* when in hand.

Nesting.—Yarrell (1871) says:

The white-winged black tern nests in marshes, sometimes in company with the black tern, where, as in Central Europe the latter preponderates, but in large colonies of its own in southeastern Russia and Siberia, where it is the dominant species. Its eggs, deposited on the floating vegetation in May and June, are usually three in number, of an olivaceous-buff, boldly blotched, and streaked with dark brown, and spotted with gray of different shades. Average measurements about 1.35 by 1 inch.

Eggs.—Morris (1903) states:

They arrive at their summer haunts in the month of May and disappear in July and August. The eggs of this species are three or four in number, with many grayish spots, and some larger blackish red ones, the ground color being dull yellowish olive. They are of a rotund form. The male and female birds sit on them in turn and show much anxiety for their safety, flying at and about all intruders.

The eggs of this species seem to be indistinguishable from those of the common black tern. The measurements of 42 eggs, in various collections, averaged 34.9 by 24.9 millimeters; the eggs showing the four extremes measure **37** by 25.1, 35 by **26, 32.5** by 24.4 and 33.5 by **23** millimeters.

Plumages.—Yarrell (1871) describes the plumage changes as follows:

The nestling is of a nearly uniform rufous-buff, slightly darker on the throat; the crown and back streaked and mottled with blackish-brown. The immature bird in August has the bill livid brown; lores and forehead white; crown and nape brownish-gray; a dark streak behind the ear-coverts. Sides of the neck white, tinted with buff; upper back and scapulars slate-gray, tipped or overlaid with brown, which gradually wears off; back gray, mottled with brown, rump white, passing to gray on the tail-coverts; tail feathers gray, darker and browner at tips; primaries darker on inner webs than in the adults; under wing-coverts and under parts white. By the end of the following summer the brown tips have completely passed away, leaving only a mottled bar along the carpals to indicate immaturity; and in the following spring, when the bird is nearly 2 years old, it assumes the black nuptial garb. The tail feathers, however, do not become quite white for some years, and it may be that this takes longer with the females than with the males; otherwise there appear to be no appreciable external differences between the sexes when fully matured. In the autumn molt the black portions of the plumage become white on the head, neck, and underparts, and slate-gray on the mantle. A specimen in the editor's collection, obtained near Valencia, in Spain, on the 25th of July, presents a remarkably piebald appearance. Some black is never absent from the nape and ear coverts, and in mature and vigorous birds the black of the under parts soon begins to make its reappearance.

Food.—Macgillivray (1852) says:

It is said to feed chiefly on aquatic insects and worms, especially dragon-lies, moths, and other winged insects, seldom on fishes.

Yarrell (1871) adds "the larvae of water insects," and Morris (1903) includes "the fry of fish."

Behavior.—Yarrell (1871) says:

In its flight it is more rapid than the black tern, and it is said to have a louder and harsher voice than that species.

Evidently it is closely related to the black tern, and apparently a detailed account of its life history would agree very closely with what we know of our own familiar bird of the western sloughs.

DISTRIBUTION.

Breeding range.—Central and southeastern Europe from central Russia southward, also westward in Galicia, Hungary, and occasionally Bavaria; in Asia, across Siberia to the Amur Valley and southward to Turkestan; in Africa, said to breed in Algeria. The Australian bird has been separated as a distinct subspecies.

Winter range.—In Africa, south to Cape Colony; in southern Asia and south to Australia and New Zealand.

Casual records.—Accidental in Denmark, Sweden, and Great Britain. Taken once in West Indies (Barbados, October 24, 1888) and once in Wisconsin (Lake Koshkonong, July 5, 1873).

Egg dates.—Central Europe: Twenty records, May 17 to June 14; ten records, May 28 to June 9.

ANOUS STOLIDUS (Linnaeus).

NODDY.

HABITS.

This dusky tropical species enjoys a wide distribution on both sides of the Equator in both of our great oceans, and shows so little geographical variation that our Atlantic and Pacific birds are scarcely separable. It resorts to many different islands throughout its range to breed, and its nesting habits vary considerably in different localities. Although much has been published regarding its habits during the breeding season we know very little about its life history at other seasons.

Spring.—Mr. W. E. D. Scott (1891) has published some interesting notes by Mr. Charles B. Taylor, regarding the arrival of the noddies on Morant Cays, near Jamaica, from which I quote, as follows:

At the time of my arrival at the Cays (2d of April) there were no sooty terns there and very few noddies, but these latter increased in numbers daily, until by the 19th of April, the date of my departure, they had assembled in hundreds and were evidently preparing to lay, yet in two females taken two or three days after my arrival the eggs in the ovaries were very small.

Soon after sunset the birds came in to roost among the low bushes fringing the shore, and up to a late hour many kept arriving. They flew very swiftly, just skimming the surface of the water, and standing on the shore at dusk (the time they began to arrive) it was rarely possible to see the birds coming until they were actually on the island. They alighted noiselessly and instantly on gaining the fringing bushes; later in the month, however, as their numbers increased, belated birds found difficulty in effecting an easy landing among the branches, those already in possession pecking right and left at all newcomers and croaking harshly. Each day, as their numbers increased, they became more vociferous, until at last the melancholy wail of those flying overhead and the croak of the sitting birds was kept up without intermission all through the night. On moonlight nights they appeared unusually abundant and restless.

I have watched them there until far into the night, as in scores they kept flying to and from the bushes. Although up and about before dawn on most mornings, I was seldom in time to watch the noddies leave their roost. One morning, however, I got a good idea of their numbers. It wanted about an hour or so of daybreak, and the moon was still bright, when someone walking along the shore appeared to give a general alarm. Scores of birds got up and went swiftly out to sea, and for some little time a constant stream poured out from the bushes along the shores in every direction, as far as it was possible to see; flying before the wind, they went out of sight in an instant. They left the land always in the same manner in which they came in to roost, dropping to the surface of the water immediately on clearing the shore. Notwithstanding their apparent abundance, the noddies, in point of numbers, sink into comparative insignificance after the arrival of the sooty terns.

Prof. John B. Watson (1908) has made a most thorough and scientific study of the behavior of this species and the sooty tern on their famous breeding grounds in the Dry Tortugas and I shall quote freely from the published results of his observations. He describes the island on which they nest as follows:

Bird Key is a small coral island about 300 yards wide (east and west) by 400 yards long (north and south). It is 65.8 statute miles due west from Key West. The island is partially sheltered on the east and on the northeast by a coral reef. Northeast of the island, about 1.125 statute miles distant, stands Fort Jefferson, now practically deserted. Still farther to the northeast other low coral islands are to be found. Loggerhead Key lies about 4 statute miles to the west of Bird Key. Immediately outside of these islands is to be found the water of the Gulf of Mexico. The situation of the island shows that it is adequately protected from all but the severest southwest storms. The Tortugas as a whole are rarely subject to heavy storms during the nesting period of the birds. During the past season (1907) only one severe storm visited the island, and this was not very destructive to the life of the birds.

Owing to its juxta-tropical location, its slight elevation, and the condition of its surface (largely coral sand) the actual surface temperature of this island is very high, ranging at times during the hottest days from 124° to 143° F.

With the exception of the bay-cedar bushes, which are very abundant upon the central and western parts of this island, little vegetation exists. On a certain limited portion of its surface (southeastern) a dense growth of cactus is to be found. Both cactus and bay cedars are utilized by the noddies for nesting places.

No accurate data exist concerning the number of years these two species have migrated to this island for the purpose of rearing their young. The oldest inhabitants of the neighborhood say that as long as they can remember the birds have been going there year after year. The terns arrive at approximately the same time each year (during the last week in April), live there until toward the 1st of September, and then begin their southern migration.

Courtship.—The birds are said to be mated before they arrive on the island, and, as he did not arrive until five days later than the birds, Prof. Watson was unable to observe their earlier actions; but he tentatively presents the following account of what is probably a mating performance:

One day I observed several noddies " sunning " upon the wire covering of one of my large experimental cages. Suddenly, one of the birds (male) began nodding and bowing to a bird standing near (female). The female gave immediate attention and began efforts to extract fish from the throat of the male. The male would first make efforts to disgorge, then put the tip of the beak almost to the ground and incline it to the angle most suitable to admit her beak. She would then thrust her beak into his (the ordinary feeding reaction). The feeding reaction was alternated with the nodding. After this series of acts had been repeated 20 times the male flew off and brought a stick. He deposited this near the female and then again offered to feed her. She again tried to feed; then the male attempted sexual relations. She immediately flew away, but almost immediately returned and alighted at a slightly different place. The male again brought the stick and again bowed and offered to feed her. She accepted the food, but again flew away when the male attempted to mount her. At this juncture the island was disturbed and my observations could not continue.

Nesting.—During his sojourn on Bird Key in 1907 he made an accurate count of the noddies' nests " by means of a mechanical counting device," which gave a total of 603 active nests. A large majority of the nests are built in the bay-cedar bushes at varying heights up to about 12 feet. About 20 per cent of them are in the cactus growth.

Very often the nest has the appearance of being constructed directly upon the ground, but a closer examination usually shows that it has been built upon a tuft of grass or upon the stem of a bush, the branches of which have been broken off close to the ground. * * * The noddies apparently do not seek to nest in the thickest parts of the bushes. Although isolated nests are present even where the shrubs are most dense, by far the majority of them are to be found in bushes which border upon open spaces.

Of the construction of the nest he says:

The noddy constructs its nest from (1) loose dead branches of the bay-cedar bushes; (2) of seaweed; (3) of a combination of these; (4) of a combination of either or both of these with various kinds of sea shells and coral. When the shells and coral are employed they are often placed as an inner lining to the nest and the egg is deposited directly upon them. The nest itself is a quite variable structure and usually loosely put together. It is very shallow, and this is rather singular, since the wind often blows the egg or the young to the ground.

The nests remaining from year to year are utilized by the birds at successive nesting periods; whether or not by the same pair can not with certainty be answered at present. On account of this utilization of the old nest from year to year some of the oldest nests have grown to enormous size, due to the addition of new materials at each successive season.

Professor Watson (1908) made an interesting series of observations on the methods of nest building and the daily routine of activities during this period, but I shall attempt to quote only part of what he says about it:

Both birds work, bringing sticks, seaweed, shells, and coral. Both birds shape the nest clumsily by pecking and pulling at the sticks. They never weave the sticks so as to form a compact and durable nest. The stick is dropped on the rim, then drawn into position. Frequently first one bird then the other sits in the nest and shapes it. In order to do this, the bird rises on its feet and depresses its breast and turns round and round. The material is obtained both far and near. Floating sticks and seaweed are gathered from the water. They frequently alight under the nests of other birds and gather up the fallen branches. They even take the material from other nests which are left momentarily unguarded. Frequent fights ensue. The birds work neither steadily nor rapidly; 10, 15, 20 minutes may elapse before either makes a trip.

The male feeds the female while she is building the nest, consequently it is necessary for him to cease from his labors in assisting her and absent himself in search of food. During his absence she also ceases her activities, but remains at the nest to guard it from her pilfering neighbors and to repel the advances of other males. On his return she is fed as follows:

The male returns with a full-laden crop. He alights directly upon the nest or near the female. The female at once shows signs of life, and as they approach each other they beginning nodding. Then the male invites the female to feed by putting his beak down to a position convenient to her. She gets the food by taking it directly from the mouth of the male, the male disgorging it by successive muscular contractions of the throat and abdomen. The impression one gets from this ludicrous performance is that the bird is choking to death. During the whole of the process of feeding, a soft, nasal, rattling purr is emitted, presumably by the female. This purring sound is an invariable indication that feeding is taking place. It is to be heard on no other occasion.

Professor Watson (1908) noted the first eggs on May 4 and found that the majority were laid between the 11th and the 16th. He says further:

After the egg is laid a marked change appears in the behavior of both the male and the female. The birds will now attack even a human intruder, and their defense of the nest against their own kind becomes even more strict than before. Oftentimes the birds will sit on the egg and allow themselves to be caught, striking viciously all the while with their long, keen, pointed beaks. Individuals vary greatly in this respect. On my daily rounds, as I approached the vicinity of a group of nests, several noddies would usually advance to meet me, striking viciously at my head. Their attacks would continue until I withdrew. Many times I have had my hat knocked off and the blood brought from my scalp by their vicious attacks.

Still another marked change occurs in the habits of the birds. The male no longer feeds the female. Each bird takes equal turns at brooding the egg. My attention was first called to this while I was watching the habits of the birds before the egg was laid. Several nests in the vicinity of the place of observation already contained eggs. At these nests I was never able to observe the feeding of the female by the male. At this period the two birds became practically automata. Their life is taken up in alternately brooding the egg and in feeding. The birds spend little or no time together except at night. The one comes to the nest; the other flies away to feed.

The egg is generally covered day and night. Occasional trips are made to the water for drinking and for wetting the breast feathers. This latter reaction has its value possibly in keeping the egg at the proper temperature. The sun is so hot that if the egg were left uncovered for any great length of time it probably would not incubate.

The period of incubation is 35 or 36 days.

Professor Watson (1908) conducted some interesting experiments to test the ability of the birds to recognize their mates, their eggs, and their nests. Painting or dyeing the plumage disturbed them greatly and upset their powers of recognition, but they were " not at all affected by changing the hue, brightness, and markings" of the eggs, showing that the egg itself is not recognizable. The noddies were very much puzzled by moving the nest, which shows that it is not the nest that they recognize but its position.

After the young bird is hatched the parents are still more interested in defending the nest. "They will now attack with vigor other noddies which approach too near the nest—the sooties and the frigate birds." Both parents help in feeding the young coming alternately at intervals varying from two to four hours. Professor Watson (1908) further says:

The young are cared for in the nest until they become strong enough to leave it and live upon the ground. The young birds born in low nests, even at a very early age (20 days and even earlier) clamber from them with alacrity and hide in near-by bushes when danger is imminent. In many cases these young birds can not get back into the nest. Under these circumstances they remain near the nest locality, and the parents on returning first alight on or near the nest and later hop to the ground and feed the young bird. It is interesting to speculate upon the method of recognition between parent and young. There can be no doubt at least of an accurate functional recognition. Since the noddy is always silent when contented, the evidence is good that recognition occurs wholly in terms of vision. Whether recognition of young (or of mate by mate) would take place outside of the nest locality is a problem which ought to be solved.

An entirely different method of nesting has been noted by several observers in the West Indies. Mr. George N. Lawrence (1864) published the following interesting notes made by Dr. A. A. Julien on the island of Sombrero:

Their nests are of two kinds. For the first the noddy gathers together, by carrying in its bill, a considerable quantity of bits of shells, deposits them in a shallow cavity of the rock, say 8 to 12 inches in diameter, deepens a little the center of the basin, and thereon lays her egg. Occasionally such a nest is also encircled with a few twigs; sometimes it consists of over 50 pieces of shell but more frequently the shells and twigs are so scant that the egg lies upon the bare rock. The nests built in the crevices of the cliff, however, consist chiefly of twigs, though even these are frequently capped by a few bits of shell, upon which the egg immediately lies. The noddies are often thievish when building their nests; where two pair are thus engaged in close proximity, the one will often repeatedly carry off to their own nest from that of the other in their absence.

Eggs.—Although the noddy has been said to lay from two to three eggs in a set, such cases must be decidedly exceptional, for one egg only seems to be the almost invariable rule. If the egg is taken or destroyed it will soon be replaced by another, but evidently only one young bird is reared in a season by each pair of birds. The egg is ovate or slightly elliptical ovate in shape. The shell is thin, smooth, and without luster. The ground color varies but slightly, from " pale-pinkish buff " to " cartridge buff." It is sparingly spotted with small spots or dots, usually more thickly at the larger end, with at least two distinct colors. The underlying spots are of various pale shades of lilac or lavender and the overlying, more conspicuous, spots are of bright shades of deep reddish brown. Some of the brown spots seem to be superimposed over the lilac spots or blended with them. The eggs can be readily distinguished from those of the sooty tern by being much less heavily spotted. The measurements of 44 eggs, in the United States National Museum, average 52 by 35 millimeters; the eggs showing the four extremes measure **58** by 37, 54 by **37.5, 49.5** by 35.5 and 51 by **33** millimeters.

Young.—According to Professor Watson (1908):

The young noddies began to appear on the island about June 9. The first few hours after birth they are extremely helpless. During the first day of their life they exhibit few signs of fear, making little effort to shrink away from the hand. * * * At the end of the first day the birds were able to stand fairly erect and to move their heads with some freedom. * * * They can not swim at the end of the first day. * * * The note of the young noddy is very different from the hoarse, rattling sound of the adult. It is a soft, liquid, slow, plaintive "querk-querk-querk." * * * It is absolutely imperative for them to have the free use of the head and eyes and to be able to stand erect and to peck during the first day. The feeding parent on returning alights near the young bird, puts down its beak, and successively touches and taps the beak of the young bird; then its part of the reaction is at an end, provided by successive disgorgements it keeps its beak and throat filled with small minnows. The young bird must stand up and strike the beak of the parent until the parent opens its beak sufficiently wide to admit the beak of the young bird. When the fish in the mouth of the parent come in contact with the buccal cavity of the young, the swallowing reflex follows perfectly.

He reared three young noddies, feeding them by hand, until they were 30 days old, and his detailed notes are well worth reading. On the fourth day they began to learn to swim; after the eleventh day they were able to eat food deposited near them, as the adult often disgorges the food on the rim of the nest. They also soon learn to keep the nest clean by forcing their fecal matter far out over the rim of the nest. At just what age they learn to fly he does not state.

Plumages.—The downy young seems to have two color phases— a dusky phase and a white phase. The only specimen that I have seen is sparingly covered with short, dirty white down, tinged with buffy, with signs of a few black feathers coming in on the center of the back, the wings, and the crown. Two of the specimens shown in Professor Watson's (1908) plate seem to be quite dusky. At an age of 18 days the young bird seems to be about half fledged, and at 30 days practically fully feathered. This juvenal plumage much resembles that of the adult; it is " bone brown " above and " fuscous " below; the feathers of the back, scapulars, and wing-coverts are tipped with " wood brown," which fades later to buffy white; the pale gray cap is acquired and the throat is largely grayish white.

Yarrell (1871) says:

In birds which are not fully mature the black loral streaks are less defined; the gray of the forehead and throat is less pronounced, and the general tint is browner. Birds of the first year have very little white on the forehead; the mantle and wing coverts are of a lighter brown, the secondaries and tail feathers showing slight bars of umber-brown near the tips; underparts pale brown.

As to subsequent molts we have very little data, but there seems to be no conspicuous seasonal change, except on the crown. In winter this is nearly as brown as the back, with only a narrow white supraloral line. The material examined seems to indicate a complete postnuptial molt and probably a complete prenuptial molt.

Food.—In regard to the feeding habits of these terns, Professor Watson (1908) says:

In a locality where marine forms are so abundant as in this favored Gulf region, the terns collect their food with little difficulty. They feed upon small fish of different kinds, which are present in great abundance. Examination of the stomach contents of both young noddies and sooties showed the presence of representatives of the two families of fish Carangidae and Clupeidae.

To my great surprise I found that the birds never swim nor dive. As a matter of fact, they never touch the water except when drinking or bathing. The bird drinks the seawater as it skims the surface of the water with open beak. Bathing they perform in much the same way, never coming to a stop in the water nor completely immersing the body; usually the breast and head are the only parts dipped into the water.

The birds fish by following schools of minnows which are being attacked by larger fish. The minnow, in its efforts to escape, jumps out of the water and skims the surface for a short distance. The terns pick off these minnows as they hop up above and over the surface of the water. The rapidity and accuracy of visual-motor adjustment in this reaction is wonderful.

The birds feed singly or in groups; usually in groups. The group may be composed of both noddies and sooties and may contain sometimes as many as

50 to 100 individuals. All during the day groups of noddies and sooties may be seen at work. As the minnows cease to jump above the surface of the water, the group disbands and scatters in every direction. An instant later, as an attack is made upon the minnows in some other locality, the birds immediately rush there and renew their feeding.

He also discovered that most of their fishing is done within 9 or 10 knots of the island, and that they seldom venture more than 15 knots away from it. Mr. B. S. Bowdish (1902) found in the stomach of a noddy "an entire flying fish about 4 inches long and remains of others.

Behavior.—Audubon (1840) writes of the flight of the noddy:

The flight of this bird greatly resembles that of the nighthawk when passing over meadows or rivers. When about to alight on the water the noddy keeps its wings extended upward and touches it first with its feet. It swims with considerable buoyancy and grace, and at times immerses its head to seize on a fish. It does not see well by night, and it is perhaps for this reason that it frequently alights on the spars of vessels, where it sleeps so soundly that the seamen often catch them.

Dr. Frank M. Chapman (1908) gives a different impression of it. He says:

As the only tern with a rounded, instead of forked tail, the noddy might be expected to differ in flight from other members of its family. In fact, it suggested, when in the air, a light-bodied, long-winged, long-tailed pigeon. They fly rapidly, never hovering with the sooties, and they were often seen pursuing each other high in the air in what were doubtless mating flights.

Professor Watson's (1908) interesting experiments show that the noddy is a swift and powerful flier, with strong powers of orientation. Birds which he transported and liberated at Key West, Cuba, and even Cape Hatteras returned directly and promptly to their breeding grounds in the Dry Tortugas. He says that in flying at night they "break their graceful flight into short, ungraceful, and ill-directed choppy swoops, very similar to the way the nighthawk breaks its flight when flying after dark."

In spite of the statement of some other writers to the contrary, Professor Watson (1908) says that these "birds never swim nor dive * * *. During my three months' stay I never saw one of these birds in the water, except by accident, and then the bird, if the tide is against it, can never reach the shore, so poorly does it swim."

Mr. Bowdish (1902) says that "the common note resembles the clamor of young crows, and is often heard, more or less, throughout the night." There has been so little published on this subject that I infer that the vocal performances of this species are not elaborate.

Of their behavior with relation to other species Professor Watson (1908) writes:

From the writings of others I had drawn the conclusion that the frigate bird attacks the terns and forces them to disgorge, and that it feeds upon their young. I spent many weary hours in attempting to discover the relation of the frigate bird to the terns, especially its relation to the noddies. Since the noddies build their nests in the bushes where the frigate birds roost, it was presumed that there, if anywhere, the devouring tendency of the frigate bird ought to appear. I found that the cause of the disturbance between noddy and frigate bird lies chiefly in the fact that the latter, in attempting to find a bush in which to rest, sun, or roost, will oftentimes alight upon or very near to a noddy nest, whereupon the noddy most immediately concerned and those near by will attack the frigate bird, and at times even rout him. It is a common occurrence especially late in the afternoon when the frigate birds are returning to see hundreds of such fights. The noddy is always careful to attack the frigate birds by sudden thrusts (usually made from below), dodging quickly to avoid their fearful and powerful beaks.

Mr. Edward W. Gifford (1913) says:

It was not uncommon to see a noddy sitting on the head of a brown pelican, while the latter was resting on the water swallowing fish. Once I saw two on a pelican's head at one time. Several often accompanied the young pelicans in their excursions along the coasts.

Gathering the eggs of this and other sea birds for food has long since been stopped in the Dry Tortugas by including the islands on which they breed in a reservation and by protecting them; but the practice still continues in the West Indies, where the eggs are considered a legitimate food supply and are gathered in large numbers.

Fall.—According to Dr. Joseph Thompson, United States Navy, (1903), " toward the end of September the birds begin to leave. They leave in great flocks and at night. The entire exodus consumes, apparently, but two or three days; and some morning the observer will find the island absolutely deserted, save for a few crippled birds that have been injured and are unable to follow their comrades." Just where they go or how they spend the winter months does not seem to be very well known. They are probably scattered widely along the tropical coast of South America and among the numerous islands inclosing the Caribbean Sea.

DISTRIBUTION.

Breeding range.—The Atlantic form breeds from the Florida Keys (Dry Tortugas) and the Bahamas (Atwood's and Gaulding's Keys, Dry and Booby Rocks, Acklin, and Berry Islands, etc.), eastward and southward throughout the West Indies (Cuba, Jamaica, Haiti, Porto Rico, Dominica, Carriacou, etc.), to Venezuela (Margarita Island). South in the Atlantic Ocean to St. Helena, Tristan da Cunha, and Ascension Islands. West to the coast of British Honduras (Glover's Reef and Cay Dolores). North, formerly and perhaps now, to southern Texas. Pacific birds are supposed to be subspecifically distinct and have been split into several subspecies.

Breeding grounds protected in the following national reservation: In Florida, Tortugas Keys.

Winter range.—Practically the same as the breeding range.

Casual records.—One record for Bermuda (September 12, 1884).

Egg dates.—Bahama Islands: Forty-three records, May 5 to July 1; twenty-two records, May 16 to June 2. West Indies and Florida: Ten records, February 17 to July 6; five records, May 20 to June 24.

Family RYNCHOPIDAE, Skimmers.

RYNCHOPS NIGRA Linnaeus.

BLACK SKIMMER.

HABITS.

The coasts of Virginia and the Carolinas are fringed with chains of low, sandy islands, many of them lying far out from the shores, with broad, flat, sandy beaches on the ocean side, and often on the inner side with extensive salt marshes which are intersected by numerous creeks and shallow estuaries. Although practically worthless for human occupancy, these islands form ideal resorts for several species of water birds and shore birds. Cobb's Island, undoubtedly the most famous and perhaps the most typical of this class of islands, has for many years been a popular resort for sportsmen and bird lovers, though its bird population has been sadly depleted during recent years. The countless thousands of least terns, which once enlivened its sandy shores, have all disappeared into the capacious maw of the millinery trade. The gull-billed terns have been nearly exterminated and the common terns much reduced in numbers by the same agency. Only a few nests of each are still to be found on the pebbly sand flats. The laughing gulls still breed in fair numbers on the salt marshes, but they are persistently robbed by egg-hunting fishermen, and the once populous breeding colonies of willets have been nearly annihilated by sportsmen, who shoot the local breeding birds as well as the migrants. Fortunately the black skimmers are not regarded as game birds and their plumage is not in demand for millinery purposes, so that they still frequent their favorite breeding grounds in large numbers.

When the rising tide flows in around the island, covering the outer sand bars, driving the birds from their low-tide roosting and feeding places and flooding the shallow estuaries, then the " flood gulls," as they are called, may be seen skimming over the muddy shallows, about the mouths of the creeks, or up into the narrow inlets, gracefully gliding on their long, slender wings close to the surface in search of their finny prey, the tiny minnows, which have followed the advancing tide into the protecting, grassy shallows. It is a pleasure to sit and watch their graceful evolution in their untiring efforts to secure a meal, as they quarter back and forth over the same ground again and again, cutting the smooth surface of the water with their razor-like bills, scaling, wheeling, and turning like giant swallows, silently engrossed in their occupation for which they are so highly specialized.

Spring.—The black skimmers arrive on their breeding grounds on Cobb's Island and in its vicinity late in April or early in May but they are late breeders. For several weeks they roam about in large flocks or roost on the sand bars in masses so dense that they blacken the ground, every bird facing the wind. When resting or sleeping in such situations they squat closely or sit upon the sand for hours, but if approached every bird rises to its feet and simultaneously all mount suddenly into the air, flying straight toward the intruder with a chorus of peculiar barking yelps; wheeling just in time they circle over his head, perform a series of aerial evolutions, now high in the air and again close to the water, until they finally settle again on the sand. Their mating performances show off their marvelous powers of flight to advantage and are most exciting as two or more males give chase to the coveted female.

The coy one, shooting aslant to either side, dashes along with marvelous speed, flying hither and thither, upward, downward, in all directions. Her suitors strive to overtake her; they emit their love cries with vehemence; you are gladdened by their softly and tenderly enunciated *ha, ha,* or the *hack, hack, cae, cae,* of the last in the chase. Like the female, they all perform the most curious zigzags as they follow in close pursuit, and as each beau at length passes her in succession he extends his wings for an instant, and in a manner struts by her side. (Audubon, 1840.)

Nesting.—In 1907 I spent the last week in June on Cobb's Island and other islands in its vicinity where I found several large colonies of black skimmers just beginning their breeding operations. On Pig Island, a low, flat, sandy island, entirely devoid of vegetation and barely above high-water mark during the spring tides, I found two large colonies. They had chosen for their breeding grounds the higher portions of the sand flats beyond the reach of high tides, where numerous oyster, clam, and scallop shells were scattered about, half buried in the sand, among which the eggs were not conspicuous. Large numbers of little hollows had been scraped out in the sand, but, even at that late date, June 24, laying had only just begun; two nests were seen with one egg each and one with two eggs. Many of the birds were already squatting on the empty hollows or were busy with their courtships. They were very solicitous, flying out to meet us or circling about in flocks, uttering their characteristic notes of protest. A few days later, June 28, we visited another large colony of black skimmers in a similar situation on Wreck Island. They had evidently begun laying at about the same time, for many of the nests contained two or three eggs and one nest held four. The nest hollows measured from 4 to 5 inches in diameter and from 1 to 2 inches in depth; the nests were all entirely devoid of any attempt at lining. Several pairs of gull-billed terns and a few common terns were nesting in the midst of this colony.

Black skimmers formerly bred commonly on low sandy islands on the coast of New Jersey, but the encroachments of civilization have driven them away to more secluded spots. They still breed abundantly at certain points on the coasts of the Carolinas. Messrs. B. S. Bowdish (1910) and P. B. Philipp in 1909 found about 200 nesting on Royal Shoals, North Carolina, with a number of common and least terns, where on June 24, they were just beginning to lay; and at Bull's Bay, South Carolina, they found about a thousand beginning to lay between June 10 and 15. Mr. Arthur T. Wayne (1910) writes as follows regarding their breeding habits in South Carolina:

Twenty years age these curious birds used to breed regularly on Sullivans Island, and by May 15 full complements of eggs could be procured. At present, however, the breeding season is much later than formerly, and the birds, as a rule, have forsaken the coast islands (including Sullivans, Long, and Capers) and breed, or try to, mainly on the larger keys. As fast as the eggs are laid they are taken by any boatman who happens to discover them. The birds are thus forced to lay again and again in order to raise a brood, and hence the breeding season is a long one, being protracted through August.

In the Breton Island and other reservations off the coast of Louisiana I found a number of interesting skimmer colonies in 1910, where they have flourished under the adequate protection afforded them. On Grand Cochere, the outermost island, a low, flat sand bar, about 300 pairs were breeding a little apart from the large colonies of royal and Cabot's terns, nesting in hollows in the sand, as usual. The largest colony, and the one most typical of the region, was found on Battledore Island, where I spent the whole of one day (June 21), and, as the birds were very tame under the constant protection of the resident warden, I was able to study them at close range from my blind. On this little island, not over 4 acres in extent, I estimated that fully 5,000 pairs of laughing gulls, 1,000 pairs of black skimmers, 50 pairs of Louisiana herons, 30 pairs of Forster's terns, and 25 pairs of common terns were breeding. A large number of skimmers were nesting by themselves on an open beach of finely broken oyster shells which formed a long narrow point at one end of the island. They were also nesting at several places with the laughing gulls on the high ridges of broken oyster shells back of the beaches, which were more or less covered with scattered clumps of beach grass and small mangrove bushes. The gulls' nests were usually concealed among the vegetation, but the skimmers selected the more open spaces. The skimmers' nests were merely hollows scooped out in the loose shells, where the eggs were almost invisible. Nearly all the nests contained full sets of four or five eggs, but no young were seen; I saw only one young skimmer on the whole trip—a newly hatched chick, picked up on Hog Island, on June 22. The impression seems to have prevailed among the earlier writers that the black skimmers do not sit on their eggs in the daytime; it is true that they may, under favorable circumstances, leave their eggs uncovered for considerable periods, but they certainly protect their eggs from the sun's rays on hot days and keep them warm in cold or wet weather. I believe that they incubate most of the time. On Breton Island they certainly returned quickly to their eggs and sat upon them almost constantly within a few feet of my blind. The male usually stands besides his mate while she is incubating.

Life in these closely populated colonies is never dull; birds are constantly coming and going, skimming close over the heads of their sitting companions, causing frequent snappings of beaks or, if they come too near, grunts of protest or even little squabbles. When approaching her nest the bird alights 3 or 4 feet away, looks around carefully, walks slowly to her nest with her head held high, and gradually settles down on the eggs, working them under her plumage with the aid of wings and feet. She is restless and uneasy, craning her neck and looking about at every new comer. She may leave and return to the nest several times before settling down to quiet incubation. On this and other islands in the reservations the black skimmers seemed to be living in perfect harmony with their neighbors, the laughing gulls, and were apparently never robbed by them.

The following extract from some notes, sent to me by Mr. Stanley C. Arthur, is worth quoting, as illustrating the nervous restlessness of this species:

One pair of skimmers immediately in front of my blind afforded me a great deal of amusement during the entire afternoon. The female was very much scared, it seemed to me, and watched the blind into which I had disappeared, although the rest of the colony paid no attention to the khaki-colored tent that had been erected on their home grounds. This particular skimmer can best be described as being " skerry," and her lord and master was very much exercised over her behavior. She would wing her way over the nesting grounds, then swoop down over her nest of eggs, and when just about to alight would give her long black wings a flap and soon be soaring again into the air. Her mate would watch her approach and departure with sundry twistings of the head, and at times I feared he would twist his neck off, as he endeavored to follow her flight as she would rapidly circle over the eggs. He would run over to the eggs with little mincing footsteps and indicate by example how she should come and sit on them. In this performance the male bird did not wholly cover the eggs with his breast feathers, as the incubating birds usually do, but rather squatted over them and followed the aerial revolutions of his mate with a constantly moving head. The wife made several stops as though intending to alight on her eggs, and finally did so, coming lightly to the ground and running up to the eggs and covering them properly with her breast feathers. There would be peace and quiet until some (to me) undiscovered alarm would send the whole colony into the air " baying like a pack of hounds." After several sweeping flights through the air the whole skimmer colony would settle back on the eggs and remain quiet, except for the thin yelps that went on all the time, whether there was anything untoward to excite them or not.

Although the breeding season is often much prolonged by various disasters only one brood is raised in a season. The normal set consists of four or five eggs, though three often constitute a complete set, and sometimes as many as six or seven are laid. In the Breton Island reservation egg laying begins the very last of May or first of June; on the Virginia coast the laying season begins fully three weeks later; the black skimmer is therefore one of the last of the sea birds to lay. The period of incubation seems to be unknown; so far as I have been able to observe only the female incubates.

Eggs.—A series of black skimmer's eggs makes a striking feature in a collection, showing many interesting variations of bold and picturesque color patterns. The ground color is rarely pure white, but usually pale bluish white or creamy white, varying on the one hand to pale greenish blue, almost a heron's egg color, and on the other hand to deep " cream buff " or " pinkish buff." They are usually heavily marked with various shades of brown, from " tawny olive " and " burnt umber " to " seal brown " or " clove brown "; sometimes fairly evenly distributed as small spots, but more often in large irregular blotches or splashes in an endless variety of patterns. Nearly all of the eggs are more or less heavily spotted or blotched, and some are very prettily marked, with various shades of " lilac gray," " lavender gray," or " olive gray." In shape they vary from rounded ovate to elongate ovate, with a prevailing tendency toward the former shape. The measurements of 58 eggs in the United States National Museum average 45 by 33.5 millimeters; the eggs showing the four extremes measure **51** by 32, 45 by **36, 41.5** by 31, and 43 by **30.5** millimeters.

Young.—Mr. Arthur has sent me the following notes on the behavior of young skimmers:

While the colony under observation were still incubating their eggs I had an excellent opportunity to note the young in all stages, from those almost ready to fly to the young just out of the shell, and I also had an opportunity of noting the way the young skimmers are fed. This is done in two ways: The downy young are fed by regurgitation, the food being dropped by the parent bird on the ground; but so avid are the little ones for food that they pick at the parent bird's bill as the fish is being dropped, and then pick it up as a tiny chicken would pick up moistened bread. When the young birds commence to show their feathers they are fed whole fish by the parent bird. The fish is carried crosswise in the bill of the parent from where they are secured to the nesting grounds and is handed direct to the young bird. If by chance the parent bird drops the fish before its young can take it from the bill, the little one will pick it up from the ground by turning its head and bill sidewise. This is not a difficult accomplishment, as the difference in length between the upper and lower mandibles is very slight at this period.

From their earliest stage the young skimmers have a habit of scratching themselves into a hollow and lying absolutely flat upon the shell-covered beach. While this habit is displayed mostly by the downy young, I have seen it exhibited to a great extent by the feathered young when the young birds are able to run about and danger threatens. Then they will throw themselves flat on the shells of the beach and scratch alternately with their little webbed feet backward. They make about 15 or 20 movements before they snuggle down to rest, and while their legs are in action they make the shells fly most energetically. When the hollow is dug sufficiently to allow them to lie flush with the surrounding beach they remain absolutely motionless, and as their coloration is such as to indicate that nature has provided a protective mimicry, yet they are not difficult to detect; and, as the accompanying photographs show, they stand away from their surroundings most vividly. The chirp of the young is no different from that of the other sea birds, such as the laughing gulls and the terns, and they show the same marked instinct of recognizing their parents' raucous cries from the other alarms.

Plumages.—The young skimmer when first hatched is completely covered with soft, thick down, pale " vinaceous buff " above, lightly mottled with dusky on the back, and only faintly so mottled on the head, the under parts being pure white. As the youngster spends most of its time lying flat on the sand, its protective coloration conceals it admirably. It fades so invisibly into its surroundings that it is hard to realize that it is a living bird. During the downy stage it well knows the value of the hiding pose, and lies prostrate on the sand with head outstretched and eyes closed until touched, when it runs away with surprising agility. The razor-shaped bill is apparent even in the youngest chick, but the specialized bill of the adult is not fully developed until the flight stage is reached. The youngest birds are fed on semidigested food from the parent's throat, but after a few days they learn to run about, and are gradually taught to feed on more solid food, principally small fish. When the young birds have attained their growth and have acquired the juvenal plumage, before they learn to fly, they gather in flocks and learn to feed on what they can pick up along the water's edge. At this time the mandibles are of equal length. The long lower mandible of the adult would be a serious handicap in feeding, and therefore it is not developed until the bird has learned to skim the surface of the water for its food.

The juvenal plumage is handsomely and boldly marked; the upper half of the head is "pale ochraceous salmon" colored and the feathers of the back, scapulars, and wing-coverts are broadly tipped and edged with the same color, each feather being centrally dusky. These edgings, which are fully a quarter of an inch broad on the scapulars, soon fade out to white and wear away, leaving a dingy mottled effect on the upper parts. During the winter some progress is made toward maturity, and at the first prenuptial molt, which is complete, young birds become practically indistinguishable from adults. Adults have two complete molts each year, a prenuptial in February and March and a postnuptial in August and September. The adult winter plumage is similar to the nuptial, but the upper parts are browner, and there is a more or less distinct nuchal collar of whitish feathers.

Food.—The food of the black skimmer consists mainly of small fish, and to some extent shrimps and other small crustaceans. It feeds largely on the wing by skimming close to the smooth water, cutting with its long, rigid lower mandible the surface, from which it scoops into the small mouth the animal food to be found there. The upper mandible, which is movable, can plainly be seen to close down upon any morsel of food which is picked up. That it feeds largely at night everyone knows who has lain at anchor among the shoals of the South Atlantic coast and seen the shadowy forms flitting by in the gloom, but it does not do so exclusively, as has been stated. I have frequently seen it feeding in broad daylight, and think that it is more influenced by the tides than by anything else, for these at certain stages make its food more accessible. It is never seen to dive for its food, and its bill is not adapted for picking it up on the shore.

Mr. Arthur seems to have discovered another method of feeding, about which he writes me:

According to my observations the birds seek shallow water of not over 3 inches depth and pick up minnows and other small fish by a direct forward movement of the head and bill, in no way differing from a chick picking up a worm on dry land. Skimmers I have had in captivity, where fish was thrown to them on a hard surface, were compelled to turn their heads sideways to pick up the fish; but the skimmers I had under observation were working on a soft mud bottom, and I did not observe a single instance of the head being turned sideways to pick up the food. It was very noticeable at this time that while some of the birds were fishing in the shallow water other skimmers would come skimming over the water in the characteristic manner, but when they came to a stop they, too, began wading around and fishing in the manner I have just described.

Stomachs collected and sent to the United States Bureau of Biological Survey for identification of contents very unfortunately proved to be empty, and I have no positive data from this source as to what constituted the skimmer's food at this time of the year, but on July 5, while on Alexander Island, there occurred an unusual incident, in which a fish, a Forster tern, and a birdologist all figured. Making my way along a stretch of sandy beach I noted a skimmer flying toward the island holding crosswise in its bill a small fish. The reflections of the bright sun rays from the scales of the fish first attracted my attention. I was next attracted by a series of muffled "*yap-yap-yap's*," intermingled with several "*tear-tear-tear-tear-r-r-r-r's*" of a very active Forster tern that was pursuing the skimmer and intent upon forcing the big black bird to drop its lawfully acquired prey. The Forster's efforts were without any great success, however, until the two birds performed the aerial fracas just above my head and about 100 feet in the air. At this juncture the tern succeeded in scaring the skimmer by a very quick and vigorous dart aimed at the back of the black bird's head, which caused it to drop the fish, which fell in the mud at the edge of a shallow pond about 75 feet from where I was standing. Recognizing an opportunity to secure positive evidence of the food of the skimmer, I dropped the camera I was carrying and it was "nip and tuck" between the tern and me who would get the fish. I got the fish, but I have never before received such a scolding from a bird. The Forster tern seemed absolutely beside itself with rage, and followed me for over a mile along the beach, where the captain of our patrol boat was waiting for me with a small motor boat. It was not until we had put off from the island and headed in the direction of our large boat that the tern decided that there was no way of bullying me into returning the fish that he felt he had earned by right of combat. I identified the fish, which was about 2½ inches long, as a squeteague, or so-called sea trout, and evidently *Cynoscion nothus*, the so-called "bastard" weak fish; and this information was afterwards concurred in by the United States Bureau of Fisheries.

Behavior.—In flight the black skimmer is one of the most graceful of sea birds and the most highly specialized. Its slender build, its long, powerful wings and its broad forked tail are perfectly adapted to its modes of life. The strongest winds offer but little resistance to the little ball of feathers, supported by two long, slender blades which cut the air like the keenest razor. It has a strong combination of buoyancy and strength; it is swift and skillful on the wing, and always holds itself in perfect control. When flying in a flock, as is customary, its movements are synchronous to a high degree of perfection, the whole flock twisting, turning, wheeling, rising, or falling in perfect unison.

Of its voice not much can be said in the way of praise, for it is harsh and grating and far from pleasing. When flying out to meet the intruder on its breeding grounds it indulges in a chorus of peculiar nasal barking notes or grunting sounds, like the syllables, "Kak, kak, kak," or "Kuk, kuk, kuk," in a low, guttural tone. It also has a variety of soft love notes, sounding like "Kow, kow," or "Keow, keow," suggestive of certain gull notes.

Winter.—Although gregarious at all seasons the black skimmers are especially so in the fall and winter, when they gather in large flocks, flying in close formation, or roosting in dense masses on the sand bars or beaches. It is only when they are feeding that they are scattered out over the shoals. As soon as the young are able to fly in September the fall migration begins, and they retire from the northern portions of their range to spend the winter about the numerous shallow bays, estuaries, and creeks on the coasts of Florida and the Gulf States. They are never seen far out at sea and are seldom driven inland.

DISTRIBUTION.

Breeding range.—On the Atlantic coast from Virginia (Northampton County) to northeastern Florida (Nassau and Dowal Counties). On the Gulf coast from the Florida Keys to Louisiana and southern Texas (Cameron County). Formerly north to New Jersey and still earlier to Massachusetts. Present in summer and probably breeding on the coasts of Venezuela (Margarita) and Yucatan (Progreso).

Breeding grounds protected in the following national reservations: In Alabama, Petit Bois Island; in Louisiana, Breton Island and Tern Islands.

Winter range.—From northern Florida (mouth of St. Johns River) and from the coast of Louisiana southward, all around the Gulf of Mexico, and along the northern and eastern coasts of South America.

Spring migration.—Arrives in South Carolina about the middle of April and in Virginia about the last of April, or first week of May.

Fall migration.—Leaves Virginia about September 10 and South Carolina by November 15 at the latest.

Casual records.—Has wandered as far north and east as the Bay of Fundy (Grand Manan, August, 1879). Accidental inland: New York (Whitesboro, October, 1893); South Carolina (Chester, September 10, 1882); and Tennessee (Obion County). One record for Bermuda (October, 1876).

Egg dates.—Virginia: Thirty-two records, June 2 to July 20; sixteen records, June 18 to 26. South Carolina: Twenty records, May 15 to July 16; ten records, June 23 to July 4. Texas: Twenty records, May 10 to July 4; ten records, June 1 to 15.

REFERENCES TO BIBLIOGRAPHY.

ALLEN, FRANCIS HENRY.
  1908—Larus kumlieni and other Northern Gulls in the Neighborhood of
      Boston. The Auk, vol. 25, p. 296.
ALLEN, JOEL ASAPH.
  1905—Report on the Birds Collected in Northeastern Siberia by the Jesup
      North Pacific Expedition. Bulletin of the American Museum of
      Natural History, vol. 21, p. 219.
ANDERSON, RUDOLPH MARIA.
  1907—The Birds of Iowa. Proceedings of the Davenport Academy of
      Sciences, vol. 11, p. 125.
  1913—Report on the Natural History Collections of the Expedition, in "My
      Life with the Eskimo," by Vilhjalmur Stefansson.
ANTHONY, ALFRED WEBSTER.
  1898—Terns of Socorro Island. The Osprey, vol. 2, p. 123.
  1906—Random Notes on Pacific Coast Gulls. The Auk, vol. 23, p. 129.
ARNOLD, EDWARD.
  1912—A Short Summer Outing in Newfoundland, 1911. The Auk, vol. 29,
      p. 72.
ASTLEY, HUBERT DELAVAL.
  1901—My Birds in Freedom and Captivity.
AUDUBON, JOHN JAMES.
  1840—The Birds of America.
BAILEY, HAROLD HARRIS.
  1906—Ornithological Notes from Western Mexico and the Tres Marias and
      Isabella Islands. The Auk, vol. 23, p. 369.
  1913—The Birds of Virginia.
BAILEY, HARRY BALCH.
  1876—Notes on Birds Found Breeding on Cobb's Island, Va., between May
      25 and May 29, 1875. Quarterly Bulletin of the Nuttall Ornith-
      ological Club, vol. 1, p. 24.
BAIRD, SPENCER FULLERTON, BREWER, THOMAS MAYO, and RIDGWAY, ROBERT.
  1884—The Water Birds of North America.
BENDIRE, CHARLES EMIL.
  1888—Eggs of the Ivory Gull (Gavia alba). The Auk, vol. 5, p. 202.
BARROWS, WALTER BRADFORD.
  1912—Michigan Bird Life.
BEYER, GEORGE E., ALLISON, ANDREW, and KOPMAN, HENRY H.
  1906—List of the Birds of Louisiana. The Auk, vol. 23, p. 1 and p. 275;
      vol. 24, p. 314.
BISHOP, WATSON L.
  1888—Breeding Dates of Birds in Kings County, Nova Scotia. Ornitholo-
      gist and Oologist, vol. 13, p. 44.

BLANCHAN, NELTJE.
    1898—Birds that Hunt and are Hunted.
BOWDISH, BEECHER SCOVILLE.
    1900—A Day on De Cicheo Island. The Oologist, vol. 17, p. 117.
    1902—Birds of Porto Rico. The Auk, vol. 19, p. 356.
    1910—Bird Photographing in the Carolinas. The Auk, vol. 27, p. 305.
BOWLES, JOHN HOOPER.
    1909—The Birds of Washington.
BRAISLIN, WILLIAM COUGHLIN.
    1903—Notes Concerning Certain Birds of Long Island, N. Y. The Auk, vol.
        20, p. 50.
BREWSTER, WILLIAM.
    1878—The Short-tailed Tern (*Hydrochelidon fissipes*) in Massachusetts.
        Bulletin of the Nuttall Ornithological Club, vol. 3, p. 190.
    1879—The Terns of the New England Coast. Bulletin of the Nuttall Ornith-
        ological Club, vol. 4, p. 13.
    1883—Notes on the Birds Observed During a Summer Cruise in the Gulf
        of St. Lawrence. Proceedings of the Boston Society of Natural
        History, vol. 22, p. 364.
    1883a—On an Apparently New Gull from Eastern North America. Bulle-
        tin of the Nuttall Ornithological Club, vol. 8, p. 214.
    1902—Birds of the Cape Region of Lower California. Bulletin of the
        Museum of Comparative Zoology at Harvard College, vol. 41, no. 1.
    1912—Notes on the Flight of Gulls. The Auk, vol. 29, p. 85.
BROOKS, WINTHROP SPRAGUE.
    1915—Notes on Birds from East Siberia and Arctic Alaska. Bulletin of
        the Museum of Comparative Zoology at Harvard College, vol. 59,
        no. 5.
BRYANT, WALTER [PIERC] E.
    1888—Birds and Eggs from the Farallone Islands. Proceedings of the
        California Academy of Sciences; second series, vol. 1, p. 25.
BUTURLIN, SERGIUS ALEKSANDROVICH.
    1906—The Breeding Grounds of the Rosy Gull. The Ibis, 1906, p. 131.
CAHOON, JOHN CYRUS.
    1890—The Shore Bird Migration at Monomoy Island, Cape Cod, Mass.,
        Summer of 1888. Ornithologist and Oologist, vol. 15, p. 49.
CHAMBERLAIN, MONTAGUE.
    1891—A Popular Handbook of the Ornithology of the United States and
        Canada, based on Nuttall's Manual.
CHAMBERS, WILLIE LEE.
    1908—The Present Status of the Least Tern in Southern California. The
        Condor, vol. 10, p. 237.
CHAPMAN, FRANK MICHLER.
    1903—The Bird Life of Cobb's Island. Bird-Lore, vol. 5, p. 109.
    1904—The Black Tern at Home. Bird-Lore, vol. 6, p. 1.
    1908—Camps and Cruises of an Ornithologist.
CLARK, WILLIAM EAGLE.
    1898—On the Avifauna of Franz Josef Land. The Ibis, 1898, p. 249.
COLE, ARTHUR A.
    1910—Early Appearance of Gulls on Cobalt Lake, Ontario, Canada. Bird-
        Lore, vol. 12, p. 146.
COLLETT, ROBERT.
    1888—On a Breeding colony of Larus eburneus on Spitsbergen. The Ibis,
        1888, p. 440.

COLLINS, WILLIAM H.

 1880—Notes on the Breeding Habits of some of the Water-Birds of St. Clair Flats, Michigan. Bulletin of the Nuttall Ornithological Club, vol. 5, p. 61.

COOKE, WELLS WOODBRIDGE.

 1911—Our Greatest Travelers. The National Geographic Magazine, vol. 22, p. 346.

 1915—Distribution and Migration of North American Gulls and their Allies. United States Department of Agriculture Bulletin, No. 292.

COUES, ELLIOTT.

 1877—Birds of the North-West.

 1903—Key to North American Birds, Fifth Edition.

DAGGETT, FRANK SLATER.

 1890—Isle Royale. Ornithologist and Oologist, vol. 15, p. 99.

DALGLEISH, JOHN JAMES.

 1886—Discovery of the Nest of *Larus rossii* in Greenland. The Auk, vol. 3, p. 273.

DALL, WILLIAM HEALEY.

 1873—Notes on the Avifauna of the Aleutian Islands, from Unalaska, Eastward.

DAVIE, OLIVER.

 1889—Nests and Eggs of North American Birds, third edition.

DAWSON, WILLIAM LEON.

 1908—The New Reserves on the Washington Coast. The Condor, vol. 10, p. 45.

 1908a—The Bird Colonies of the Olympiades. The Auk, vol. 25, p. 153.

 1909—The Birds of Washington.

DILL, HOMER R., and BRYAN, WILLIAM ALANSON.

 1912—Report on Conditions on the Hawaiian Bird Reservation with List of the Birds found on Laysan. United States Department of Agriculture, Biological Survey, Bulletin No. 42.

DRESSER, HENRY EELES.

 1871—A History of the Birds of Europe.

DUTCHER, WILLIAM.

 1888—Bird notes from Long Island, N. Y. The Auk, vol. 5, p. 169.

 1901—Results of Special Protection to Gulls and Terns obtained through the Thayer Fund. The Auk, vol, 18, p. 76.

 1903—Report of the A. O. U. Committee on the Protection of North American Birds. The Auk, vol. 20, p. 101.

 1905—Report of the National Association of Audubon Societies. Bird-lore, vol. 7, p. 43.

 1905a—Gulls Destroy Insects and Mice. Bird-lore, vol. 7, p. 280.

DUTCHER, WILLIAM and BAILY, WILLIAM LLOYD.

 1903—A Contribution to the Life History of the Herring Gull in the United States. The Auk, vol. 20, p. 417.

DWIGHT, JONATHAN.

 1901—The Sequence of Moults and Plumages of the Laridae (Gulls and Terns). The Auk, vol. 18, p. 49.

 1906—Status and Plumages of the White-winged Gulls of the Genus Larus. The Auk, vol, 23, p. 26.

 1917—The Status of "Larus thayeri, Thayer's Gull." The Auk, vol. 34, p. 413.

EIFRIG, CHARLES WILLIAM GUSTAVE.

    1905—Ornithological Results of the Canadian "Neptune" Expedition to Hudson Bay and Northward. The Auk, vol 22, p. 233.

ELLIOTT, HENRY WOOD.

    1875—A Report upon the Condition of Affairs in the Territory of Alaska, chap. 10, p. 194, Ornithology of the Prybilov Islands, by Elliott Coues.

    1880—Report on the Seal Islands of Alaska.

EVANS, WILLIAM.

    1891—On the Periods occupied by Birds in the Incubation of their Eggs. The Ibis, 1891, p. 52.

EVERMANN, BARTON WARREN.

    1913—Eighteen Species of Birds New to the Pribilof Islands, Including Four New to North America. The Auk, vol. 30, p. 15.

FEILDEN, HENRY WEMYSS.

    1877—List of Birds Observed in Smith Sound and in the Polar Basin during the Arctic Expedition of 1875–76. The Ibis, 1877, p. 401.

FERRY, JOHN FARWELL.

    1910—Birds Observed in Saskatchewan during the Summer of 1909. The Auk, vol. 27, p. 185.

FIELD, GEORGE WILTON.

    1894—Notes on the Birds of Port Henderson, Jamaica, West Indies. The Auk, vol. 11, p. 117.

FINLEY, WILLIAM LOVELL.

    1905—Among the Seabirds off the Oregon Coast. The Condor, vol. 7, pp. 119 and 161.

    1907—Among the Gulls on Klamath Lake. The Condor, vol. 9, p. 12.

FISHER, ALBERT KENRICK.

    1893—The Death Valley Expedition. North American Fauna, No. 7.

FISHER, WALTER KENRICK.

    1906—Birds of Laysan and the Leeward Islands, Hawaiian Group. Bulletin of the United States Fish Commission, vol. 23, pt. 3, p. 769.

FISHER, WILLIAM HARMANUS.

    1897—Cobb's Island, Virginia. The Osprey, vol. 1, p. 107.

FORBES, ALEXANDER.

    1913—Concerning the Flight of Gulls. The Auk, vol. 30, p. 359.

FORBES, HENRY OGG.

    1898—British Birds, with their Nests and Eggs, Order Gaviae, vol. 6, p. 1.

FRAZAR, MARTIN ABBOTT.

    1887—An Ornithologist's Summer in Labrador. Ornithologist and Oologist vol. 12, p. 1.

GÄTKE, HEINRICH.

    1895—Heligoland as an Ornithological Observatory.

GIFFORD, EDWARD WINSLOW.

    1913—The Birds of the Galapagos Islands. Proceedings of the California Academy of Sciences, Fourth Series, vol. 2, p. 1.

GOODWIN, S. H.

    1904—About the Utah Gulls. The Condor, vol. 6, p. 99.

GOSS, NATHANIEL STICKNEY.

    1891—History of the Birds of Kansas.

GOSSE, PHILIP HENRY.

    1847—The Birds of Jamaica.

GRINNELL, JOSEPH.
  1900—Birds of the Kotzebue Sound Region. Pacific Coast Avifauna, No. 1.
  1915—A Distributional List of the Birds of California. Pacific Coast
    Avifauna, No. 11.
HAGERUP, ANDREAS THOMSEN.
  1891—The Birds of Greenland.
HATCH, PHILO LUOIS.
  1892—Notes on the Birds of Minnesota.
HEADLEY, FREDERICK WEBB.
  1912—The Flight of Birds.
HEERMANN, ADOLPHUS L.
  1859—Report upon Birds Collected on the Survey. U. S. Explorations and
    Surveys for a Railroad to the Pacific, vol. 10, p. 29.
HENNINGER, WALTHER FRIEDRICH.
  1910—On Some Eggs Supposed to be New to Science. The Wilson Bulletin,
    vol. 22. Old series, No. 71, p. 119.
HILL, C. BOYCE.
  1900—Notes on the Nesting of the Pomatorhine Skua. The Ibis, 1900,
    p. 526.
HINCKLEY, F. C.
  1900—Notes on the Animal and Vegetable Life of the region of Sushitna
    and Kuskokwim Rivers. U. S. Geological Survey, 1898–1899,
    pt. 7, p. 76.
HOLLAND, ARTHUR H.
  1890—On Some Birds of the Argentine Republic, with Notes by P. L.
    Sclater. The Ibis, 1890, p. 424.
  1892—Short Notes on the Birds of Estancia Espartilla, Argentine Republic,
    The Ibis, 1892, p. 193.
HOWELL, ALFRED BRAZIER.
  1911—A Comparative Study at Cobb's Island, Va. The Auk, vol. 28, p. 449.
ISELY, DWIGHT.
  1912—A List of the Birds of Sedgwick County, Kansas. The Auk, vol. 29,
    p. 25.
JOB, HERBERT KEIGHTLEY.
  1898—The Enchanted Isles. The Osprey, vol. 3, p. 37.
  1910—The Franklin's Gull. National Association of Audubon Societies,
    Educational Leaflet No. 44, Bird-Lore, vol. 12, p. 124.
JONES, LYNDS.
  1903—The Terns of the Weepecket Islands, Massachusetts. The Wilson
    Bulletin, No. 44, vol. 10, p. 94.
  1906—A Contribution to the Life History of the Common and Roseate
    Terns. The Wilson Bulletin, vol. 18, p. 35.
  1908—June with the Birds of the Washington Coast. The Wilson Bulletin,
    vol. 20, pp. 19, 57, and 189, and vol. 21, p. 3.
  1909—The Birds of Cedar Point and Vicinity. The Wilson Bulletin, No.
    67, vol. 21, p. 55.
JORDAN, A. H.
  1888—A Visit to the Four Brothers, Lake Champlain. Ornithologist and
    Oologist, vol. 13, p. 138.
KEELER, CHARLES AUGUSTUS.
  1892—On the Natural History of the Farallone Islands. Zoe, vol. 3, p. 144.
KELSEY, FREDERICK WILLIS.
  1902—The Least Tern at San Diego. The Condor, vol. 4, p. 144.

KING, RICHARD.
    1836—Narrative of a Journey to the Shores of the Arctic Ocean in 1833,
        1834, and 1835, Under the Command of Captain Back, R. N.
KNIGHT, ORA WILLIS.
    1908—The Birds of Maine.
KNOX, JOHN COWING.
    1899—My First Trip in '99. The Oologist, vol. 16, pp. 118 and 131.
KOBBÉ, WILLIAM HOFFMAN.
    1902—The Status of Certain Supposed Species of the Genus Larus. The
        Auk, vol. 19, p. 19.
KUMLIEN, LUDWIG.
    1879—Contributions to the Natural History of Arctic America. Bulletin
        of the United States National Museum, No. 15.
KUMLIEN, LUDWIG, and HOLLISTER, NED.
    1903—The Birds of Wisconsin. Bulletin of the Wisconsin Natural His-
        tory Society, vol. 3, new ser., p. 5.
LANGILLE, JAMES HIBBERT.
    1884—Our Birds and Their Haunts.
LAWRENCE, GEORGE NEWBOLD.
    1864—Catalogue of Birds Collected at the Island of Sombrero, W. I., with
        Observations by A. A. Julien. Annals of the Lyceum of Natural
        History in New York, vol. 8, p. 93.
McCLINTOCK, LEOPOLD.
    1856—His diary, June 21, 1853. The Natural History Review, vol. 3, p. 40.
McCORMICK, ALOYSIUS IGNATIUS STANISLAUS.
    1894—Breeding Habits of the Least Tern in Los Angeles County, Cali-
        fornia. Bulletin of the Cooper Ornithological Club, vol. 1, p. 49.
McGREGOR, RICHARD CRITTENDEN.
    1902—A List of Birds Collected in Norton Sound, Alaska. The Condor,
        vol. 4, p. 135.
McILWRAITH, THOMAS.
    1894—The Birds of Ontario.
MACFARLANE, RODERICK ROSS.
    1891—Notes on and List of Birds and Eggs Collected in Arctic America,
        1861–1866. Proceedings of the United States National Museum,
        vol. 14, p. 412.
    1908—List of Birds and Eggs Observed and Collected in the Northwest
        Territories of Canada, between 1880 and 1894, in "Through the
        Mackenzie Basin," by Charles Mair.
MACGILLIVRAY, WILLIAM.
    1852—A History of British Birds.
MACKAY, GEORGE HENRY.
    1892—Habits of the American Herring Gull. The Auk, vol. 9, p. 221.
    1893—Observations on the Breeding Habits of Larus atricilla in Massa-
        chusetts. The Auk, vol. 10, p. 333.
    1895—The Terns of Muskeget Island, Massachusetts. The Auk, vol. 12,
        p. 32.
    1897—The Terns of Muskeget Island, Massachusetts, pt. 3. The Auk, vol.
        14, p. 383.
    1898—The Terns of Muskeget Island, Massachusetts, pt. 4. The Auk,
        vol. 15, p. 168.
MACOUN, JOHN.
    1909—Catalogue of Canadian Birds, second edition.

MANNICHE, A. L. V.

    1910—The Terrestrial Mammals and Birds of Northeast Greenland. Mede-
        lelser om Grønland, vol. 45.

MARS, F. ST.

    1912—The Eagle Guard. The Outing Magazine, vol. 59, p. 676, No. 6,
        March, 1912.

MAYNARD, CHARLES JOHNSON.

    1896—The Birds of Eastern North America.

MORRIS, FRANCIS ORPEN.

    1903—A History of British Birds, fifth edition.

MURDOCH, JOHN.

    1885—Report of the International Polar Expedition to Point Barrow,
        Alaska, part 4, Natural History, p. 91.

NANSEN, FRIDTJOF.

    1899—The Norwegian North Polar Expedition, 1893–1896, Scientific Re-
        sults, vol. 4.

NELSON, EDWARD WILLIAM.

    1883—The Birds of Bering Sea and the Arctic Ocean.

    1887—Report upon Natural History Collections made in Alaska.

    1899—Birds of the Tres Marias Islands. North American Fauna, No. 14,
        p. 21.

NOBLE, GEORGE KINGSLEY.

    1916—The Resident Birds of Guadeloupe. Bulletin of the Museum of Com-
        parative Zoology at Harvard College, vol. 60, No. 10.

NORTON, ARTHUR HERBERT.

    1909—The Food of Several Maine Water-Birds. The Auk, vol. 26, p. 439.

    1910—The Little Gull, Larus minutus Pall., in Maine, with remarks on
        its distribution and its occurrence in America. The Auk, vol. 27,
        pp. 447–450.

    1918—The Ivory Gull (Pagophila alba) at Portland, Me. The Auk, vol.
        35, p. 220.

NUTTALL, THOMAS.

    1834—A Manual of the Ornithology of the United States and Canada.
        Water Birds.

OBERHOLSER, HARRY CHURCH.

    1918—The Subspecies of Larus hyperboreus Gunnerus. The Auk, vol. 35,
        p. 467.

OSBURN, PINGREE I.

    1909—The Nesting of the Heermann Gull. The Condor, vol. 11, p. 151.

PALMER, WILLIAM.

    1890—Notes on the Birds observed during the Cruise of the United States
        Fish Commission Schooner Grampus in the summer of 1887. Pro-
        ceedings of the United States National Museum, vol. 13, p. 249.

    1899—The Avifauna of the Pribilof Islands. The Fur-Seals and Fur-Seal
        Islands of the North Pacific Ocean, Part 3, p. 355.

PARRY, WILLIAM EDWARD.

    1824—Journal of a second voyage for the discovery of a Northwest Passage.

PEABODY, PUTNAM BURTON.

    1896—A Tern Study. The Osprey, vol. 1, p. 1.

PEARSON, THOMAS GILBERT.

    1908—Cabot's Tern (Sterna sandvicensis acuflavida) Breeding in North
        Carolina. The Auk, vol. 25, p. 312.

PREBLE, EDWARD ALEXANDER.
   1908—A Biological Investigation of the Athabaska-Mackenzie Region. North American Fauna, No. 27.

PRESTON, J. W.
   1886—Breeding of Franklin's Gull in Minnesota. Ornithologist and Oologist, vol. 11, p. 54.

RAY, MILTON SMITH.
   1903—A List of Water Birds of Lake Valley, Central Sierra Nevada Mountains, California. The Condor, vol. 5, p. 47.

   1904—A Fortnight on the Farallones. The Auk, vol. 21, p. 425.

RAY, PATRICK HENRY.
   1885—Report of the International Polar Expedition to Point Barrow, Alaska. Part 4, Natural History. p. 91.

REED, CHESTER ALBERT.
   1904—North American Birds' Eggs.

RICHARDSON, JOHN.
   1825—Appendix to Capt. Parry's Journal of Second Voyage for the Discovery of a Northwest Passage.

   1851—Arctic Searching Expedition.

RIDGWAY, ROBERT.
   1880—Description of the Eggs of the Caspian Tern (Sterna caspia). Bulletin of the Nuttall Ornithological Club, vol. 5, p. 221.

   1886—On the Glaucous Gull of Bering Sea and Contiguous Waters. The Auk, vol. 3, p. 330.

   1887—A Manual of North American Birds.

RIVES, WILLIAM CABELL.
   1890—A Catalogue of the Birds of the Virginias. Proceedings of the Newport Natural History Society, no. 7.

ROBERTS, THOMAS SADLER.
   1877—Notes on the Breeding of the Black Tern (Hydrochelidon lariformis) in Minnesota. Bulletin of the Nuttall Ornithological Club, vol. 2, p. 34.

   1900—An Account of the Nesting Habits of Franklin's Rosy Gull (Larus franklinii), as Observed at Heron Lake in Southern Minnesota. The Auk, vol. 17, p. 272.

ROCKWELL, ROBERT BLANCHARD.
   1911—Notes on the Nesting of the Forster and Black Terns in Colorado. The Condor, vol. 13, p. 57.

ROSS, JAMES CLARK.
   1835—Natural History, in Appendix to the narrative of a second voyage in search of a Northwest Passage, by Sir John Ross.

RUSSELL, FRANK.
   1898—Explorations in the Far North.

SAUNDERS, HOWARD.
   1889—An Illustrated Manual of British Birds.

SCOTT, WILLIAM EARL DODGE.
   1887—The Present Conditions of Some of the Bird Rookeries of the Gulf Coast of Florida. The Auk, vol. 4, pp. 135, 213, and 273.

   1888—A Summary of Observations on the Birds of the Gulf Coast of Florida. The Auk, vol. 5, p. 373.

   1891—Observations on the Birds of Jamaica, West Indies. The Auk, vol. 8, p. 249 and p. 353.

SELBY, PRIDEAUX JOHN.
    1833—Illustrations of British Ornithology.
SELOUS, EDMUND.
    1905—The Bird Watcher in the Shetlands.
SENNETT, GEORGE BURRITT.
    1878—Notes on the Ornithology of the Lower Rio Grande of Texas. Bul-
        letin of the United States Geological and Geographical Survey,
        vol. 4, p. 1.
SETON, ERNEST THOMPSON.
    1908—Bird Records from Great Slave Lake Region. The Auk, vol. 25,
        p. 68.
STEJNEGER, LEONHARD.
    1885—Results of Ornithological Explorations in the Commander Islands
        and in Kamtschatka. Bulletin of the United States National
        Museum, No. 29.
STONE, WITMER.
    1909—The Birds of New Jersey, Their Nests and Eggs. Annual Report of
        the New Jersey State Museum.
STRONG, REUBEN MYRON.
    1914—On the Habits and Behaviour of the Herring Gull, Larus argentatus
        Pont. The Auk, vol. 31, pp. 22 and 178.
SUCKLEY, GEORGE, and COOPER, JAMES GRAHAM.
    1860—The Natural History of Washington Territory and Oregon.
SWAINSON, WILLIAM, and RICHARDSON, JOHN.
    1831—Fauna Boreali-Americana, vol. 2, Birds.
THAYER, JOHN ELIOT.
    1911—A Nesting Colony of Heermann Gulls and Brewster Boobies. The
        Condor, vol. 13, p. 104.
    1911a—Eggs of the Elegant Tern (Sterna elegans). The Oologist, vol. 28,
        p. 171.
THAYER, JOHN ELIOT, and BANGS, OUTRAM.
    1914—Notes on the Birds and Mammals of the Arctic Coast of East
        Siberia—Birds. Proceedings of the New England Zoological Club,
        vol. 5, p. 1.
THOMPSON, ERNEST EVAN.
    1890—The Birds of Manitoba. Proceedings of the United States National
        Museum, vol. 13, p. 457.
THOMPSON, JOSEPH.
    1903—The Tortugas Tern Colony. Bird-Lore, vol. 5, p. 77.
TOWNSEND, CHARLES WENDELL.
    1905—The Birds of Essex County, Massachusetts. Memoirs of the Nuttall
        Ornithological Club, No. 3.
TOWNSEND, CHARLES WENDELL, and ALLEN, GLOVER MORRILL.
    1907—Birds of Labrador. Proceedings of the Boston Society of Natural
        History, vol. 33, p. 277.
TURNER, LUCIEN MCSHAN.
    1886—Contributions to the Natural History of Alaska.
TUTTLE, ALBERT W.
    1911—Pomarine Jaeger Capturing a Phalarope. The Auk, vol. 28, p. 482.
WARD, HENRY LEVI.
    1906—Notes on the Herring Gull and the Caspian Tern. Bulletin of the
        Wisconsin Natural History Society, vol. 4, p. 113.
    1906a—Why Do Herring Gulls Kill Their Young? Science, new ser., vol.
        24, p. 593.

WARREN, BENJAMIN HARRY.
    1890—Report on the Birds of Pennsylvania.
WATSON, JOHN BROADUS.
    1908—The Behaviour of Noddy and Sooty Terns. Papers from the Tortugas
        Laboratory of the Carnegie Institution of Washington, vol. 2,
        p. 187.
WAYNE, ARTHUR TREZEVANT.
    1910—Birds of South Carolina. Contributions from the Charleston
        Museum, 1.
WELLS, JOHN GRANT.
    1902—Birds of the Island of Carriacou. The Auk, vol. 19, p. 239.
WETMORE, ALEXANDER.
    1916—Birds of Porto Rico. U. S. Department of Agriculture Bulletin,
        No. 326.
WILLETT, GEORGE.
    1912—Report of G. Willett, Agent and Warden Stationed on St. Lazaria
        Bird Reservation, Alaska. Bird-Lore, vol. 14, p. 419.
WILSON, ALEXANDER.
    1832—American Ornithology. Jardine edition.
YARRELL, WILLIAM.
    1871—History of British Birds, Fourth Edition, 1871–1885, Revised and En-
        larged by Alfred Newton and Howard Saunders.

EXPLANATION OF PLATES 78-93

The eggs illustrated were selected from the collection of the United States National Museum, except where otherwise indicated. After the Museum catalogue number of each specimen is given the locality, the date, and the name of the collector as far as known.

PLATE 78.

1. Pomarine jaeger, 18458, Greenland, Governor Fencker.
2. Pomarine jaeger, 18459, Greenland, Governor Fencker.
3. Skua, 24541, Shetland Islands, June 28, 1884, A. Hopeland.
4. Parasitic jaeger, 24542, Monsay coast of Shetland Islands, June 2, 1881, R. Turnbull.
5. Parasitic jaeger, 22155, Kodiak Island, Alaska, June 19, 1884, W. J. Fisher.

PLATE 79.

1. Long-tailed jaeger, 21434, Saint Michael, Alaska, June 16, 1880, E. W. Nelson.
2. Long-tailed jaeger, 11688, Arctic coast, east of Anderson River, R. McFarlane.
3. Ivory gull, 23598, Storöen, Spitzbergen, August 8, 1887, M. Foslic.
4. Glaucous-winged gull, 19061, Kodiak Island, Alaska, July, 1883, W. J. Fisher.
5. Glaucous-winged gull, 19061, Kodiak Island, Alaska, July, 1883, W. J. Fisher.

PLATE 80.

1. Kittiwake, 21512, Greenland, Governor Fencker.
2. Kittiwake, 23257, Bird Rock, Quebec, July 9, 1887, W. Palmer.
3. Pacific Kittiwake, 16739, Saint George Island, Alaska, June 24, 1873, H. W. Elliott.
4. Pacific Kittiwake, 16739, Saint George Island, Alaska, June 24, 1873, H. W. Elliott.
5. Red-legged Kittiwake, 16735, Saint George Island, Alaska, June 25, 1873, H. W. Elliott.
6. Red-legged Kittiwake, 16737, Saint George Island, Alaska, 1873, H. W. Elliott.

PLATE 81.

1. Glaucous gull, 18713, Afognak Island, Alaska, July 12, 1882, W. J. Fisher.
2. Glaucous gull, 21451, Yukon Delta, Alaska, June 4, 1879, E. W. Nelson.
3. Iceland gull, 18446, Christianshaab, Greenland, Governor Fencker.
4. Iceland gull, 18447, Christianshaab, Greenland, 1880, Governor Fencker.

329

PLATE 82.

1. Great black-backed gull, 18450, Christianshaab, Greenland, Governor Fencker.
2. Great black-backed gull, 24426, Southeast Labrador, June 6, 1884, M. A. Frazar.
3. Western gull, 26442, Tomales Point, California, May 24, 1885, A. M. Ingersoll.
4. Western gull, 26443, Tomales Point, California, May 24, 1885, A. M. Ingersoll.

PLATE 83.

1. Herring gull, 27573, Islin, Midkiff Lake, Hamilton County, New York, May 13, 1894, C. Haskell.
2. Herring gull, 27577, Islin, Midkiff Lake, Hamilton County, New York, May 13, 1894, C. Haskell.
3. Vega gull, A. C. Bent collection, Kolyma River, Siberia, July 10, 1916, J. Koren.
4. Vega gull, A. C. Bent collection, Kolyma River, Siberia, July 6, 1917, J. Koren.

PLATE 84.

1. Ring-billed gull, 3598, Fort George, Hudson Bay, C. Drexler.
2. Ring-billed gull, 6074, Lake Winnipeg, Manitoba, Donald Gunn.
3. California gull, 13721, Pyramid Lake, Nevada, May 16, 1868, R. Ridgway.
4. California gull, 13700, Pyramid Lake, Nevada, May 16, 1868, R. Ridgway.
5. California gull, 24676, Pyramid Lake, Nevada, June 4, 1891.

PLATE 85.

1. Short-billed gull, 19064, Kodiak Island, Alaska, 1883, W. J. Fisher.
2. Short-billed gull, 29218, Prince William Sound, Alaska, June 26, 1899, A. K. Fisher.
3. Mew gull, 24544, Murray Islands, Fleet Bay, Scotland, May 6, 1885, R. Sevell.
4. Heermann's gull, 32004, Ildefonso Island, Lower California, April 8, 1909, W. W. Brown, jr.
5. Heermann's gull, 31965, Ildefonso Island, Lower California, April 8, 1909, W. W. Brown, jr.

PLATE 86.

1. Laughing gull, 23332, Cobb Island, Virginia, July 16, 1884, H. M. Smith.
2. Laughing gull, 23331, Cobb Island, Virginia, July 16, 1884, H. M. Smith.
3. Laughing gull, 18139, Rapeza Marsh, Virginia, R. Ridgway.
4. Franklin's gull, 14212, Red River Settlements, 1865, D. Gunn.
5. Franklin's gull, 12735, Lake Manitoba, Manitoba, D. Gunn.
6. Franklin's gull, 24431, Jackson County, Minnesota, May 18, 1890, O. L. Bullis.

PLATE 87.

1. Bonaparte's gull, 15745, Fort Anderson, Mackenzie, 1866, R. McFarlane.
2. Bonaparte's gull, 15744, Fort Anderson, Mackenzie, 1866, R. McFarlane.
3. Bonaparte's gull, 11484, Fort Anderson, Mackenzie, 1866, R. McFarlane.
4. Little gull, 15572, North Ladoga, Russia, June 1, 1869, H. E. Dresser.
5. Ross's gull, 31096, Kolyma Delta, Siberia, June 13, 1905, S. Buturlin.

6. Sabine's gull, 21401, Saint Michael, Alaska, 1877, E. W. Nelson.
7. Sabine's gull, 11529, Franklin Bay, Mackenzie, 1865, R. McFarlane.
8. Sabine's gull, 21408, Saint Michael, Alaska, 1877, E. W. Nelson.

PLATE 88.

1. Caspian tern, 22556, Corpus Christi, Texas, June 15, 1883, B. F. Goss.
2. Caspian tern, 22560, Corpus Christi, Texas, May 6, 1883, B. F. Goss.
3. Royal tern, 26303, San Antonio Bay, Texas, May 12, 1892, H. P. Attwater.
4. Royal tern, 26303, San Antonio Bay, Texas, May 12, 1892, H. P. Attwater.
5. Royal tern, 21589, Clearwater, Florida, S. T. Walker.

PLATE 89.

1. Elegant tern, J. E. Thayer collection, Cerralvo Island, Lower California, April 10, 1910, W. W. Brown, jr.
2. Elegant tern, J. E. Thayer collection, Cerralvo Island, Lower California, April 10, 1910, W. W. Brown, jr.
3. Elegant tern, J. E. Thayer collection, Cerralvo Island, Lower California, April 10, 1910, W. W. Brown, jr.
4. Cabot's tern, 26317, San Antonio Bay, Texas, May 12, 1892, H. P. Attwater.
5. Cabot's tern, 25359, Hog Island, Bahamas, May 16, 1892, D. P. Ingraham.
6. Cabot's tern, 25359, Hog Island, Bahamas, May 16, 1892, D. P. Ingraham.
7. Cabot's tern, 25359, Hog Island, Bahamas, May 16, 1892, D. P. Ingraham.

PLATE 90.

1. Gull-billed tern, 21522, Cobb Island, Virginia, May 30, 1871, Rev. C. M. Jones.
2. Gull-billed tern, 21539, Texas, Dr. J. C. Merrill.
3. Forster's tern, 18124, Rapeza Marsh, Virginia, July, 1880, R. Ridgway.
4. Forster's tern, 21543, Minneapolis, Minn., 1876, E. Dickinson.
5. Common tern, A. C. Bent collection, Lake Winnepegosis, Manitoba, June 19, 1913, A. C. Bent.
6. Common tern, A. C. Bent collection, Chatham, Mass., June 29, 1916, A. C. Bent.
7. Common tern, A. C. Bent collection, Jericho Bay, Maine, June 17, 1899, A. C. Bent.
8. Common tern, A. C. Bent collection, Chatham, Mass., May 26, 1916, A. C. Bent.

PLATE 91.

1. Arctic tern, 7831, Anderson River, MacKenzie, June 23, 1865, R. McFarlane.
2. Arctic tern, 23333, Muskeget Island, Massachusetts, June 21, 1884, J. C. Cahoon.
3. Arctic tern, 15183, Sable Island, Nova Scotia, P. S. Dodd.
4. Roseate tern, 12795, East Windsor Hill, Connecticut, Dr. Wood.
5. Roseate tern, 21521, Cobb Island, Virginia, May 31, 1871, C. M. Jones.
6. Roseate tern, 21521, Cobb Island, Virginia, May 31, 1871, C. M. Jones.
7. Aleutian tern, 13471, Kodiak Island, Alaska, 1868, F. Bischoff.
8. Aleutian tern, 17228, Saint Michael, Alaska, July 1, 1875, L. M. Turner.
9. Trudeau's tern, J. E. Thayer collection, Saint Ambrose Island, Saint Felix Group, Chile, December 17, 1907, H. Ozan.

PLATE 92.

1. Sooty tern, 23917, Ship Channel Keys, Bahamas, May 28, 1889, D. P. Ingraham.
2. Sooty tern, 9751, Jamaica, 1864, W. T. March.
3. Sooty tern, 9790, Dry Tortugas, Florida, L. Greenwood.
4. Sooty tern, 1751, Dry Tortugas, Florida, L. Greenwood.
5. Bridled tern, 24823, Atwoods Island, Bahamas, May 14, 1891.
6. Bridled tern, 24362, Samona Keys, Bahamas, June 14, 1891, D. P. Ingraham.
7. Bridled tern, 24839, Atwoods Island, Bahamas, June 10, 1891.
8. Bridled tern, 33060, Desecheo Island, Porto Rico, June 15, 1912, A. Wetmore.

PLATE 93.

1. Noddy, 4989, Dry Tortugas, Florida, T. J. Greenwood.
2. Least tern, 2948, Saint Georges Island, Florida, G. W. Maslin.
3. Noddy, 4989, Dry Tortugas, Florida, T. J. Greenwood.
4. Black tern, 21527, Camp Harney, Oregon, June 1, 1876, C. Bendire.
5. Black tern, 21523, Pewaukee, Wisconsin, May 27, 1872, B. F. Goss.
6. Black tern, 15177, Pewaukee, Wisconsin, 1869, B. F. Goss.
7. White-winged black tern, A. C. Bent collection, Ungane, Hungary, May 28, 1906. Kudeldorff collection.
8. Black skimmer, 23318, Galveston, Texas, July 1, 1878, N. S. Goss.
9. Least tern, 24349, Chincoteague, Virginia, June 5, 1888, M. H. Bickley.
10. Black skimmer, 18147, Bone Island, Virginia, R. Ridgway.

INDEX.

333

PLATES

PLATE 1. LAUGHING GULL. Group of laughing gulls on beach, Battledore Island, Louisiana, June, 1905; photo presented by Mr. Herbert K. Job.

PLATE 2. *Left*: SKUA. Nest and eggs of skua, Kaldafarnes, Iceland, photo presented by Mr. J. Wilkinson. *Right*: POMARINE JAEGER. Pomarine jaeger, Chatham, Massachusetts, August 31, 1904, photo presented by Mr. Herbert K. Job.

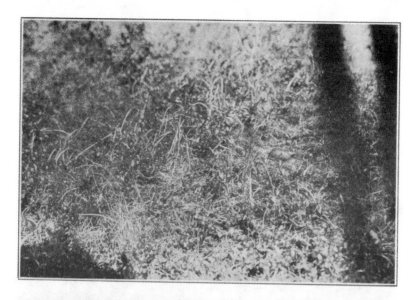

PLATE 3. PARASITIC JAEGER. *Upper:* Nest and egg of parasitic jaeger, Kolyma Delta, Siberia, June 27, 1917, from a negative taken by Mr. Johan Koren for the author. *Lower:* Nest and eggs of parasitic jaeger, Point Barrow, Alaska, June 25, 1917, from a negative taken by Mr. T. L. Richardson for the author.

PLATE 4. LONG-TAILED JAEGER. *Upper:* Nest and eggs of long-tailed jaeger, St. Michael, Alaska, June 19, 1915, from a negative taken by Mr. F. S. Hersey for the author. *Lower:* A nearer view of the same nest, referred to on page 22.

PLATE 5. LONG-TAILED JAEGER. *Upper:* Nest and eggs of long-tailed jaeger, Kolyma Delta, Siberia, June 22, 1917, from a negative taken by Mr. Johan Koren for the author. *Lower:* Long-tailed jaeger on its nest, northeast Greenland, courtesy of Mr. A. L. V. Manniche, Meddelelser om Gronland.

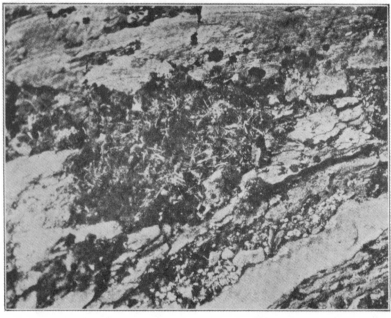

PLATE 6. IVORY GULL. *Upper:* Nesting site of ivory gull, north-east Greenland, July 18, 1908. *Lower:* Nest in above locality. Both courtesy of Mr. A. L. V. Manniche, Meddelelser om Grønland.

PLATE 7. KITTIWAKE. *Upper:* Kittiwake on its nest, Bird Rock, Quebec, June 25, 1904, photo presented by Mr. Herbert K. Job. *Lower:* Kittiwakes on their nests, Bird Rock, Quebec, June 24, 1904, referred to on page 38.

PLATE 8. KITTIWAKE. *Upper:* Nests and eggs of kittiwakes, Bird Rock, Quebec, June 25, 1904, referred to on page 38. *Lower:* Young kittiwakes, just prior to the flight stage, Bird Rock, Quebec, July 24, 1915, referred to on page 39.

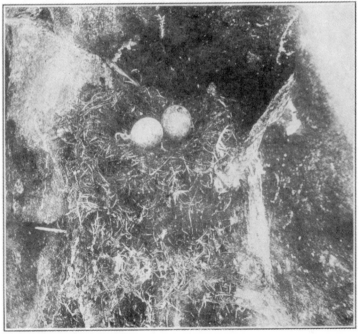

PLATE 9. PACIFIC KITTIWAKE. *Upper:* Pacific kittiwakes on their nests, Walrus Island, Alaska, July 7, 1911. *Lower:* Nest and eggs of same in the above locality. Both referred to on page 46.

PLATE 10. RED-LEGGED KITTIWAKE. Nesting colony of red-legged kittiwakes, Saint George Island, Alaska, photo presented by Dr. Charles H. Townsend.

PLATE 11. GLAUCOUS GULL. *Upper:* Nest and eggs of glaucous gull, Borup Glenn, Greenland. *Lower:* Nearer view of another nest, Sutherland Island, Greenland. Both photos presented by Mr. Donald B. MacMillan, courtesy of the American Museum of Natural History.

PLATE 12. GLAUCOUS GULL. *Upper:* Nest and young of glaucous gull, Sulwuddy, Greenland. *Lower:* Young glaucous gulls, Cape Kendrick, Greenland. Both photos presented by Mr. Donald B. Mac-Millan, courtesy of the American Museum of Natural History.

PLATE 13. GLAUCOUS-WINGED GULL. *Upper:* Nesting colony of glaucous-winged gulls, Walrus Island, Alaska, July 7, 1911, referred to on page 68. *Lower:* Nest and eggs of same, Bogoslof Island, Alaska, July 4, 1911, referred to on page 67.

PLATE 14. GLAUCOUS-WINGED GULL. *Upper:* Nesting resort of glaucous-winged gulls, Flattery Rocks, Reservation, Washington. *Lower:* Nest and eggs of same, Carroll Islet, Washington. Both photos presented by Mr. W. L. Dawson.

PLATE 15. GREAT BLACK-BACKED GULL. *Upper:* Distant view of nest of great black-backed gull, south coast of Labrador, May 25, 1909. *Lower:* Nearer view of same nest, referred to on page 77.

PLATE 16. GREAT BLACK-BACKED GULL. *Upper:* Great black-backed gull, trumpeting, Lake George, Nova Scotia, July 28, 1912, referred to on page 84. *Lower:* Adult and young bird, one year old, same locality and date. Both photos presented by Mr. H. H. Cleaves.

PLATE 17. WESTERN GULLS. *Upper:* Western gulls in breeding colony, Farallon Islands, August 10, 1919; photo presented by Mr. Oluf J. Heinemann. *Lower:* Breeding colony of same, Humboldt County, California; photo presented by Mr. W. L. Dawson.

PLATE 18. WESTERN GULL. *Upper:* Nest and young of western gull, Farallon Islands, July 3, 1914, photo presented by Mr. Oluf J. Heinemann. *Lower:* Nest and eggs of same, Los Coronados Islands, Lower California, photo presented by Mr. Donald R. Dickey.

PLATE 19. HERRING GULL. *Upper:* Nesting site of herring gulls, Heron Island, Maine, July 11, 1915. *Lower:* Herring gulls in breeding colony, Little Spoon Island, Maine, July 12, 1915.

PLATE 20. HERRING GULL. *Upper:* Nest and eggs of herring gull, Seal Island, Nova Scotia, July 4, 1904. *Lower:* Another nest of same, Heron Island, Maine, July 11, 1915.

PLATE 21. HERRING GULL. *Upper:* Nest and young of herring gull, Heron Island, Maine, July 11, 1915. *Lower:* Young herring gull, half fledged, Matinicus Rock, Maine, July, 1906; photo presented by Mr. Herbert K. Job.

PLATE 22. VEGA GULL. *Upper:* Nest and eggs of Vega gull, Kolyma Delta, Siberia, July, 1916. *Lower:* Another nest in same locality, July 6, 1917. Both from negatives taken by Mr. Johan Koren for the author.

PLATE 23. *Upper:* RING-BILLED GULL. Nesting colony of California and ring-billed gulls, Big Stick Lake, Saskatchewan, June 14, 1906, referred to on page 125. *Lower:* CALIFORNIA GULL. Nests of California gulls, in shallow water, in same colony.

PLATE 24. CALIFORNIA GULL. *Upper:* Nest and eggs of California gull, Big Stick Lake, Saskatchewan, June 14, 1906, referred to on page 126. *Lower:* Nest and young of same in same colony.

PLATE 25. RING-BILLED AND CALIFORNIA GULLS. *Upper:*
Nesting colony of ring-billed and California gulls, Big Stick Lake,
Saskatchewan, June 14, 1906, referred to on page 133. *Lower:* Nests
and eggs of ring-billed gull in same colony.

PLATE 26. RING-BILLED GULL. *Upper:* Nest and eggs of ring-billed gull, Prince William Sound, Alaska, June, 1912; photo presented by Mr. George G. Cantwell, referred to on page 135. *Lower:* Nest and young of same, Big Stick Lake, Saskatchewan, June 14, 1906.

PLATE 27. SHORT-BILLED GULL. *Upper:* Nesting site of short-billed gull, Lake Athabaska, Saskatchewan, June 27, 1914. *Lower:* Nest and egg in above locality. Both photos presented by Mr. Francis Harper, courtesy of the Geological Survey of Canada.

PLATE 28. SHORT-BILLED GULL. *Upper:* Nesting site of short-billed gull, St. Michael, Alaska, June 19, 1915, referred to on page 141. *Lower:* Nest, egg, and young of same in above locality. Both photos by Mr. F. S. Hersey for the author.

PLATE 29. HEERMANN'S GULL. *Upper:* Nesting colony of Heermann's gulls, Ildefonso Island, Lower California, March 23, 1909, referred to on page 148. *Lower:* Another view in same colony April 8, 1909. Both photos by Mr. W. W. Brown for Col. John E. Thayer; courtesy of *The Condor*.

PLATE 30. LAUGHING GULL. *Upper:* Nest and eggs of laughing gull, Muskeget Island, Massachusetts, June 22, 1902, referred to on page 155. *Lower:* Nest and young of same in above locality, July 4, 1904.

PLATE 31. LAUGHING GULL. *Upper:* Young laughing gull, hiding in grass, Muskeget Island, Massachusetts, August 3, 1916, referred to on page 158. *Lower:* Young laughing gull, just prior to flight stage, same locality, August 4, 1916; photo presented by Dr. Alfred O. Gross.

PLATE 32. LAUGHING GULL. *Upper:* Pair of laughing gulls at the nest, Louisiana, June, 1908; photo presented by Mr. Herbert K. Job. *Lower:* Laughing gull on its nest, Louisiana; photo presented by Mr. Alfred M. Bailey.

PLATE 33. FRANKLIN'S GULL. *Upper:* Nesting colony of Franklin's gulls, Lake of the Narrows, Saskatchewan, June 9, 1905; photo presented by Mr. Herbert K. Job. *Lower:* Gull alighting on nest in above colony, referred to on page 164.

PLATE 34. FRANKLIN'S GULL. *Upper*: Nest and eggs of Franklin's gull, Lake of the Narrrows, Saskatchewan, June 9, 1905. *Lower*: Nest and young of same, in above locality, referred to on page 165.

PLATE 35. FRANKLIN'S GULL. *Upper*: Pair of Franklin's gulls on their nest, North Dakota. *Lower*: Group of Franklin's gulls in nesting colony, Lake of the Narrrows, Saskatchewan, June 9, 1905. Both photos presented by Mr. Herbert K. Job.

PLATE 36. SABINE'S GULL. *Upper*: Nesting site of Sabine's gull, Saint Michael, Alaska, June 5, 1915, referred to on page 192. *Lower*: Nest and eggs of same in above locality. Both from negatives taken by Mr. F. S. Hersey for the author.

PLATE 37. SABINE'S GULL. *Upper:* Nest and eggs of Sabine's gull,
Saint Michael, Alaska, June 5, 1915, referred to on page 192. *Lower:*
Young Sabine's gull, Saint Michael, Alaska, June 19, 1915. Both from
negatives taken by Mr. F. S. Hersey for the author.

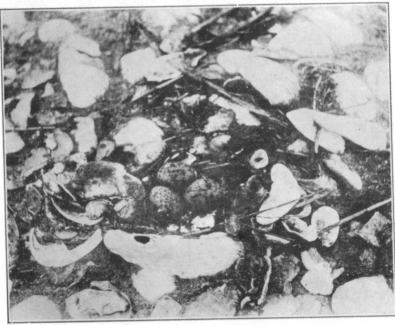

PLATE 38. GULL-BILLED TERN. *Upper*: Nesting site of gull-billed
tern, Cobb Island, Virginia, June 26, 1907, referred to on page 198.
Lower: Nest and eggs of same in above locality.

PLATE 39. GULL-BILLED TERN. *Upper:* Gull-billed tern in its nest, Cobb Island, Virginia, July, 1902; photo by Dr. Frank M. Chapman, courtesy of D. Appleton & Co. *Lower:* Young gull-billed tern, Cobb Island, Virginia, photo presented by Mr. Herbert K. Job.

PLATE 40. CASPIAN TERN. *Upper:* Nests and eggs of Caspian tern, Grand Cochere, Louisiana, June 19, 1910, referred to on page 204. *Lower:* One of above nests.

PLATE 41. CASPIAN TERN. Caspian tern on its nest, Alexander Island, Louisiana, July 3, 1918, photo presented by Mr. Stanley C. Arthur.

PLATE 42. CASPIAN TERN. *Upper:* Nesting colony of Caspian terns, Lower Klamath Lake, Oregon, referred to on page 205. *Lower:* Old and young birds in above colony. Both photos presented by Mr. William L. Finley.

PLATE 43. ROYAL TERN. *Upper:* Flock of royal terns, Grand Cochere, Louisiana, June 19, 1910. *Lower:* Eggs in above colony, referred to on page 213.

PLATE 44. ROYAL TERN. *Upper:* Nesting colony of royal terns, Grand Cochere, Louisiana, June 19, 1910, referred to on page 214. *Lower:* Pair of royal terns and young, Louisiana; photo presented by Mr. Alfred M. Bailey.

PLATE 45. ROYAL TERN. *Upper:* Flock of young royal terns, Louisiana, July 5, 1918. *Lower:* Young royal terns, Louisiana, June 15, 1918. Both photos presented by Mr. Stanley C. Arthur.

PLATE 46. CABOT'S TERN. *Upper:* Nesting colony of Cabot's terns, Grand Cochere, Louisiana, June 19, 1910, referred to on page 222. *Lower:* Eggs of Cabot's tern in same locality.

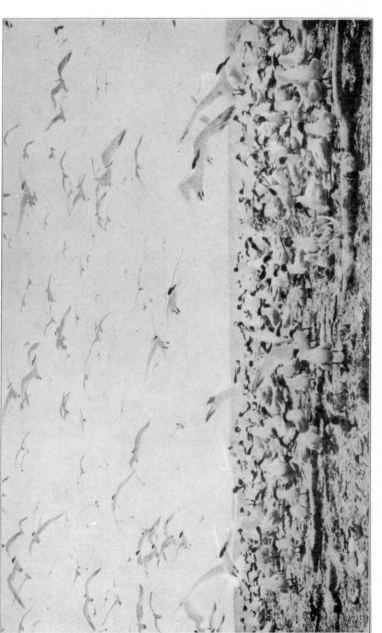

PLATE 47. CABOT'S TERN. Nesting colony of Cabot's terns, with a few royal terns, Louisiana; photo presented by Mr. Alfred M. Bailey.

PLATE 48. CABOT'S TERN. *Upper:* Nesting colony of Cabot's terns, with one royal tern, Southwest Key, Louisiana, June, 1908; photo presented by Mr. Herbert K. Job. *Lower:* Young Cabot's tern, Louisiana, June 16, 1918; photo presented by Mr. Stanley C. Arthur.

PLATE 49. FORSTER'S TERN. *Upper:* Nests of Forster's tern, Wreck Island, Virginia, June 28, 1907, referred to on page 230. *Lower:* One of above nests.

PLATE 50. FORSTER'S TERN. *Upper:* Nests of Forster's terns, Barr Lake, Colorado, May 24, 1907. *Lower:* Young Forster's terns in above colony. Both photos presented by Mr. Robert B. Rockwell, referred to on page 231.

PLATE 51. FORSTER'S TERN. *Upper:* Nest and eggs of Forster's tern, Barr Lake, Colorado; photo presented by the Colorado Museum of Natural History. *Lower:* Forster's tern on its nest, Malheur Lake, Oregon; photo presented by Mr. W. L. Finley.

PLATE 52. COMMON TERN. *Upper:* Nest and eggs of common tern, Penobscot Bay, Maine, June 12, 1900, referred to on page 240. *Lower:* Another nest of same, Muskeget Island, Massachusetts, June 22, 1902, referred to on page 239.

PLATE 53. COMMON TERN. *Upper:* Young common terns, recently hatched, Chatham, Massachusetts, June 29, 1916. *Lower:* Older young of same, Muskeget Island, Massachusetts, July 4, 1903.

PLATE 54. COMMON TERN. *Upper:* Common tern on its nest, Chatham, Massachusetts, June 13, 1919. *Lower:* Nesting colony of same in above locality, same date.

PLATE 55. ARCTIC TERN. *Upper:* Nest and eggs of arctic tern, Chatham, Massachusetts, June 29, 1916. *Lower:* Another nest of same, Yukon Delta, Alaska, June 19, 1914, from negative taken by Mr. F. S. Hersey for the author.

PLATE 56. ARCTIC TERN. *Upper:* Arctic tern at its nest, Matinicus Rock, Maine, July, 1906. *Lower:* Another nest of same in above locality. Both photos presented by Mr. Herbert K. Job.

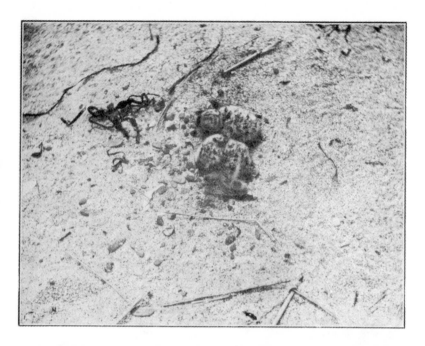

PLATE 57. ARCTIC TERN. *Upper:* Young arctic terns, recently hatched, Chatham, Massachusetts, June 29, 1916. *Lower:* Two older young of same, Matinicus Rock, Maine, July, 1906; photo presented by Mr. Herbert K. Job.

PLATE 58. ROSEATE TERN. *Upper:* Nests and eggs of roseate tern, Muskeget Island, Massachusetts, June 22, 1902. *Lower:* Another nest of same in above locality, referred to on page 257.

PLATE 59. ROSEATE TERN. *Upper:* Nesting colony of roseate terns, Muskeget Island, Massachusetts, June 10, 1919, referred to on page 257. *Lower:* Roseate tern on its nest, above locality and date.

PLATE 60. ROSEATE TERN. *Upper:* Roseate tern and young, Weepecket Island, Massachusetts, July 1, 1919. *Lower:* Roseate tern, same locality and date.

PLATE 61. ROSEATE TERN. *Upper:* Young roseate tern, about 5 days old, Dry Tortugas, Florida. *Lower:* Young roseate tern, about 3 weeks old, same locality. Both photos by Dr. Paul Bartsch.

PLATE 62. ALEUTIAN TERN. *Upper:* Nest and eggs of Aleutian tern, Saint Michael, Alaska, June 23, 1915, referred to page 266. *Lower:* Nearer view of same nest. Both from negatives taken by Mr. F. S. Hersey for the author.

PLATE 63. LEAST TERN. *Upper:* Nesting site of least terns, Dartmouth, Massachusetts, June 14, 1919. *Lower:* Nest and eggs of same, in above locality, June 16, 1916.

PLATE 64. LEAST TERN. *Upper:* Nest and eggs of least tern, Newport Beach, Orange County, California; photo presented by Mr. Wright M. Pierce. *Lower:* Least terns and young, Louisiana; photo presented by Mr. Alfred M. Bailey.

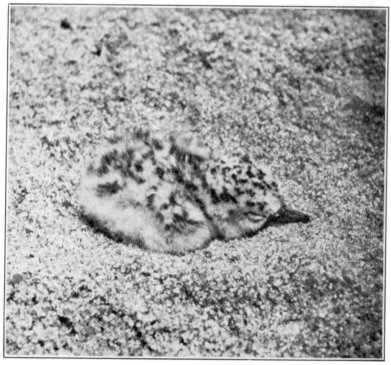

PLATE 65. LEAST TERN. *Upper:* Young least tern, half grown. *Lower:* Young least tern, recently hatched. Both photos presented by Mr. Edward H. Forbush.

PLATE 66. SOOTY TERN. *Upper:* Nesting colony of sooty terns,
Bird Key, Dry Tortugas, Florida. *Lower:* Bird on its nest in above
locality. Both photos presented by Mr. Herbert K. Job.

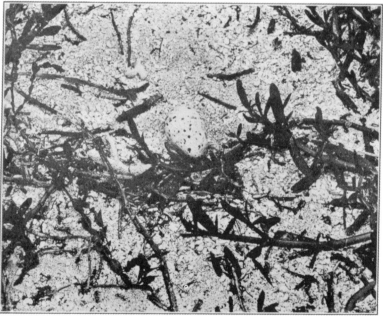

PLATE 67. SOOTY TERN. *Upper:* Nest and two eggs of sooty tern, Bird Key, Dry Tortugas, Florida. *Lower:* Ordinary nest of same in above locality. Both photos presented by Mr. Herbert K. Job.

PLATE 68. SOOTY TERN. *Upper:* Young sooty tern, 8 days old, Dry Tortugas, Florida. *Lower:* An older bird, 25 days old. Both photos by Prof. John B. Watson, courtesy of *Bird-Lore*.

PLATE 69. BLACK TERN. *Upper:* Nesting site of black terns, Steele County, North Dakota, June 9, 1901, referred to on page 291. *Lower:* Nest and eggs of same in above locality.

PLATE 70. BLACK TERN. *Upper:* Nesting site of black tern, Barr Lake, Colorado. *Lower:* Nest and eggs of same in above locality. Both photos presented by Mr. Robert B. Rockwell.

PLATE 71. BLACK TERN. *Upper:* Black tern at its nest, Minneapolis, Minnesota, June, 1918. *Lower:* Another bird and nest. Both photos by Mr. Jenness Richardson and presented by the University of Minnesota.

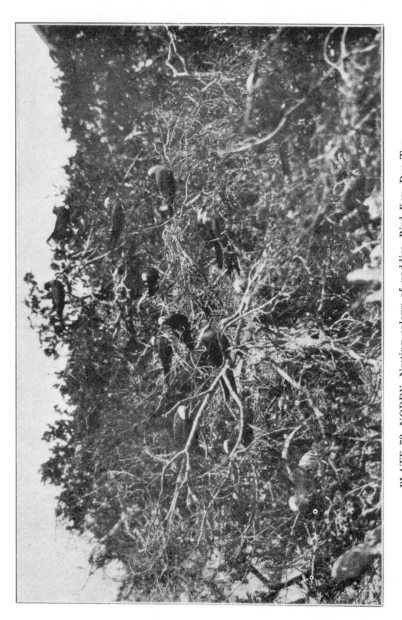

PLATE 72. NODDY. Nesting colony of noddies, Bird Key, Dry Tortugas, Florida; photo presented by Mr. Herbert K. Job.

PLATE 73. NODDY. *Upper:* Nest and egg of noddy, Bird Key, Dry Tortugas, Florida. *Lower:* Pair of noddies at their nest in same locality. Both photos presented by Mr. Herbert K. Job.

PLATE 74. NODDY. *Upper:* Young noddy in its nest, Dry Tortugas, Florida. *Lower:* An older bird in same locality. Both from photos by Dr. Joseph Thompson, courtesy of *Bird-Lore*.

PLATE 75. BLACK SKIMMER. *Upper:* Black skimmers flying over their nesting colony, Battledore Island, Louisiana, June 21, 1910, referred to on page 312. *Lower:* View in above colony.

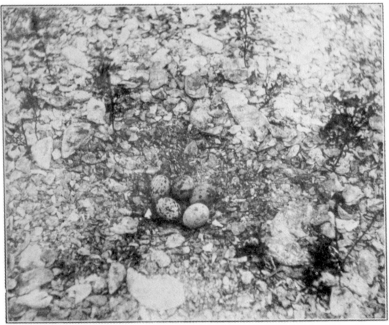

PLATE 76. BLACK SKIMMER. *Upper:* Nest and eggs of black skimmer on sandy beach, Wreck Island, Virginia, June 28, 1907, referred to on page 312. *Lower:* Nest and eggs of same on shell beach, Battledore Island, Louisiana, June 21, 1910, referred to on page 312.

PLATE 77. BLACK SKIMMER. *Upper:* Young black skimmer, recently hatched, Cobb Island, Virginia; photo by Dr. Frank M. Chapman, courtesy of D. Appleton & Co. *Lower:* Young black skimmer in juvenal plumage, September 19, 1895; photo slightly retouched on top of head and back, presented by Dr. R. W. Shufeldt.

PLATE 78. 1 and 2, Pomarine Jaeger; 3, Skua; 4 and 5, Parasitic Jaeger. For description, see page 329.

PLATE 79. 1 and 2, Long-tailed Jaeger; 3, Ivory Gull; 4 and 5, Glaucous-winged Gull. For description, see page 329.

PLATE 80. 1 and 2, Kittiwake; 3 and 4, Pacific Kittiwake; 5 and 6, Red-legged Kittiwake. For description, see page 329.

PLATE 81. 1 and 2, Glaucous Gull; 3 and 4, Iceland Gull. For description, see page 329.

PLATE 82. 1 and 2, Great Black-backed Gull; 3 and 4, Western Gull.
For description, see page 330.

PLATE 83. 1 and 2, Herring Gull; 3 and 4, Vega Gull. For description, see page 330.

PLATE 84. 1 and 2, Ring-billed Gull; 3, 4 and 5, California Gull. For description, see page 330.

PLATE 85. 1 and 2, Short-billed Gull; 3, Mew Gull; 4 and 5, Heermann's Gull. For description, see page 330.

PLATE 86. 1, 2 and 3, Laughing Gull; 4, 5 and 6, Franklin's Gull.
For description, see page 330.

PLATE 87. 1, 2 and 3, Bonaparte's Gull; 4, Little Gull; 5, Ross's Gull; 6, 7 and 8, Sabine's Gull. For description, see pages 330 and 331.

PLATE 88. 1 and 2, Caspian Tern; 3, 4 and 5, Royal Tern. For description, see page 331.

PLATE 89. 1, 2 and 3, Elegant Tern; 4, 5, 6 and 7, Cabot's Tern. For description, see page 331.

PLATE 90. 1 and 2, Gull-billed Tern; 3 and 4, Forster's Tern; 5, 6, 7 and 8, Common Tern. For description, see page 331.

PLATE 91. 1, 2 and 3, Arctic Tern; 4, 5 and 6, Roseate Tern; 7 and 8, Aleutian Tern; 9, Trudeau's Tern. For description, see page 331.

PLATE 92. 1, 2, 3 and 4, Sooty Tern; 5, 6, 7 and 8, Bridled Tern. For description, see page 332.

PLATE 93. 1 and 3, Noddy; 2 and 9, Least Tern; 4, 5 and 6, Black Tern; 7, White-winged Black Tern; 8 and 10, Black Skimmer. For description, see page 332.

A CATALOG OF SELECTED
DOVER BOOKS
IN ALL FIELDS OF INTEREST

A CATALOG OF SELECTED DOVER
BOOKS IN ALL FIELDS OF INTEREST

DRAWINGS OF REMBRANDT, edited by Seymour Slive. Updated Lippmann, Hofstede de Groot edition, with definitive scholarly apparatus. All portraits, biblical sketches, landscapes, nudes. Oriental figures, classical studies, together with selection of work by followers. 550 illustrations. Total of 630pp. 9⅛ × 12¼.
21485-0, 21486-9 Pa., Two-vol. set $29.90

GHOST AND HORROR STORIES OF AMBROSE BIERCE, Ambrose Bierce. 24 tales vividly imagined, strangely prophetic, and decades ahead of their time in technical skill: "The Damned Thing," "An Inhabitant of Carcosa," "The Eyes of the Panther," "Moxon's Master," and 20 more. 199pp. 5⅜ × 8½. 20767-6 Pa. $3.95

ETHICAL WRITINGS OF MAIMONIDES, Maimonides. Most significant ethical works of great medieval sage, newly translated for utmost precision, readability. Laws Concerning Character Traits, Eight Chapters, more. 192pp. 5⅜ × 8½.
24522-5 Pa. $4.50

THE EXPLORATION OF THE COLORADO RIVER AND ITS CANYONS, J. W. Powell. Full text of Powell's 1,000-mile expedition down the fabled Colorado in 1869. Superb account of terrain, geology, vegetation, Indians, famine, mutiny, treacherous rapids, mighty canyons, during exploration of last unknown part of continental U.S. 400pp. 5⅜ × 8½. 20094-9 Pa. $7.95

HISTORY OF PHILOSOPHY, Julián Marías. Clearest one-volume history on the market. Every major philosopher and dozens of others, to Existentialism and later. 505pp. 5⅜ × 8½. 21739-6 Pa. $9.95

ALL ABOUT LIGHTNING, Martin A. Uman. Highly readable non-technical survey of nature and causes of lightning, thunderstorms, ball lightning, St. Elmo's Fire, much more. Illustrated. 192pp. 5⅜ × 8½. 25237-X Pa. $5.95

SAILING ALONE AROUND THE WORLD, Captain Joshua Slocum. First man to sail around the world, alone, in small boat. One of great feats of seamanship told in delightful manner. 67 illustrations. 294pp. 5⅜ × 8½. 20326-3 Pa. $4.95

LETTERS AND NOTES ON THE MANNERS, CUSTOMS AND CONDITIONS OF THE NORTH AMERICAN INDIANS, George Catlin. Classic account of life among Plains Indians: ceremonies, hunt, warfare, etc. 312 plates. 572pp. of text. 6⅛ × 9¼. 22118-0, 22119-9, Pa. Two-vol. set $17.90

ALASKA: The Harriman Expedition, 1899, John Burroughs, John Muir, et al. Informative, engrossing accounts of two-month, 9,000-mile expedition. Native peoples, wildlife, forests, geography, salmon industry, glaciers, more. Profusely illustrated. 240 black-and-white line drawings. 124 black-and-white photographs. 3 maps. Index. 576pp. 5⅜ × 8½. 25109-8 Pa. $11.95

THE BOOK OF BEASTS: Being a Translation from a Latin Bestiary of the Twelfth Century, T. H. White. Wonderful catalog real and fanciful beasts: manticore, griffin, phoenix, amphivius, jaculus, many more. White's witty erudite commentary on scientific, historical aspects. Fascinating glimpse of medieval mind. Illustrated. 296pp. 5⅜ × 8¼. (Available in U.S. only) 24609-4 Pa. $6.95

FRANK LLOYD WRIGHT: ARCHITECTURE AND NATURE With 160 Illustrations, Donald Hoffmann. Profusely illustrated study of influence of nature—especially prairie—on Wright's designs for Fallingwater, Robie House, Guggenheim Museum, other masterpieces. 96pp. 9¼ × 10¾. 25098-9 Pa. $7.95

FRANK LLOYD WRIGHT'S FALLINGWATER, Donald Hoffmann. Wright's famous waterfall house: planning and construction of organic idea. History of site, owners, Wright's personal involvement. Photographs of various stages of building. Preface by Edgar Kaufmann, Jr. 100 illustrations. 112pp. 9¼ × 10.
23671-4 Pa. $8.95

YEARS WITH FRANK LLOYD WRIGHT: Apprentice to Genius, Edgar Tafel. Insightful memoir by a former apprentice presents a revealing portrait of Wright the man, the inspired teacher, the greatest American architect. 372 black-and-white illustrations. Preface. Index. vi + 228pp. 8¼ × 11. 24801-1 Pa. $10.95

THE STORY OF KING ARTHUR AND HIS KNIGHTS, Howard Pyle. Enchanting version of King Arthur fable has delighted generations with imaginative narratives of exciting adventures and unforgettable illustrations by the author. 41 illustrations. xviii + 313pp. 6⅛ × 9¼. 21445-1 Pa. $6.95

THE GODS OF THE EGYPTIANS, E. A. Wallis Budge. Thorough coverage of numerous gods of ancient Egypt by foremost Egyptologist. Information on evolution of cults, rites and gods; the cult of Osiris; the Book of the Dead and its rites; the sacred animals and birds; Heaven and Hell; and more. 956pp. 6⅛ × 9¼.
22055-9, 22056-7 Pa., Two-vol. set $21.90

A THEOLOGICO-POLITICAL TREATISE, Benedict Spinoza. Also contains unfinished *Political Treatise*. Great classic on religious liberty, theory of government on common consent. R. Elwes translation. Total of 421pp. 5⅜ × 8½.
20249-6 Pa. $6.95

INCIDENTS OF TRAVEL IN CENTRAL AMERICA, CHIAPAS, AND YUCATAN, John L. Stephens. Almost single-handed discovery of Maya culture; exploration of ruined cities, monuments, temples; customs of Indians. 115 drawings. 892pp. 5⅜ × 8½. 22404-X, 22405-8 Pa., Two-vol. set $15.90

LOS CAPRICHOS, Francisco Goya. 80 plates of wild, grotesque monsters and caricatures. Prado manuscript included. 183pp. 6⅜ × 9⅜. 22384-1 Pa. $5.95

AUTOBIOGRAPHY: The Story of My Experiments with Truth, Mohandas K. Gandhi. Not hagiography, but Gandhi in his own words. Boyhood, legal studies, purification, the growth of the Satyagraha (nonviolent protest) movement. Critical, inspiring work of the man who freed India. 480pp. 5⅜ × 8½. (Available in U.S. only)
24593-4 Pa. $6.95

ILLUSTRATED DICTIONARY OF HISTORIC ARCHITECTURE, edited by Cyril M. Harris. Extraordinary compendium of clear, concise definitions for over 5,000 important architectural terms complemented by over 2,000 line drawings. Covers full spectrum of architecture from ancient ruins to 20th-century Modernism. Preface. 592pp. 7½ × 9⅝. 24444-X Pa. $15.95

THE NIGHT BEFORE CHRISTMAS, Clement Moore. Full text, and woodcuts from original 1848 book. Also critical, historical material. 19 illustrations. 40pp. 4⅝ × 6. 22797-9 Pa. $2.50

THE LESSON OF JAPANESE ARCHITECTURE: 165 Photographs, Jiro Harada. Memorable gallery of 165 photographs taken in the 1930's of exquisite Japanese homes of the well-to-do and historic buildings. 13 line diagrams. 192pp. 8⅜ × 11¼. 24778-3 Pa. $10.95

THE AUTOBIOGRAPHY OF CHARLES DARWIN AND SELECTED LET-TERS, edited by Francis Darwin. The fascinating life of eccentric genius composed of an intimate memoir by Darwin (intended for his children); commentary by his son, Francis; hundreds of fragments from notebooks, journals, papers; and letters to and from Lyell, Hooker, Huxley, Wallace and Henslow. xi + 365pp. 5⅜ × 8. 20479-0 Pa. $6.95

WONDERS OF THE SKY: Observing Rainbows, Comets, Eclipses, the Stars and Other Phenomena, Fred Schaaf. Charming, easy-to-read poetic guide to all manner of celestial events visible to the naked eye. Mock suns, glories, Belt of Venus, more. Illustrated. 299pp. 5¼ × 8¼. 24402-4 Pa. $7.95

BURNHAM'S CELESTIAL HANDBOOK, Robert Burnham, Jr. Thorough guide to the stars beyond our solar system. Exhaustive treatment. Alphabetical by constellation: Andromeda to Cetus in Vol. 1; Chamaeleon to Orion in Vol. 2; and Pavo to Vulpecula in Vol. 3. Hundreds of illustrations. Index in Vol. 3. 2,000pp. 6⅛ × 9¼. 23567-X, 23568-8, 23673-0 Pa., Three-vol. set $38.85

STAR NAMES: Their Lore and Meaning, Richard Hinckley Allen. Fascinating history of names various cultures have given to constellations and literary and folkloristic uses that have been made of stars. Indexes to subjects. Arabic and Greek names. Biblical references. Bibliography. 563pp. 5⅜ × 8½. 21079-0 Pa. $8.95

THIRTY YEARS THAT SHOOK PHYSICS: The Story of Quantum Theory, George Gamow. Lucid, accessible introduction to influential theory of energy and matter. Careful explanations of Dirac's anti-particles, Bohr's model of the atom, much more. 12 plates. Numerous drawings. 240pp. 5⅜ × 8½. 24895-X Pa. $5.95

CHINESE DOMESTIC FURNITURE IN PHOTOGRAPHS AND MEASURED DRAWINGS, Gustav Ecke. A rare volume, now affordably priced for antique collectors, furniture buffs and art historians. Detailed review of styles ranging from early Shang to late Ming. Unabridged republication. 161 black-and-white drawings, photos. Total of 224pp. 8⅜ × 11¼. (Available in U.S. only) 25171-3 Pa. $13.95

VINCENT VAN GOGH: A Biography, Julius Meier-Graefe. Dynamic, penetrating study of artist's life, relationship with brother, Theo, painting techniques, travels, more. Readable, engrossing. 160pp. 5⅜ × 8½. (Available in U.S. only) 25253-1 Pa. $4.95

HOW TO WRITE, Gertrude Stein. Gertrude Stein claimed anyone could understand her unconventional writing—here are clues to help. Fascinating improvisations, language experiments, explanations illuminate Stein's craft and the art of writing. Total of 414pp. 4⅜ × 6⅜.   23144-5 Pa. $6.95

ADVENTURES AT SEA IN THE GREAT AGE OF SAIL: Five Firsthand Narratives, edited by Elliot Snow. Rare true accounts of exploration, whaling, shipwreck, fierce natives, trade, shipboard life, more. 33 illustrations. Introduction. 353pp. 5⅜ × 8½.   25177-2 Pa. $8.95

THE HERBAL OR GENERAL HISTORY OF PLANTS, John Gerard. Classic descriptions of about 2,850 plants—with over 2,700 illustrations—includes Latin and English names, physical descriptions, varieties, time and place of growth, more. 2,706 illustrations. xlv + 1,678pp. 8½ × 12¼.   23147-X Cloth. $75.00

DOROTHY AND THE WIZARD IN OZ, L. Frank Baum. Dorothy and the Wizard visit the center of the Earth, where people are vegetables, glass houses grow and Oz characters reappear. Classic sequel to *Wizard of Oz.* 256pp. 5⅜ × 8.
24714-7 Pa. $4.95

SONGS OF EXPERIENCE: Facsimile Reproduction with 26 Plates in Full Color, William Blake. This facsimile of Blake's original "Illuminated Book" reproduces 26 full-color plates from a rare 1826 edition. Includes "The Tyger," "London," "Holy Thursday," and other immortal poems. 26 color plates. Printed text of poems. 48pp. 5¼ × 7.   24636-1 Pa. $3.50

SONGS OF INNOCENCE, William Blake. The first and most popular of Blake's famous "Illuminated Books," in a facsimile edition reproducing all 31 brightly colored plates. Additional printed text of each poem. 64pp. 5¼ × 7.
22764-2 Pa. $3.50

PRECIOUS STONES, Max Bauer. Classic, thorough study of diamonds, rubies, emeralds, garnets, etc.: physical character, occurrence, properties, use, similar topics. 20 plates, 8 in color. 94 figures. 659pp. 6⅛ × 9¼.
21910-0, 21911-9 Pa., Two-vol. set $15.90

ENCYCLOPEDIA OF VICTORIAN NEEDLEWORK, S. F. A. Caulfeild and Blanche Saward. Full, precise descriptions of stitches, techniques for dozens of needlecrafts—most exhaustive reference of its kind. Over 800 figures. Total of 679pp. 8⅛ × 11. Two volumes.   Vol. 1 22800-2 Pa. $11.95
Vol. 2 22801-0 Pa. $11.95

THE MARVELOUS LAND OF OZ, L. Frank Baum. Second Oz book, the Scarecrow and Tin Woodman are back with hero named Tip, Oz magic. 136 illustrations. 287pp. 5⅜ × 8½.   20692-0 Pa. $5.95

WILD FOWL DECOYS, Joel Barber. Basic book on the subject, by foremost authority and collector. Reveals history of decoy making and rigging, place in American culture, different kinds of decoys, how to make them, and how to use them. 140 plates. 156pp. 7⅞ × 10¾.   20011-6 Pa. $8.95

HISTORY OF LACE, Mrs. Bury Palliser. Definitive, profusely illustrated chronicle of lace from earliest times to late 19th century. Laces of Italy, Greece, England, France, Belgium, etc. Landmark of needlework scholarship. 266 illustrations. 672pp. 6⅛ × 9¼.   24742-2 Pa. $14.95

ILLUSTRATED GUIDE TO SHAKER FURNITURE, Robert Meader. All furniture and appurtenances, with much on unknown local styles. 235 photos. 146pp. 9 × 12. 22819-3 Pa. $8.95

WHALE SHIPS AND WHALING: A Pictorial Survey, George Francis Dow. Over 200 vintage engravings, drawings, photographs of barks, brigs, cutters, other vessels. Also harpoons, lances, whaling guns, many other artifacts. Comprehensive text by foremost authority. 207 black-and-white illustrations. 288pp. 6 × 9. 24808-9 Pa. $8.95

THE BERTRAMS, Anthony Trollope. Powerful portrayal of blind self-will and thwarted ambition includes one of Trollope's most heartrending love stories. 497pp. 5⅜ × 8½. 25119-5 Pa. $9.95

ADVENTURES WITH A HAND LENS, Richard Headstrom. Clearly written guide to observing and studying flowers and grasses, fish scales, moth and insect wings, egg cases, buds, feathers, seeds, leaf scars, moss, molds, ferns, common crystals, etc.—all with an ordinary, inexpensive magnifying glass. 209 exact line drawings aid in your discoveries. 220pp. 5⅜ × 8½. 23330-8 Pa. $4.95

RODIN ON ART AND ARTISTS, Auguste Rodin. Great sculptor's candid, wide-ranging comments on meaning of art; great artists; relation of sculpture to poetry, painting, music; philosophy of life, more. 76 superb black-and-white illustrations of Rodin's sculpture, drawings and prints. 119pp. 8⅜ × 11¼. 24487-3 Pa. $7.95

FIFTY CLASSIC FRENCH FILMS, 1912–1982: A Pictorial Record, Anthony Slide. Memorable stills from Grand Illusion, Beauty and the Beast, Hiroshima, Mon Amour, many more. Credits, plot synopses, reviews, etc. 160pp. 8¼ × 11. 25256-6 Pa. $11.95

THE PRINCIPLES OF PSYCHOLOGY, William James. Famous long course complete, unabridged. Stream of thought, time perception, memory, experimental methods; great work decades ahead of its time. 94 figures. 1,391pp. 5⅜ × 8½. 20381-6, 20382-4 Pa., Two-vol. set $23.90

BODIES IN A BOOKSHOP, R. T. Campbell. Challenging mystery of blackmail and murder with ingenious plot and superbly drawn characters. In the best tradition of British suspense fiction. 192pp. 5⅜ × 8½. 24720-1 Pa. $3.95

CALLAS: PORTRAIT OF A PRIMA DONNA, George Jellinek. Renowned commentator on the musical scene chronicles incredible career and life of the most controversial, fascinating, influential operatic personality of our time. 64 black-and-white photographs. 416pp. 5⅜ × 8¼. 25047-4 Pa. $8.95

GEOMETRY, RELATIVITY AND THE FOURTH DIMENSION, Rudolph Rucker. Exposition of fourth dimension, concepts of relativity as Flatland characters continue adventures. Popular, easily followed yet accurate, profound. 141 illustrations. 133pp. 5⅜ × 8½. 23400-2 Pa. $3.95

HOUSEHOLD STORIES BY THE BROTHERS GRIMM, with pictures by Walter Crane. 53 classic stories—Rumpelstiltskin, Rapunzel, Hansel and Gretel, the Fisherman and his Wife, Snow White, Tom Thumb, Sleeping Beauty, Cinderella, and so much more—lavishly illustrated with original 19th century drawings. 114 illustrations. x + 269pp. 5⅜ × 8½. 21080-4 Pa. $4.95

SUNDIALS, Albert Waugh. Far and away the best, most thorough coverage of ideas, mathematics concerned, types, construction, adjusting anywhere. Over 100 illustrations. 230pp. 5⅜ × 8½. 22947-5 Pa. $4.95

PICTURE HISTORY OF THE NORMANDIE: With 190 Illustrations, Frank O. Braynard. Full story of legendary French ocean liner: Art Deco interiors, design innovations, furnishings, celebrities, maiden voyage, tragic fire, much more. Extensive text. 144pp. 8⅞ × 11¾. 25257-4 Pa. $10.95

THE FIRST AMERICAN COOKBOOK: A Facsimile of "American Cookery," 1796, Amelia Simmons. Facsimile of the first American-written cookbook published in the United States contains authentic recipes for colonial favorites—pumpkin pudding, winter squash pudding, spruce beer, Indian slapjacks, and more. Introductory Essay and Glossary of colonial cooking terms. 80pp. 5⅜ × 8½. 24710-4 Pa. $3.50

101 PUZZLES IN THOUGHT AND LOGIC, C. R. Wylie, Jr. Solve murders and robberies, find out which fishermen are liars, how a blind man could possibly identify a color—purely by your own reasoning! 107pp. 5⅜ × 8½. 20367-0 Pa. $2.50

THE BOOK OF WORLD-FAMOUS MUSIC—CLASSICAL, POPULAR AND FOLK, James J. Fuld. Revised and enlarged republication of landmark work in musico-bibliography. Full information about nearly 1,000 songs and compositions including first lines of music and lyrics. New supplement. Index. 800pp. 5⅜ × 8¼. 24857-7 Pa. $15.95

ANTHROPOLOGY AND MODERN LIFE, Franz Boas. Great anthropologist's classic treatise on race and culture. Introduction by Ruth Bunzel. Only inexpensive paperback edition. 255pp. 5⅜ × 8½. 25245-0 Pa. $6.95

THE TALE OF PETER RABBIT, Beatrix Potter. The inimitable Peter's terrifying adventure in Mr. McGregor's garden, with all 27 wonderful, full-color Potter illustrations. 55pp. 4¼ × 5½. (Available in U.S. only) 22827-4 Pa. $1.75

THREE PROPHETIC SCIENCE FICTION NOVELS, H. G. Wells. *When the Sleeper Wakes, A Story of the Days to Come* and *The Time Machine* (full version). 335pp. 5⅜ × 8½. (Available in U.S. only) 20605-X Pa. $6.95

APICIUS COOKERY AND DINING IN IMPERIAL ROME, edited and translated by Joseph Dommers Vehling. Oldest known cookbook in existence offers readers a clear picture of what foods Romans ate, how they prepared them, etc. 49 illustrations. 301pp. 6⅛ × 9¼. 23563-7 Pa. $7.95

SHAKESPEARE LEXICON AND QUOTATION DICTIONARY, Alexander Schmidt. Full definitions, locations, shades of meaning of every word in plays and poems. More than 50,000 exact quotations. 1,485pp. 6½ × 9¼. 22726-X, 22727-8 Pa., Two-vol. set $29.90

THE WORLD'S GREAT SPEECHES, edited by Lewis Copeland and Lawrence W. Lamm. Vast collection of 278 speeches from Greeks to 1970. Powerful and effective models; unique look at history. 842pp. 5⅜ × 8½. 20468-5 Pa. $11.95

THE BLUE FAIRY BOOK, Andrew Lang. The first, most famous collection, with many familiar tales: Little Red Riding Hood, Aladdin and the Wonderful Lamp, Puss in Boots, Sleeping Beauty, Hansel and Gretel, Rumpelstiltskin; 37 in all. 138 illustrations. 390pp. 5⅜ × 8½. 21437-0 Pa. $6.95

THE STORY OF THE CHAMPIONS OF THE ROUND TABLE, Howard Pyle. Sir Launcelot, Sir Tristram and Sir Percival in spirited adventures of love and triumph retold in Pyle's inimitable style. 50 drawings, 31 full-page. xviii + 329pp. 6½ × 9¼. 21883-X Pa. $7.95

AUDUBON AND HIS JOURNALS, Maria Audubon. Unmatched two-volume portrait of the great artist, naturalist and author contains his journals, an excellent biography by his granddaughter, expert annotations by the noted ornithologist, Dr. Elliott Coues, and 37 superb illustrations. Total of 1,200pp. 5⅜ × 8.
Vol. I 25143-8 Pa. $8.95
Vol. II 25144-6 Pa. $8.95

GREAT DINOSAUR HUNTERS AND THEIR DISCOVERIES, Edwin H. Colbert. Fascinating, lavishly illustrated chronicle of dinosaur research, 1820's to 1960. Achievements of Cope, Marsh, Brown, Buckland, Mantell, Huxley, many others. 384pp. 5¼ × 8¼. 24701-5 Pa. $7.95

THE TASTEMAKERS, Russell Lynes. Informal, illustrated social history of American taste 1850's–1950's. First popularized categories Highbrow, Lowbrow, Middlebrow. 129 illustrations. New (1979) afterword. 384pp. 6 × 9.
23993-4 Pa. $8.95

DOUBLE CROSS PURPOSES, Ronald A. Knox. A treasure hunt in the Scottish Highlands, an old map, unidentified corpse, surprise discoveries keep reader guessing in this cleverly intricate tale of financial skullduggery. 2 black-and-white maps. 320pp. 5⅜ × 8½. (Available in U.S. only) 25032-6 Pa. $6.95

AUTHENTIC VICTORIAN DECORATION AND ORNAMENTATION IN FULL COLOR: 46 Plates from "Studies in Design," Christopher Dresser. Superb full-color lithographs reproduced from rare original portfolio of a major Victorian designer. 48pp. 9¼ × 12¼. 25083-0 Pa. $7.95

PRIMITIVE ART, Franz Boas. Remains the best text ever prepared on subject, thoroughly discussing Indian, African, Asian, Australian, and, especially, Northern American primitive art. Over 950 illustrations show ceramics, masks, totem poles, weapons, textiles, paintings, much more. 376pp. 5⅜ × 8. 20025-6 Pa. $6.95

SIDELIGHTS ON RELATIVITY, Albert Einstein. Unabridged republication of two lectures delivered by the great physicist in 1920–21. *Ether and Relativity* and *Geometry and Experience*. Elegant ideas in non-mathematical form, accessible to intelligent layman. vi + 56pp. 5⅜ × 8½. 24511-X Pa. $2.95

THE WIT AND HUMOR OF OSCAR WILDE, edited by Alvin Redman. More than 1,000 ripostes, paradoxes, wisecracks: Work is the curse of the drinking classes, I can resist everything except temptation, etc. 258pp. 5⅜ × 8½. 20602-5 Pa. $4.95

ADVENTURES WITH A MICROSCOPE, Richard Headstrom. 59 adventures with clothing fibers, protozoa, ferns and lichens, roots and leaves, much more. 142 illustrations. 232pp. 5⅜ × 8½. 23471-1 Pa. $3.95

PLANTS OF THE BIBLE, Harold N. Moldenke and Alma L. Moldenke. Standard reference to all 230 plants mentioned in Scriptures. Latin name, biblical reference, uses, modern identity, much more. Unsurpassed encyclopedic resource for scholars, botanists, nature lovers, students of Bible. Bibliography. Indexes. 123 black-and-white illustrations. 384pp. 6 × 9. 25069-5 Pa. $8.95

FAMOUS AMERICAN WOMEN: A Biographical Dictionary from Colonial Times to the Present, Robert McHenry, ed. From Pocahontas to Rosa Parks, 1,035 distinguished American women documented in separate biographical entries. Accurate, up-to-date data, numerous categories, spans 400 years. Indices. 493pp. 6½ × 9¼. 24523-3 Pa. $10.95

THE FABULOUS INTERIORS OF THE GREAT OCEAN LINERS IN HISTORIC PHOTOGRAPHS, William H. Miller, Jr. Some 200 superb photographs capture exquisite interiors of world's great "floating palaces"—1890's to 1980's: *Titanic, Ile de France, Queen Elizabeth, United States, Europa,* more. Approx. 200 black-and-white photographs. Captions. Text. Introduction. 160pp. 8⅞ × 11¾. 24756-2 Pa. $9.95

THE GREAT LUXURY LINERS, 1927–1954: A Photographic Record, William H. Miller, Jr. Nostalgic tribute to heyday of ocean liners. 186 photos of Ile de France, Normandie, Leviathan, Queen Elizabeth, United States, many others. Interior and exterior views. Introduction. Captions. 160pp. 9 × 12. 24056-8 Pa. $10.95

A NATURAL HISTORY OF THE DUCKS, John Charles Phillips. Great landmark of ornithology offers complete detailed coverage of nearly 200 species and subspecies of ducks: gadwall, sheldrake, merganser, pintail, many more. 74 full-color plates, 102 black-and-white. Bibliography. Total of 1,920pp. 8⅝ × 11¼. 25141-1, 25142-X Cloth. Two-vol. set $100.00

THE SEAWEED HANDBOOK: An Illustrated Guide to Seaweeds from North Carolina to Canada, Thomas F. Lee. Concise reference covers 78 species. Scientific and common names, habitat, distribution, more. Finding keys for easy identification. 224pp. 5⅜ × 8½. 25215-9 Pa. $6.95

THE TEN BOOKS OF ARCHITECTURE: The 1755 Leoni Edition, Leon Battista Alberti. Rare classic helped introduce the glories of ancient architecture to the Renaissance. 68 black-and-white plates. 336pp. 8⅜ × 11¼. 25239-6 Pa. $14.95

MISS MACKENZIE, Anthony Trollope. Minor masterpieces by Victorian master unmasks many truths about life in 19th-century England. First inexpensive edition in years. 392pp. 5⅜ × 8½. 25201-9 Pa. $8.95

THE RIME OF THE ANCIENT MARINER, Gustave Doré, Samuel Taylor Coleridge. Dramatic engravings considered by many to be his greatest work. The terrifying space of the open sea, the storms and whirlpools of an unknown ocean, the ice of Antarctica, more—all rendered in a powerful, chilling manner. Full text. 38 plates. 77pp. 9¼ × 12. 22305-1 Pa. $4.95

THE EXPEDITIONS OF ZEBULON MONTGOMERY PIKE, Zebulon Montgomery Pike. Fascinating first-hand accounts (1805–6) of exploration of Mississippi River, Indian wars, capture by Spanish dragoons, much more. 1,088pp. 5⅜ × 8½. 25254-X, 25255-8 Pa. Two-vol. set $25.90

A CONCISE HISTORY OF PHOTOGRAPHY: Third Revised Edition, Helmut Gernsheim. Best one-volume history—camera obscura, photochemistry, daguerreotypes, evolution of cameras, film, more. Also artistic aspects—landscape, portraits, fine art, etc. 281 black-and-white photographs. 26 in color. 176pp. 8⅜ × 11¼. 25128-4 Pa. $13.95

THE DORÉ BIBLE ILLUSTRATIONS, Gustave Doré. 241 detailed plates from the Bible: the Creation scenes, Adam and Eve, Flood, Babylon, battle sequences, life of Jesus, etc. Each plate is accompanied by the verses from the King James version of the Bible. 241pp. 9 × 12. 23004-X Pa. $9.95

HUGGER-MUGGER IN THE LOUVRE, Elliot Paul. Second Homer Evans mystery-comedy. Theft at the Louvre involves sleuth in hilarious, madcap caper. "A knockout."—Books. 336pp. 5⅜ × 8½. 25185-3 Pa. $5.95

FLATLAND, E. A. Abbott. Intriguing and enormously popular science-fiction classic explores the complexities of trying to survive as a two-dimensional being in a three-dimensional world. Amusingly illustrated by the author. 16 illustrations. 103pp. 5⅜ × 8½. 20001-9 Pa. $2.50

THE HISTORY OF THE LEWIS AND CLARK EXPEDITION, Meriwether Lewis and William Clark, edited by Elliott Coues. Classic edition of Lewis and Clark's day-by-day journals that later became the basis for U.S. claims to Oregon and the West. Accurate and invaluable geographical, botanical, biological, meteorological and anthropological material. Total of 1,508pp. 5⅜ × 8½. 21268-8, 21269-6, 21270-X Pa. Three-vol. set $26.85

LANGUAGE, TRUTH AND LOGIC, Alfred J. Ayer. Famous, clear introduction to Vienna, Cambridge schools of Logical Positivism. Role of philosophy, elimination of metaphysics, nature of analysis, etc. 160pp. 5⅜ × 8½. (Available in U.S. and Canada only) 20010-8 Pa. $3.95

MATHEMATICS FOR THE NONMATHEMATICIAN, Morris Kline. Detailed, college-level treatment of mathematics in cultural and historical context, with numerous exercises. For liberal arts students. Preface. Recommended Reading Lists. Tables. Index. Numerous black-and-white figures. xvi + 641pp. 5⅜ × 8½. 24823-2 Pa. $11.95

HANDBOOK OF PICTORIAL SYMBOLS, Rudolph Modley. 3,250 signs and symbols, many systems in full; official or heavy commercial use. Arranged by subject. Most in Pictorial Archive series. 143pp. 8⅛ × 11. 23357-X Pa. $6.95

INCIDENTS OF TRAVEL IN YUCATAN, John L. Stephens. Classic (1843) exploration of jungles of Yucatan, looking for evidences of Maya civilization. Travel adventures, Mexican and Indian culture, etc. Total of 669pp. 5⅜ × 8½. 20926-1, 20927-X Pa., Two-vol. set $11.90

DEGAS: An Intimate Portrait, Ambroise Vollard. Charming, anecdotal memoir by famous art dealer of one of the greatest 19th-century French painters. 14 black-and-white illustrations. Introduction by Harold L. Van Doren. 96pp. 5⅜ × 8½.
25131-4 Pa. $4.95

PERSONAL NARRATIVE OF A PILGRIMAGE TO ALMANDINAH AND MECCAH, Richard Burton. Great travel classic by remarkably colorful personality. Burton, disguised as a Moroccan, visited sacred shrines of Islam, narrowly escaping death. 47 illustrations. 959pp. 5⅜ × 8½. 21217-3, 21218-1 Pa., Two-vol. set $19.90

PHRASE AND WORD ORIGINS, A. H. Holt. Entertaining, reliable, modern study of more than 1,200 colorful words, phrases, origins and histories. Much unexpected information. 254pp. 5⅜ × 8½. 20758-7 Pa. $5.95

THE RED THUMB MARK, R. Austin Freeman. In this first Dr. Thorndyke case, the great scientific detective draws fascinating conclusions from the nature of a single fingerprint. Exciting story, authentic science. 320pp. 5⅜ × 8½. (Available in U.S. only) 25210-8 Pa. $6.95

AN EGYPTIAN HIEROGLYPHIC DICTIONARY, E. A. Wallis Budge. Monumental work containing about 25,000 words or terms that occur in texts ranging from 3000 B.C. to 600 A.D. Each entry consists of a transliteration of the word, the word in hieroglyphs, and the meaning in English. 1,314pp. 6⅜ × 10.
23615-3, 23616-1 Pa., Two-vol. set $31.90

THE COMPLEAT STRATEGYST: Being a Primer on the Theory of Games of Strategy, J. D. Williams. Highly entertaining classic describes, with many illustrated examples, how to select best strategies in conflict situations. Prefaces. Appendices. xvi + 268pp. 5⅜ × 8½. 25101-2 Pa. $5.95

THE ROAD TO OZ, L. Frank Baum. Dorothy meets the Shaggy Man, little Button-Bright and the Rainbow's beautiful daughter in this delightful trip to the magical Land of Oz. 272pp. 5⅜ × 8. 25208-6 Pa. $5.95

POINT AND LINE TO PLANE, Wassily Kandinsky. Seminal exposition of role of point, line, other elements in non-objective painting. Essential to understanding 20th-century art. 127 illustrations. 192pp. 6½ × 9¼. 23808-3 Pa. $4.95

LADY ANNA, Anthony Trollope. Moving chronicle of Countess Lovel's bitter struggle to win for herself and daughter Anna their rightful rank and fortune—perhaps at cost of sanity itself. 384pp. 5⅜ × 8½. 24669-8 Pa. $8.95

EGYPTIAN MAGIC, E. A. Wallis Budge. Sums up all that is known about magic in Ancient Egypt: the role of magic in controlling the gods, powerful amulets that warded off evil spirits, scarabs of immortality, use of wax images, formulas and spells, the secret name, much more. 253pp. 5⅜ × 8½. 22681-6 Pa. $4.50

THE DANCE OF SIVA, Ananda Coomaraswamy. Preeminent authority unfolds the vast metaphysic of India: the revelation of her art, conception of the universe, social organization, etc. 27 reproductions of art masterpieces. 192pp. 5⅜ × 8½.
24817-8 Pa. $5.95

CHRISTMAS CUSTOMS AND TRADITIONS, Clement A. Miles. Origin, evolution, significance of religious, secular practices. Caroling, gifts, yule logs, much more. Full, scholarly yet fascinating; non-sectarian. 400pp. 5⅜ × 8½.
23354-5 Pa. $6.95

THE HUMAN FIGURE IN MOTION, Eadweard Muybridge. More than 4,500 stopped-action photos, in action series, showing undraped men, women, children jumping, lying down, throwing, sitting, wrestling, carrying, etc. 390pp. 7⅞ × 10⅝.
20204-6 Cloth. $21.95

THE MAN WHO WAS THURSDAY, Gilbert Keith Chesterton. Witty, fast-paced novel about a club of anarchists in turn-of-the-century London. Brilliant social, religious, philosophical speculations. 128pp. 5⅜ × 8½.   25121-7 Pa. $3.95

A CEZANNE SKETCHBOOK: Figures, Portraits, Landscapes and Still Lifes, Paul Cezanne. Great artist experiments with tonal effects, light, mass, other qualities in over 100 drawings. A revealing view of developing master painter, precursor of Cubism. 102 black-and-white illustrations. 144pp. 8¾ × 6⅝.   24790-2 Pa. $5.95

AN ENCYCLOPEDIA OF BATTLES: Accounts of Over 1,560 Battles from 1479 B.C. to the Present, David Eggenberger. Presents essential details of every major battle in recorded history, from the first battle of Megiddo in 1479 B.C. to Grenada in 1984. List of Battle Maps. New Appendix covering the years 1967–1984. Index. 99 illustrations. 544pp. 6½ × 9¼.   24913-1 Pa. $14.95

AN ETYMOLOGICAL DICTIONARY OF MODERN ENGLISH, Ernest Weekley. Richest, fullest work, by foremost British lexicographer. Detailed word histories. Inexhaustible. Total of 856pp. 6½ × 9¼.
21873-2, 21874-0 Pa., Two-vol. set $17.00

WEBSTER'S AMERICAN MILITARY BIOGRAPHIES, edited by Robert McHenry. Over 1,000 figures who shaped 3 centuries of American military history. Detailed biographies of Nathan Hale, Douglas MacArthur, Mary Hallaren, others. Chronologies of engagements, more. Introduction. Addenda. 1,033 entries in alphabetical order. xi + 548pp. 6½ × 9¼. (Available in U.S. only)
24758-9 Pa. $13.95

LIFE IN ANCIENT EGYPT, Adolf Erman. Detailed older account, with much not in more recent books: domestic life, religion, magic, medicine, commerce, and whatever else needed for complete picture. Many illustrations. 597pp. 5⅜ × 8½.
22632-8 Pa. $8.95

HISTORIC COSTUME IN PICTURES, Braun & Schneider. Over 1,450 costumed figures shown, covering a wide variety of peoples: kings, emperors, nobles, priests, servants, soldiers, scholars, townsfolk, peasants, merchants, courtiers, cavaliers, and more. 256pp. 8⅜ × 11¼.   23150-X Pa. $9.95

THE NOTEBOOKS OF LEONARDO DA VINCI, edited by J. P. Richter. Extracts from manuscripts reveal great genius; on painting, sculpture, anatomy, sciences, geography, etc. Both Italian and English. 186 ms. pages reproduced, plus 500 additional drawings, including studies for *Last Supper, Sforza* monument, etc. 860pp. 7⅞ × 10¾. (Available in U.S. only) 22572-0, 22573-9 Pa., Two-vol. set $31.90

THE ART NOUVEAU STYLE BOOK OF ALPHONSE MUCHA: All 72 Plates from "Documents Decoratifs" in Original Color, Alphonse Mucha. Rare copyright-free design portfolio by high priest of Art Nouveau. Jewelry, wallpaper, stained glass, furniture, figure studies, plant and animal motifs, etc. Only complete one-volume edition. 80pp. 9⅜ × 12¼. 24044-4 Pa. $9.95

ANIMALS: 1,419 COPYRIGHT-FREE ILLUSTRATIONS OF MAMMALS, BIRDS, FISH, INSECTS, ETC., edited by Jim Harter. Clear wood engravings present, in extremely lifelike poses, over 1,000 species of animals. One of the most extensive pictorial sourcebooks of its kind. Captions. Index. 284pp. 9 × 12.
23766-4 Pa. $9.95

OBELISTS FLY HIGH, C. Daly King. Masterpiece of American detective fiction, long out of print, involves murder on a 1935 transcontinental flight—"a very thrilling story"—NY Times. Unabridged and unaltered republication of the edition published by William Collins Sons & Co. Ltd., London, 1935. 288pp. 5⅜ × 8½. (Available in U.S. only) 25036-9 Pa. $5.95

VICTORIAN AND EDWARDIAN FASHION: A Photographic Survey, Alison Gernsheim. First fashion history completely illustrated by contemporary photographs. Full text plus 235 photos, 1840-1914, in which many celebrities appear. 240pp. 6½ × 9¼. 24205-6 Pa. $6.95

THE ART OF THE FRENCH ILLUSTRATED BOOK, 1700-1914, Gordon N. Ray. Over 630 superb book illustrations by Fragonard, Delacroix, Daumier, Doré, Grandville, Manet, Mucha, Steinlen, Toulouse-Lautrec and many others. Preface. Introduction. 633 halftones. Indices of artists, authors & titles, binders and provenances. Appendices. Bibliography. 608pp. 8⅜ × 11¼. 25086-5 Pa. $24.95

THE WONDERFUL WIZARD OF OZ, L. Frank Baum. Facsimile in full color of America's finest children's classic. 143 illustrations by W. W. Denslow. 267pp. 5⅜ × 8½. 20691-2 Pa. $7.95

FRONTIERS OF MODERN PHYSICS: New Perspectives on Cosmology, Relativity, Black Holes and Extraterrestrial Intelligence, Tony Rothman, et al. For the intelligent layman. Subjects include: cosmological models of the universe; black holes; the neutrino; the search for extraterrestrial intelligence. Introduction. 46 black-and-white illustrations. 192pp. 5⅜ × 8½. 24587-X Pa. $7.95

THE FRIENDLY STARS, Martha Evans Martin & Donald Howard Menzel. Classic text marshalls the stars together in an engaging, non-technical survey, presenting them as sources of beauty in night sky. 23 illustrations. Foreword. 2 star charts. Index. 147pp. 5⅜ × 8½. 21099-5 Pa. $3.95

FADS AND FALLACIES IN THE NAME OF SCIENCE, Martin Gardner. Fair, witty appraisal of cranks, quacks, and quackeries of science and pseudoscience: hollow earth, Velikovsky, orgone energy, Dianetics, flying saucers, Bridey Murphy, food and medical fads, etc. Revised, expanded In the Name of Science. "A very able and even-tempered presentation."—The New Yorker. 363pp. 5⅜ × 8.

20394-8 Pa. $6.95

ANCIENT EGYPT: ITS CULTURE AND HISTORY, J. E Manchip White. From pre-dynastics through Ptolemies: society, history, political structure, religion, daily life, literature, cultural heritage. 48 plates. 217pp. 5⅜ × 8½. 22548-8 Pa. $5.95

CATALOG OF DOVER BOOKS

SIR HARRY HOTSPUR OF HUMBLETHWAITE, Anthony Trollope. Incisive, unconventional psychological study of a conflict between a wealthy baronet, his idealistic daughter, and their scapegrace cousin. The 1870 novel in its first inexpensive edition in years. 250pp. 5⅜ × 8½. 24953-0 Pa. $5.95

LASERS AND HOLOGRAPHY, Winston E. Kock. Sound introduction to burgeoning field, expanded (1981) for second edition. Wave patterns, coherence, lasers, diffraction, zone plates, properties of holograms, recent advances. 84 illustrations. 160pp. 5⅜ × 8¼. (Except in United Kingdom) 24041-X Pa. $3.95

INTRODUCTION TO ARTIFICIAL INTELLIGENCE: SECOND, ENLARGED EDITION, Philip C. Jackson, Jr. Comprehensive survey of artificial intelligence—the study of how machines (computers) can be made to act intelligently. Includes introductory and advanced material. Extensive notes updating the main text. 132 black-and-white illustrations. 512pp. 5⅜ × 8½. 24864-X Pa. $8.95

HISTORY OF INDIAN AND INDONESIAN ART, Ananda K. Coomaraswamy. Over 400 illustrations illuminate classic study of Indian art from earliest Harappa finds to early 20th century. Provides philosophical, religious and social insights. 304pp. 6⅜ × 9⅜. 25005-9 Pa. $9.95

THE GOLEM, Gustav Meyrink. Most famous supernatural novel in modern European literature, set in Ghetto of Old Prague around 1890. Compelling story of mystical experiences, strange transformations, profound terror. 13 black-and-white illustrations. 224pp. 5⅜ × 8½. (Available in U.S. only) 25025-3 Pa. $6.95

ARMADALE, Wilkie Collins. Third great mystery novel by the author of *The Woman in White* and *The Moonstone*. Original magazine version with 40 illustrations. 597pp. 5⅜ × 8½. 23429-0 Pa. $9.95

PICTORIAL ENCYCLOPEDIA OF HISTORIC ARCHITECTURAL PLANS, DETAILS AND ELEMENTS: With 1,880 Line Drawings of Arches, Domes, Doorways, Facades, Gables, Windows, etc., John Theodore Haneman. Sourcebook of inspiration for architects, designers, others. Bibliography. Captions. 141pp. 9 × 12. 24605-1 Pa. $7.95

BENCHLEY LOST AND FOUND, Robert Benchley. Finest humor from early 30's, about pet peeves, child psychologists, post office and others. Mostly unavailable elsewhere. 73 illustrations by Peter Arno and others. 183pp. 5⅜ × 8½. 22410-4 Pa. $4.95

ERTÉ GRAPHICS, Erté. Collection of striking color graphics: *Seasons, Alphabet, Numerals, Aces* and *Precious Stones*. 50 plates, including 4 on covers. 48pp. 9⅜ × 12¼. 23580-7 Pa. $6.95

THE JOURNAL OF HENRY D. THOREAU, edited by Bradford Torrey, F. H. Allen. Complete reprinting of 14 volumes, 1837–61, over two million words; the sourcebooks for *Walden*, etc. Definitive. All original sketches, plus 75 photographs. 1,804pp. 8½ × 12¼. 20312-3, 20313-1 Cloth., Two-vol. set $120.00

CASTLES: THEIR CONSTRUCTION AND HISTORY, Sidney Toy. Traces castle development from ancient roots. Nearly 200 photographs and drawings illustrate moats, keeps, baileys, many other features. Caernarvon, Dover Castles, Hadrian's Wall, Tower of London, dozens more. 256pp. 5⅜ × 8¼. 24898-4 Pa. $6.95

CATALOG OF DOVER BOOKS

AMERICAN CLIPPER SHIPS: 1833–1858, Octavius T. Howe & Frederick C. Matthews. Fully-illustrated, encyclopedic review of 352 clipper ships from the period of America's greatest maritime supremacy. Introduction. 109 halftones. 5 black-and-white line illustrations. Index. Total of 928pp. 5⅜ × 8½.
25115-2, 25116-0 Pa., Two-vol. set $17.90

TOWARDS A NEW ARCHITECTURE, Le Corbusier. Pioneering manifesto by great architect, near legendary founder of "International School." Technical and aesthetic theories, views on industry, economics, relation of form to function, "mass-production spirit," much more. Profusely illustrated. Unabridged translation of 13th French edition. Introduction by Frederick Etchells. 320pp. 6⅛ × 9¼. (Available in U.S. only)
25023-7 Pa. $8.95

THE BOOK OF KELLS, edited by Blanche Cirker. Inexpensive collection of 32 full-color, full-page plates from the greatest illuminated manuscript of the Middle Ages, painstakingly reproduced from rare facsimile edition. Publisher's Note. Captions. 32pp. 9⅜ × 12¼.
24345-1 Pa. $4.95

BEST SCIENCE FICTION STORIES OF H. G. WELLS, H. G. Wells. Full novel The Invisible Man, plus 17 short stories: "The Crystal Egg," "Aepyornis Island," "The Strange Orchid," etc. 303pp. 5⅜ × 8½. (Available in U.S. only)
21531-8 Pa. $6.95

AMERICAN SAILING SHIPS: Their Plans and History, Charles G. Davis. Photos, construction details of schooners, frigates, clippers, other sailcraft of 18th to early 20th centuries—plus entertaining discourse on design, rigging, nautical lore, much more. 137 black-and-white illustrations. 240pp. 6⅛ × 9¼.
24658-2 Pa. $6.95

ENTERTAINING MATHEMATICAL PUZZLES, Martin Gardner. Selection of author's favorite conundrums involving arithmetic, money, speed, etc., with lively commentary. Complete solutions. 112pp. 5⅜ × 8½.
25211-6 Pa. $2.95

THE WILL TO BELIEVE, HUMAN IMMORTALITY, William James. Two books bound together. Effect of irrational on logical, and arguments for human immortality. 402pp. 5⅜ × 8½.
20291-7 Pa. $7.95

THE HAUNTED MONASTERY and THE CHINESE MAZE MURDERS, Robert Van Gulik. 2 full novels by Van Gulik continue adventures of Judge Dee and his companions. An evil Taoist monastery, seemingly supernatural events; overgrown topiary maze that hides strange crimes. Set in 7th-century China. 27 illustrations. 328pp. 5⅜ × 8½.
23502-5 Pa. $6.95

CELEBRATED CASES OF JUDGE DEE (DEE GOONG AN), translated by Robert Van Gulik. Authentic 18th-century Chinese detective novel; Dee and associates solve three interlocked cases. Led to Van Gulik's own stories with same characters. Extensive introduction. 9 illustrations. 237pp. 5⅜ × 8½.
23337-5 Pa. $4.95

Prices subject to change without notice.

Available at your book dealer or write for free catalog to Dept. GI, Dover Publications, Inc., 31 East 2nd St., Mineola, N.Y. 11501. Dover publishes more than 175 books each year on science, elementary and advanced mathematics, biology, music, art, literary history, social sciences and other areas.